Economic Trends

No. 628, March 2006

Regulars

Features

Tables

Publications

national STATISTICS

ISSN 0013-0400

ISBN 0-230-00268-4

Contacts
For enquiries about this publication, contact the Editor, David Harper.
Telephone: 020 7533 5914
E-mail: david.harper@ons.gsi.gov.uk

For general enquiries, contact the National Statistics Customer Contact Centre on **0845 601 3034** (minicom: 01633 812399)

E-mail: info@statistics.gsi.gov.uk
Facsimile: 01633 652747
Letters: Customer Contact Centre,
Room 1015,
Government Buildings,
Cardiff Road,
Newport NP10 8XG

You can also find National Statistics on the Internet at www.statistics.gov.uk

About the Office for National Statistics
The Office for National Statistics (ONS) is the government agency responsible for compiling, analysing and disseminating many of the United Kingdom's economic, social and demographic statistics, including the retail prices index, trade figures and labour market data, as well as the periodic census of the population and health statistics. It is also the agency that administers the statutory registration of births, marriages and deaths in England and Wales. The Director of ONS is also the National Statistician and the Registrar General for England and Wales.

A National Statistics Publication
National Statistics are produced to high professional standards set out in the National Statistics Code of Practice. They undergo regular quality assurance reviews to ensure that they meet customer needs. They are produced free from any political influence.

palgrave macmillan

in brief

At a glance – economic summaries recently released on the National Statistics website.

GDP growth

GDP, chained volume measure

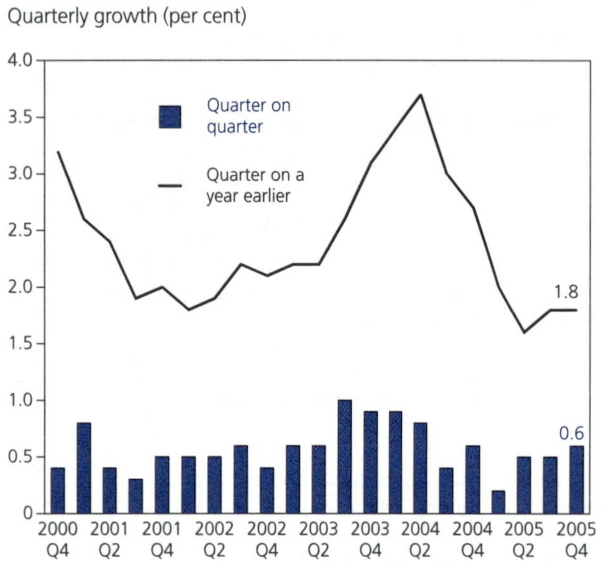

GDP grew by 0.6 per cent in the fourth quarter of 2005. This compares with growth of 0.5 per cent in the previous quarter. For the year 2005 as a whole GDP rose by 1.8 per cent over 2004.

Growth in the latest quarter is driven by a rise of 0.9 per cent in the service sector with strength across transport, storage and communication, and financial and business services.

Output of the production sector fell by 0.8 per cent, driven by a 1.0 per cent decline in manufacturing output, partly offset by a 0.4 per cent rise in energy extraction and a 0.1 per cent rise in utilities.

Construction output rose by 0.3 per cent in the fourth quarter of 2005 and is now 1.0 per cent above the level seen in the fourth quarter of 2004.

Household expenditure rose by 0.7 per cent, reflecting expenditure on both goods and services.

General government final consumption expenditure rose by 0.8 per cent in the latest quarter and is now 2.8 per cent above the level seen in the fourth quarter of 2004

Exports rose by 1.1 per cent over the quarter, within which exports of goods rose by 1.7 per cent and exports of services remained unchanged. Imports rose by 0.3 per cent, with imports of goods up 0.7 per cent and imports of services down 0.9 per cent.

Compensation of employees, measured at current prices, rose by 0.7 per cent, and is now 4.6 per cent above the level seen in the fourth quarter of 2004.

Released: 24 February 2006

Business investment

Total business investment percentage change, quarter on corresponding quarter of previous year (1980 Q1 to 2005 Q4)

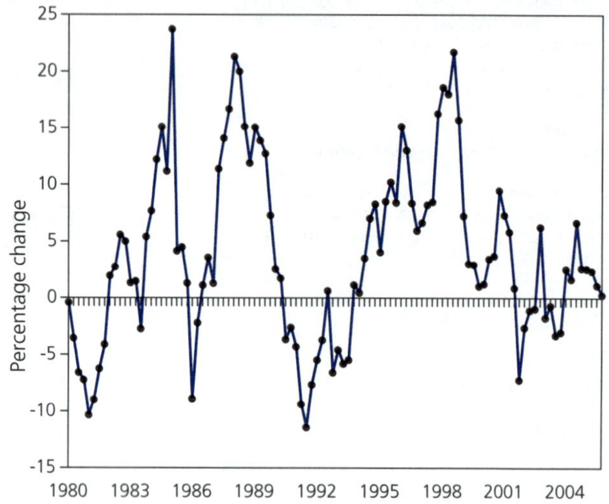

Business investment in the fourth quarter of 2005 is provisionally estimated to be 0.3 per cent higher than in the same period a year earlier and 1.0 per cent lower than in the previous quarter.

The quarterly fall in business investment is due to reduced capital spending by industries classified as private sector manufacturing, other production, construction, and distribution services. This decrease was slightly offset by increased capital spending by industries classified within private sector other services.

The quarterly fall in private sector manufacturing investment stems from lower capital expenditure across most industry groups with falls in the engineering and vehicles industries (down 3.8 per cent), the chemicals and man made fibres industries (down 5.8 per cent) the food, drink and tobacco industries (down 4.9 per cent), and the other manufacturing industries (down 14.4 per cent). The solid and nuclear fuels, and oil refining industries showed a rise for the fourth quarter (up 9.0 per cent).

By asset, the fall in private sector manufacturing investment was driven by lower capital expenditure on new building work (down 18.5 per cent) and other capital equipment (down 6.4 per cent).

Compared with the fourth quarter of 2004, total manufacturing investment fell by 8.3 per cent, construction and other production fell by 12.1 per cent and services rose by 4.0 per cent.

Released: 23 February 2006

Inflation

Annual inflation rates – 12 month

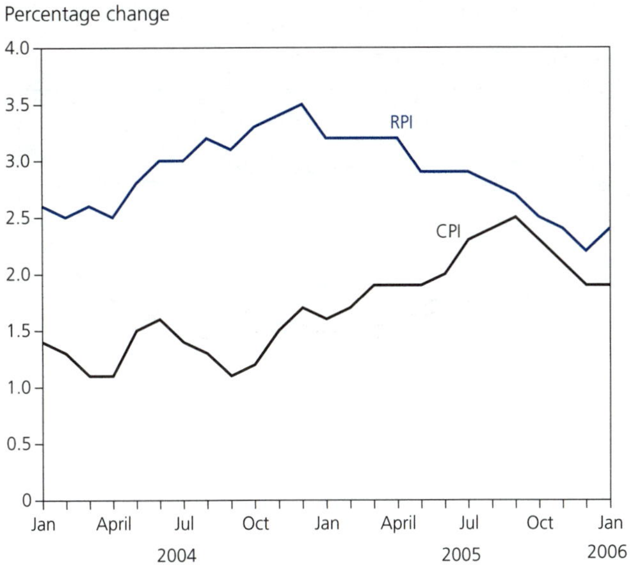

CPI annual inflation – the Government's target measure – remained unchanged at 1.9 per cent in January.

The largest upward effect on the CPI annual rate came from transport. Fuel prices rose this year, with the average price for a litre of ultra-low sulphur petrol up by around 1.7p; last year prices fell by around 3p per litre. In addition, airfares fell by less than last year, back close to their November levels. This followed a smaller than usual increase in fares in December 2005, particularly on international routes.

A further large upward effect came from changes in the cost of fixed landline telephone charges this year.

Downward pressure on the CPI annual rate came from furniture and furnishings, where prices fell by more than a year ago, and from miscellaneous goods and services mainly due to financial services, where last year's increases in overdraft fees were not repeated this year, and other miscellaneous services.

Further downward pressure came from recreation and culture, in particular games, toys and hobbies and, to a lesser extent, cultural services, major durables for outdoor recreation and package holidays. A large partially offsetting upward effect came from recording media.

Additional downward contributions came from changes in the price of food, in particular vegetables, and from clothing and footwear, with prices for women's and children's outerwear falling by more than a year ago.

RPI inflation rose in January to 2.4 per cent from 2.2 per cent in December. Upward pressures were similar to the CPI but some downward pressures were less pronounced, particularly the contributions from financial services and other miscellaneous services, which are both lower weighted in the RPI, and furniture where the downward pressure in the CPI was amplified by an increase in the weights. RPIX inflation – the all items RPI excluding mortgage interest payments – rose to 2.3 per cent in January, from 2.0 per cent in December.

As an internationally comparable measure of inflation, the CPI shows that the UK inflation rate is around the average for the European Union as a whole. The provisional inflation rate for the enlarged EU 25 in December was 2.1 per cent, compared with the UK figure for the same month of 1.9 per cent.

Released: 14 February 2006

Employment

Working age employment rate

Sampling variability ± 0.3 per cent

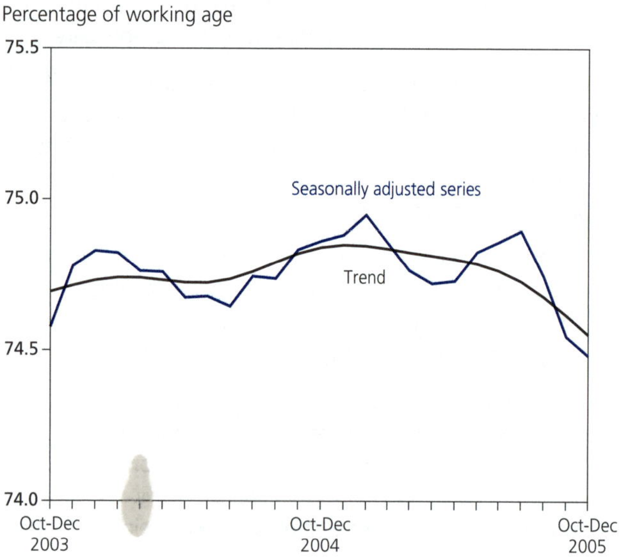

Unemployment rate

Sampling variability ± 0.2 per cent

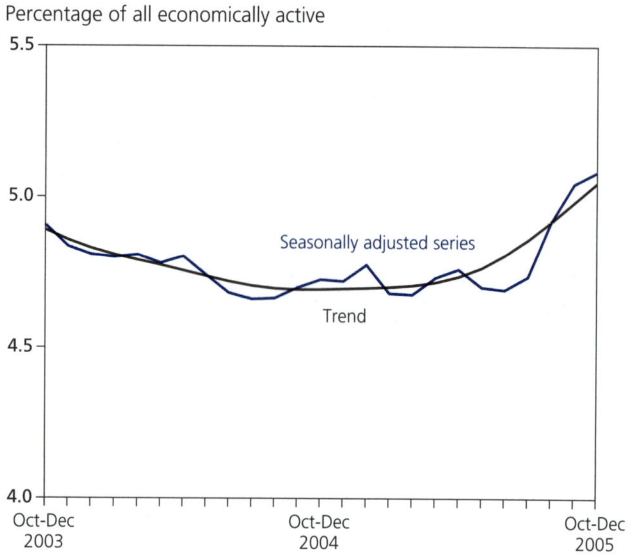

The trend in the employment rate is falling while the trend in the unemployment rate is increasing. However, the number of people claiming Jobseeker's Allowance benefit has fallen. The number of job vacancies has increased. Growth in average earnings excluding bonuses is unchanged while growth in average earnings including bonuses has increased.

The employment rate for people of working age was 74.5 per cent for the three months ending in December 2005, down from 74.9 per cent both over the quarter and over the year.

The number of people in employment was 28.77 million, down 57,000 over the quarter but up 183,000 over the year. The quarterly fall in total employment was due to a fall in the number of employees, particularly women.

Total hours worked per week was 922.0 million, down 2.7 million over the quarter but up 5.0 million over the year.

The unemployment rate was 5.1 per cent, up from 4.7 per cent both over the quarter and over the year. The number of unemployed people increased by 108,000 over the quarter and by 123,000 over the year, to reach 1.54 million.

The claimant count was 904,200 in January 2006, down 2,000 on the previous month. This is the first time the claimant count has fallen since January 2005.

The inactivity rate for people of working age was 21.4 per cent for the three months ending in December 2005, up from 21.3 per cent both over the quarter and over the year. The number of economically inactive people of working age rose by 59,000, to reach 7.95 million, the highest figure since comparable records began in 1971. This quarterly increase in inactivity was mainly due to more people, particularly women, looking after the family or home.

The annual rate of growth in average earnings (the AEI), excluding bonuses, was 3.8 per cent in December 2005, unchanged from the previous month. Including bonuses, it was 3.6 per cent, up from 3.4 per cent the previous month.

The average number of job vacancies for the three months to January 2006 was 616,800. This was up 12,100 on the previous quarter but down 34,200 over the year. This quarterly increase was largely due to more vacancies in the finance and business services sector.

The redundancy rate for the three months to December 2005 was 5.7 per 1,000 employees, down from 6.3 the previous quarter.

Released: 15 February 2006

Changes to tables

With effect from the April edition of *Economic Trends*, **Table 2.15 Measures of UK competitiveness in trade in manufactures** and its associated charts will be dropped, as the information shown is no longer being updated.

Summaries on other economic topics as well as social subjects can be found at www.statistics.gov.uk/glance

Economic update March 2006

Anis Chowdhury
Office for National Statistics

Overview

- The GDP growth in the fourth quarter of 2005 was 0.6 per cent, higher than the 0.5 per cent growth in the previous quarter.
- There was an acceleration in service sector growth and positive growth in oil production in quarter four. This was offset in part by negative growth in manufacturing production.
- From the demand perspective, consumer spending appears to have picked up in quarter four. Government expenditure shows modest growth. Business investment fell.
- The public sector finances deficit showed an improvement in 2005 quarter four.
- Net trade made a positive contribution to GDP growth in 2005 quarter four.
- Labour market shows mixed conditions in the fourth quarter but overall remains weak. The employment rate decreased whilst the unemployment rate increased in the three months to December. Average earnings growth, excluding bonuses, remained stable whilst average earnings including bonuses rose in the three months to December.
- Producer output price inflation showed a modest increase, whilst high input price fell in January compared to December.
- Consumer price inflation decreased in January, undershooting the Government's 2 per cent target.

GDP activity – overview

The GDP growth for the fourth quarter of 2005 is estimated to have grown by 0.6 per cent, unchanged from the preliminary estimate, after the release of the national accounts figures for that quarter. This is a slight acceleration from the 0.5 per cent growth in quarter three. The annual rate of growth rose to 1.8 per cent, unchanged from the previous quarter (Figure 1). This latest release contains more information than that contained in the preliminary one. It gives first estimates for the main expenditure categories and more complete information on the output side. It is still however, based on as yet incomplete information.

Preliminary data for 2005 quarter four are available for the other major OECD economies, except Italy. Data for quarter four shows a mixed , but overall a weak picture of the world economy. US GDP growth for the fourth quarter of 2005 recorded a subdued growth rate of 0.4 per cent. This is a marked deceleration from the 1.0 per cent growth in the previous quarter. The lower growth was mainly driven by lower consumer and government expenditure. There was also a negative contribution from net trade with imports

Figure 1
GDP

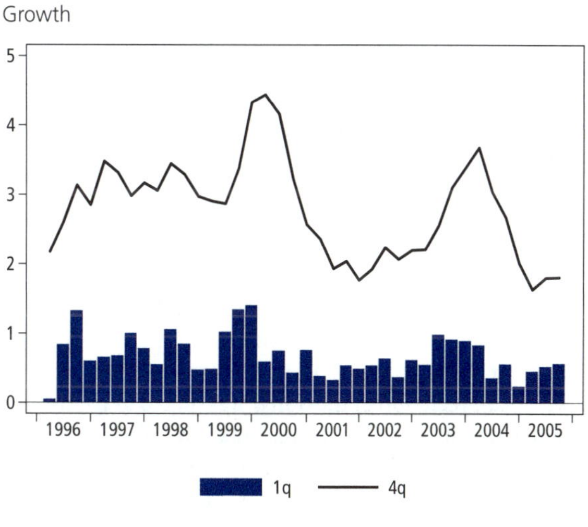

rising much strongly than exports. Japan's output in contrast increased substantially in 2005 quarter four. Growth was 1.4 per cent compared to 0.4 per cent in 2005 quarter three. The acceleration was partly due to a moderate increase in private consumption. There were also positive contributions from business investment, partly reflecting an improvement in corporate profits and from a pick up in exports, mainly to Asia and the US.

Growth in the three biggest mainland EU economies – France, Germany and Italy – shows a weakening picture. Growth in the euro zone was 0.3 per cent compared to 0.6 per cent in the previous quarter. German GDP growth was flat in quarter four having grown by 0.6 per cent in quarter three. The deceleration was mainly due to lower household and government consumption expenditure. This was offset by a positive contribution from growth in capital formation, particularly construction. Net trade, which was the main driver of growth for the past three quarters showed a neutral contribution, with imports rising strongly on the quarter. France GDP was 0.2 per cent in quarter four, a deceleration from 0.7 per cent growth in quarter three. This was mainly due to a slowing of household consumption expenditure. There was also a fall in manufacturing output, together with a weaker performance in net exports. Quarter four figures at the time of writing this article, were not yet available for Italy. Indications are that growth is likely to be similar to the picture in the previous quarter. Italy recorded a growth rate of 0.3 per cent in quarter three. Industrial output was the main contributor to the growth rate. Services output was flat whilst agricultural output continues to remain weak.

Financial Market activity

Equity performance was positive as a whole in 2005, although stock prices have been volatile. This positive performance has continued in the beginning of 2006 with the FTSE All - Share index increasing by around 3 per cent in January 2006, similar to the growth rate in 2005 quarter four.

As for currency markets, January 2006 saw sterling's average value appreciate by around 1 per cent against the dollar having depreciated by 2 per cent in 2005 quarter four. Against the euro, sterling 's value appreciated by around 1 per cent, after flat growth in 2005 quarter four. Overall, the quarterly effective exchange rate decreased by around 1 per cent in January 2006 after having been flat in the previous quarter (Figure 2).

The recent movements in the exchange rate might be linked to a number of factors. Firstly, exchange rate movements can be related to the perceptions of the relative strengths of the US and UK economy. The movements in January may partly reflect the weakening US economy as against a slightly strenthening UK economy. This is in contrast to quarter four where appreciation of the dollar was linked to robust US economic growth. Secondly, the recent appreciation of the dollar may have been due to the hikes in interest rates in the US, particularly as rates have been stable elsewhere. In the UK, interest rates were lowered in August 2005 by 0.25 per cent to stand at 4.50 per cent, well above rates in the euro zone at 2.5 per cent but at a similar level to the US. However, as the US economy has seem to have weakened in quarter four, with

Figure 2
Exchange rates

£ equals

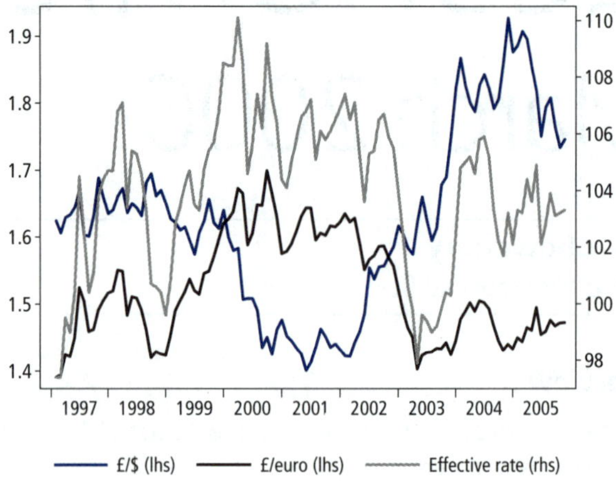

the UK economy growing modestly , the possible chances of an interest rate cut in the UK may have somewhat receded, therefore boosting sterling. The appreciation of sterling against the euro in January partly reflects the weakening economic picture in the euro zone.

Output

GDP growth in 2005 quarter four is estimated to be 0.6 per cent, unchanged from the preliminary estimate. On an annual basis, it was 1.8 per cent, unchanged from 2005 quarter three.

According to the 2005 quarter four GDP figures, the growth rate of 0.6 per cent in the UK economy was due to a combination of factors. Industrial production fell. Construction output grew at a slower rate than the previous quarter. Service sector output however accelerated. Service output remains robust and continues to lead economic growth.

Construction is estimated to have grown by 0.3 per cent following 0.4 per cent growth in the previous quarter. Comparing the quarter on the quarter a year ago, growth was 1.0 per cent, down from 1.4 per cent in the previous quarter. (Figure 3).

Figure 3
Construction output

Growth

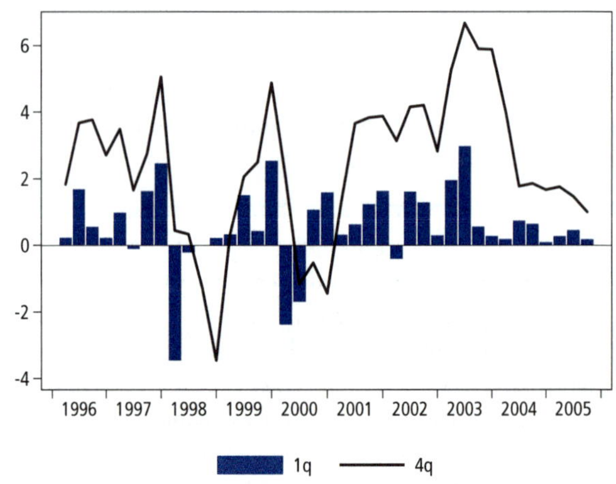

As for external surveys of construction, the CIPS survey echoes the subdued growth with the measure showing a slowdown in the average growth of the headline index in quarter four to 53.6, down from 56.4 in quarter three, reflecting weaker growth in new orders. The commercial and housing sectors also saw slower growth. In January 2006, the headline index decreased further to 50.7. The RICS survey reported steady growth with a workload balance of plus 39. The RICS reported a rebound in commercial and industrial activity, partly offset by slower growth in private housing activity.

Total output from the production industries fell by 0.8 per cent in 2005 quarter four, a further fall from 0.6 per cent in quarter three. The main contribution to the decrease came from a fall in manufacturing output of 1.0 per cent following a muted rise of 0.3 per cent in the previous quarter (Figure 4). This was partly offset by mining and quarrying (including oil & gas extraction) output which increased by 0.4 per cent in quarter four, reversing the large decrease of 8.3 per cent of the previous quarter, suggesting the extended maintenance issues of the third quarter are no longer a factor. It is worth noting that production growth in the mining and quarrying industries and electricity, gas and water supply industries has been volatile in recent quarters. Agriculture, forestry and fishing output decreased by 0.5 per cent, a lower rate of decline compared to fall of 1.1 per cent in the previous quarter.

Figure 4
Manufacturing output

Growth

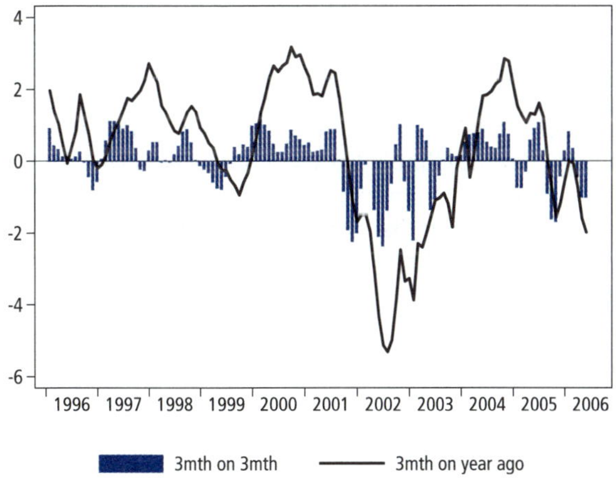

External surveys of manufacturing for 2005 quarter four (Figure 5) show some signs of improvement compared to the third quarter, but overall remain subdued. The gap between external surveys and official data has narrowed recently as the external surveys have become more pessimistic. It is worth noting that it is not unusual for the path of business indicators and official data to diverge over the short term. These differences happen partly because the series are not measuring exactly the same thing. External surveys measure the direction rather than the magnitude of a change in output and often enquire into expectations rather than actual activity.

The CIPS headline index for manufacturing signalled an increase in activity in 2005 quarter four. The headline index was 51.4 in 2005 quarter four compared to 50.6 in quarter

Figure 5
External manufacturing

Balances

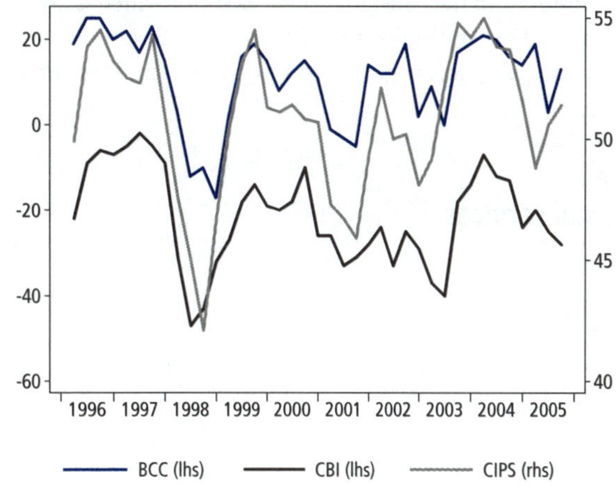

three. In January 2006, the headline index remained roughly unchanged at 51.7. The 2005 quarter four BCC survey also reports a modest improvement but overall a weak picture. The headline index improved to plus 13 from plus 3 in quarter three. The CBI in its quarter four Industrial Trends Survey generally reports a weak picture. The total orders index deteriorated to minus 28 from minus 25 in quarter three. The February monthly survey shows a slight improvement in the orders index.

Overall, the service sector, by far the largest part of the UK economy and the main driver of UK growth recently, continues to grow. The growth rate was 1.0 per cent, up from 0.7 per cent in the previous quarter. Within the sector, contributions to the growth rate appear broad based with distribution, hotels and catering, financial and business services and transport and communication services making major contributions (Figure 6).

The external surveys on services show a mixed picture in quarter four, but show an improvement overall. The CIPS Index of Services rose strongly to 57.5 from 54.8 in quarter three, mirroring the trend in official figures. Positive new orders growth was partly offset by expectations, which although high, fell from quarter three. In January 2006, the

Figure 6
Services output

Growth

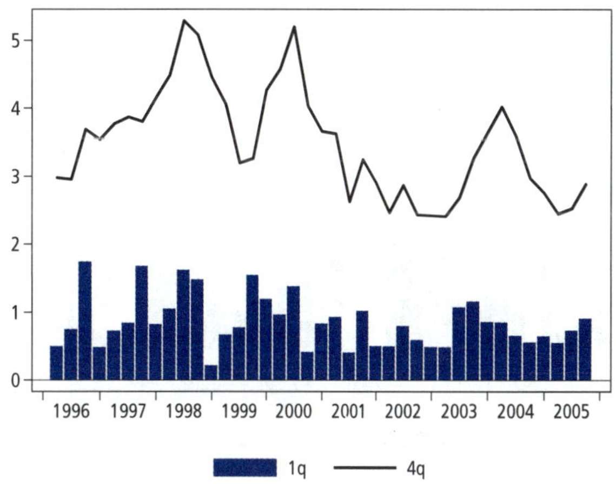

headline index fell to 52.9. The CBI in its latest (November) services sector survey make the distinction between the business and professional services sector who reported robust results and the consumer services sector which is characterised by continuing sluggishness. The BCC also report a modest improvement in output, but overall remains low (Figure 7).

Figure 7
External services

Balances

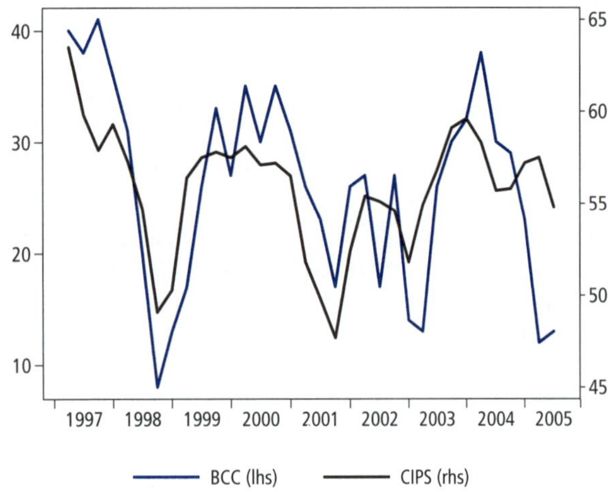

Household demand

There was a further slight pick up in household consumption expenditure in quarter four. Growth was 0.7 per cent in 2005 quarter four, up from 0.6 per cent in the previous quarter. Although this does represent a pick up, it is still subdued when compared to the first three quarters of 2004. Growth compared with the same quarter a year ago was 1.7 per cent, up from 1.4 per cent in the previous quarter. The increase in expenditure in the fourth quarter is in part due to higher expenditure on semi-durable goods, with modest growth in durable and non durable goods expenditure and on services (Figure 8).

Figure 8
Household demand

Growth

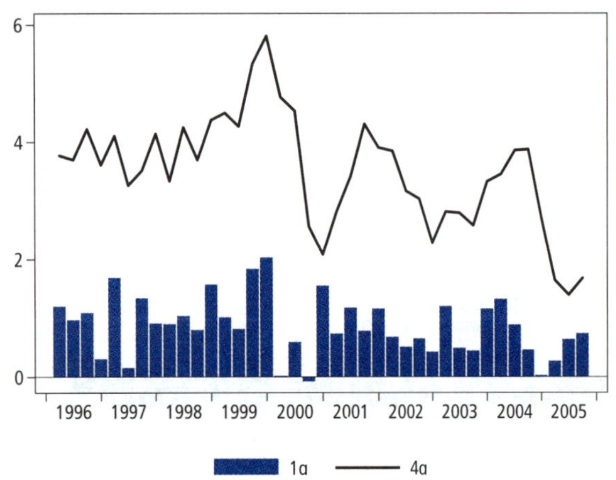

Figure 9
Retail sales

Growth

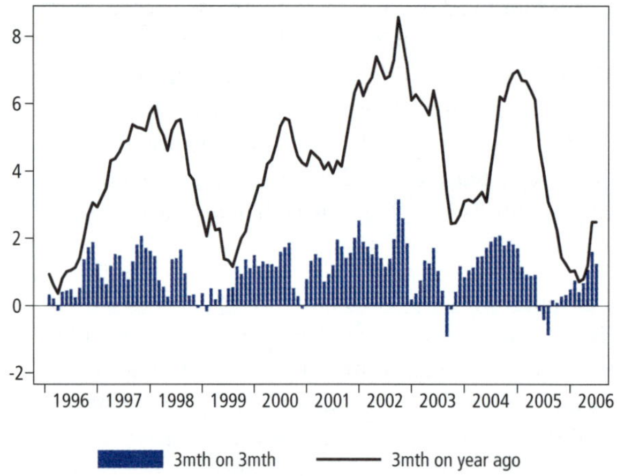

Retail sales figures are published on a monthly basis and the latest available figures are for January and show a decrease (Figure 9). According to the latest figures, the volume of retail sales in the three months to January 2006 was 1.3 per cent higher than the previous three months. This follows particularly strong growth of 1.6 per cent in the three months to December. The decrease in January may imply a post Christmas effect. On an underlying basis, growth was a robust 2.6 per cent in the three months to January compared to three months a year ago.

At a dis-aggregated level, during the three months to the end of January, sales volume for food stores was 1.0 per cent and 1.3 per cent for non-food stores. Non specialised stores showed growth of 1.3 per cent with household goods stores showing the largest growth of 3.2 per cent.

External surveys for retail sales confirm the official picture. The CBI in its monthly distributive trades survey reported that a surge in retail sales around Christmas was not sustained in January. The headline balance was minus 11 in January down from zero in December. The British Retail Consortium (BRC) also report a similar story. They report that like-for-like retail sales was 0.2 per cent in January, sharply down from 2.6 per cent in December. However, the three month trend rate of growth improved to 1.1 per cent from 0.2 per cent for like-for-like sales (Figure 10).

Figure 10
External retailing

Balances, 3 month moving average

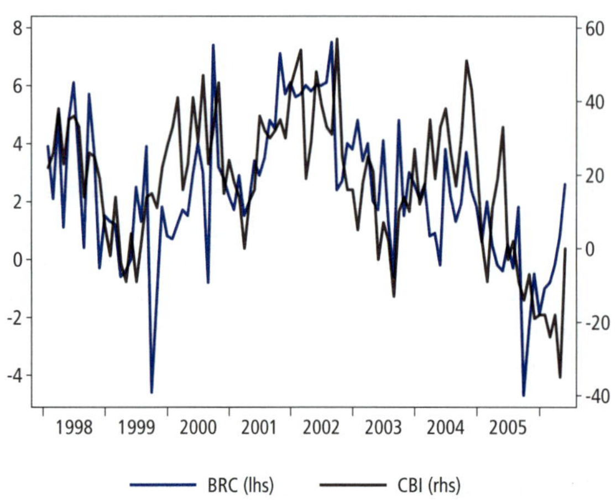

Indicators for consumer expenditure in 2005 quarter four appear mixed. Consumer spending as mentioned earlier picked up slightly in the fourth quarter. This may be in part to the lagged effect of the Bank of England's interest rate cut of 0.25 per cent starting to feed through. Retail sales show modest growth. The stock market grew further albeit modestly in quarter four and this has continued in January 2006. There are signs of a tentative recovery in the housing market. Allied to this, mortgage lending according to an annual basis showed strong growth in recent months, according to the Council of Mortgage Lenders.

Potential negatives include a weakening in the labour market and subdued wage growth. Indices of consumer confidence such as MORI and GfK generally report a negative picture for quarter four. However, figures for January 2006, despite showing negative balances, show some improvement with the GfK balance improving by six points to minus 3. The prospect of higher utility and council tax bills may dampen household expenditure. Higher oil prices could also be a factor in terms of displacing expenditure on certain durable goods.

As household consumption has risen faster than disposable income in recent years the household sector has become a considerable net borrower. It is possible, that due to relatively high debt levels, consumer expenditure growth will be more tied to the growth of personal disposable income in the future. As a major part of personal debt is tied up in equity release, the lower rate of growth in house prices, may lower personal disposable income. Consumer credit growth showed weakness in 2005 quarter four.

Business demand

The provisional estimate of business investment for the fourth quarter of 2005 shows a weakening picture. Business investment for the fourth quarter of 2005 was 1.0 per cent lower than the previous quarter and 0.3 per cent higher than the fourth quarter of 2004 (Figure 11).

Looking at business investment on a more dis-aggregated level shows that the fall in investment was mainly due to a large fall in construction and 'other' production and private sector manufacturing investment.

Figure 11
Total fixed business investment

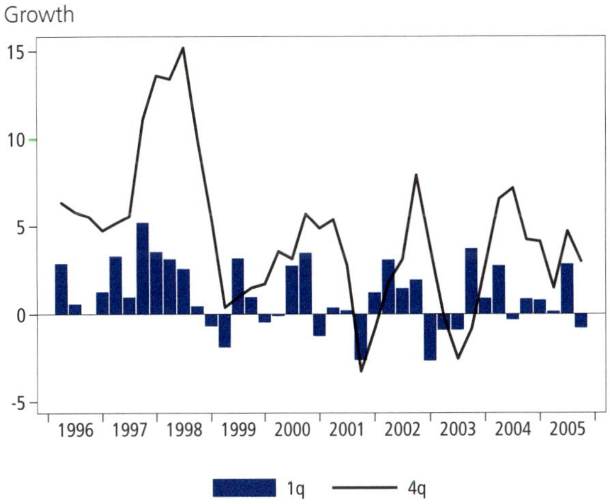

Investment in private sector services is the most important component representing around three quarters of total business investment. Private sector services rose by 2.5 per cent in 2005 quarter four, compared with the fourth quarter of 2004, services rose by 4.0 per cent.

Manufacturing investment according to the provisional estimate for the fourth quarter shows a modest fall. The manufacturing sector accounts for a little over one tenth of total business investment. This has tended to be fairly volatile, but since 1999 manufacturing investment has undergone a persistent contraction. In 2005 quarter four private sector manufacturing investment fell by 7.2 per cent and by 8.6 per cent compared to 2004 quarter four.

Construction and other production investment fell by 14.1 per cent on the quarter and decreased by 12.1 per cent compared with the fourth quarter of 2004.

Evidence on investment intentions from the latest BCC and CBI surveys does not show an inconsistent picture. According to the quarterly BCC survey, the balance of manufacturing firms planning to increase investment in plant and machinery fell by one point to plus eight. The CBI in its 2005 quarter four Industrial Survey also report a weak investment position. The balance for investment in plant and machinery was minus 14, partly reflecting a downturn in manufacturing capacity requirements.

Despite the rise in spending over the last twelve months, the environment still remains a mixed one for investment. Some consider that subdued investment sits oddly with low interest rates by historical standards. A more pessimistic view of global demand may have dampened investment as may have subdued domestic demand. Profitability though is also likely to be an important factor determining investment, which has been relatively high in recent quarters.

Government demand

Government final consumption expenditure shows moderate growth in 2005 quarter four. Growth was 0.8 per cent, unchanged from the previous quarter. Growth compared to a year ago was 2.8 per cent, up from 2.3 per cent in the previous quarter. However, government spending now is a little more subdued following strong growth of 3.2 per cent for the whole of 2004 (Figure 12).

Figure 12
Government spending

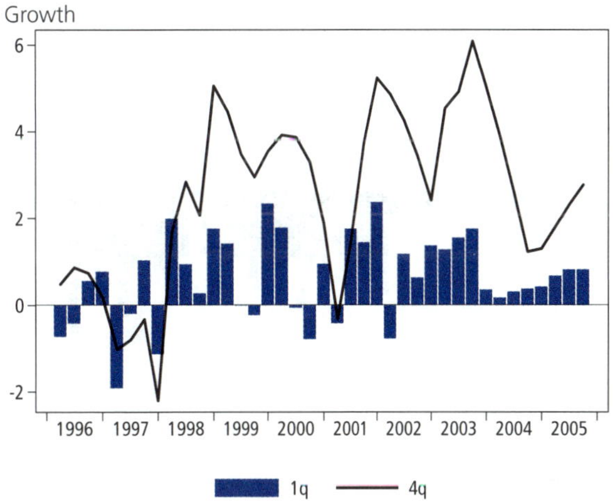

The latest figures on the public sector finances report up to January and show a slight improvement from a year ago. It is worth noting that monthly data are volatile. The financial year to date provides a better picture. The figures for the current financial year to date (April 2005 to January 2006) shows net borrowing presently stands at £29.8 billion compared to £30.0 billion in the same period in 2004/05. The current budget deficit stands at £7.8 billion; this is a £7.2 billion lower deficit than in the same period of 2004/05 when there was a deficit of £15.0 billion. The improved public sector finance position mainly reflects buoyant corporate tax revenues, in part due to strong profits made by North Sea oil companies. There was also an increase in income tax and VAT receipts.

Since net borrowing became positive in 2002, following the current budget moving from surplus into deficit, net debt as a proportion of annual GDP has risen steadily. Public sector net debt by the end of January 2006, was 35.6 per cent of GDP; down from 37.2 per cent of GDP in December, but up from 35.1 per cent in 2004/05.

Trade and the Balance of Payments

The UK continues to have a trade deficit in goods with imports rising faster than exports. However, the latest quarter suggests some slight improvement with net trade making a positive contribution to GDP growth in quarter four.

In quarter four, growth in total exports of goods in volume terms increased by 1.7 per cent. Total exports (excluding oil & erratics) rose by 1.2 per cent. Total imports in volume terms rose by 0.7 per cent. Total imports (excluding oil & erratics) rose by 1.2 per cent.

In the fourth quarter, the deficit on trade in goods and services narrowed to £12.3 billion from £14.4 billion deficit in the previous quarter. This was in part due to a higher surplus on services which was £4.9 billion in the fourth quarter compared to £2.9 billion in quarter three. These figures are flattered by the reversal in the newly established oil deficit in quarter four which was £0.1 billion in quarter four, compared to a deficit of £1.2 billion in the previous quarter (Figure 13).

Figure 13
Balance of payments

£ million

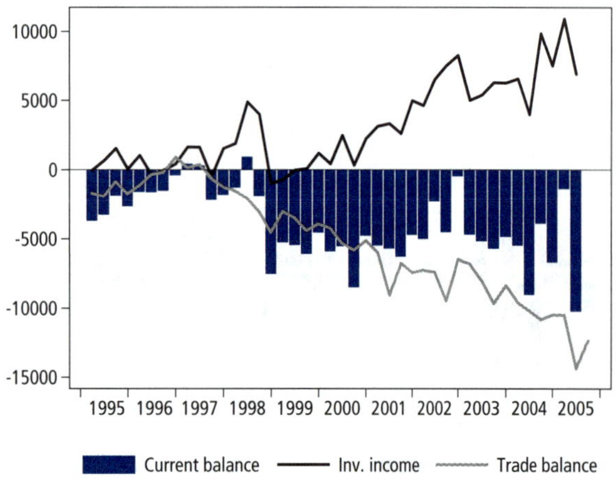

These figures need to be treated with caution as they may have been distorted by VAT Missing Trader Intra- Community (MTIC) Fraud. The effect of this fraud would lead to an over recording of exports and under recording of imports. For instance, traders import goods, mainly on high value and easily transportable goods such as mobile phones and computer chips VAT free, sell them on for a sum including VAT, and then disappear before passing the VAT to HMRC. A more sophisticated version of the fraud known as 'carousel fraud' enables goods to be imported and passed through a series of companies- before being exported out of the UK. The same goods are then re-imported, replicating the fraud. There are some indications that this type of fraud is now taking place to non- EU destinations and may be partially responsible for inflating recent non-EU export figures.

The run of current account deficits since 1998 reflects the sustained deterioration in the trade balance. The UK has traditionally run a surplus on the trade in services, but this has been more than offset by the growing deficit in trade in goods. The latest figures may seem to suggest that the UK is beginning to take advantage of growth opportunities worldwide helped by a lower pound – but the narrowing in the deficit can be partly accounted for by a positive services trade balance. The narrowing in the deficit may also be explained in terms of subdued domestic demand having the effect of restricting import growth. Oil could be another factor. In quarter four, the oil trade was in surplus from a deficit in quarter three. This may indicate that the maintenance shutdowns in the North Sea in quarter three which were preventing exports may have been to some extent overcome with oil rigs back in operational mode, leading to resumption in oil exports.

External surveys on exports show a generally weak picture. The BCC reported that the export sales net balance fell by 2 points to plus 12. The CBI quarterly Industrial Trends Survey reports that the balance for export orders was minus 5.

Labour Market

In recent years the strength of the UK economy has been clearly reflected in the labour market statistics. The latest figures from the Labour Force Survey (LFS) pertain to the three- month period up to December 2005 and show a mixed picture but overall a weakening in the Labour Market compared to quarter three. The employment rate was down whilst the unemployment rate increased. The claimant count fell. Average earnings (excluding bonuses) remained unchanged.

The current working age employment rate is 74.5 per cent, down 0.4 percentage points in the three months to December. The number of people in employment decreased by 27,000 over the quarter to currently stand at 21.47 million. The unemployment rate was 5.1 per cent, up 0.3 percentage points from the three months to September (Figure 14). The number of unemployed rose by 108,000 over the quarter to stand at

Figure 14
Unemployment and economically inactive
Per cent

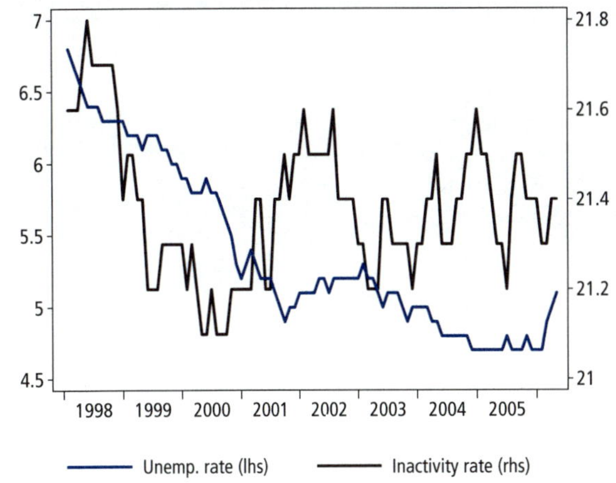

1.54 million. The claimant count measures the number of people receiving the job-seekers allowance. The latest figures for January show the claimant count level at 904,200, down 2,000 on the month but up 90,400 on a year earlier.

According to the LFS, in the period October to December 2005, 57,000 jobs were lost. In the same reference period, employee jobs fell by 96,000 while self-employed jobs rose by 40,000 reversing the trend of previous recent quarters where generation of jobs came from employees. From another perspective, full-time jobs was down by 27,000 and part-time jobs down by 30,000.

The industry dis-aggregation from 'workforce jobs' is only available for the three months to September 2005, up to which point, 9,000 jobs were created on the quarter – unchanged from the previous quarter. The largest job losses occurred in manufacturing of 20,000 followed by agriculture and distribution, hotels & catering, which both fell by 6,000. Total services on the other hand rose by 22,000, followed by construction on 11,000.

Average earnings growth shows moderate but stable growth in the latest reference period. Average earnings growth, excluding bonuses, was 3.8 per cent in December, unchanged from November. Average earnings growth, including bonuses, grew by a rate of 3.6 per cent in December, up from 3.4 per cent in November, but this is still a subdued rate of growth.

In terms of the public and private sector split, the gap in earnings growth excluding bonuses shows a slight widening in quarter four after signs of narrowing towards the end of quarter three. Public sector wage growth in the three months to December stood at 4.1 per cent (down from 4.8 per cent in June), compared to growth of 3.7 per cent in the private sector.

Overall, the numbers point to a weaker labour market, with unemployment levels increasing and employment levels decreasing, which is consistent with subdued wage growth.

Prices

The divergence between input and output price inflation for producers has continued at the beginning of 2006 from quarter four 2005. Input prices grew by 16.2 per cent in the year to January, down from 18.1 per cent in December. The average quarterly growth in 2005 quarter four was 13.3 per cent on the year ago, up from 12.4 per cent in the previous quarter. The main driver of growth remains energy, particularly oil prices, which neared $70 a barrel in January. (Figure 15). On the core measure, input price inflation increased by 10.4 per cent in the year to January, down from 12.2 per cent in December. However, producer output inflation, which has been considerably lower, jumped up to 2.9 per cent in the year to January, up from 2.4 per cent in December. The average 2005 quarter four growth compared to a year ago was 2.4 per cent, a deceleration from the 3.1 per cent growth in the previous quarter. On the core measure, output prices increased by 1.6 per cent in January, down from 1.7 per cent in December. This jump in output prices suggests that producers were able to pass on part of the increase in input prices to customers, somewhat reversing the position of recent months where producers were more willing to absorb costs into their profit margins rather than pass them on.

Figure 15
Oil prices
Brent crude per barrel

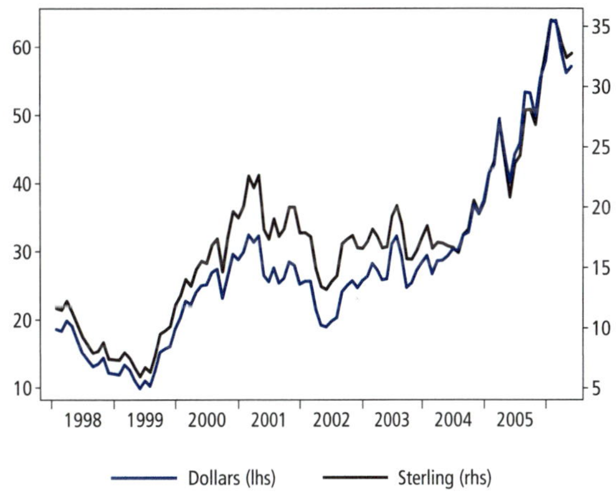

Growth in the consumer price index (CPI) – the Government's target measure of inflation rose by 1.9 per cent in January, unchanged from December. This fall just under the Bank of England's 2.0 per cent inflation target.

The largest upward effect on the CPI came from transport, due to large upward contributions from air travel and fuels and lubricants. Airfares fell by less than a year ago and prices of sulphur petrol and diesel rose by more than a year ago. A further large upward effect came from changes in fixed telephone charges. This was offset by large downward effects from furniture, due to sales. There were also large downward effects from financial services, where last years increases in overdraft fees were not repeated this year; recreation and culture, particularly games and toys; food, with prices on some vegetables falling and clothing and footwear, due partly to sales. The RPI rose to 2.4 per cent from 2.2 per cent in December. The RPIX also increased in January, to 2.3 per cent, up from 2.0 per cent in December (Figure 16).

Figure 16
Inflation

Growth, month on month a year ago

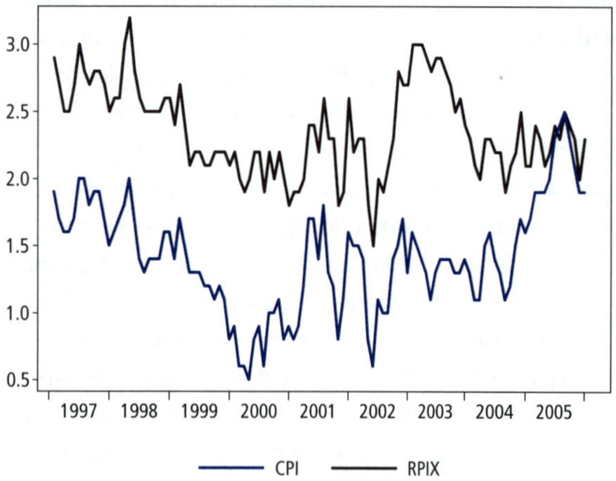

Forecasts for the UK economy

A comparison of independent forecasts, February 2006

The tables below are extracted from HM Treasury's Forecasts for the UK Economy and summarise the average and range of independent forecasts for 2006 and 2007, updated monthly.

Independent forecasts for 2006

	Average	Lowest	Highest
GDP growth (per cent)	2.1	0.6	2.8
Inflation rate (Q4 per cent)			
CPI	1.9	1.4	2.9
RPI	2.2	1.5	3.5
Claimant unemployment (Q4, million)	0.99	0.83	1.10
Current account (£ billion)	–27.5	–42.5	–17.2
Public Sector Net Borrowing (2005–06, £ billion)	38.2	33.3	47.4

Independent forecasts for 2007

	Average	Lowest	Highest
GDP growth (per cent)	2.5	1.4	2.9
Inflation rate (Q4 per cent)			
CPI	1.9	1.6	2.6
RPI	2.5	1.7	3.6
Claimant unemployment (Q4, million)	0.98	0.80	1.20
Current account (£ billion)	–29.5	–44.3	–12.8
Public Sector Net Borrowing (2007–08, £ billion)	37.4	28.7	55.6

NOTE Forecasts for the UK Economy gives more detailed forecasts, covering 27 variables and is published monthly by HM Treasury, available on annual subscription, price £75. Subscription enquiries should be addressed to Claire Coast-Smith, Public Enquiry Unit 2/S2, HM Treasury, 1 Horse Guards Road, London, SW1A 2HQ (Tel 020 7270 4558). It is also available at the Treasury's internet site: http://www.hm-treasury.gov.uk under 'Economic Data and Tools'.

**PSNB: Public Sector Net Borrowing.*

Corporate services price index (experimental) Quarter 4, 2005

What is the CSPI?

The experimental Corporate Services Price Index (CSPI) measures movements in prices charged for services supplied by businesses to other businesses, local and national government. The data produced are used internally by the Office for National Statistics (ONS) as a deflator for the Index of Services and the quarterly measurement of Gross Domestic Product (GDP). It is also used by the Treasury and Bank of England to help monitor inflation in the economy.

Results for quarter 4, 2005

Prices of business-to-business services rose by 3.8 per cent in the year to the fourth quarter of 2005. This is based on a comparison of the change in the top-level CSPI on the *net* sector basis.

Figure 1 shows how the percentage change for the top-level CSPI (net sector) compares with the Retail Prices Index (RPI) and the Producer Price Index (PPI) for all manufactured goods (net sector).

The top-level results, on both gross and net sector bases, are shown in Table 1. In 2005 Q4, the top-level CSPI (net sector) rose by 0.6 per cent compared with the previous quarter.

Figure 1
Experimental top-level CSPI compared with the Retail Prices Index (RPI) for services and the Producer Price Index (PPI)

Percentage change on the same quarter a year earlier

United Kingdom

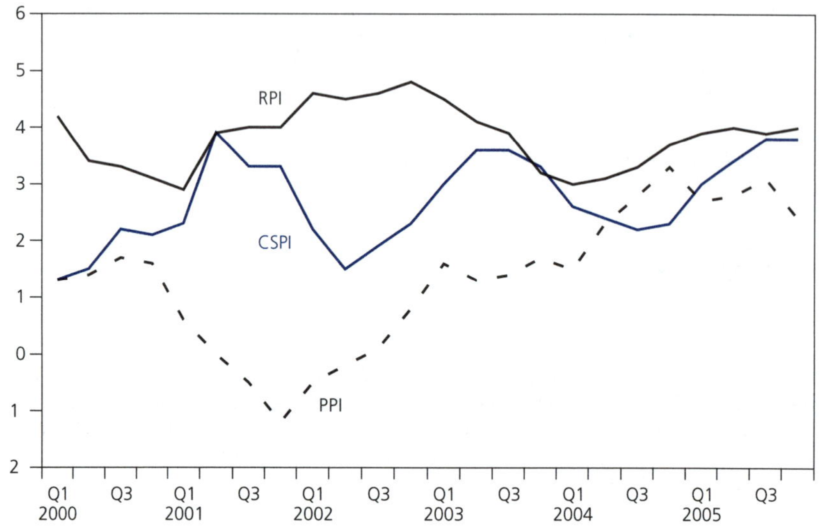

Table 1
CSPI results

		CSPI quarterly index values 2000=100		Percentage change on same quarter in previous year	
		Gross	Net	Gross	Net
2000	Q1	99.8	99.5	*–0.6*	*1.3*
	Q2	99.6	99.5	*–0.3*	*1.5*
	Q3	100.2	100.3	*0.9*	*2.2*
	Q4	100.4	100.7	*1.0*	*2.1*
2001	Q1	101.4	101.8	*1.5*	*2.3*
	Q2	102.9	103.4	*3.3*	*3.9*
	Q3	103.5	103.7	*3.2*	*3.3*
	Q4	103.8	104.1	*3.4*	*3.3*
2002	Q1	103.8	104.1	*2.4*	*2.2*
	Q2	104.7	105.0	*1.8*	*1.5*
	Q3	105.6	105.6	*2.0*	*1.9*
	Q4	106.1	106.4	*2.2*	*2.3*
2003	Q1	106.6	107.2	*2.7*	*3.0*
	Q2	108.1	108.8	*3.2*	*3.6*
	Q3	108.7	109.3	*3.0*	*3.6*
	Q4	109.2	109.9	*2.9*	*3.3*
2004	Q1	109.3	110.1	*2.5*	*2.6*
	Q2	110.6	111.4	*2.4*	*2.4*
	Q3	111.0	111.8	*2.1*	*2.2*
	Q4	111.6	112.5	*2.3*	*2.3*
2005	Q1	112.3	113.4	*2.7*	*3.0*
	Q2	113.7	115.1	*2.7*	*3.4*
	Q3	114.5	116.0	*3.1*	*3.8*
	Q4	115.5	116.8	*3.5*	*3.8*

Figure 2 shows the CSPI annual growths for both the net and gross sector time series. The annual growth for the CSPI net sector remains at 3.8 per cent, the same as for 2005 Q3. The annual growth for the CSPI gross series is 3.5 per cent in 2005 Q4 compared with 3.1 per cent in 2005 Q3. The difference in annual growth between the gross and net sector CSPI is 0.3 per cent in 2005 Q4.

Figure 2
Experimental top-level CSPI (gross and net sector)

Percentage change on the same quarter a year earlier

United Kingdom

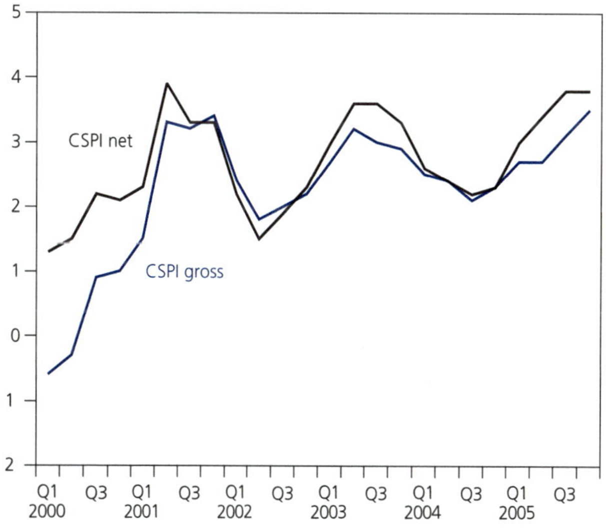

Industry-specific indices

The tables at the end of this article contain the data for the 31 industries for which indices of corporate services prices are currently available. The weights for each industry index are shown at both gross and net sector levels. Some key points to note are:

- *banking* prices rose by 4.6 per cent on the previous quarter, based on calculations using data provided by the Bank of England
- *real estate* prices rose by 3.2 per cent on the previous quarter, as reported by the Investment Property Databank

- *business telecoms* prices rose by 2.7 per cent on the previous quarter, based on calculations using Ofcom data
- *bus and coach hire* prices rose by 2.0 per cent on the previous quarter, reportedly due to an increase in fuel and wage costs
- *sea and coastal* prices rose by 1.8 per cent on the previous quarter, reportedly due to an increase in fuel costs
- *security services* prices rose by 1.1 per cent on the previous quarter, reportedly due to general price increases across the industry
- *construction plant hire* prices fell by 1.2 per cent on the previous quarter, reportedly due to the competitiveness of the industry

Background notes

1. The experimental Corporate Services Price Index (CSPI) was rebased to the year 2000 and released on 20 February 2004. Many aspects of the methods and sources used to compile the CSPI have been reviewed and updated in the rebasing. For more information on the methodology and associated impact of the rebasing see www.statistics.gov.uk/downloads/experimental/CSPI_Rebasing_Methodology_and_Impact.pdf.
2. The February 2004 release of the rebased CSPI also introduced a redeveloped business telecommunications index and new banking (loans and interest bearing deposits) index. ONS has also expanded substantially the survey of businesses on which the CSPI is based. We now survey 1,500 businesses, seeking price quotes for 5,000 service products. For further information on the redeveloped business telecommunications CSPI see www. statistics. gov .uk / downloads/experimental/Redeveloped_Business_Telecommunications.pdf. For further information on the new banking CSPI see www.statistics.gov.uk/downloads/experimental/New_Banking_CSPI.pdf.
3. The CSPI is shown in this release as both net and gross sector time series, aligning with the PPI release format. The net series is scoped to monitor the corporate-service activity provided to other businesses and government organisations, outside the corporate services sector. The gross series is scoped to monitor the provision of corporate services to all businesses and government organisations.
4. Indices relate to average prices for a quarter. The full effect of a price change, occurring part-way through any quarter, will only be reflected in the following quarter's index. All index numbers exclude VAT.
5. Some back data for a few industry-specific indices have been revised. The figures previously published are now found to have included transcription errors. Many of the revisions are very small, either 0.1 or 0.2 index points, although some are larger. The largest revisions are to the 2003 index number level and growth rate for hotels, and technical testing (around 1 index point). The largest revisions to quarterly growth rates are for bus and coach hire in 2000 Q3 (revision of 1 index point) and to banking services in 2002 Q3 (revision of 2 index points). There were no errors in the top-level CSPI index number levels or growth rates. The index numbers in this publication have now been subject to a further quality assessment and improvements to operational procedures are being put in place as a result.

Note: measurement of service sector prices is inherently difficult and challenging. When viewing the results, *it should be borne in mind that the indices shown are regarded as experimental.* This is particularly true of those that have been added to the series most recently. Therefore, some of the results will be subject to revision before the completion of the CSPI development project. The top-level index should also be viewed as *experimental.*

6. *Review of car contract hire.* ONS contract a private agency to provide price information on the car contract hire industry for inclusion in the experimental CSPI. In 2005 Q1, the agency made changes to their weighting patterns which has led to a significant jump in the level of their index. ONS has reviewed the way in which this index is calculated and has decided to withdraw it from the CSPI until further notice. This has increased the industry weights for the remaining components of the index and has caused slight revisions to the net and gross top-level CSPI back to 2000 Q1.
7. *Index weighting methodology.* Enhancements have been made to the CSPI weighting calculations and are now ready to be implemented into the series. This follows research into the 2000=100 rebasing exercise and will incorporate improvements to the way in which the experimental index is compiled. At the request of ONS National Accountants, this methodological change will not now be introduced until mid-2006 in order to fit in with the publication of the 2006 Blue Book.
8. *Presentation of future experimental releases.* Following the withdrawal of the car contract hire index from the CSPI, improvements to the way in which CSPI results are presented will now be introduced in February 2006, alongside the existing publication. These will include additional commentary on index movements together with accompanying charts and the introduction of industry family grouping to aid interpretation.
9. *Employment agencies.* The CSPI for employment agencies has been revised over the last six quarters to take account of updated salary information from the ONS Annual Survey of Hours and Earnings (ASHE).

Note to the main table:

There are external sources for the indices denoted by an asterisk, as follows:

Index	Source
Banking services	Bank of England
Property rental payments	Investment Property Databank (IPD)
Maintenance and repair of motor vehicles	Yewtree.com Ltd
Construction plant hire	Construction Plant-hire Association (CPA) up to Quarter 2 of 2002
Business telecommunications	Ofcom (Office of Communications)
Sewerage services	Ofwat (Office of Water Services)
National post parcels	Parcelforce
Business rail fares	Strategic Rail Authority (SRA)

Next results

The next set of CSPI results will be issued on 12 May 2006 via the National Statistics website www.statistics.gov.uk/cspi

Further information

- Articles on the methodology and impact of rebasing the CSPI, the redevelopment of an index for business telecommunications and the introduction of an index for banking services (together with more general information on the CSPI) are available at www.statistics.gov.uk/cspi
- Survey contact:

  Tim Clode

  Office for National Statistics

  Tel: (01633) 813493

  E-mail: cspi@ons.gsi.gov.uk

Table 2

Corporate Services Price Indices (experimental) (2000=100)

		Maintenance and repair of motor vehicles*	Hotels	Canteens and catering	Business rail fares*	Rail freight	Bus and coach hire	Freight transport by road Total	Freight transport by road International component
SIC(2003)		50.2	55.1	55.50	60.10/1	60.10/9	60.23/1	60.24/9	
2000 weights per cent									
Gross sector		3.01	3.78	3.11	0.33	0.64	0.12	13.05	
Net sector		2.15	4.23	3.48	0.17	1.07	0.20	21.93	
Annual									
	2000	100.0	100.0	100.0	100.0	100.0	100.0	100.0	100.0
	2001	102.9	104.3	104.2	103.1	100.5	106.8	102.9	100.3
	2002	106.1	104.3	105.4	106.1	102.1	114.7	103.9	99.3
	2003	110.2	108.6	106.6	109.8	103.5	120.8	106.2	99.3
	2004	115.2	111.8	107.6	114.4	104.1	123.9	108.4	99.8
	2005	119.8	114.3	110.4	120.0	106.3	128.2	113.3	105.3
Percentage change, latest year on previous year									
	2000	*2.3*	*2.3*	*0.1*	*4.5*	*–1.0*	*6.5*	*4.6*	*2.6*
	2001	*2.9*	*4.3*	*4.2*	*3.1*	*0.5*	*6.8*	*2.9*	*0.3*
	2002	*3.1*	*0.0*	*1.1*	*2.9*	*1.6*	*7.4*	*1.0*	*–1.0*
	2003	*3.9*	*4.2*	*1.1*	*3.5*	*1.4*	*5.3*	*2.2*	*0.1*
	2004	*4.5*	*2.9*	*1.0*	*4.2*	*0.6*	*2.5*	*2.1*	*0.4*
	2005	*4.0*	*2.2*	*2.6*	*4.9*	*2.1*	*3.5*	*4.6*	*5.6*
Quarterly (not seasonally adjusted)									
2000	Q1	99.1	98.8	99.1	100.0	101.8	98.1	98.9	99.5
	Q2	99.6	100.1	100.1	100.0	99.4	99.9	99.3	99.5
	Q3	100.2	100.7	100.1	100.0	99.4	100.6	100.2	100.0
	Q4	101.2	100.5	100.7	100.0	99.4	101.4	101.6	101.0
2001	Q1	102.0	102.9	103.2	103.1	100.3	103.4	102.5	100.9
	Q2	102.8	104.7	104.4	103.1	101.1	105.1	103.0	100.2
	Q3	103.5	104.5	104.5	103.1	100.5	108.1	103.1	99.8
	Q4	103.3	104.9	104.6	103.1	100.1	110.8	103.0	100.1
2002	Q1	104.9	103.7	104.7	106.1	101.3	111.7	102.9	99.6
	Q2	105.5	103.4	105.3	106.1	102.1	113.3	103.6	99.4
	Q3	106.6	104.0	105.7	106.1	102.4	116.4	104.3	99.7
	Q4	107.4	106.0	105.7	106.1	102.5	117.4	104.9	98.3
2003	Q1	108.9	107.2	106.1	109.8	102.7	119.2	105.6	99.3
	Q2	109.8	107.2	106.4	109.8	103.4	120.8	106.1	99.3
	Q3	110.4	109.1	106.7	109.8	103.6	121.6	106.3	99.5
	Q4	111.7	110.9	107.0	109.8	104.2	121.7	106.8	99.2
2004	Q1	113.3	110.5	107.2	114.4	103.7	122.4	107.1	99.0
	Q2	114.6	112.3	107.4	114.4	104.1	123.4	107.8	99.1
	Q3	115.9	112.0	108.0	114.4	104.3	124.6	108.7	100.3
	Q4	116.8	112.4	107.9	114.4	104.5	125.2	110.0	100.7
2005	Q1	118.9	114.1	108.8	120.0	105.6	125.9	111.8	103.4
	Q2	119.0	114.2	109.9	120.0	105.8	127.8	113.0	105.1
	Q3	119.8	114.4	111.4	120.0	106.6	128.2	114.3	106.5
	Q4	121.5	114.4	111.5	120.0	107.4	130.7	114.3	106.4
Percentage change, latest quarter on previous quarter									
2000	Q1	*0.3*	*1.7*	*–0.4*	*4.5*	*0.5*	*1.6*	*1.3*	*2.2*
	Q2	*0.5*	*1.3*	*1.1*	*0.0*	*–2.3*	*1.9*	*0.5*	*0.0*
	Q3	*0.6*	*0.6*	*0.0*	*0.0*	*0.0*	*0.7*	*0.9*	*0.5*
	Q4	*1.0*	*–0.2*	*0.5*	*0.0*	*0.0*	*0.8*	*1.4*	*0.9*

Table 2 - *continued*

		Maintenance and repair of motor vehicles*	Hotels	Canteens and catering	Business rail fares*	Rail freight	Bus and coach hire	Freight transport by road Total	Freight transport by road International component
SIC(2003)		50.2	55.1	55.50	60.10/1	60.10/9	60.23/1	60.24/9	
2001	Q1	*0.8*	*2.4*	*2.5*	*3.1*	*0.9*	*1.9*	*0.9*	*–0.1*
	Q2	*0.8*	*1.8*	*1.2*	*0.0*	*0.8*	*1.7*	*0.5*	*–0.6*
	Q3	*0.6*	*–0.2*	*0.1*	*0.0*	*–0.6*	*2.8*	*0.1*	*–0.4*
	Q4	*–0.2*	*0.3*	*0.1*	*0.0*	*–0.4*	*2.5*	*0.0*	*0.3*
2002	Q1	*1.5*	*–1.1*	*0.0*	*2.9*	*1.2*	*0.9*	*–0.1*	*–0.5*
	Q2	*0.6*	*–0.3*	*0.6*	*0.0*	*0.8*	*1.4*	*0.7*	*–0.2*
	Q3	*1.0*	*0.6*	*0.4*	*0.0*	*0.2*	*2.8*	*0.6*	*0.3*
	Q4	*0.8*	*1.9*	*0.0*	*0.0*	*0.1*	*0.9*	*0.5*	*–1.4*
2003	Q1	*1.5*	*1.2*	*0.4*	*3.5*	*0.2*	*1.5*	*0.7*	*1.0*
	Q2	*0.8*	*0.0*	*0.2*	*0.0*	*0.7*	*1.3*	*0.5*	*0.0*
	Q3	*0.6*	*1.8*	*0.3*	*0.0*	*0.2*	*0.6*	*0.2*	*0.1*
	Q4	*1.2*	*1.6*	*0.2*	*0.0*	*0.5*	*0.1*	*0.5*	*–0.3*
2004	Q1	*1.4*	*–0.4*	*0.2*	*4.2*	*–0.5*	*0.6*	*0.3*	*–0.2*
	Q2	*1.1*	*1.6*	*0.2*	*0.0*	*0.4*	*0.8*	*0.6*	*0.1*
	Q3	*1.2*	*–0.3*	*0.5*	*0.0*	*0.2*	*0.9*	*0.8*	*1.3*
	Q4	*0.7*	*0.4*	*0.0*	*0.0*	*0.2*	*0.5*	*1.2*	*0.4*
2005	Q1	*1.8*	*1.6*	*0.8*	*4.9*	*1.1*	*0.6*	*1.6*	*2.7*
	Q2	*0.1*	*0.0*	*1.0*	*0.0*	*0.2*	*1.5*	*1.1*	*1.6*
	Q3	*0.7*	*0.2*	*1.4*	*0.0*	*0.8*	*0.3*	*1.2*	*1.4*
	Q4	*1.3*	*0.0*	*0.0*	*0.0*	*0.7*	*2.0*	*0.0*	*–0.2*
Percentage change, latest quarter on corresponding quarter of previous year									
2000	Q1	*2.5*	*–1.3*	*–0.8*	*4.5*	*1.3*	*6.3*	*5.2*	*1.9*
	Q2	*2.0*	*3.3*	*–0.2*	*4.5*	*–1.7*	*7.3*	*4.3*	*2.2*
	Q3	*2.2*	*4.0*	*0.4*	*4.5*	*–1.8*	*7.2*	*4.6*	*2.7*
	Q4	*2.5*	*3.4*	*1.2*	*4.5*	*–1.8*	*5.1*	*4.1*	*3.7*
2001	Q1	*2.9*	*4.2*	*4.2*	*3.1*	*–1.4*	*5.4*	*3.7*	*1.4*
	Q2	*3.2*	*4.7*	*4.3*	*3.1*	*1.6*	*5.3*	*3.7*	*0.7*
	Q3	*3.3*	*3.8*	*4.3*	*3.1*	*1.1*	*7.4*	*2.8*	*–0.2*
	Q4	*2.1*	*4.4*	*4.0*	*3.1*	*0.7*	*9.2*	*1.4*	*–0.9*
2002	Q1	*2.8*	*0.7*	*1.4*	*2.9*	*1.0*	*8.1*	*0.4*	*–1.2*
	Q2	*2.6*	*–1.3*	*0.9*	*2.9*	*1.0*	*7.7*	*0.6*	*–0.8*
	Q3	*3.0*	*–0.5*	*1.2*	*2.9*	*1.9*	*7.7*	*1.2*	*–0.2*
	Q4	*3.9*	*1.0*	*1.0*	*2.9*	*2.4*	*6.0*	*1.8*	*–1.8*
2003	Q1	*3.9*	*3.3*	*1.4*	*3.5*	*1.3*	*6.7*	*2.6*	*–0.3*
	Q2	*4.0*	*3.7*	*1.0*	*3.5*	*1.3*	*6.7*	*2.3*	*–0.1*
	Q3	*3.6*	*5.0*	*1.0*	*3.5*	*1.2*	*4.4*	*1.9*	*–0.2*
	Q4	*4.1*	*4.7*	*1.2*	*3.5*	*1.6*	*3.6*	*1.9*	*0.9*
2004	Q1	*4.0*	*3.1*	*1.0*	*4.2*	*0.9*	*2.7*	*1.5*	*–0.4*
	Q2	*4.4*	*4.8*	*0.9*	*4.2*	*0.7*	*2.1*	*1.6*	*–0.3*
	Q3	*5.0*	*2.6*	*1.1*	*4.2*	*0.6*	*2.5*	*2.2*	*0.9*
	Q4	*4.5*	*1.3*	*0.9*	*4.2*	*0.3*	*2.9*	*2.9*	*1.5*
2005	Q1	*4.9*	*3.3*	*1.5*	*4.9*	*1.8*	*2.9*	*4.3*	*4.5*
	Q2	*3.8*	*1.7*	*2.3*	*4.9*	*1.6*	*3.6*	*4.8*	*6.1*
	Q3	*3.4*	*2.2*	*3.2*	*4.9*	*2.2*	*2.9*	*5.2*	*6.2*
	Q4	*4.0*	*1.8*	*3.3*	*4.9*	*2.8*	*4.5*	*3.9*	*5.6*

Table 2 – *continued*

	Commercial vehicle ferries	Sea and coastal water freight	Business air fares	Freight forwarding	National post parcels*	Courier services	Business telecoms services*	Banking services*
SIC(2003)	61.10/1	61.10/2	62.10/1	63.4	64.11	64.12	64.2	65.121
2000 weights per cent								
Gross sector	0.30	0.75	3.37	7.67	3.57	2.48	12.15	2.98
Net sector	0.38	0.95	1.65	6.43	1.88	1.31	5.59	3.35
Annual								
2000	100.0	100.0	100.0	100.0	100.0	100.0	100.0	100.0
2001	98.7	100.7	115.1	100.4	103.1	102.7	92.6	108.2
2002	100.6	95.0	122.8	99.8	107.1	107.1	90.6	116.5
2003	102.8	96.1	127.1	104.3	113.3	109.2	87.8	125.6
2004	102.6	95.2	129.6	107.6	119.5	112.7	85.6	126.7
2005	104.8	99.7	134.3	112.6	123.2	116.7	82.8	126.5
Percentage change, latest year on previous year								
2000	1.9	2.8	5.6	0.9	4.1	0.2	–16.0	10.2
2001	–1.3	0.7	15.1	0.4	3.1	2.7	–7.4	8.2
2002	2.0	–5.7	6.7	–0.6	3.9	4.2	–2.2	7.7
2003	2.1	1.1	3.5	4.4	5.9	2.0	–3.0	7.8
2004	–0.2	–0.9	2.0	3.2	5.4	3.2	–2.5	0.9
2005	2.1	4.7	3.6	4.6	3.1	3.6	–3.2	–0.2
Quarterly (not seasonally adjusted)								
2000 Q1	100.9	96.8	96.2	98.9	96.5	98.6	107.0	94.9
Q2	99.8	98.8	98.0	99.3	101.2	99.2	99.6	99.3
Q3	100.4	101.7	100.0	100.5	101.2	100.0	99.1	103.8
Q4	98.9	102.7	105.8	101.2	101.2	102.2	94.3	102.0
2001 Q1	101.5	103.9	111.9	102.2	101.2	100.4	93.1	101.4
Q2	99.0	101.6	113.1	100.6	103.7	101.5	92.8	109.0
Q3	97.0	99.9	116.8	99.4	103.7	104.2	93.7	106.7
Q4	97.3	97.5	118.5	99.4	103.7	104.8	90.8	115.7
2002 Q1	101.8	96.4	120.7	98.5	103.7	106.0	88.3	113.6
Q2	100.5	94.1	122.2	99.5	108.2	106.6	89.5	117.8
Q3	100.6	94.1	123.3	100.4	108.2	107.7	93.0	113.4
Q4	99.6	95.4	124.8	100.9	108.2	107.9	91.4	121.3
2003 Q1	102.6	98.8	124.9	102.2	108.2	108.6	88.2	122.5
Q2	102.8	97.0	127.1	104.4	115.0	109.4	87.3	125.8
Q3	102.8	94.5	128.1	105.0	115.0	109.3	88.2	125.7
Q4	102.8	94.0	128.2	105.5	115.0	109.4	87.6	128.4
2004 Q1	102.6	95.4	129.1	104.9	115.0	110.9	86.1	127.3
Q2	102.5	94.1	129.5	107.5	121.0	112.1	85.8	128.4
Q3	102.6	93.9	129.6	109.3	121.0	113.4	85.6	125.1
Q4	102.7	97.3	130.3	108.7	121.0	114.3	85.0	126.0
2005 Q1	104.8	96.7	132.3	109.9	121.0	115.0	83.4	125.5
Q2	104.7	97.7	133.5	111.9	124.0	116.2	82.7	127.0
Q3	104.8	101.2	134.9	113.9	124.0	117.6	81.5	123.8
Q4	104.8	103.1	136.3	114.7	124.0	118.1	83.7	129.5
Percentage change, latest quarter on previous quarter								
2000 Q1	5.6	2.1	0.8	0.7	0.0	–0.9	–3.2	3.2
Q2	–1.0	2.1	2.0	0.4	4.8	0.6	–6.9	4.7
Q3	0.6	2.9	2.0	1.2	0.0	0.8	–0.6	4.5
Q4	–1.4	1.0	5.8	0.7	0.0	2.1	–4.8	–1.7
2001 Q1	2.6	1.2	5.8	1.0	0.0	–1.8	–1.3	–0.5
Q2	–2.5	–2.2	1.1	–1.6	2.5	1.1	–0.3	7.4
Q3	–2.0	–1.7	3.3	–1.2	0.0	2.6	1.0	–2.1
Q4	0.3	–2.4	1.4	–0.1	0.0	0.6	–3.2	8.5

Table 2 – *continued*

		Commercial vehicle ferries	Sea and coastal water freight	Business air fares	Freight forwarding	National post parcels*	Courier services	Business telecoms services*	Banking services*
SIC(2003)		61.10/1	61.10/2	62.10/1	63.4	64.11	64.12	64.2	65.121
2002	Q1	*4.6*	*–1.1*	*1.9*	*–0.9*	*0.0*	*1.2*	*–2.7*	*–1.8*
	Q2	*–1.3*	*–2.4*	*1.2*	*1.0*	*4.4*	*0.6*	*1.3*	*3.6*
	Q3	*0.1*	*0.1*	*0.9*	*0.9*	*0.0*	*0.9*	*4.0*	*–3.7*
	Q4	*–1.0*	*1.3*	*1.2*	*0.5*	*0.0*	*0.2*	*–1.8*	*6.9*
2003	Q1	*3.0*	*3.6*	*0.1*	*1.3*	*0.0*	*0.6*	*–3.5*	*1.0*
	Q2	*0.2*	*–1.8*	*1.7*	*2.2*	*6.3*	*0.7*	*–1.0*	*2.7*
	Q3	*0.0*	*–2.6*	*0.8*	*0.5*	*0.0*	*–0.1*	*1.0*	*–0.1*
	Q4	*0.0*	*–0.5*	*0.1*	*0.5*	*0.0*	*0.1*	*–0.6*	*2.2*
2004	Q1	*–0.2*	*1.5*	*0.7*	*–0.6*	*0.0*	*1.3*	*–1.7*	*–0.9*
	Q2	*–0.1*	*–1.3*	*0.3*	*2.5*	*5.1*	*1.1*	*–0.4*	*0.9*
	Q3	*0.0*	*–0.2*	*0.1*	*1.6*	*0.0*	*1.2*	*–0.2*	*–2.6*
	Q4	*0.1*	*3.7*	*0.6*	*–0.5*	*0.0*	*0.8*	*–0.7*	*0.7*
2005	Q1	*2.1*	*–0.6*	*1.5*	*1.1*	*0.0*	*0.5*	*–1.8*	*–0.4*
	Q2	*–0.1*	*1.0*	*0.9*	*1.7*	*2.5*	*1.1*	*–0.8*	*1.2*
	Q3	*0.1*	*3.5*	*1.1*	*1.8*	*0.0*	*1.2*	*–1.5*	*–2.5*
	Q4	*0.0*	*1.8*	*1.0*	*0.7*	*0.0*	*0.4*	*2.7*	*4.6*
Percentage change, latest quarter on corresponding quarter of previous year									
2000	Q1	*0.2*	*–3.1*	*2.5*	*–2.6*	*2.0*	*–0.7*	*–17.5*	*5.3*
	Q2	*1.2*	*0.2*	*3.4*	*0.2*	*4.8*	*–0.7*	*–17.8*	*11.6*
	Q3	*2.8*	*6.1*	*5.5*	*3.0*	*4.8*	*–0.2*	*–13.8*	*12.7*
	Q4	*3.6*	*8.3*	*10.9*	*3.0*	*4.8*	*2.6*	*–14.7*	*10.9*
2001	Q1	*0.6*	*7.3*	*16.4*	*3.4*	*4.8*	*1.7*	*–13.0*	*6.9*
	Q2	*–0.9*	*2.8*	*15.4*	*1.3*	*2.5*	*2.3*	*–6.9*	*9.7*
	Q3	*–3.4*	*–1.8*	*16.8*	*–1.1*	*2.5*	*4.1*	*–5.4*	*2.8*
	Q4	*–1.6*	*–5.1*	*12.0*	*–1.8*	*2.5*	*2.6*	*–3.8*	*13.5*
2002	Q1	*0.3*	*–7.2*	*7.8*	*–3.6*	*2.5*	*5.7*	*–5.1*	*12.0*
	Q2	*1.5*	*–7.5*	*8.0*	*–1.1*	*4.4*	*5.1*	*–3.6*	*8.1*
	Q3	*3.7*	*–5.8*	*5.6*	*0.9*	*4.4*	*3.3*	*–0.7*	*6.3*
	Q4	*2.4*	*–2.1*	*5.3*	*1.5*	*4.4*	*3.0*	*0.7*	*4.8*
2003	Q1	*0.8*	*2.5*	*3.5*	*3.7*	*4.4*	*2.4*	*–0.1*	*7.8*
	Q2	*2.3*	*3.1*	*4.0*	*4.9*	*6.3*	*2.6*	*–2.4*	*6.8*
	Q3	*2.2*	*0.3*	*3.9*	*4.6*	*6.3*	*1.5*	*–5.2*	*10.8*
	Q4	*3.2*	*–1.5*	*2.8*	*4.6*	*6.3*	*1.4*	*–4.1*	*5.9*
2004	Q1	*0.0*	*–3.4*	*3.4*	*2.6*	*6.3*	*2.1*	*–2.4*	*3.9*
	Q2	*–0.3*	*–3.0*	*1.9*	*3.0*	*5.1*	*2.5*	*–1.8*	*2.1*
	Q3	*–0.3*	*–0.6*	*1.2*	*4.1*	*5.1*	*3.8*	*–3.0*	*–0.5*
	Q4	*–0.1*	*3.6*	*1.6*	*3.1*	*5.1*	*4.5*	*–3.0*	*–1.9*
2005	Q1	*2.1*	*1.4*	*2.4*	*4.8*	*5.1*	*3.7*	*–3.1*	*–1.4*
	Q2	*2.1*	*3.8*	*3.1*	*4.0*	*2.5*	*3.6*	*–3.5*	*–1.1*
	Q3	*2.2*	*7.8*	*4.1*	*4.2*	*2.5*	*3.7*	*–4.7*	*–1.0*
	Q4	*2.1*	*5.9*	*4.6*	*5.4*	*2.5*	*3.3*	*–1.5*	*2.8*

Table 2 – *continued*

		Property rental payments*	Real estate agency	Construction plant hire*	Market research	Technical testing	Employment agencies	Security services	Industrial cleaning	Commercial film processing
SIC(2003)		70.2	70.3	71.32	74.13	74.3	74.5	74.60/2	74.7	74.81/9
2000 weights per cent										
Gross sector		8.08	3.81	2.44	1.18	0.79	14.77	2.03	2.41	0.16
Net sector		12.79	1.62	5.90	1.02	1.00	6.83	2.57	2.45	0.20
Annual										
2000		100.0	100.0	100.0	100.0	100.0	100.0	100.0	100.0	100.0
2001		106.5	101.9	104.2	102.6	103.8	107.1	104.4	101.1	99.9
2002		111.0	102.6	102.0	107.0	107.2	112.0	108.2	104.0	99.9
2003		115.6	105.8	108.2	109.8	111.0	115.5	113.8	106.9	103.4
2004		120.2	114.6	106.8	111.4	112.7	117.4	117.7	109.3	107.7
2005		124.1	123.7	106.8	114.7	114.1	120.8	121.4	111.1	105.9
Percentage change, latest year on previous year										
2000		*5.7*	*6.5*	*5.1*	*2.4*	*1.3*	*2.3*	*2.1*	*0.7*	*0.2*
2001		*6.5*	*1.9*	*4.2*	*2.6*	*3.8*	*7.1*	*4.4*	*1.1*	*–0.1*
2002		*4.3*	*0.7*	*–2.1*	*4.3*	*3.3*	*4.6*	*3.6*	*2.9*	*0.0*
2003		*4.1*	*3.1*	*6.1*	*2.6*	*3.6*	*3.1*	*5.2*	*2.7*	*3.5*
2004		*4.0*	*8.4*	*–1.3*	*1.4*	*1.5*	*1.7*	*3.5*	*2.3*	*4.1*
2005		*3.2*	*7.9*	*0.0*	*3.0*	*1.2*	*2.9*	*3.1*	*1.6*	*–1.6*
Quarterly (not seasonally adjusted)										
2000	Q1	98.0	98.5	96.6	99.7	99.3	99.3	99.0	99.9	99.9
	Q2	99.3	99.7	100.8	100.0	99.6	99.9	99.7	100.0	100.0
	Q3	100.6	100.6	101.7	100.5	100.0	100.1	100.4	100.0	100.0
	Q4	102.2	101.3	100.9	99.8	101.1	100.7	100.9	100.1	100.0
2001	Q1	104.1	101.9	101.8	102.3	101.7	102.7	102.1	99.9	100.0
	Q2	105.7	101.9	108.0	102.6	104.2	106.8	103.8	100.6	100.1
	Q3	107.2	101.9	105.0	102.7	104.3	108.7	105.4	100.9	99.8
	Q4	108.8	101.8	101.9	103.0	104.9	110.0	106.3	103.1	99.8
2002	Q1	109.6	101.5	100.3	106.4	106.0	111.6	107.4	103.5	99.9
	Q2	110.7	102.0	101.4	106.5	106.3	111.9	107.7	103.9	99.9
	Q3	111.3	103.0	102.9	106.9	107.6	112.4	108.3	104.0	99.9
	Q4	112.5	103.8	103.3	108.3	108.9	112.2	109.3	104.8	99.9
2003	Q1	113.4	103.9	106.5	109.1	109.9	113.4	111.8	105.6	100.1
	Q2	115.5	104.9	108.4	109.3	110.5	116.0	113.0	105.8	99.5
	Q3	116.3	106.7	108.8	110.3	111.7	116.4	114.2	107.8	105.4
	Q4	117.1	107.5	109.1	110.6	111.9	116.2	116.2	108.3	108.8
2004	Q1	118.3	110.2	107.0	110.8	112.4	116.1	117.2	108.3	109.3
	Q2	119.4	113.6	107.8	111.1	112.3	117.6	117.7	109.3	107.1
	Q3	120.9	116.0	106.2	111.4	112.9	117.5	117.8	109.6	107.1
	Q4	122.2	118.8	106.1	112.2	113.2	118.5	118.2	110.0	107.1
2005	Q1	122.5	120.9	106.5	113.3	113.3	118.7	119.6	110.7	105.7
	Q2	123.8	121.2	107.1	114.7	113.5	120.1	120.4	110.9	105.9
	Q3	124.4	124.3	107.4	115.3	114.6	121.9	122.2	110.9	106.0
	Q4	125.5	128.3	106.1	115.5	114.9	122.4	123.5	111.8	106.0
Percentage change, latest quarter on previous quarter										
2000	Q1	*1.2*	*2.6*	*0.7*	*1.4*	*0.4*	*0.9*	*0.4*	*0.2*	*0.1*
	Q2	*1.3*	*1.2*	*4.3*	*0.3*	*0.2*	*0.6*	*0.7*	*0.2*	*0.1*
	Q3	*1.3*	*0.9*	*0.8*	*0.5*	*0.5*	*0.2*	*0.7*	*0.0*	*0.0*
	Q4	*1.6*	*0.7*	*–0.7*	*–0.7*	*1.1*	*0.6*	*0.5*	*0.1*	*0.0*
2001	Q1	*1.9*	*0.6*	*0.9*	*2.5*	*0.6*	*2.0*	*1.2*	*–0.2*	*0.0*
	Q2	*1.5*	*0.0*	*6.1*	*0.3*	*2.5*	*4.0*	*1.7*	*0.7*	*0.0*
	Q3	*1.4*	*0.0*	*–2.7*	*0.0*	*0.1*	*1.8*	*1.5*	*0.3*	*–0.3*
	Q4	*1.5*	*–0.1*	*–3.0*	*0.4*	*0.6*	*1.2*	*0.9*	*2.2*	*0.0*

Table 2 - *continued*

		Property rental payments*	Real estate agency	Construction plant hire*	Market research	Technical testing	Employment agencies	Security services	Industrial cleaning	Commercial film processing
SIC(2003)		70.2	70.3	71.32	74.13	74.3	74.5	74.60/2	74.7	74.81/9
2002	Q1	*0.8*	*–0.3*	*–1.5*	*3.2*	*1.0*	*1.4*	*1.0*	*0.4*	*0.2*
	Q2	*1.0*	*0.5*	*1.0*	*0.1*	*0.3*	*0.3*	*0.3*	*0.4*	*0.0*
	Q3	*0.5*	*0.9*	*1.5*	*0.4*	*1.2*	*0.4*	*0.5*	*0.1*	*0.0*
	Q4	*1.1*	*0.8*	*0.4*	*1.2*	*1.3*	*–0.2*	*0.9*	*0.8*	*0.0*
2003	Q1	*0.8*	*0.1*	*3.1*	*0.8*	*0.9*	*1.1*	*2.3*	*0.8*	*0.1*
	Q2	*1.8*	*1.0*	*1.9*	*0.2*	*0.6*	*2.3*	*1.0*	*0.2*	*–0.6*
	Q3	*0.7*	*1.7*	*0.3*	*0.9*	*1.1*	*0.3*	*1.1*	*1.8*	*6.0*
	Q4	*0.7*	*0.8*	*0.3*	*0.2*	*0.2*	*–0.1*	*1.8*	*0.5*	*3.2*
2004	Q1	*1.0*	*2.5*	*–1.9*	*0.2*	*0.4*	*–0.1*	*0.8*	*0.0*	*0.5*
	Q2	*1.0*	*3.1*	*0.8*	*0.3*	*–0.1*	*1.3*	*0.4*	*0.9*	*–2.0*
	Q3	*1.3*	*2.1*	*–1.5*	*0.2*	*0.5*	*–0.1*	*0.2*	*0.3*	*0.0*
	Q4	*1.1*	*2.5*	*–0.1*	*0.7*	*0.3*	*0.8*	*0.3*	*0.3*	*0.0*
2005	Q1	*0.2*	*1.7*	*0.3*	*1.0*	*0.1*	*0.2*	*1.1*	*0.6*	*–1.2*
	Q2	*1.1*	*0.3*	*0.6*	*1.3*	*0.2*	*1.2*	*0.7*	*0.2*	*0.2*
	Q3	*0.5*	*2.6*	*0.3*	*0.5*	*0.9*	*1.5*	*1.5*	*0.1*	*0.1*
	Q4	*0.9*	*3.2*	*–1.2*	*0.2*	*0.3*	*0.5*	*1.1*	*0.8*	*0.0*
Percentage change, latest quarter on corresponding quarter of previous year										
2000	Q1	*5.9*	*8.3*	*0.3*	*2.6*	*0.7*	*2.5*	*1.7*	*1.0*	*0.1*
	Q2	*5.9*	*6.5*	*7.4*	*2.8*	*1.0*	*2.1*	*2.1*	*0.9*	*0.1*
	Q3	*5.4*	*5.7*	*7.8*	*2.7*	*1.3*	*2.2*	*2.3*	*0.5*	*0.2*
	Q4	*5.5*	*5.6*	*5.1*	*1.5*	*2.1*	*2.4*	*2.3*	*0.4*	*0.2*
2001	Q1	*6.3*	*3.5*	*5.4*	*2.6*	*2.4*	*3.5*	*3.1*	*0.0*	*0.1*
	Q2	*6.5*	*2.3*	*7.1*	*2.6*	*4.7*	*7.0*	*4.2*	*0.5*	*0.1*
	Q3	*6.6*	*1.4*	*3.3*	*2.1*	*4.3*	*8.6*	*5.0*	*0.8*	*–0.3*
	Q4	*6.5*	*0.5*	*1.0*	*3.3*	*3.8*	*9.3*	*5.3*	*3.0*	*–0.3*
2002	Q1	*5.3*	*–0.4*	*–1.4*	*4.0*	*4.2*	*8.6*	*5.2*	*3.6*	*–0.1*
	Q2	*4.7*	*0.1*	*–6.1*	*3.8*	*2.0*	*4.8*	*3.8*	*3.3*	*–0.1*
	Q3	*3.8*	*1.0*	*–2.0*	*4.2*	*3.1*	*3.4*	*2.8*	*3.1*	*0.2*
	Q4	*3.4*	*2.0*	*1.4*	*5.1*	*3.8*	*1.9*	*2.9*	*1.7*	*0.2*
2003	Q1	*3.5*	*2.4*	*6.1*	*2.6*	*3.7*	*1.6*	*4.1*	*2.1*	*0.1*
	Q2	*4.3*	*2.8*	*7.0*	*2.6*	*4.0*	*3.7*	*4.8*	*1.9*	*–0.5*
	Q3	*4.6*	*3.6*	*5.7*	*3.2*	*3.8*	*3.6*	*5.4*	*3.7*	*5.4*
	Q4	*4.1*	*3.6*	*5.6*	*2.2*	*2.8*	*3.6*	*6.3*	*3.3*	*8.8*
2004	Q1	*4.3*	*6.0*	*0.5*	*1.5*	*2.2*	*2.3*	*4.8*	*2.6*	*9.2*
	Q2	*3.4*	*8.3*	*–0.5*	*1.7*	*1.6*	*1.4*	*4.2*	*3.3*	*7.7*
	Q3	*4.0*	*8.7*	*–2.3*	*0.9*	*1.0*	*1.0*	*3.2*	*1.7*	*1.6*
	Q4	*4.4*	*10.5*	*–2.7*	*1.4*	*1.1*	*2.0*	*1.7*	*1.5*	*–1.6*
2005	Q1	*3.6*	*9.7*	*–0.5*	*2.3*	*0.8*	*2.3*	*2.0*	*2.1*	*–3.3*
	Q2	*3.7*	*6.7*	*–0.7*	*3.2*	*1.1*	*2.1*	*2.3*	*1.4*	*–1.1*
	Q3	*2.9*	*7.2*	*1.1*	*3.5*	*1.5*	*3.7*	*3.7*	*1.2*	*–1.0*
	Q4	*2.7*	*8.0*	*0.0*	*3.0*	*1.5*	*3.3*	*4.4*	*1.6*	*–1.0*

Table 2 – *continued*

		Contract packaging	Direct marketing/ secretarial	Translation and interpretation services	Adult education	Sewerage services*	Waste disposal	Commercial washing and dry cleaning	TOP–LEVEL CSPI Gross sector	Net sector
SIC(2003)		74.82	74.83(pt)	74.83(pt)	80.42	90.00/1	90.00/2	93.01		
2000 weights per cent										
Gross sector		0.60	0.34	0.05	1.57	2.33	1.47	0.69	100	
Net sector		1.38	0.35	0.05	1.59	4.14	2.61	0.70		100
Annual										
2000		100.0	100.0	100.0	100.0	100.0	100.0	100.0	100.0	100.0
2001		101.8	101.2	99.6	103.9	98.3	105.3	101.2	102.9	103.2
2002		103.1	99.7	101.5	106.8	99.1	111.3	102.0	105.1	105.3
2003		109.3	100.4	102.6	111.5	102.7	118.6	102.4	108.1	108.8
2004		111.4	101.5	107.1	117.4	108.8	124.1	104.7	110.6	111.4
2005		121.0	102.2	106.2	118.5	121.4	136.5	105.5	114.0	115.3
Percentage change, latest year on previous year										
2000		*1.2*	*1.3*	*–0.2*	*2.3*	*–8.7*	*4.9*	*–0.3*	*0.2*	*1.8*
2001		*1.8*	*1.2*	*–0.4*	*3.9*	*–1.7*	*5.3*	*1.2*	*2.9*	*3.2*
2002		*1.3*	*–1.5*	*1.9*	*2.7*	*0.8*	*5.7*	*0.9*	*2.1*	*2.0*
2003		*6.0*	*0.7*	*1.1*	*4.5*	*3.7*	*6.5*	*0.3*	*2.9*	*3.4*
2004		*1.9*	*1.0*	*4.4*	*5.2*	*5.9*	*4.6*	*2.3*	*2.3*	*2.4*
2005		*8.6*	*0.7*	*–0.9*	*1.0*	*11.6*	*10.0*	*0.7*	*3.0*	*3.5*
Quarterly (not seasonally adjusted)										
2000	Q1	99.6	99.9	100.2	99.5	110.4	99.2	99.7	99.8	99.5
	Q2	99.4	99.9	100.2	99.5	96.5	100.4	100.2	99.6	99.5
	Q3	100.7	100.3	99.9	100.3	96.5	100.2	100.4	100.2	100.3
	Q4	100.3	99.9	99.6	100.8	96.5	100.2	99.8	100.4	100.7
2001	Q1	101.1	100.6	99.7	101.4	96.5	101.8	100.3	101.4	101.8
	Q2	101.3	101.5	99.7	104.6	98.9	104.7	101.1	102.9	103.4
	Q3	102.3	101.3	99.4	104.6	98.9	106.8	101.2	103.5	103.7
	Q4	102.4	101.5	99.5	105.1	98.9	107.9	102.0	103.8	104.1
2002	Q1	102.5	100.9	101.4	106.0	98.9	108.0	102.4	103.8	104.1
	Q2	102.4	99.3	101.5	106.3	99.1	110.9	102.1	104.7	105.0
	Q3	103.2	99.3	101.4	107.3	99.1	111.3	102.5	105.6	105.6
	Q4	104.2	99.3	101.6	107.4	99.1	115.0	101.1	106.1	106.4
2003	Q1	105.0	99.7	102.3	108.1	99.1	115.7	102.4	106.6	107.2
	Q2	109.7	99.6	102.7	110.3	104.0	119.8	102.2	108.1	108.8
	Q3	110.9	100.9	102.7	112.9	104.0	119.4	102.2	108.7	109.3
	Q4	111.6	101.5	102.7	114.8	104.0	119.5	102.7	109.2	109.9
2004	Q1	112.0	101.5	108.0	117.3	104.0	120.0	105.0	109.3	110.1
	Q2	110.8	101.4	108.0	117.3	110.4	124.8	104.9	110.6	111.4
	Q3	111.3	101.5	106.2	117.5	110.4	124.9	104.3	111.0	111.8
	Q4	111.5	101.5	106.1	117.4	110.4	126.6	104.7	111.6	112.5
2005	Q1	120.5	101.0	106.2	117.5	110.4	126.1	104.8	112.3	113.4
	Q2	120.6	102.2	106.2	118.5	125.1	136.3	105.5	113.7	115.1
	Q3	121.5	102.7	106.2	118.7	125.1	141.2	105.7	114.5	116.0
	Q4	121.4	102.8	106.2	119.3	125.1	142.5	106.0	115.5	116.8
Percentage change, latest quarter on previous quarter										
2000	Q1	*0.8*	*1.1*	*0.0*	*1.2*	*0.0*	*3.0*	*0.6*	*0.4*	*0.8*
	Q2	*–0.2*	*0.0*	*0.0*	*0.1*	*–12.5*	*1.2*	*0.5*	*–0.3*	*0.0*
	Q3	*1.3*	*0.5*	*–0.4*	*0.8*	*0.0*	*–0.2*	*0.2*	*0.7*	*0.8*
	Q4	*–0.4*	*–0.4*	*–0.2*	*0.5*	*0.0*	*–0.1*	*–0.6*	*0.1*	*0.4*
2001	Q1	*0.8*	*0.7*	*0.0*	*0.7*	*0.0*	*1.6*	*0.5*	*1.0*	*1.1*
	Q2	*0.2*	*0.9*	*0.0*	*3.1*	*2.5*	*2.9*	*0.8*	*1.5*	*1.6*
	Q3	*1.0*	*–0.2*	*–0.3*	*0.0*	*0.0*	*2.0*	*0.1*	*0.5*	*0.2*
	Q4	*0.1*	*0.2*	*0.2*	*0.5*	*0.0*	*1.0*	*0.8*	*0.3*	*0.4*

Table 2 – *continued*

		Contract packaging	Direct marketing/ secretarial	Translation and interpretation services	Adult education	Sewerage services*	Waste disposal	Commercial washing and dry cleaning	TOP–LEVEL CSPI Gross sector	TOP–LEVEL CSPI Net sector
SIC(2003)		74.82	74.83(pt)	74.83(pt)	80.42	90.00/1	90.00/2	93.01		
2002	Q1	*0.1*	*–0.6*	*1.8*	*0.8*	*0.0*	*0.1*	*0.4*	*0.0*	*0.0*
	Q2	*0.0*	*–1.6*	*0.1*	*0.3*	*0.2*	*2.7*	*–0.2*	*0.9*	*0.9*
	Q3	*0.8*	*–0.1*	*0.0*	*0.9*	*0.0*	*0.3*	*0.4*	*0.8*	*0.6*
	Q4	*0.9*	*0.0*	*0.2*	*0.1*	*0.0*	*3.3*	*–1.4*	*0.5*	*0.8*
2003	Q1	*0.8*	*0.4*	*0.6*	*0.6*	*0.0*	*0.6*	*1.3*	*0.5*	*0.8*
	Q2	*4.5*	*–0.1*	*0.5*	*2.1*	*4.9*	*3.6*	*–0.2*	*1.4*	*1.4*
	Q3	*1.0*	*1.3*	*0.0*	*2.4*	*0.0*	*–0.3*	*0.0*	*0.6*	*0.5*
	Q4	*0.6*	*0.6*	*0.0*	*1.6*	*0.0*	*0.0*	*0.5*	*0.4*	*0.5*
2004	Q1	*0.4*	*0.0*	*5.2*	*2.2*	*0.0*	*0.4*	*2.2*	*0.1*	*0.1*
	Q2	*–1.0*	*–0.1*	*0.0*	*0.0*	*6.2*	*4.0*	*0.0*	*1.2*	*1.2*
	Q3	*0.5*	*0.0*	*–1.7*	*0.1*	*0.0*	*0.1*	*–0.6*	*0.3*	*0.4*
	Q4	*0.2*	*0.0*	*0.0*	*–0.1*	*0.0*	*1.3*	*0.4*	*0.6*	*0.6*
2005	Q1	*8.1*	*–0.5*	*0.0*	*0.1*	*0.0*	*–0.4*	*0.1*	*0.6*	*0.8*
	Q2	*0.1*	*1.2*	*0.0*	*0.8*	*13.3*	*8.1*	*0.6*	*1.2*	*1.6*
	Q3	*0.7*	*0.4*	*0.0*	*0.2*	*0.0*	*3.6*	*0.2*	*0.8*	*0.8*
	Q4	*–0.1*	*0.1*	*0.0*	*–0.2*	*0.0*	*0.9*	*0.3*	*0.9*	*0.6*
Percentage change, latest quarter on corresponding quarter of previous year										
2000	Q1	*0.7*	*2.2*	*0.1*	*2.2*	*3.0*	*6.5*	*–0.3*	*–0.6*	*1.3*
	Q2	*0.6*	*0.4*	*0.0*	*2.0*	*–12.5*	*5.1*	*–0.8*	*–0.3*	*1.5*
	Q3	*1.9*	*1.5*	*–0.3*	*2.5*	*–12.5*	*4.1*	*–0.7*	*0.9*	*2.2*
	Q4	*1.5*	*1.1*	*–0.6*	*2.5*	*–12.5*	*4.0*	*0.7*	*1.0*	*2.1*
2001	Q1	*1.5*	*0.7*	*–0.6*	*2.0*	*–12.5*	*2.6*	*0.6*	*1.5*	*2.3*
	Q2	*1.9*	*1.7*	*–0.6*	*5.1*	*2.5*	*4.3*	*0.9*	*3.3*	*3.9*
	Q3	*1.6*	*1.0*	*–0.5*	*4.3*	*2.5*	*6.6*	*0.9*	*3.2*	*3.3*
	Q4	*2.1*	*1.6*	*–0.1*	*4.3*	*2.5*	*7.7*	*2.2*	*3.4*	*3.3*
2002	Q1	*1.4*	*0.3*	*1.7*	*4.5*	*2.5*	*6.1*	*2.1*	*2.4*	*2.2*
	Q2	*1.1*	*–2.1*	*1.8*	*1.7*	*0.2*	*5.9*	*1.0*	*1.8*	*1.5*
	Q3	*0.9*	*–2.0*	*2.1*	*2.6*	*0.2*	*4.2*	*1.3*	*2.0*	*1.9*
	Q4	*1.7*	*–2.2*	*2.1*	*2.2*	*0.2*	*6.6*	*–0.9*	*2.2*	*2.3*
2003	Q1	*2.5*	*–1.2*	*0.9*	*2.0*	*0.2*	*7.1*	*0.0*	*2.7*	*3.0*
	Q2	*7.1*	*0.3*	*1.3*	*3.8*	*4.9*	*7.9*	*0.1*	*3.2*	*3.6*
	Q3	*7.4*	*1.7*	*1.3*	*5.3*	*4.9*	*7.3*	*–0.3*	*3.0*	*3.6*
	Q4	*7.1*	*2.3*	*1.1*	*6.8*	*4.9*	*3.9*	*1.5*	*2.9*	*3.3*
2004	Q1	*6.6*	*1.8*	*5.6*	*8.6*	*4.9*	*3.7*	*2.5*	*2.5*	*2.6*
	Q2	*1.0*	*1.8*	*5.2*	*6.3*	*6.2*	*4.2*	*2.7*	*2.4*	*2.4*
	Q3	*0.4*	*0.5*	*3.3*	*4.0*	*6.2*	*4.6*	*2.0*	*2.1*	*2.2*
	Q4	*0.0*	*–0.1*	*3.3*	*2.3*	*6.2*	*6.0*	*2.0*	*2.3*	*2.3*
2005	Q1	*7.6*	*–0.6*	*–1.7*	*0.2*	*6.2*	*5.1*	*–0.1*	*2.7*	*3.0*
	Q2	*8.9*	*0.8*	*–1.7*	*1.0*	*13.3*	*9.3*	*0.5*	*2.7*	*3.4*
	Q3	*9.2*	*1.2*	*0.0*	*1.0*	*13.3*	*13.0*	*1.3*	*3.1*	*3.8*
	Q4	*8.9*	*1.3*	*0.0*	*0.9*	*13.3*	*12.5*	*1.2*	*3.5*	*3.8*

Public Service Productivity: Health

UK Centre for the Measurement of Government Activity

This article presents various estimates of change in productivity in public expenditure on health. One of these uses the output estimates included in the current National Accounts. Recognising that these estimates make no allowance for quality change, a distinct drawback, the article then goes on to present additional sets of productivity estimates implied by newly proposed methodologies for taking account of quality change. These draw on work published by the Centre for Health Economics (University of York) and the National Institute for Economics and Social Research, and by the Department of Health in 2005.

The article also presents an improvement to the wider set of evidence that helps build up an overall picture of Health Service performance. The intention is now to engage in a public consultation about the new methodologies proposed to help evaluate how health productivity should best be assessed. The article should be seen as a staging post in a continuing journey to improve measurement of public sector productivity. This article is the third in an ongoing series of Public Service Productivity articles following the first Health and Education articles published in October 2004 and October 2005, respectively.

- Measuring the productivity of public services is complex. The estimates of National Health Service (NHS) productivity presented in this article build on those in the first health productivity article published in October 2004. This article is one of a series that is developing and improving productivity information in light of the best sources of data and methodologies available.
- The ideas and methods presented in this article, particularly those on the quality adjustment of NHS output, are presented as a basis for further public consultation and debate.
- The primary aim of the NHS is to improve and maintain the health of the population. However, health outcomes, such as increases in life expectancy, and reductions in mortality rates, are also influenced by factors outside the control of the NHS, such as diet, housing and smoking habits. NHS output is therefore best defined as the contribution of the NHS to improved health outcomes, that is excluding improvements in outcomes due to other factors.
- NHS productivity is estimated by dividing NHS output by NHS inputs. Key to this calculation is the appropriate coverage and quality adjustment of output, and the conversion of expenditure into volumes of inputs.
- The first set of NHS productivity estimates presented are based on NHS output as currently published in the National Accounts. On this basis, NHS productivity fell from 1995 to 2004 by an average of between 0.6 and 1.3 per cent per year. This compares with an average fall of between 0 and 1 per cent per year as presented by the Office for National Statistics (ONS) in October 2004. However, these estimates make no allowance for quality change, although the *Atkinson Review* recommended that productivity estimates should take account of quality change.
- So further sets of estimates are presented that do have regard for quality change, based on research by the Centre for Health Economics at the University of York and the National Institute of Economic and Social Research, and by the Department of Health.
- A related key issue to take into account is the argument that health and NHS output become increasingly valuable in material terms over time, in an increasingly prosperous economy. The *Atkinson Review* recommended such an adjustment but suggested it should be used cautiously pending further debate. Accordingly, this article presents estimates both with and without this adjustment.
- Including adjustments for quality change but not for increasing value of health, NHS productivity could have changed on average by between +0.2 per cent or -0.5 per cent per year from 1999 to 2004, the period for which the quality change information is available.
- Including adjustments for quality change and for increasing value of health, NHS productivity is estimated to have risen on average by between 0.9 and 1.6 per cent per year over the same 1999 to 2004 period.
- Finally, estimates of productivity need to be interpreted alongside other forms of corroborative evidence, for example, information on average length of stay in hospital, or elective day case rates. It is unlikely that a single number for productivity will ever capture all the costs and benefits of the NHS. The methodologies and estimates presented here should be regarded as a staging point in an ongoing agenda to refine the measurement of NHS productivity.

1 Executive summary

1.1 This article estimates the change in productivity associated with public expenditure on health using National Accounts data from 1995 to 2004, in the context of wider information about health spending, output, outcomes and measurement issues. It is the third in the Office for National Statistics' (ONS) series of articles on Public Service Productivity. The first in the series, also on health, was published in October 2004. The second in the series, on education, was published in October 2005.

1.2 Measuring productivity for public services is complex. The information presented in this article should therefore be regarded as a staging point in moving steadily towards better and more comprehensive measurement of National Health Service (NHS) productivity. Public debate and scrutiny are now needed to help move this process forward with as wide a consensus as possible. ONS, in association with the Department of Health (DH) will be facilitating consultation to this end.

1.3 The primary aim of the NHS is to improve and maintain the health of the population served. However, health outcomes and the overall health of the population are only in part due to the activities performed by the NHS. They are also due to other factors, such as housing, diet, smoking, as well as change in demography, for example, the effects of an ageing population and population movements. NHS output is best regarded as the improvement in health outcomes directly attributable to the NHS.

1.4 One set of estimates of NHS productivity is based on current National Accounts estimates of output as in *Blue Book 2005*. Using this measure, NHS output is estimated to have increased during the period 1995 to 2004 by an average of 3.2 per cent per year, with the volume of NHS inputs rising over the same period by an average of between 3.9 and 4.6 per cent per year. This means that NHS productivity is estimated to have fallen during the period 1995 to 2004 by an average of between 0.6 and 1.3 per cent per year. This set of estimates takes no account of quality change, however, and must be firmly understood as such. Figure 1 presents this first set of estimates.

1.5 By contrast, the *Atkinson Review* recommended that NHS output should be adjusted to take into account quality change, where quality is based on health outcomes directly attributable to NHS output, as well as other measures of change in the NHS. This is a complex procedure and the data and methodology necessary for quality adjustment are still developing. However, using new research by the Centre for Health Economics (CHE) at the University of York and the National Institute of Economic and Social Research (NIESR), and by DH, significant advances have been made possible. The ideas and methods presented in this article, particularly those on the quality adjustment of NHS output, are presented as a basis for further public consultation and debate.

Figure 1.

NHS productivity *excluding* quality change in NHS output, 1995 to 2004

United Kingdom

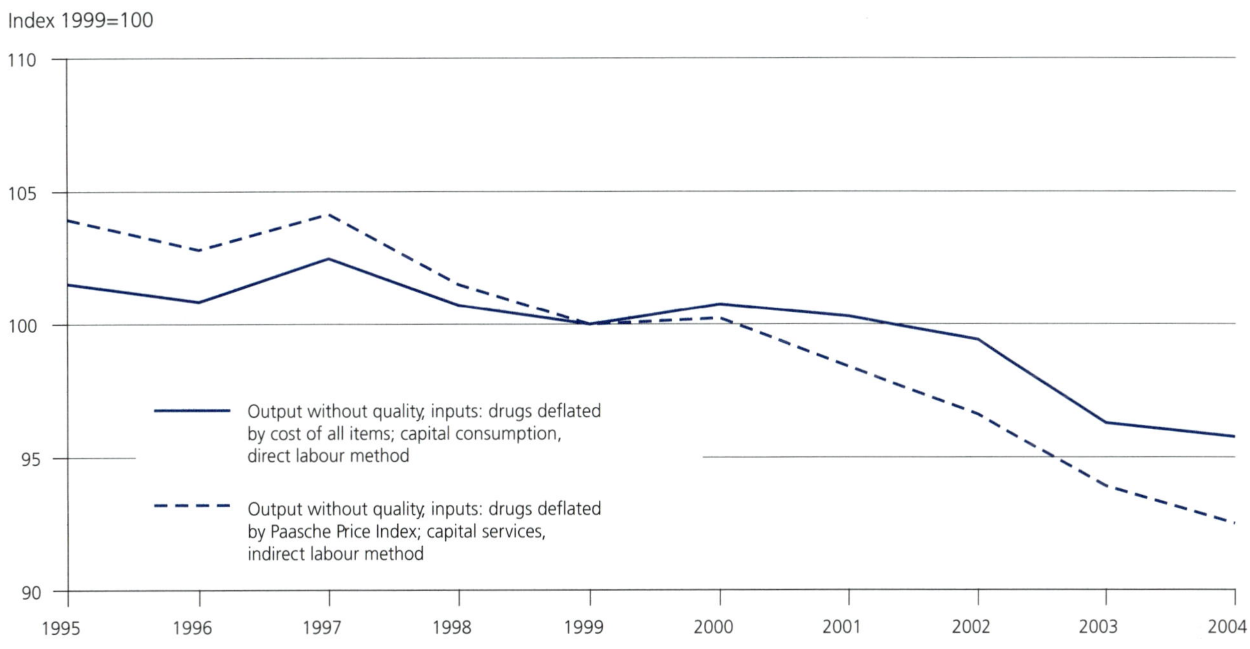

Source: ONS

1.6 A number of quality indicators are used to build up more relevant estimates of NHS output growth:

- survival rates;
- health effects;
- an adjustment for life expectancy for survival rates and health effects;
- waiting times;
- improvements in primary medical care;
- longer term survival rates for myocardial infarction; and
- patient experience.
- In addition, DH proposes a new quality measure that uses value weights instead of cost weights for statins used to treat patients with coronary heart disease (CHD). This impact is also included in quality adjustments.

1.7 NHS output growth with all these quality adjustments during the period 1999 to 2004 is estimated to have increased by an average of around 5 per cent per year. With the volume of NHS inputs rising at between 4.8 and 5.5 per cent during this period, this leads to a second set of estimates which suggests that NHS productivity is estimated to have either increased by an average of 0.2 per cent per year, or has fallen by an average of 0.5 per cent per year, over the same period. Figure 2 presents this second set of estimates.

1.8 The *Atkinson Review* also recommended adjusting the value of NHS output by rising real earnings in the economy (estimated to be 1.5 per cent per year) to reflect the fact that health becomes increasingly valuable in a growing and increasingly productive economy, but at the same time suggested this adjustment should be used cautiously pending further debate. DH includes this value of health adjustment in their total estimates for quality adjusted NHS output growth.

1.9 This leads to a third set of estimates. NHS output growth with all of the quality adjustments listed above, and an allowance for the increasing value of health, is estimated to have increased by an average of around 6.5 per cent per year during the period 1999 to 2004. With the volume of NHS inputs rising at between 4.8 and 5.5 per cent during this period, NHS productivity is estimated to have increased by an average of between 0.9 and 1.6 per cent per year. Figure 3 presents this third set of estimates.

1.10 Finally, the article provides corroborative evidence to support the existing estimates. Section 9 shows that since 1991/92 the average length of stay in hospital has been falling steadily (apart from a small rise between 1999/2000 and 2000/01); and there has been a steady increase in the rate for elective day case treatments. This suggests a shift towards more cost-effective treatment and would be consistent with a productivity increase from NHS resources. At the same time, emergency readmission rates have increased very slightly over the period. If this requires additional NHS

Figure 2

NHS productivity *including* quality change in NHS output but no allowance for increasing value of health, 1999 to 2004

United Kingdom

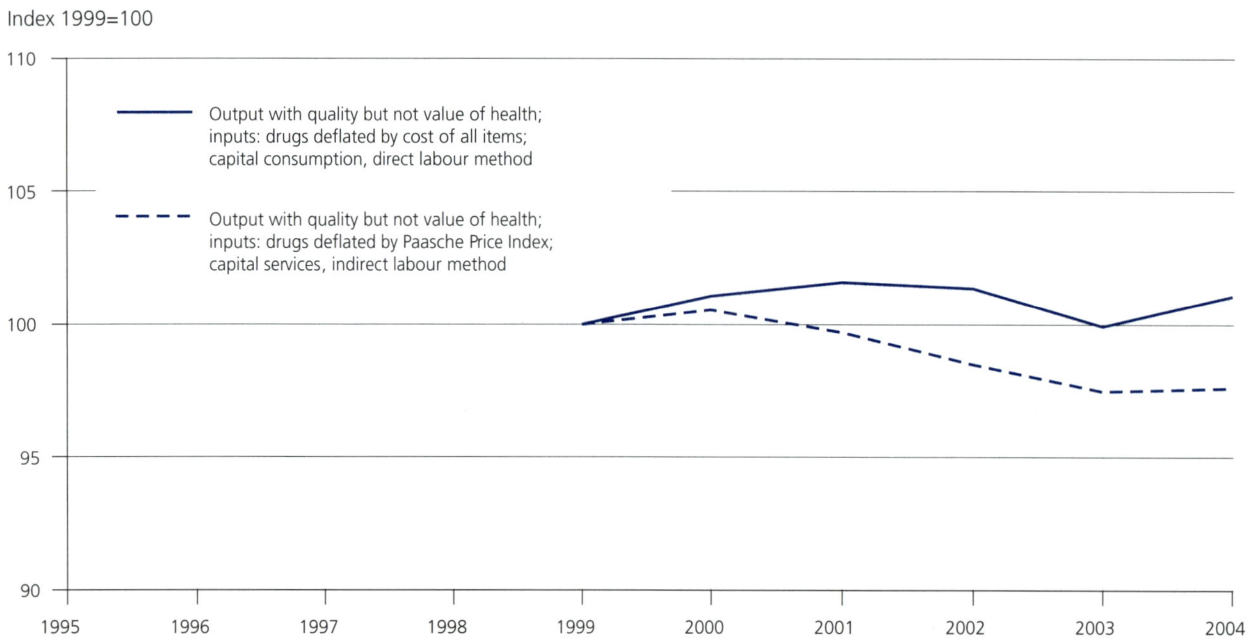

Source: ONS

Figure 3.

NHS productivity *including* quality change in NHS output and allowance for increasing value of health, 1999 to 2004

United Kingdom

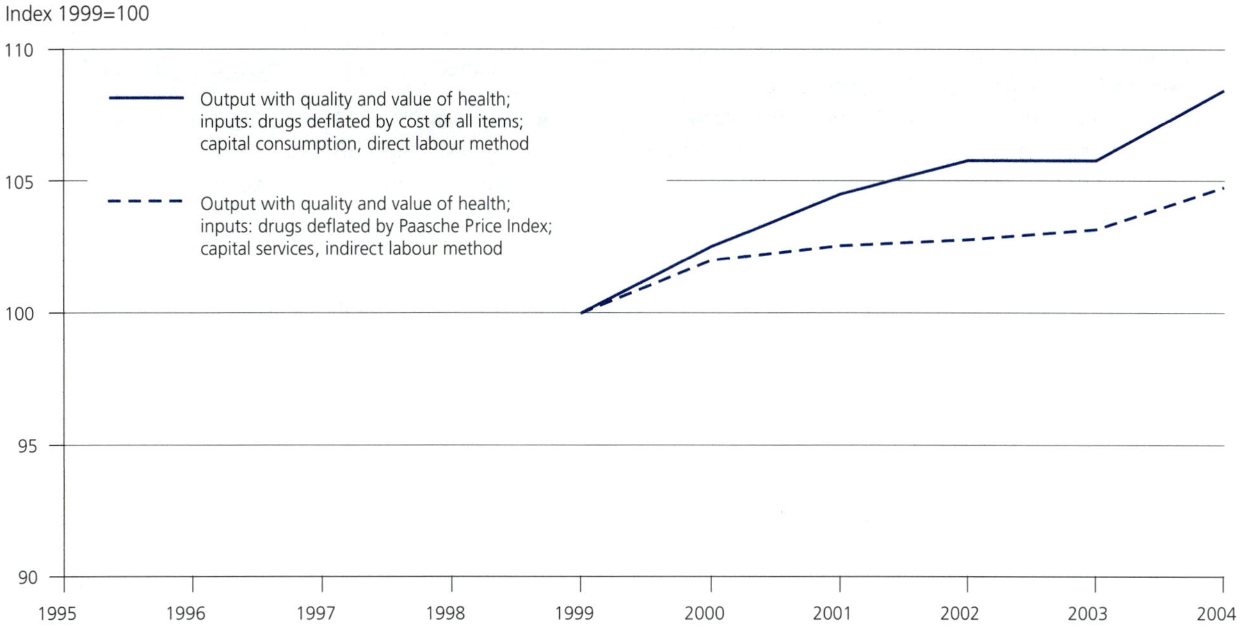

Source: ONS

resources, this could dampen down productivity. More information is needed to check on this impact.

1.11 These new estimates of NHS productivity are based on significant methodological improvements compared with those reported in the first health productivity article published in October 2004. The main improvements which have been made for measuring NHS output are:

- the coverage of the output measure for England has been widened;
- information on activity in Northern Ireland has been included for the first time; and
- NHS output has been quality adjusted using the latest research available.

1.12 The main improvements which have been made for measuring NHS inputs are:

- in the deflation methods; and
- two new measures for estimating the volume of labour inputs.

1.13 However, there is still more work to do:

- further improvements in measuring the quality of NHS output remains a priority;
- data on GP contacts continue to be derived from a household survey which does not provide accurate estimates of growth from one year to the next;
- notwithstanding wider coverage introduced by the new methodology in June 2004 and further in June 2005, the output estimates are still based on a subset of activities carried out by the NHS, and growth in these may not be representative of all activities;
- the output estimates are calculated using data from the NHS in England and Northern Ireland, and growth for these two countries may not be representative of the UK overall; and
- information systems do not necessarily reflect the most recent changes in the structure of, and practice in, the NHS. For example, much activity that was once carried out in hospital inpatient settings is now carried out in outpatient settings or in general practice. But information systems do not yet identify the extent of this change.

2 Introduction

2.1 This is the third in a series of articles that examines public service productivity within the context of the National Accounts, painting a broader picture of public service output and productivity than the National Accounts alone. More precisely, the focus is on productivity associated with money spent by the public sector, including central and local government, in providing health care services to the public.

2.2 This means, therefore, that private purchases from government providers are excluded (for example, figures in this article are net of prescription and dental charges paid by patients). On the other hand, government purchases from the private sector are included (for example, NHS contracts with private companies to provide, say, hip replacement and cataract operations).

2.3 ONS has drawn the material required to estimate NHS productivity from a wide range of sources and used expert advice[1] according to the principles set out in the National Statistics Code of Practice, particularly regarding relevance, fitness for purpose and production with integrity in the interests of all.

2.4 In compiling estimates of NHS productivity, ONS has aimed for conformity with the guidance available from the international community. In particular, the Organisation for Economic Cooperation and Development (OECD) has published *Measuring Productivity* (OECD, 2001) and Eurostat has published a *Handbook on price and volume measures in national accounts* (Eurostat 2001).

2.5 Health is the subject of two of the first three in this series of productivity articles. Health expenditure is important as it constitutes the largest single item of expenditure on public services (social security has a larger share of overall public expenditure, but the majority of this is payment of benefits rather than government providing goods and services).

2.6 The general framework for measuring productivity in the public sector is based on the relationship between inputs, activities, output and outcomes. In health, inputs are the resources used to produce NHS activities, for example, medical staff, prescription drugs, and hospitals. Health outcomes are the final events produced by NHS output, for example, increased life expectancy. However, it is important to recognise that other factors outside the control of the NHS also impact on health outcomes, such as smoking habits, diet and lifestyle. Accordingly, NHS output should be regarded as only the improvement in health outcomes directly attributable to the NHS.

2.7 An overview of the process of measuring NHS productivity is as follows:

- NHS treatment activities are weighted by their relative costs to measure volume growth in NHS output in a cost weighted activity index;
- the cost weighted activity index is then adjusted to take into account quality, using, for example, data that are available for NHS outcomes;
- expenditure on NHS inputs is divided into three main categories: labour, procurement (goods and services) and capital, and then converted into volumes of inputs by taking into account pay and price increases, and changes in the rental value of capital;
- a direct measure of labour input is also used. This involves counting the volume of NHS labour, for example, using number of staff;
- NHS productivity is estimated by dividing NHS output by NHS inputs, using volume measures;
- growth in NHS productivity is estimated as the change in NHS productivity over time; and
- estimates of NHS productivity are tested against wider corroborative evidence that was not used directly in the productivity estimates. This procedure of cross-checking is called 'triangulation'.

2.8 ONS has already published aggregate estimates of government inputs and output in the *United Kingdom National Accounts Blue Book* (ONS 2005a); and inputs, output and implied productivity in *Public Service Productivity: Health* (ONS 2004a). These estimates form the starting point for new estimates of NHS productivity in this paper.

2.9 Sir Tony Atkinson published the final report of his review of the *Measurement of Government Output and Productivity for the National Accounts* (Atkinson 2005) in January 2005. The final report set out a number of recommendations and suggestions for further work for measuring government output and productivity in general as well as specifically for health. This article draws on these recommendations and suggestions.

2.10 A joint project by CHE at the University of York and NIESR has produced a set of estimates of quality change in NHS services which were published in *Developing New Approaches to Measuring NHS Output and Productivity* (York 2005). DH has been working in parallel and has published estimates of quality change in NHS services which complement and broaden the York / NIESR estimates, in *Healthcare Output and Productivity: Accounting for Quality Change* (DH 2005a). All of these estimates are taken into account in this article, and are complemented by other sources of information.

2.11 As the productivity series is developed, ONS will draw further on available information including, for example, material in the various reports published by government and associated institutions such as the Healthcare Commission, and in studies conducted by academic institutions.

2.12 In many cases, analysis is limited to England, or to financial years. As the work continues, ONS intends to expand the analysis to include all constituent parts of the UK, as well as to consider calendar year information, in order for there to be full consistency with the estimates from the National Accounts.

2.13 Annual information is presented in this article, as in articles previously published by ONS in *Economic Trends*. ONS will consider whether to widen the analysis presented in this productivity series to include quarterly information, but publication of quarterly figures would depend on fitness for purpose.

2.14 Triangulation evidence is intended to corroborate (or otherwise) the estimated productivity figures. At the same time, this evidence helps to paint a broader picture of productivity in the NHS. Triangulation material is presented separately in section 9 but sections 3 (Health outcomes) and 5 (Quality of NHS output) also help paint a wider picture of productivity in the NHS.

2.15 The first *Public Service Productivity: Health* article was explicit in recognising that the output and productivity estimates made no allowance for changes in health care quality over time. This article presents a range of estimates which do allow for various dimensions of quality change. They are presented as one stage in an ongoing programme to understand this better. The sources and methodologies presented now need public scrutiny and discussion.

2.16 The rest of this article is as follows:

- section 3 presents the health outcomes that are the prime focus of the NHS but which are also affected by factors outside the control of the NHS;
- section 4 sets out the measurement of NHS output as currently in the National Accounts and also outlines some potential improvements not involving incorporation of quality change. Estimates of output form the starting point for measuring productivity;
- section 5 presents the quality adjusted estimates of output in light of research published in 2005;
- section 6 gives estimates of inputs at current prices in the National Accounts;
- section 7 sets out various estimates of NHS inputs in volume terms, based on improved methodologies;
- section 8 shows new measures of NHS productivity in light of the material presented in sections 4 to 7;
- section 9 describes additional evidence on triangulation not covered in earlier sections; and
- section 10 outlines the next steps in measuring NHS output and productivity.

2.17 This article is also accompanied by *Sources and Methods* (ONS 2006), a supporting article that describes the data, sources and methods used in compiling the estimates in this article.

3 Health outcomes

3.1 The primary aim of the NHS is to improve and maintain the health of the population served. The NHS is therefore mainly concerned with delivery of improved health outcomes.

3.2 This section sets out some information on key health outcomes covering infant mortality, life and healthy life expectancy, and mortality rates. But it is important to recognise that health outcomes are influenced by many factors and are not solely, or even mainly, due to the activities or output of the NHS. Smoking, housing, the environment, diet, changes in demography, socio-economic status, education levels and so on also play their part. Estimates of NHS output need to focus on the improvements in outcomes solely attributable to the NHS, abstracting from the wider factors.

3.3 Nevertheless, as a starting point, it is useful to consider how overall health outcomes have evolved. It is then necessary to consider the extent to which these outcomes are directly affected by the NHS. Principle B in the *Atkinson Review* states that 'the output of the government sector should in principle be measured in a way that is adjusted for quality, taking account of the attributable incremental contribution of the service to the outcome'. Section 4, therefore, presents how NHS output is currently measured in the National Accounts, and section 5 provides an account of how NHS output can be adjusted to take into account quality, based on some of the outcomes described in this section but also on wider criteria.

3.4 ONS, health departments and other authorities publish a range of health statistics on how health outcomes such as mortality and life expectancy have changed over the last century, for example, see *Twentieth Century Mortality Trends in England and Wales* (ONS 2003). This section will limit information on health outcomes to 1980 onwards.

Infant mortality

3.5 Figure 4 shows the reduction in the rate of infant mortality between 1980 and 2004. Infant mortality has fallen throughout this period with the exception of a rise in 1986 which was associated with the exceptionally cold weather in February of that year (MacFarlane A and Mugford M, 2000). In 2004, the infant mortality rate was five per 1,000 live births compared to 12 in 1980.

3.6 Over two thirds of the decline in infant mortality during this period took place in two relatively short intervals. The first, between 1980 and 1984, was predominantly associated with a reduction of around a quarter in mortality rates in the first four weeks of life. It is thought that this was due to the increased survival rate of low birth weight babies as a result of advances in neonatal special and intensive care (MacFarlane A and Mugford M 2000). The second large reduction was between 1988 and 1992. This was associated mainly

Figure 4

Infant mortality (deaths within one year of birth), 1980 to 2004

United Kingdom

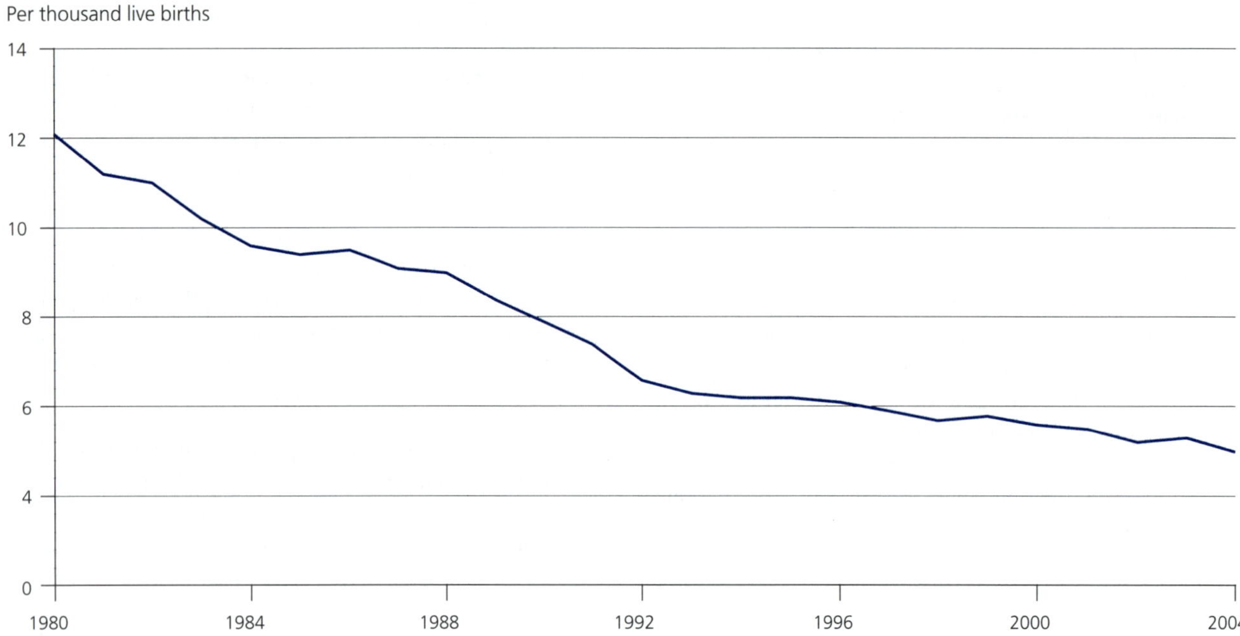

Source: ONS; General Register Office for Scotland; Northern Ireland Statistics and Research Agency; Government Actuary's Department

with a reduction, of just under a half, in death rates of babies aged between four weeks and a year. This followed advice to mothers on avoiding cot deaths (such as that given in the DH campaign 'Back to sleep') (OPCS 1995). The decrease in the infant mortality rate can also be attributed to other factors such as better antenatal, postnatal and medical care; and the development and use of vaccine and immunisation programmes in the NHS. The reduction could also be attributed to factors outside the control of the NHS such as diet. The reduction in the infant mortality rate has been a contributing factor to the overall increase in life expectancy.

Life expectancy

3.7 Life expectancy is a widely used indicator of health status. Healthy life expectancy partitions total life expectancy into years free of health-related problems, and it includes a quality of life aspect that life expectancy does not. As Figure 5 shows, there has been an increase in life expectancy at birth for both males and females during the period presented.

3.8 Female life expectancy at birth has continued to be higher than that for males, though the gap narrowed by one year from six years in 1981 to just under five years in 2001. During this period, life expectancy for men increased by five years, one year more than for women. Healthy life expectancy during the same period increased by just under three years for men – again, around one year more than for women. Therefore, for both sexes, not all the gains in life expectancy were gains in healthy life years.

3.9 A possible explanation for the absolute difference in male and female life and healthy life expectancy may be the result of differences in their chosen lifestyles. For example, men are more likely to adopt behaviour considered risky, such as heavy smoking, drinking and having an unhealthy diet. Men are also less likely to use health services for prevention of diseases. However, as the trend in healthy life expectancy shows, there has been a narrowing in the gap between men and women.

Mortality rates

3.10 Figure 6 presents age-standardised mortality rates by sex for the major causes of death. Since the early 1970s, circulatory diseases (including both heart disease and stroke) have remained the most common cause of death in the UK, but they have also shown the greatest decline. The three major risk factors for CHD are smoking, high cholesterol and high blood pressure. A recent study (BMJ 2005a) looked at contributory factors to explain the 54 per cent fall in CHD mortality rates during the period 1981 to 2000. The study found that approximately half of this fall can be attributed to primary prevention which is aimed at reducing the three major risk factors in people without known CHD. This is four times the impact on mortality rates from secondary prevention which is aimed at reducing risk factors for known CHD patients.

3.11 Cancer is the second most common cause of death, and there have been reductions in mortality from cancer over the last two decades or so. Breast cancer is the most common type of cancer among women. Since a peak in 1988, the mortality rate has declined as a

Figure 5

Life expectancy and healthy life expectancy at birth, by sex, 1981 to 2001

Great Britain

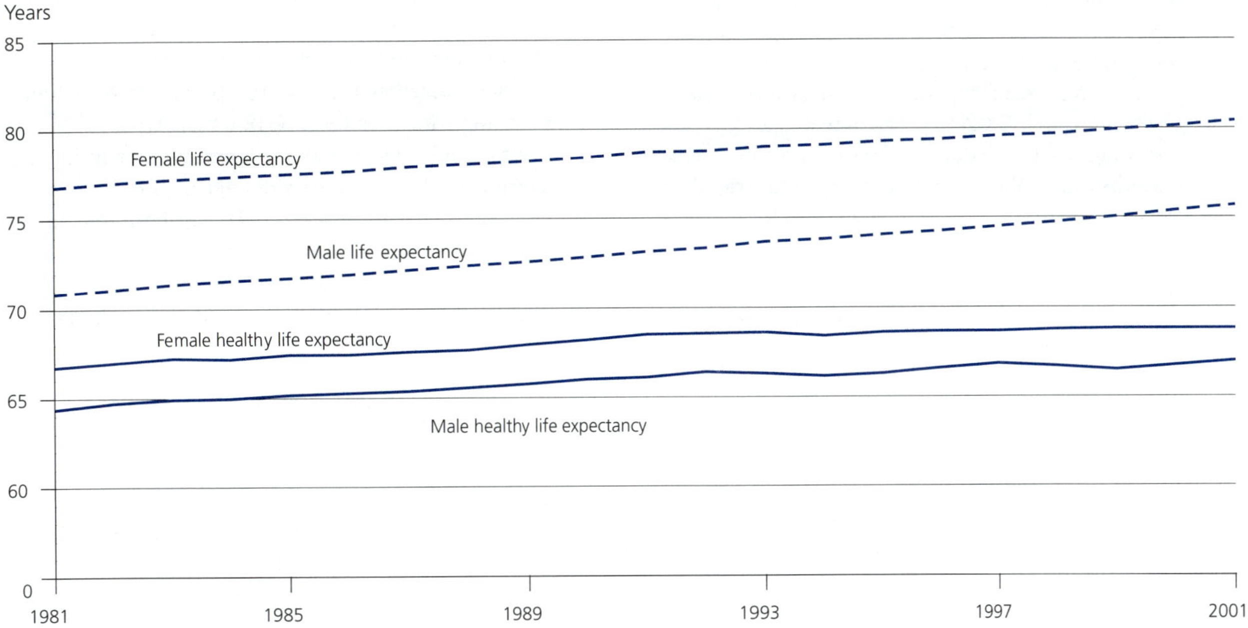

Source:* *Government Actuary's Department; ONS

Figure 6

Standardised mortality rates by sex and major cause, 1980 to 2003

United Kingdom

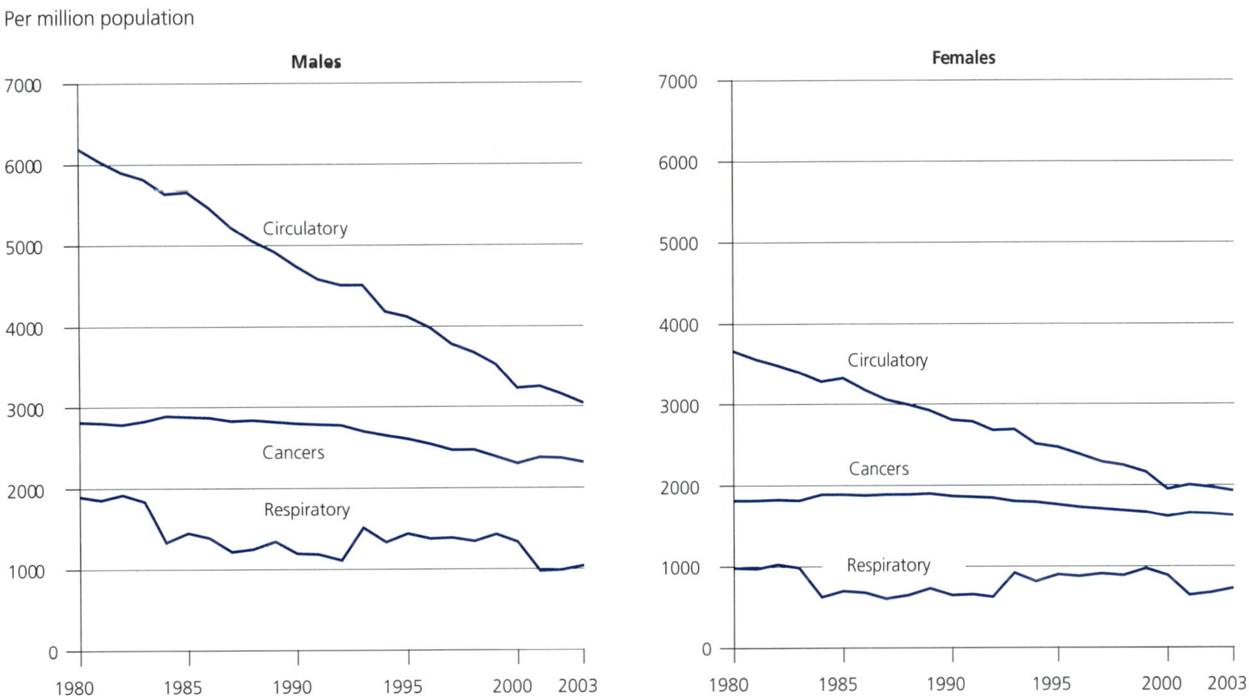

Note: Data for 2000 are for Wales and England only.

Source:* *ONS; General Register Office for Scotland; Northern Ireland Statistics and Research Agency

result of better breast self-examination and because of treatments, including the use of Tamoxifen, and to a lesser extent, earlier diagnosis by breast screening (BMJ 1994, BMJ 2000).

3.12 Many major causes of death, such as heart disease, respiratory diseases and lung cancer, are affected by smoking trends. For example, smoking is estimated to be the main cause of 90 per cent of lung cancer cases (Cancer Research UK 2002). The time it takes for changes in smoking habits to affect such major causes of deaths is thought to differ by cause: from a rapid effect for heart disease, to around 20 years for lung cancer.

3.13 Numerous anti-smoking campaigns and other measures have influenced the proportion of adults who smoke cigarettes, which has fallen from 45 per cent in the early 1970s to 26 per cent in 2003/04, and consequently have had an effect on mortality rates (ONS 2004b).

3.14 Overall, it is clear that some important health outcomes in the UK have been improving. What is less clear is what part of this improvement can be directly attributed to the NHS and thus count as output. The following two sections consider NHS output in more detail, with section 5 in particular discussing proposals for incorporating changes in health outcomes into measures of NHS output change.

4 NHS output in the National Accounts

4.1 NHS output represents the direct contribution it makes to improved health outcomes. This section:

- sets out the current methodology and output estimates used in the National Accounts. These already incorporate improvements made in the 2004 and 2005 *National Accounts Blue Books* as a result of *Atkinson Review* work; and
- then outlines further potential improvements to current methodology, other than steps to be taken to incorporate quality change into the output estimates.

4.2 Satisfactory incorporation of quality change is a substantial topic in its own right and this subject matter is the focus of the next section.

Current methods in the National Accounts

4.3 The methodology used to compile NHS output estimates for the National Accounts since June 2004 distinguishes between different types of detailed activity, and it captures the majority of, but not all, NHS activities in England. Since June 2005, the methodology has also started to capture activity in Northern Ireland. The current methodology does not include quality change as part of output, as recommended by the *Atkinson Review;* and it assumes that output change for Wales and Scotland is the same as that for England and Northern Ireland combined.

4.4 Measuring change in NHS output is based on a number of different sources: the DH National Schedule of Reference Costs (Reference Costs), the General Household Survey, information from NHS Direct, Walk-In Centres, NHS Direct Online, the Prescription Pricing Authority, General Dental Services, General Ophthalmic Services, and ambulance emergency journeys. Together, these sources provide information on changes for over 1,900 NHS activity types in the latest period. DH estimates that around four-fifths by value of all NHS activity in England is covered by the aggregate measure; and the Northern Ireland Department of Health, Social Services and Public Safety estimates that just under three quarters by value of all NHS activity in Northern Ireland is covered by the aggregate measure.

4.5 Growth in NHS output is measured using a cost weighted activity index. In simple terms, this is a large basket of treatment activities where each activity is given importance (weight) as measured by the unit cost associated with its production. As the volume of NHS activities change over time, this volume is adjusted according to the relative weight given to it.

4.6 Table 1 sets out the current *National Accounts Blue Book 2005* estimates of annual growth in NHS output for the years 1995 to 2004, during which NHS output increased by an annual average of 3.2 per cent. These estimates of NHS output growth are the starting point from which to consider how to make adjustments to incorporate NHS quality.

4.7 This average growth of 3.2 per cent per year compares with an annual average growth figure of 3.1 per cent as reported in the first *Public Service Productivity: Health* article in October 2004. The small difference is due to stronger growth between 2003 and 2004 than on average in earlier years. Growth during the period 1999 to 2004, the years for which quality adjustments to outputs are available is higher: 3.9 per cent per year. There are also some methodological improvements incorporated in the later figures. These include:

- additional coverage of a wider range of NHS activities; and
- incorporation of figures for Northern Ireland for the first time.

While these changes are important in principle, they appear to have made little quantitative difference to the estimates.

Table 1

Quantity growth in NHS output (cost weighted activity index using a Laspeyres chained volume measure)

United Kingdom

Index 1999=100 Percentages

	1995	1996	1997	1998	1999	2000	2001	2002	2003	2004	Average annual growth 1995–2003	Average annual growth 1995–2004	Average annual growth 1999–2004
Quantity growth in NHS output in *Blue Book 2005*	90.8	93.8	95.2	96.9	100.0	103.0	107.4	111.4	115.5	121.0	*3.0*	*3.2*	*3.9*
Quantity growth in NHS output October 2004 article	91.1	93.8	95.2	96.9	100.0	103.0	107.3	111.7	116.3	-	*3.1*	-	-

Source: ONS

Potential improvements for measuring NHS output, other than quality adjustment

4.8 This section discusses further potential improvements to the existing measure of NHS output, other than for quality adjustment which is covered in section 5. They cover the use of different sources of information on hospital activity and different base years for unit costs.

4.9 In addition, the impact of using different indices for measuring change in the growth of NHS activities over time is also an important topic for discussion. But given the technical content of this work, this is presented in the accompanying *Sources and Methods.*

Different sources of information on hospital activity

4.10 The most important improvement made in June 2004 was the differentiation in the NHS output index of many different types of health activity. This was made possible because of the availability of unit cost information at a disaggregated level from the Reference Costs. Information on changes in activity had been available for several years from Hospital Episode Statistics (HES), and had been the source of information on activity for the National Accounts prior to June 2004, but only at an aggregated level, and only with unit costs at the aggregate level. It was thus possible in 2004 to differentiate between some 1,700 NHS activities, compared only 16 previously. A desire to retain the consistency of the activity and unit cost information from a single source, alongside the fact that the totals reported in the Reference Costs tally with audited NHS Trusts accounts, meant that the Reference Costs became the source of both activity and unit cost estimates for the NHS output index from June 2004.

4.11 An alternative approach has been considered by the York / NIESR project, which has based estimates of NHS output on the activity figures from HES, because their proposals for incorporating quality adjustments require analysis of patient-level information which is only available from HES, and not from Reference Costs. The researchers also combined individual episodes to form continuous inpatient spells, and constructed adjusted unit costs consistent with this approach. The York / NIESR methodology is not possible using information ONS currently receives from Reference Costs.

4.12 Further discussion of the pros and cons of this change will be needed, as well as consideration of its feasibility. A project has accordingly been set up, involving the ONS, the health administrations and the Health and Social Care Information Centre to consider the most appropriate methods and source of information on NHS activity for the future.

Different base line for unit costs

4.13 A further difference in methodology in the York / NIESR project is the use of a different base year for unit costs to measure NHS output growth. To measure change in the volume of NHS output in the National Accounts, ONS, after consultation with the DH, decided to use unit costs for the most up to date period, 2002/03, as a proxy for unit costs in previous years. The York / NIESR estimates are based on the use of actual unit costs each year to measure output growth in a cost weighted activity index.

4.14 The same project group as mentioned in paragraph 4.12 will also consider which of these unit cost schemes should be preferred.

4.15 Table 2 illustrates the difference between the ONS estimates of change in NHS output growth and those from the York / NIESR project, encompassing both the use of different sources of data on hospital activities and differences in base year unit costs, as well as other more minor differences. ONS estimates of output growth are 0.2 percentage points per year higher than

Table 2:

Quantity growth in NHS output – illustration of differences between the ONS and York / NIESR estimates based on different sources and methods

England Percentages

	1999/1900	2000/2001	2001/2002	2002/2003	2003/2004	Average annual growth 98/1999–03/2004
ONS: Quantity growth in NHS output	3.4	2.9	4.4	3.7	4.3	3.8
York / NIESR project: Quantity growth in NHS output	2.6	2.1	3.9	5.1	4.4	3.6

Source: ONS, York / NIESR

the York / NIESR approach over the period 1999/00 to 2002/03. Comparing the methods and sources used by the York / NIESR model with those currently used by ONS:

- their use of different unit costs is estimated to add 0.6 percentage points to output growth;
- their use of HES rather than Reference Costs to measure activity is estimated to remove 0.5 percentage points from output growth; and
- a number of other, smaller differences are estimated to remove a further 0.3 percentage points from output growth.

4.16 Note that the two methodologies do not give systematically higher or lower growth estimates. The York / NIESR methodology gives higher growth figures for the last two years, but the reverse for the previous three.

5 Quality of NHS output

5.1 The *Atkinson Review* recognised that measuring NHS output simply on the basis of countable activities and cost-based weights ignores the quality of these activities and the contribution they make to valuable outcomes. This section summarises the recommendations made in the *Atkinson Review* for measuring the quality of NHS output, and then describes research commissioned and produced by DH for quality adjusting NHS output. A number of indicators have been developed and the individual impacts they have on NHS output growth are reported where it is possible to do so. The indicators represent the main quality adjustment factors to be considered, but the list should not be regarded as exhaustive, and they are still limited in terms of the data that are available to populate them.

5.2 The quality adjustment indicators covered in this section come from recently published research by York / NIESR on: survival rates, health effects, life expectancy and waiting times; and from additional research carried out by DH on: health gain from the use of statins to treat CHD, improved outcomes from primary medical care, survival rates from myocardial infarction, and patient experience. A further adjustment for changing value of health, proposed in the *Atkinson Review* and by DH is discussed.

5.3 The intention in this section is to consider the consequences of this research for the NHS output and productivity figures if these various adjustments are made. It is intended to set the stage for further public discussion on these methods, data and results. ONS, working with DH, will be holding consultation seminars on these issues in 2006.

The Atkinson Framework

5.4 The *Atkinson Review* set out five principles to be applied in the measurement of government output. One of these stated that the output of the government sector should be measured in a way that is adjusted for quality. More specifically, paragraph 4.25 in the *Atkinson Review* stated there are at least three different ways to approach the measurement of quality in the National Accounts:

- first, differentiate the services, with the aim of arriving at categories that can be regarded as homogenous. A quality change is then captured by changes in the proportions of different categories;
- second, define the volume measures in terms of the degree of success; and
- third, the volume measure may be based on the level of activity but the contribution to outcomes introduced in the form of a quality adjustment. The volume measure would be 'marked up or down' by a percentage reflecting indicators of success and the contribution of the service to that success.

5.5 The first aspect of quality change is covered in section 4 on measuring NHS output. In particular, the number of categories covered has increased from 16 to, first, 1,700 in 2004 and to around 1,900 since July 2005. The second and third aspects of quality change in NHS output are covered in this section, and can be linked to some of the health outcomes presented in section 3.

5.6 A further principle set out in the *Atkinson Review*, Principle C, suggested that account should be taken of the fact that the output of public services becomes increasingly valuable in material terms in an economy with rising real income. This is set forth as a general principle but elsewhere the *Atkinson Review* makes clear that this should apply to Health, as to other services.

5.7 While the *Atkinson Review* regarded an adjustment on this account as important, it also recognised that such an adjustment was not yet universally accepted and should therefore be used with caution, pending further debate.

Subsequent work

5.8 Since publication of the *Atkinson Review Final Report* in January 2005, there have been major advances in measuring the quality of NHS output. In particular, two research publications have moved the agenda forward:

- *Developing new approaches to measuring NHS output and productivity*, a paper published jointly by CHE at the University of York and NIESR on 7 December 2005; and
- *Healthcare Output and Productivity: Accounting for Quality Change*, a paper by DH, published on 7 December 2005, which includes information from the report above.

5.9 ONS has worked closely with DH, the University of York and NIESR on quality adjustment issues, but at the same time maintained an independent view of the new research findings.

5.10 Both studies are explicitly consistent with the broad framework recommended by the *Atkinson Review*. They are therefore broadly based on the proposition that the task is to measure the contribution of the NHS to improved health outcomes as a result of its activities. Higher quality, in its various manifestations, obviously produces greater health gains and benefits for patients. The exact ways in which the various dimensions come together and can be captured in a quality adjusted index of output are set out in the two research publications.

The York / NIESR Study

5.11 The York / NIESR work essentially recognises a cluster of interacting factors in arriving at an overall quality adjustment:

- taking account of improving survival rates for patients;
- taking account of improving health gains for patients;
- adjusting for the fact that both better survival and health gain will depend upon the life expectancy distribution of the patients concerned. Younger patients will enjoy the benefits for longer on average than older ones; and
- allowance for changes in waiting times. Patients enjoy gains more quickly if waiting times are shorter.

5.12 The following sections discuss each of these elements in more detail, as well as noting the comments on them from the DH publication. The adjustments proposed by York / NIESR (and DH) relate to the financial years 1999/2000 to 2003/04. For simplicity, ONS has incorporated these adjustments to the 2000 to 2004 calendar years, respectively, without adjustment.

Survival rates

5.13 Improved survival as a result of NHS interventions must obviously be considered as a quality adjustment factor, as this is a key health outcome. Several observations are relevant when using survival rates as a quality adjustment factor:

- for some health conditions, death may be an expected outcome of hospital admissions, for example, patients with terminal conditions being admitted for palliative care as they approach the end of their lives;
- by contrast, for some health conditions, death may take place but was not expected and is therefore considered avoidable. For example, most patients admitted with acute appendicitis survive, but few die; and
- for other health conditions, patients at high risk of death are admitted to hospital and the outcome will depend, in part, on the preventative treatment, for example, by major heart surgery or from successful cancer treatments.

So survival rates are, in principle, relevant as an indicator of quality mainly in the areas of avoidable deaths.

5.14 The York / NIESR research uses data on deaths within 30 days of admission, by hospital, which is produced by the National Centre for Health Outcomes Development. The 30 days cut off point is used on the basis that any period greater than 30 days makes it more difficult to attribute survival directly to NHS interventions. While the York / NIESR work makes adjustment for the fact that some health conditions have a higher death rate, the use of routine survival data means it was not possible to consider separately the impacts of avoidable deaths and for patients reaching the end of their natural life.

5.15 The DH publication agrees with the York / NIESR work, that in principle, survival rate is a valid quality adjustment for health care output but points out that this indicator still requires further development as follows:

- adjustment is needed for changes in case mix, in particular age of patient, severity of diagnosis, comorbidity and other risk factors;
- emergency admissions have been rising quickly in recent years with a shift towards 'zero day' admissions which allow observation and treatment planning. These admissions alter the denominator for survival rates, as there may be more 'low risk' admissions for patients who would previously have been assessed in Accident and Emergency departments without admission, or perhaps in primary care;
- changes in the place of death over time need to be considered, for example, if more patients choose to move to a hospice or a nursing home, this may affect comparisons of survival rates between years; and
- more consideration should be given to the balance between 'avoidable or preventable' and other deaths.

5.16 On this last point, there is no consensus on how to measure levels of avoidable and premature death. ONS is currently in the process of developing national indicators for measuring premature and avoidable mortality, details of which could be included in future productivity articles. (For further details see: www.statistics.gov.uk/about/Consultations/mortality.asp)

Health effects

5.17 The extent to which NHS activities improve the health of patients relative to the situation when no treatment is provided is an important but complex quality adjustment issue. Quality adjustment of NHS output using health effects would, ideally, make use of data collected on the health status of patients before and after all the treatment interventions included in the NHS cost weighted output index. Unfortunately such a comprehensive dataset does not exist. However, York / NIESR has been able to demonstrate the impact of using data available for 29 individual procedures. A list of the 29 individual procedures that were used by York / NIESR is provided in *Sources and Methods.* These procedures cover around $2^1/_2$ per cent of total NHS expenditure.

5.18 Health benefits data have been taken from two sources: measures of 'before and after' change in health status after treatment in BUPA hospitals, and research studies. Health benefits data are based on a simple scale between 0 and 1, where 0 represents the worst possible health state, 1 represents perfect health, following treatment for a health condition. For example, York / NIESR use a well known health measurement tool, the Short Form 36, to show that health status changes from 0.7 to 0.8 following surgery for hysterectomy. It is this type of change in health status that is used for the 29 individual procedures in *Sources and Methods.* The researchers acknowledge the limitations of their data and recommend further data collection.

5.19 The DH publication broadly agrees with the York / NIESR approach and recognises the data limitations for measuring health effects, but makes the following comments:

- it might be valid initially to use a quality adjustment based on health effects for a small number of high volume treatments, while continuing to work towards wider coverage;
- the health benefit of treatment is, in principle, a comparison between health status for the rest of the patient's life after treatment, with their health status if they had not received treatment. This needs further consideration, particularly as York / NIESR currently use only a three month period for measuring treatment effects;
- 'before and after' measures alone are not enough to estimate health gain from treatment, particularly if the 'after' treatment measure is short term. When treating serious health conditions, for example, it is also appropriate to consider longer term life expectancy, for example, successful treatment of an early cancer patient could add 20 years to life expectancy, whereas for some patients whose treatment is unsuccessful, death might be typically three months after treatment interventions; and
- the impact of treatment on patients treated under BUPA may not be the same as those who are treated under the NHS.

Adjustment for life expectancy

5.20 As outlined in section 3, the extension of life that is due to NHS activities is a key health outcome. York / NIESR adjusts their estimates for survival and health effects by taking into account life expectancy, factoring in an adjustment for age of patients at the time of treatment. Quality adjustment using life expectancy reflects the fact that older patients have less time to benefit from treatment. A discounting approach is used giving most weight to health benefits in the near future, and progressively less to health benefits in later time periods. Health benefits are assumed to be sustained for the rest of the patient's life.

5.21 The DH publication agrees with the proposals from York / NIESR but adds the following:

- there are examples (for example, chronic disease with repeated short hospital episodes) where the duration of treatment benefit is shorter than the remaining years of the patient's life. This needs to be considered further; and

- in agreement with York / NIESR, it would be preferable to use condition-specific and age-specific survival rates, rather than rely on a general life expectancy adjustment.

Waiting times

5.22 The NHS has established targets for waiting times with the aim of cutting the number of people on long waiting lists. These targets have also been built into the Performance Assessment Framework. Table 3 presents waiting time information for English inpatients and outpatients. This table shows fairly substantial decreases in the number of people experiencing long inpatient and outpatient waiting times since 1998.

5.23 The maximum waiting times for both inpatient and outpatient treatment has decreased, with the median wait for outpatient treatment falling from around 15 weeks in 1998 to 8.5 weeks in March 2005. Waiting times are an important component of the quality of care so the measure of NHS output should take them into account.

5.24 Waiting times for treatment have potentially two impacts relevant to the quality adjustment of NHS output. First, the experience of waiting may reduce health gains as the benefits of treatment to patients are deferred. Second, the waiting may not actually affect health outcomes but nevertheless the patient may find the experience associated with waiting stressful. Some of this effect has already been captured by the York / NIESR estimates, but it should be noted that the evidence base to assess and measure the two impacts more generally is weak.

5.25 The York / NIESR work concentrates on the first impact, that is, the impact that waiting times have on reducing health gains. A discount factor of 1.5 per cent per year is used to reflect the fact that distant health gains are less valuable to people; and the researchers also incorporate a 'charge for waiting' which is the equivalent of an interest payment during the waiting period, and one that increases with the length of time the patient has to wait.

5.26 The DH publication broadly supports the work of York / NIESR but has some concerns with the overall approach. In particular, the York / NIESR formula for waiting times needs to be understood in a wider context. For example, most patients who need elective treatment do not wait long; most hospital patients are admitted without ever being on a waiting list; and most NHS care takes place outside hospital. In addition, the DH publication questions whether the 'health gains' approach used by York / NIESR currently captures the wider patient experience associated with waiting for treatment.

5.27 Taking account of all of the elements in the York / NIESR cluster (survival rates, health effects – both adjusted for life expectancy and waiting times) increases NHS output growth by an average of 0.17 percentage points per year during the period 1999/2000 to 2003/04.

The DH publication

5.28 Subject to the comments summarised above, DH accept the York / NIESR analysis. The DH publication sets out other areas for which they have developed additional adjustments:

- improved health outcomes from the use of statins to treat CHD;
- improved outcomes from primary medical care;
- better survival rates as a result of higher quality treatment of myocardial infarction; and
- improving (non-clinical) patient experience.

Table 3

NHS inpatient and outpatient waiting times

England Thousands

Number of people waiting	Mar 98	Mar 99	Mar 00	Mar 01	Mar 02	Mar 03	Mar 04	Mar 05
For inpatient treatment:								
0–5 months	900	784	760	752	783	786	811	768
6–8 months	192	146	138	130	141	136	80	41
9–11 months	118	84	78	72	75	53	<1	<1
12 months plus	67	47	48	41	22	<1	<1	<1
For first outpatient appointment:								
13–25 weeks	196	292	263	200	191	120	40	30 [1]
26 weeks plus	101	144	130	80	1	<1	<1	n/a [1]

1 From Q1 2004/05 figures for 26 weeks plus are not collected separately. Figures are collected for 21 plus.

Source: DH

The DH figures come from examples of methods considered appropriate for quality adjustment and DH have plans to develop these further. The following sections discuss the DH quality adjustments in turn.

Health gain from using statins to treat CHD

5.29 The *Atkinson Review* recommended that ONS and the health departments should consider identifying treatments where marginal valuation and cost weights are very different, and explore the difference in output growth resulting from use of estimated value weights instead of cost weights. In the first instance, and considering the data available, the DH publication identifies the use of statins to treat CHD as one such example.

5.30 The National Service Framework for health recommends statin therapy for patients with evidence of occlusive arterial diseases, including CHD and stroke. Statins reduce cholesterol which can block arteries, and so reduce the risk of heart attacks, strokes, and the onset of angina (DH 2005a). In 2004, around 2.6 million patients took statins, at a cost of £738m (around 1 per cent of total NHS expenditure). The evidence on health gain from statins is outlined in more detail in a technical paper (DH 2005b).

5.31 The DH publication follows the recommendation made by the *Atkinson Review*. Instead of using cost weights, the publication proposes using value weights based on added life years as a direct result of statin therapy.

5.32 Paragraph 7.14 from the DH publication summarises the approach used to measure NHS output growth for statins:

> 'TP2 estimates that statin therapy in 2003 added 77,000 life years, compared with no therapy, for the 1.9 million patients who took the drug. It estimates that each prescription has a marginal benefit of 0.0038 life years. If each life year is valued at £30,000, the value of each prescription is £115. This compares with £27 as the unit cost used in the current output index. TP2 also argues that the marginal value has not changed over time (i.e. there is no evidence that prescriptions are being given to patients with less chance of benefiting). Using £115 instead of £27 as the weight for statins increases overall NHS output growth by, on average, 0.81 per cent a year'.

5.33 The increase in output growth estimated by the DH publication is clearly dependent on the value placed on each life year, currently estimated to be around £30,000. But this is a figure used in health economics and does not seem an unreasonable estimate.

5.34 Using value weights instead of cost weights for statins increases NHS output growth by an annual average of 0.81 percentage points during 1999 to 2004.

Improved outcomes from primary medical care

5.35 The DH publication proposes an adjustment for changing quality of primary medical care (excluding prescribed drugs) which accounts for around 12 per cent of the NHS cost weighted activity index in 2003/04. Data for a full quality adjustment based on primary medical care outcomes are still developing (DH 2005c). However, DH were able to use data on improvements in blood pressure and cholesterol control from the QRESEARCH[2] database which holds information on over three million registered patients. Those data showed:

- a 23 per cent average annual increase in cholesterol control for patients with known CHD between January 2002 and October 2004; and
- blood pressure control for patients with CHD improved by an annual rate of 11 per cent, and for patients with hypertension, by 22 per cent, over the same period.

5.36 DH 2005c sets out a general methodology for quality adjustment based on primary medical care outcomes. The approach adopted suggests that outcome indicators are weighted by the prevalence of the condition. For example, 14 per cent of the QRESEARCH patients have either CHD or hypertension or both, so would carry a weight of 14 per cent. The paper assumes there is no change in quality of care for patients with other conditions, and also applies downward weighting to allow for the fact that patients with CHD also visit the GP for treatment for other conditions.

5.37 Based on DH calculations (see table 3, p43 in the main DH publication for detail), quality adjustment based on data currently available for primary medical care increases overall NHS output growth by 0.16 percentage points per year for the two years for which data are available (2002/03 to 2003/04). Further work will be required to develop this illustrative measure and to expand on the NHS activities included in primary medical care.

Longer survival rates from myocardial infarction

5.38 The DH publication also makes use of data available on hospital episodes for patients admitted to hospital with myocardial infarction (MI), together with death certificates up to five years later for any cause. The longer term survival data expands on the analysis carried out by York / NIESR (where the survival period was restricted to the 30 day period) for this condition following hospital admission. Over the period 1998/99 to 2002/03, mortality rates, adjusted for age and sex, for patients admitted with MI in 1998/99, fell on average 3.2 per cent per year. Over the longer survival period it is possible that other factors contributed to this, for example, the clinical threshold for defining a case as MI, or the threshold for hospital admission for MI, may have changed. However, the DH publication also points out that success in treating MI is consistent with changes in clinical practice promoted in the National Service Framework.

5.39 Using additional survival benefit for patients treated with MI adds 0.01 percentage points per year to total NHS output. This adjustment is small because NHS spending on MI is small in comparison with total NHS spending. Further work is required to see if this level of adjustment could be applied more generally across the CHD programme.

Patient experience

5.40 Recommendation 8.5(i) from the *Atkinson Review* stated that ONS and DH 'should explore whether measures of quality change over time could be based on the national patient survey programme which measures aspects of patient experience'. The National Patient Experience Survey Programme was established under the 2000 NHS Plan (DH 2000), and NHS organisations are required to carry out local surveys each year, also changing the service areas that are covered each year. So far there have been two surveys in four different areas of NHS activity: inpatients, accident and emergency, outpatients and primary care.

5.41 The survey asks recent patients to reply to a range of questions about their experience of the health care they have received. Questions are mapped to five domains: access and waiting; safe, high quality co-ordinated care; better information, more choice; building closer relationships; and clean, friendly, comfortable place to be. A further DH Technical Paper (DH 2005d) provides detail on the use of these domains and how they are used for quality adjustment purposes.

5.42 There are two time points available in the survey for each of the four different areas of NHS activity, but with a missing year for three out of the four areas (there are only consecutive years for primary care). These areas cover around half the NHS cost weighted activity index. After combining domain scores and accounting for data for missing years, the quality adjustment for patient experience increases total NHS output growth by 0.17 percentage points per year during 2001/02 and 2003/04. When averaged over a five year period 1999/2000 to 2003/04 this becomes 0.07 percentage ponts, assuming there is no change in patient experience for the first three years.

5.43 Interpreting patient experience surveys is not straightforward, for example, it is difficult to fully assess how far responses actually reflect changes in the quality of NHS care. Such surveys will always contain some elements of bias, levels of expectation rather than experience, general beliefs, and so on.

Value of health adjustment based on real earnings growth

5.44 As noted earlier in paragraph 5.6, Principle C in the *Atkinson Report* stated:

> 'Account should be taken of the complementarity between public and private output, allowing for the increased real value of public services in an economy with rising real GDP'.

5.45 In the context of health, paragraph 4.38 from the *Atkinson Report* states:

> 'In the case of health, rising real wage rates means that we attach a higher valuation to days lost through sickness absence. An extra week at work today is worth more than forty years ago. The same effect may apply more generally. The literature on Quality Adjusted Life Years has considered how the financial value to be attached should be adjusted over time. The answer given by Gravelle and Smith (2001) is that it should grow at approximately 1.5 per cent per year in real terms'.

5.46 However, at the same time, the *Atkinson Report* recommended caution in implementing Principle C as it may be considered controversial. ONS will be working with DH to consult on this point specifically, in the context of wider discussion on improving the measurement of NHS output. Until consultation has taken place, this paper therefore presents estimates of NHS output and productivity growth with and without an adjustment for real earnings growth. In line with the *Atkinson Review* recommendation, for those estimates that include the adjustment, NHS output growth is adjusted to reflect real earnings growth of 1.5 per cent per year.

5.47 ONS followed the same procedure in the *Public Service Productivity: Education* article published in October 2005. Again as a basis for further discussion, estimates both with and without the real earnings adjustment are presented.

Summary of the quality adjustment impacts

5.48 Table 4 provides a summary of the impacts on growth of NHS output using the York / NIESR, DH and *Atkinson Review* adjustment indicators, and the estimated total impact on NHS output growth. In this table, the value of health effect is shown separately.

5.49 The total impacts on NHS output growth from using these quality adjustment factors are also shown in Figure 7. From 1999 to 2004, growth in NHS output is estimated to be:

- 3.9 per cent per year on average without quality adjustment;

- 5.0 per cent per year on average with quality adjustment but excluding the value of health adjustment; and
- 6.5 per cent per year on average including both quality and value of health adjustments.

Table 4

Estimated impact on growth of NHS output from various methods of quality adjustment, proposed by the York / NIESR project, DH, and the *Atkinson Review*

England — Percentage points

	Average impact on growth per year
York / NIESR effects	+0.17
DH proposals:	
Value for statins	+0.81
Improved blood pressure control[1]	+0.05
Heart attack survival	+0.01
Patient experience[1]	+0.07
Annual increase in value of health	+1.50
Total DH effect[2]	+2.51
Overall quality adjustment	+2.68

1 *Results from the two most recent years have been averaged over five years.*
2 *The total is greater than the sum of individual adjustments because of cumulative effects.*

Source: DH

6 NHS inputs in the National Accounts at current prices

6.1 This section presents estimates of expenditure on NHS inputs over time. This forms the starting point for estimating the volume of NHS inputs. NHS inputs are the resources used in the production of NHS activities and output that contribute to NHS outcomes. NHS inputs cover, for example, medical staff (labour), prescription drugs and electricity (procurement), and hospitals (capital). A key part of this section is to present the latest estimates of NHS expenditure taking into account any revisions planned to be made to previous *Blue Book* estimates. In this section, revisions to NHS expenditure include an adjustment to intermediate consumption expenditure, updating some estimates based on planned spending with actual spending, and an adjustment required for Pension Increase Payments in 1995.

6.2 The National Accounts provide information on general government final consumption expenditure (GGFCE) on health which can be converted to volume measures by taking out changes in pay and prices over time. This section presents information on GGFCE on NHS inputs at current year prices. Section 7 provides an account of how current price inputs are converted in volumes.

6.3 Different types of inputs contribute in different ways to health care production. This section and section 7 distinguish between labour, intermediate consumption and capital consumption. Labour covers NHS staff;

Figure 7

NHS output growth without quality adjustment, 1995 to 2004 and with quality adjustment, 1999 to 2004

United Kingdom

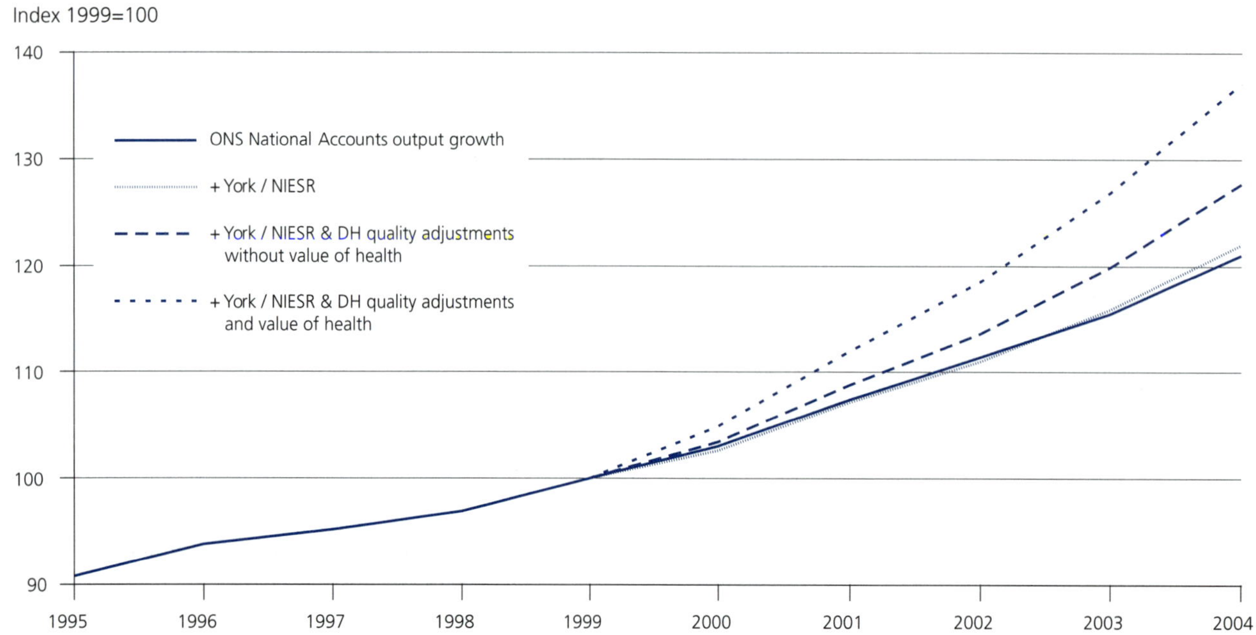

Source: ONS

intermediate consumption, also termed procurement, involves the purchase of goods and services that are used up in the production process. For example, the NHS buys drugs, pays for electricity and buys services from private sector health companies.

6.4 The NHS also buys capital assets that can be used repeatedly or continuously over the longer term, such as buildings, machinery, and vehicles. Such capital assets are distinguished from intermediate consumption because they contribute in a different way to the production of NHS output. Whereas intermediate consumption items are used up in producing NHS output in any given year, capital assets last over a number of years. The amount used up of these capital assets over a year in the production process is called capital consumption.

Changes to expenditure for measuring productivity

6.5 *Correction to NHS Trusts intermediate consumption expenditure used in National Accounts.* From 1999 onwards, estimates published in *Blue Book 2005* for intermediate consumption for the health function were under recorded by between £0.8 and £1.2 billion a year. This will be corrected in *Blue Book 2006.* It is only the functional breakdown of intermediate consumption that is affected by this revision; the overall consumption total that forms part of key public sector finance series is unaffected.

6.6 *Revisions to provisional estimates. Blue Book 2005* includes an estimate for some NHS expenditure in 2004 which was based on planned figures. This estimate has subsequently been revised with outturn (or actual) data and incorporated into the latest quarterly National Accounts. The health series is published annually in *Blue Book.* The revised estimates have been used in the productivity calculations and are presented in this article.

6.7 *Pension Increase Payments.* The pension scheme for NHS Trust staff, as well as some others in the NHS, is only notionally funded. Prior to 2003/04, actual employer contributions to the scheme did not include adjustments for inflation. *Blue Book 2005* estimates of NHS expenditure include an inflation adjustment in order to reflect true labour costs, but this inflation adjustment has been made to calendar year estimates from only 1996 onwards. For this article, an extra adjustment has been made to the *Blue Book 2005* estimate for 1995 to create a consistent series.

6.8 Table 5 presents estimates of labour, intermediate consumption and capital consumption at current year prices, taking into account the above changes and the latest available information, and as such, differ slightly from those currently published in the National Accounts.

6.9 Taking into account these revisions and other minor changes, table 6 compares total current price GGFCE on NHS inputs used in this article with the estimates used in the first *Public Service Productivity: Health* article.

Table 5

Expenditure on NHS Inputs: labour, intermediate consumption and capital consumption, current prices

United Kingdom £ million

	1995	1996	1997	1998	1999	2000	2001	2002	2003	2004
Labour	22,245	23,056	24,025	24,838	26,096	28,099	30,927	33,975	35,405	38,672
Intermediate consumption	15,853	17,591	17,608	19,611	22,703	23,550	25,535	27,765	32,947	36,601
Capital consumption	1,227	1,319	1,366	1,387	1,455	1,587	1,570	1,648	1,729	1,784
Total	39,325	41,966	42,999	45,836	50,254	53,236	58,032	63,388	70,081	77,057

Source: ONS

Table 6

Expenditure on NHS inputs: comparison of estimates in this article compared with the first *Public Service Productivity: Health* article, current prices

United Kingdom £ million

	1995	1996	1997	1998	1999	2000	2001	2002	2003	2004
This article	39,325	41,966	42,999	45,836	50,254	53,236	58,032	63,388	70,081	77,057
October 2004 article	39,508	42,282	43,369	46,185	51,155	54,880	59,098	65,089	71,194	-
Difference	–183	–316	–370	–349	–901	–1,644	–1,066	–1,701	–1,113	-

Source: ONS

7 Measuring the volume of NHS inputs

7.1 Measurement of NHS productivity is based on dividing the volume of NHS output by a volume measure for NHS inputs. This section presents the methodology on how expenditure on NHS inputs is converted into a volume measure, and the resulting estimates. Two approaches are presented:

- the first approach – the 'indirect approach' – deflates NHS expenditure by adjusting labour and procurement expenditure by pay and price indices respectively. Capital expenditure is adjusted by taking into account changes in the rental value of capital; and
- a new 'direct approach' is also used to convert expenditure on NHS staff into a volume measure by adjusting for hours worked and taking into account differences in earnings. York / NIESR carried out an alternative methodology using a different source of information on NHS labour and also considered skill mix. The estimates are very similar to those in this section, so are not reported here.

7.2 Use of these two methods is consistent with the recommendations of the *Atkinson Review*. Principle F noted that 'labour inputs should be compiled using both direct and indirect methods, compared and reconciled'. The first health productivity article presented estimates of labour inputs based only on an indirect method, that is, deflated expenditure on NHS labour. This article also presents estimates based on direct methods.

Deflating NHS Labour inputs using information on pay (indirect method)

7.3 The National Accounts convention requires a Paasche Price Index when deflating current price expenditure. The deflators used in the first *Public Service Productivity: Health* article for removing the price effect from some expenditure on NHS labour (predominantly hospital and community health staff) have been improved. The previous deflators were similar to a Laspeyres Price Index, but used current price expenditure weights rather than quantity weights. The new deflator, constructed using the same raw data, is a Paasche Price Index using quantity weights. Table 7 presents the new and old deflators (the latter have been updated using the latest available information to show differences over the 1995-2004 time period).

7.4 Using the Paasche Price Index consistent with the National Accounts, cost inflation of some NHS staff is rising less quickly than previously estimated, by just under 1 per cent per year on average.

Counting NHS Labour inputs using numbers of staff and hours worked (direct method)

7.5 The OECD manual *Measuring Productivity* recommends the number of hours worked, with suitable differentiation by skill, as the preferable measure of the quantity of labour inputs into production. This is preferred to numbers of people employed, as the contribution provided by full-time employees differs from that of part-time employees according to the number of hours worked. *Measuring Productivity* points out that "...an hour worked by a highly experienced surgeon and an hour worked by a newly hired teenager at a fast food restaurant..." should be differentiated for productivity analysis, but although desirable, this is difficult.

7.6 ONS has compiled an exploratory direct measure in accordance with the OECD manual based on available NHS sources relating to staff levels and earnings differentials by grade of staff.

7.7 Table 8 presents the estimates from both using the indirect and direct methods. Both show the growth in the volume of NHS labour to be at or just over 3 per cent per year, on average, with the indirect method showing the higher growth of the two.

Table 7

Comparison of the deflators used for removing the price effect from expenditure on hospital and community health staff: deflators consistent with those used in the first *Public Service Productivity: Health* article and the improved deflators used in this article

England

Index 1999=100 | Percentages

	1995	1996	1997	1998	1999	2000	2001	2002	2003	2004	Average annual growth 1995–2004
This article	85.9	88.6	91.0	94.3	100.0	106.6	114.1	120.3	126.4	132.6	*4.9*
October 2004 article	84.9	88.0	90.2	93.9	100.0	107.0	116.1	122.5	130.6	139.3	*5.7*

Source: ONS

Table 8

Change in NHS labour inputs using direct and indirect methods

England

Index 1999=100 Percentages

	1995	1996	1997	1998	1999	2000	2001	2002	2003	2004	Average annual change 1995–2004
ONS indirect method	94.5	95.7	96.4	97.7	100.0	102.7	108.1	114.3	119.1	127.2	*3.4*
ONS direct method	94.7	95.8	96.4	97.7	100.0	102.2	106.2	111.8	117.4	123.1	*3.0*

Source: ONS

7.8 *Sources and Methods*, provides detail on the relative advantages and disadvantages of the approaches to measurement of NHS labour inputs.

Intermediate consumption: prescription drugs

7.9 As discussed in the first *Public Service Productivity: Health* article, the identification of a suitable price deflator for expenditure on drugs dispensed outside hospitals has been problematic. DH has made a key change to its analysis so that it now links the prices of branded and generic drugs. This means that when branded drugs fall out of patent and generic drugs come onto the market that may be cheaper, this fall in cost for similar drugs is counted as part of the price change. Previously, this effect was not included as part of the price effect. A consistent series calculated in this new way would constitute an appropriate price deflator for expenditure on prescription drugs.

7.10 The new analysis has so far only been carried out for two years, 2003 and 2004, and not for previous years. ONS and DH will be looking into extending the new analysis back over time. According to the new analysis, the price of prescription drugs fell in both years, by 0.5 per cent from 2002 to 2003, and by 3.4 per cent from 2003 to 2004.

7.11 For previous years, two deflators are presented as for the first *Public Service Productivity: Health* article, reflecting uncertainty about the effect on one overall price change of branded drugs coming off patent prior to 2003. These are an index of average costs per item and a Paasche Price Index, both taken from the DH analysis of change in the net ingredient costs of prescription drugs. Table 9 presents the two alternatives. The two methods produce very different results for annual average price changes. This differential is reflected in the range of productivity estimates provided in this article, and in more detail in *Sources and Methods.*

7.12 Table 10 shows the results of adding the estimates of price change from the new analysis for the years 2003 and 2004 to each of the alternative estimates of price change for years prior to 2003, to arrive at a time series for the whole 1995 to 2004 period.

Table 9

Alternative estimates of change in price of prescription drugs

England

Index 1999=100 Percentages

	1995	1996	1997	1998	1999	2000	2001	2002	Average annual price change 1995–2004
Index of average cost per item	77.9	82.7	87.4	91.7	100.0	101.3	104.3	111.1	*5.2*
Paasche Price Index, separately accounting for branded and generic drugs	99.5	99.6	99.9	97.3	100.0	97.4	94.4	94.1	*–0.8*

Source: ONS

Table 10
Estimates of change in price of prescription drugs
England

Index 1999=100 Percentages

	1995	1996	1997	1998	1999	2000	2001	2002	2003	2004	Average annual price change 1995–2004
Index of average cost per item	77.9	82.7	87.4	91.7	100.0	101.3	104.3	111.1	110.5	106.8	*3.6*
Paasche Price Index	99.5	99.6	99.9	97.3	100.0	97.4	94.4	94.1	93.6	90.4	*-1.1*

Source: ONS

Intermediate consumption: hospitals and community health services

7.13 For the National Accounts, health expenditure on intermediate consumption at current prices is available from the detailed accounting data maintained by HM Treasury and the health administrations. Changes in the volume of intermediate consumption are calculated by deflating the total current price expenditure figures using suitable deflators. For this article, these deflators only relate to the NHS in England and not to the whole of the UK.

7.14 ONS has improved the method for calculating the deflator used to remove the price effect from expenditure on goods and services bought by hospital and community health services. The method for linking the monthly growth is now the same as that conventionally used in the National Accounts.

7.15 The York / NIESR project noted that the cost of capital items should not feature in the measure of price change for procurement items, and has excluded those capital items from the calculation of the respective deflator. This constitutes an improvement to methods, which ONS has adopted. Table 11 presents the new and old deflators (the latter have been updated using the latest available information to show differences over the 1995 to 2004 time period).

7.16 Otherwise, the sources and methods for measuring the changes in the volume of NHS procurement are as used in the first *Public Service Productivity: Health* article, and are detailed in *Sources and Methods.*

Capital

7.17 The National Accounts provide estimates of capital depreciation, which have been used by ONS as a measure of change in the volume of capital inputs. The *Atkinson Review*, by contrast, suggested that a better measure would be capital services. Moreover, for the purposes of understanding productivity, *Measuring Productivity* states that the quantity of capital input to production should be measured by capital services and the price of those services by the user costs of capital. Capital services can be thought of as the flow of productive services from the capital stock, for example the shelter and heating provided by an office building. The price of capital services can be thought of as the rental price: offices in general do have rental prices, but this is not the case for many other types of capital. Where no rental prices exist, such prices need to be estimated.

Table 11
Comparison of the deflators used for removing the price effect from expenditure on goods and services purchased by hospital and community health services: deflators consistent with those used in the first *Public Service Productivity: Health* article and the improved deflators used in this article, 1995 to 2004
England

Index 1999=100 Percentages

	1995	1996	1997	1998	1999	2000	2001	2002	2003	2004	Average annual growth 1995–2004
This article	98.1	99.0	99.7	99.2	100.0	99.5	99.0	100.3	102.4	104.2	*0.7*
October 2004 article	94.1	95.7	96.6	97.9	100.0	99.8	99.3	100.1	101.9	103.1	*1.0*

Source: ONS

7.18 ONS published experimental estimates of capital services for the whole economy in November 2005 (ONS 2005b). This did not include a distinct set of estimates for public service health. They did provide information on health and social work at the level of the total economy, therefore including private sector health (for example, private hospitals) and private sector social care (for example, residential homes for the elderly) as well as public sector hospitals and other facilities.

7.19 Table 12 presents the volume indices for capital consumption and for capital services. Care should be taken in interpreting these estimates, as the capital consumption figures are not strictly a measure of the use of capital by the NHS, and the capital services figures are not limited in coverage to the NHS.

Total NHS inputs (labour, intermediate consumption and capital)

7.20 Table 13 presents the estimates of change in NHS inputs which constitute the highest and lowest growth over the period 1995 to 2004 using the different sources, methods and assumptions. The estimates show that inputs have been increasing by an annual average of between 3.9 and 4.6 per cent. Growth during the period 1999 to 2004, the years for which quality adjustments to output are available, are higher: 4.8 and 5.5 per cent.

7.21 The estimates of change in inputs which constitute the lowest growth over the period 1995 to 2004 are based on measuring:

- the volume of growth in labour using the direct approach (counting number of staff);
- the volume of growth in intermediate consumption including an average cost of items for prescription drugs; and
- the volume of inputs from capital using estimates of capital consumption.

Table 12
Alternative measures of capital inputs to the NHS
United Kingdom

Index 1999=100 Percentages

	1995	1996	1997	1998	1999	2000	2001	2002	2003	2004	Average annual change
Capital consumption	86.8	91.3	94.9	96.1	100.0	108.3	105.1	109.6	114.0	115.8	*3.3*
Capital services	85.7	88.6	89.9	94.4	100.0	105.4	108.9	115.8	120.0	124.8	*4.3*

Source: ONS

Table 13
Growth in NHS inputs using a range of estimates of change based on different combinations of sources, methods and assumptions
United Kingdom

Index 1999=100 Percentages

											Average annual change	
	1995	1996	1997	1998	1999	2000	2001	2002	2003	2004	1995–2004	1999–2004
Lowest growth in NHS inputs based on drugs deflated using cost of all items, capital consumption, and direct labour method	89.5	93.0	92.9	96.2	100.0	102.3	107.1	112.0	120.0	126.4	*3.9*	*4.8*
Highest growth in NHS inputs based on drugs deflated by Paasche Price Index, capital services and indirect labour method	87.4	91.2	91.4	95.5	100.0	102.8	109.1	115.3	123.0	130.8	*4.6*	*5.5*

Source: ONS

Figure 8

Estimates of greatest and least change in the volume of NHS inputs, 1995 to 2004

United Kingdom

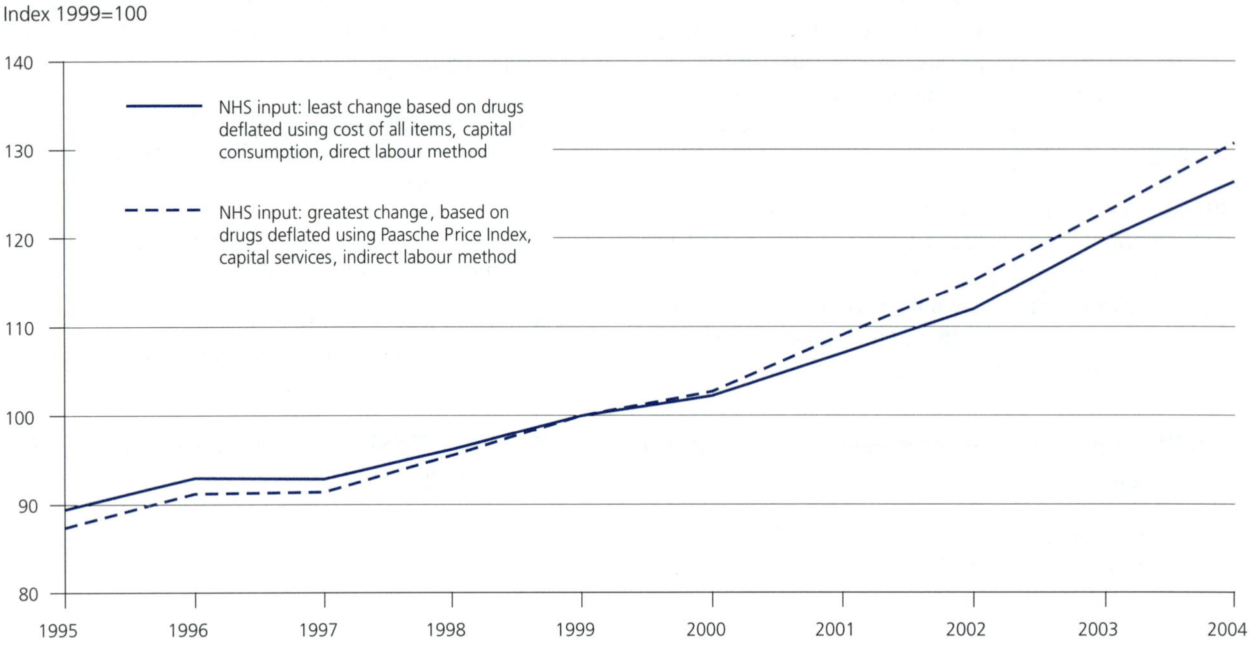

Source: ONS

7.22 The estimates of change in inputs which constitute the highest growth over the period 1995 to 2004 are based on measuring:

- the volume of growth in labour using the indirect approach (deflating expenditure on labour using price indices);
- the volume of growth in intermediate consumption including a Paasche Price Index for prescription drugs; and
- the volume of inputs from capital using estimates of capital services of total economy health and social services.

7.23 All other combinations of sources, assumptions and methods fall within the range presented by these highest and lowest series.

7.24 Figure 8 presents these estimates of greatest and least change in the volume of NHS inputs.

8 NHS productivity

8.1 This section presents estimates of productivity based on the information already presented in sections 4 to 7 on NHS output and inputs. Productivity is defined as the ratio of NHS output to NHS inputs. More important is how this ratio has changed over time. Clearly, the results will depend on which of the methodologies and resulting series discussed above are used. Not surprisingly, estimates of the change over time in NHS productivity are sensitive to the sources and methods used.

8.2 There are a range of estimates for both NHS inputs and output growth which means there are several estimates for NHS productivity. In this section, three sets of productivity figures are presented. These sets are the range of estimates of NHS productivity based on:

- output without adjustment for quality change or the value of health, and the greatest and least rises in NHS inputs;
- output with adjustment for quality change but no adjustment for the value of health, and the greatest and least rises in NHS inputs; and
- output with adjustment for both quality change and the value of health, and the greatest and least rises in NHS inputs.

Set 1: NHS productivity *excluding* quality change in NHS output and making no allowance for increasing value of health

8.3 In the first *Public Service Productivity: Health* article, ONS estimated that NHS productivity (taking no account of changing quality) fell by an annual average of between 0 and 1 per cent during the period 1995 to 2003 as presented in Figure 9. These estimates were rounded to the nearest whole number. This was based on estimates of NHS output having increased by around 3.1 per cent per year and NHS inputs having increased by between 3.5 and 4.2 per cent. It has always been clear that not taking account of quality change is unsatisfactory.

Figure 9:

NHS productivity *excluding* quality change for NHS output, 1995 to 2003, as published in October 2004

United Kingdom

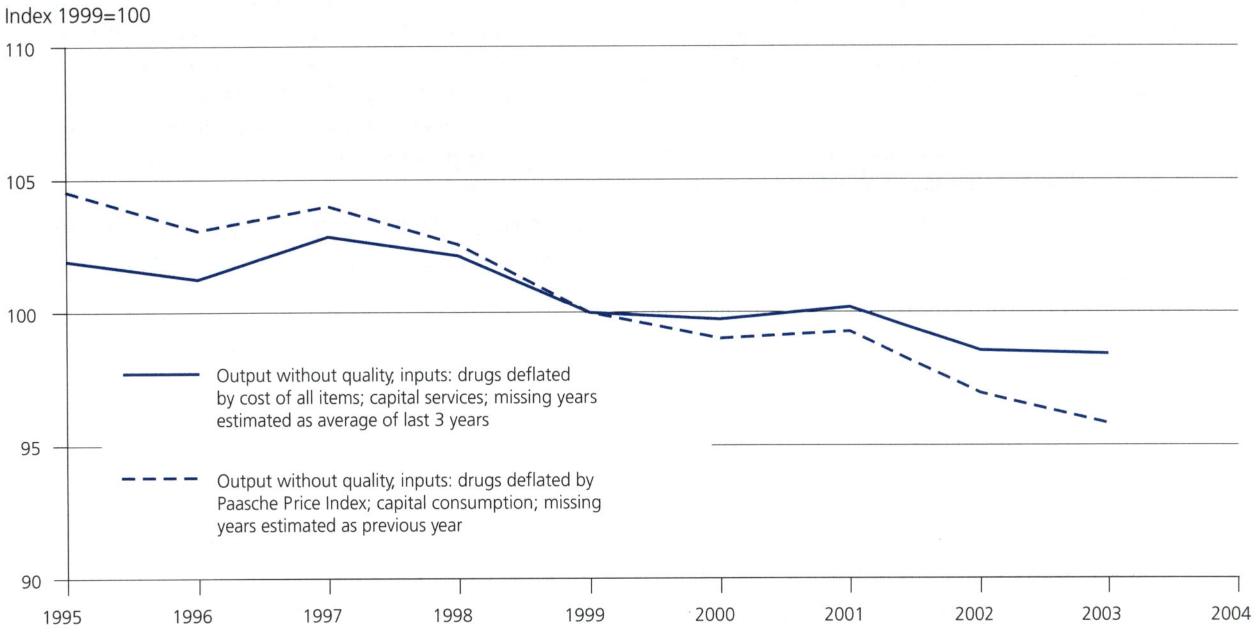

Source: ONS

8.4 Improvements have now been made to the ONS estimate of NHS output growth (not taking into account quality change) as described in section 4, and to the ONS estimates of NHS inputs as described in sections 6 and 7. The latest ONS estimate is that for the years 1995 to 2004, NHS productivity (not taking into account quality change for NHS output) has been falling by an average of between 0.6 and 1.3 per cent per year. This is based on NHS output growing by 3.2 per cent per year and NHS inputs growing by between 3.9 and 4.6 per cent per year. Figure 10 shows the latest range of NHS productivity estimates (excluding quality change for NHS output).

Figure 10

New estimate of NHS productivity, *excluding* quality change for NHS output, 1995 to 2004

United Kingdom

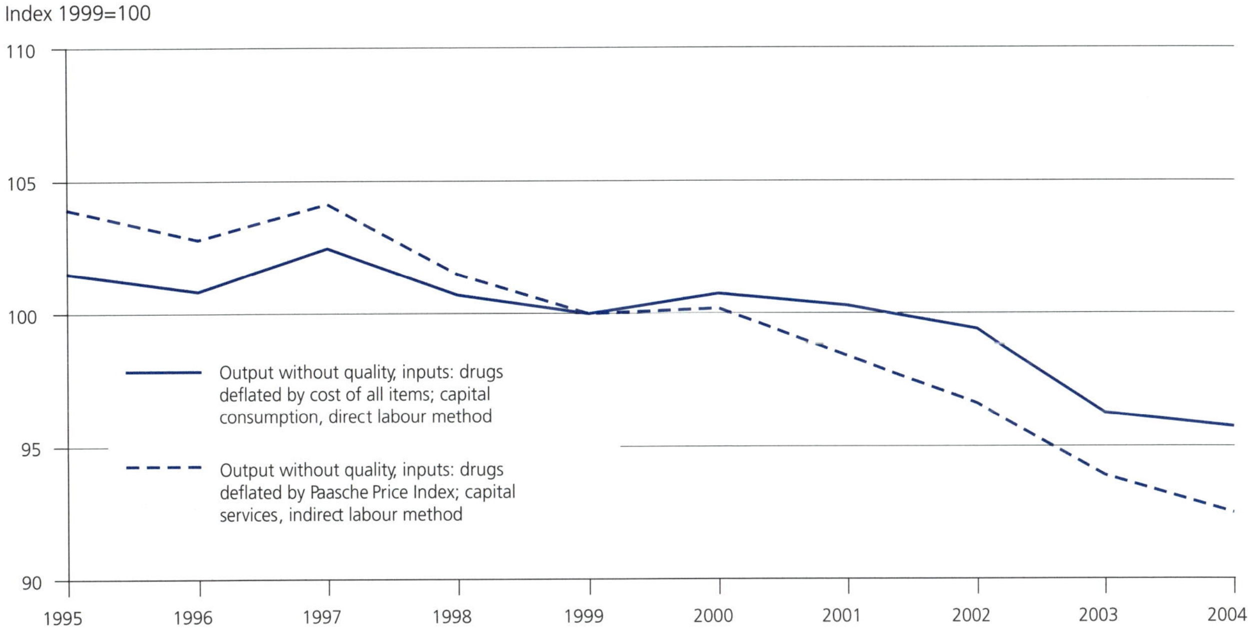

Source: ONS

8.5 These estimates are subject to a number of limitations. It remains unsatisfactory to take no account of quality change. Further, the output figures are based on a subset of activities in the NHS for England and Northern Ireland. The input figures are also not yet fully developed, with the deflators based on information relating only to changes in price in England.

8.6 Part of the difference between the annual average changes in figures on this basis and those presented in this article compared with the first *Public Service Productivity: Health* article is due to the addition of an extra year in the analysis. The annual average fall for the same period for which estimates were published in October 2004, that is 1995 to 2003, using the latest sources and methods, is estimated to have been between 0.7 and 1.3 per cent. The remainder of the difference is due to rounding differences as well as to improvements in the sources and methods described in sections 4, 6 and 7.

Set 2: NHS productivity *including* quality change in NHS output but no allowance for increasing value of health

8.7 The combined effect from adding the quality adjustments proposed in the York / NIESR and DH publications, but with no allowance for increasing value of health, add an annual average of around 1.1 percentage points to output growth during the period 1999 to 2004. NHS productivity under these conditions is estimated to have either increased by an average of 0.2 per cent per year, or fallen by an average of 0.5 per cent per year during this period. This is based on output growing by an average of 5.0 per cent per year and inputs growing by an average of between 4.8 and 5.5 per cent per year. Figure 11 presents estimates of NHS productivity on this basis and using the estimates of greatest and least change in NHS inputs as presented in section 7.

Set 3: NHS productivity *including* quality change in NHS output and also allowance for increasing value of health

8.8 The combined effect from adding the quality adjustments proposed in the York / NIESR and DH publications, including an adjustment for the increasing value of health as recommended by the *Atkinson Review* of 1.5 per cent per year, adds an annual average of 2.6 percentage points to total NHS output growth during the period 1999 to 2004. NHS productivity under these conditions is estimated to have increased by an average of between 0.9 and 1.6 per cent per year during this period. This is based on output growing by an average of around 6.5 per cent per year and inputs growing by an average of between 4.8 and 5.5 per cent per year. Figure 12 presents estimates of NHS productivity on this basis and using the estimates of greatest and least change in NHS inputs as presented in section 7.

Figure 11

NHS productivity based on output *including* quality change in NHS output but no allowance for increasing value of health, 1999 to 2004

United Kingdom

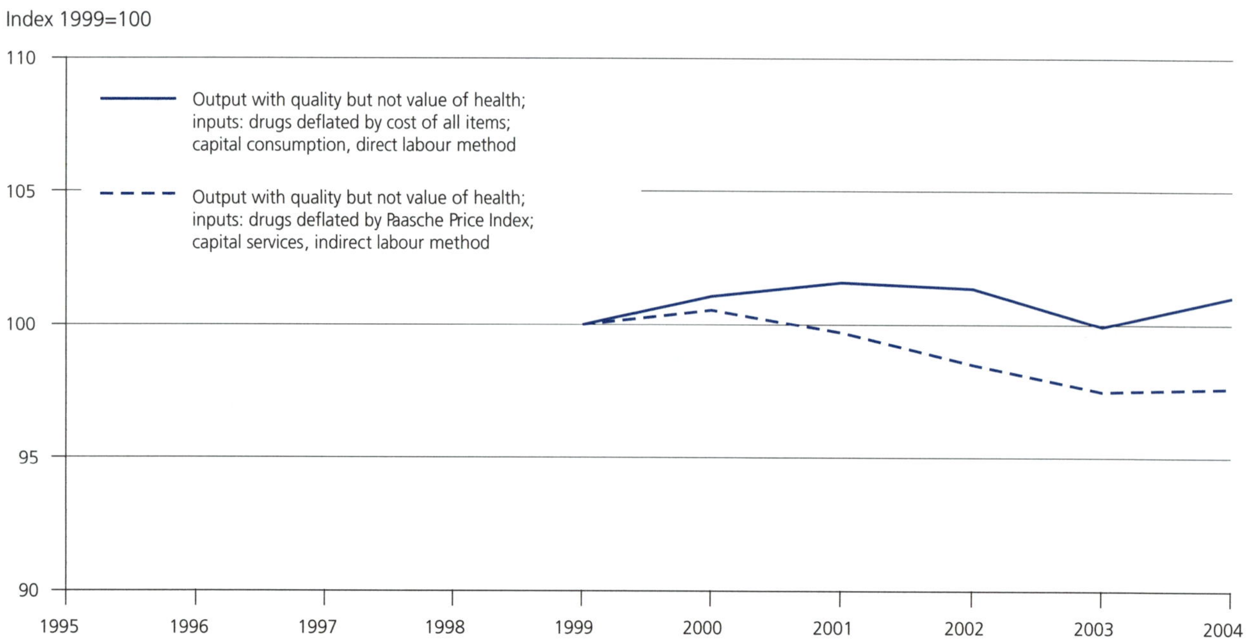

Source: ONS

Figure 12

NHS productivity *including* quality change in NHS output and allowance for increasing value of health, 1999 to 2004

United Kingdom

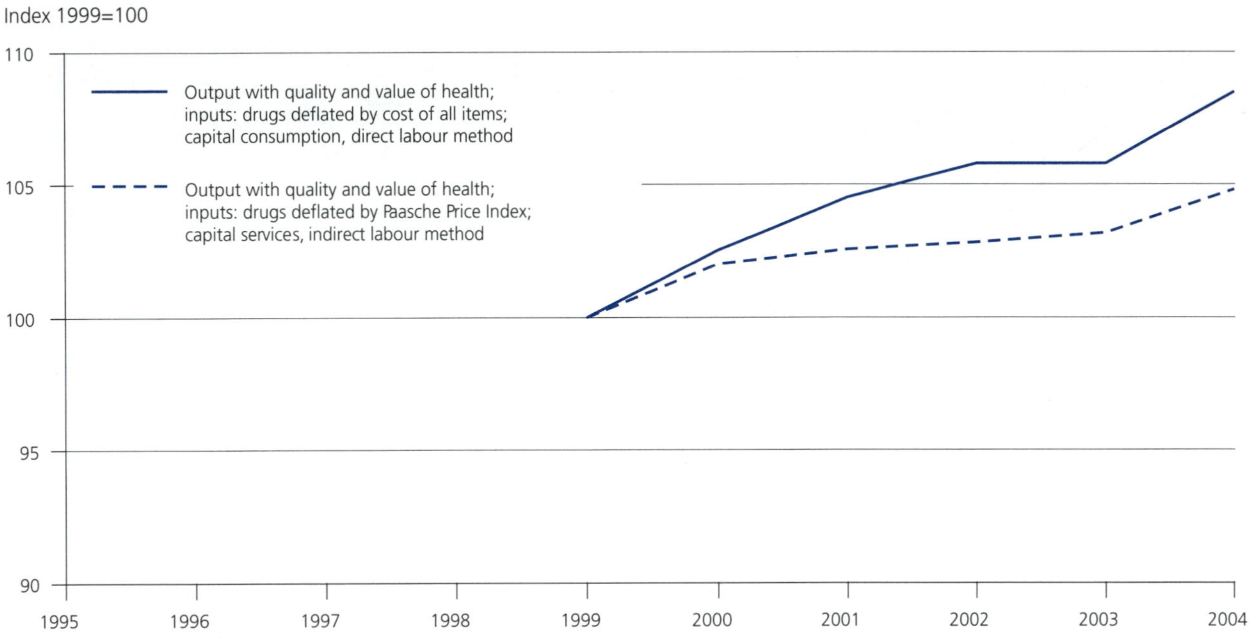

Source: ONS

9 Triangulation

9.1 The productivity figures that appear in this article are based on the best data available from the National Accounts, DH, ONS and the wider academic community. As more data become available, estimates of NHS productivity will be updated accordingly. However, estimating NHS productivity (and productivity for public services more generally) is a complex process and under constant development. It is therefore sensible to examine alternative information that helps understand productivity estimates in a wider context, as recommended by the *Atkinson Review*.

9.2 Principle H in the Report recommended:

> 'Independent corroborative evidence should be sought on government productivity, as part of a process of 'triangulation', recognising the limitations in reducing productivity to a single number'.

9.3 The *Atkinson Review* distinguishes between three levels at which the process of triangulation could be conducted (see paragraphs 4.66 to 4.71 for more detail):

- at the first level, ONS should be 'looking at the data' to see if productivity statistics, using estimates of NHS output and input, are coherent with other evidence;
- at the second level, the ONS should make an explicit attempt to relate the output and input indicators to departmental performance measures, for example, a systematic examination of the relation between direct output indicators and the Public Service Agreement targets; and
- the 'third and most ambitious level', would be to initiate a government productivity measurement programme, drawing experience from the United States. The Report suggests that it would not be necessary to collect anything like the high number of output indicators used in the US programme for there to be a major improvement in the information available on public sector performance.

9.4 In this section, triangulation evidence is presented at the 'first level', on the following:

- average length of stay in hospital;
- elective day case rates;
- emergency readmissions; and
- public attitudes to health care.

Average length of stay

9.5 Figure 13 shows that the average length of stay in hospital in England reduced from just over eight days at the beginning of the 1990s to around seven days by the mid 1990s. Since then, the average length of stay has hovered around the seven day mark, with the latest information showing a small reduction to just below seven days.

9.6 As length of stay in hospital is a major driver of costs in the NHS, the decline since 1991/92 (apart from the small rise in 2001/02) would be consistent with rising

Figure 13

Average length of stay, 1991/92 to 2003/04

England

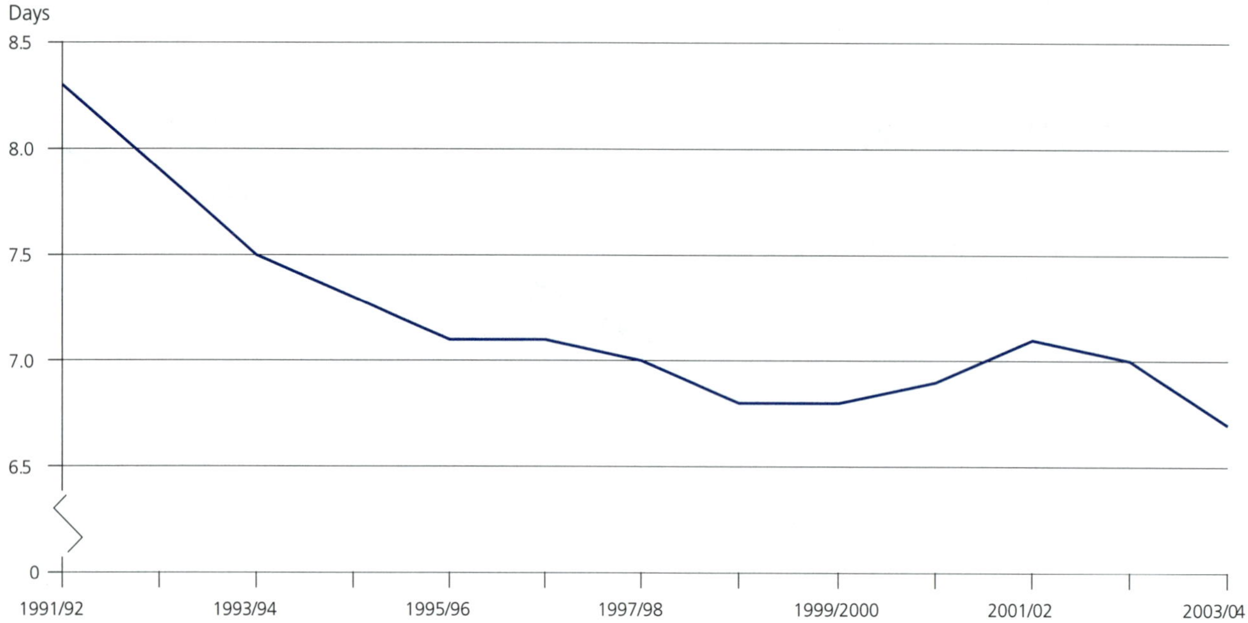

Source: HES, Health and Social Care Information Centre

productivity, particularly if the freeing up of hospital beds allows more patients to be treated. The undulation over the period since 1999/2000, however, would be more consistent with relatively stable productivity experience over this more recent period.

Elective day case rates

9.7 Day case surgery is the admission of patients into hospital for a selective planned surgical procedure, with discharge from hospital occurring on the same day. The Healthcare Commission has identified 25 types of operations for which hospitals should be able to treat 75 per cent of patients as day cases (HSJ 2005).

9.8 The elective day case rate in England, as presented in Figure 14, has risen since the 1990s from 39 per cent to 67 per cent in 2003/04. This increase has been most prominent in the over 75 age group where day cases have increased by 41 per cent since the 1990s. As with

Figure 14

Elective day case rate, 1991/92 to 2003/04

England

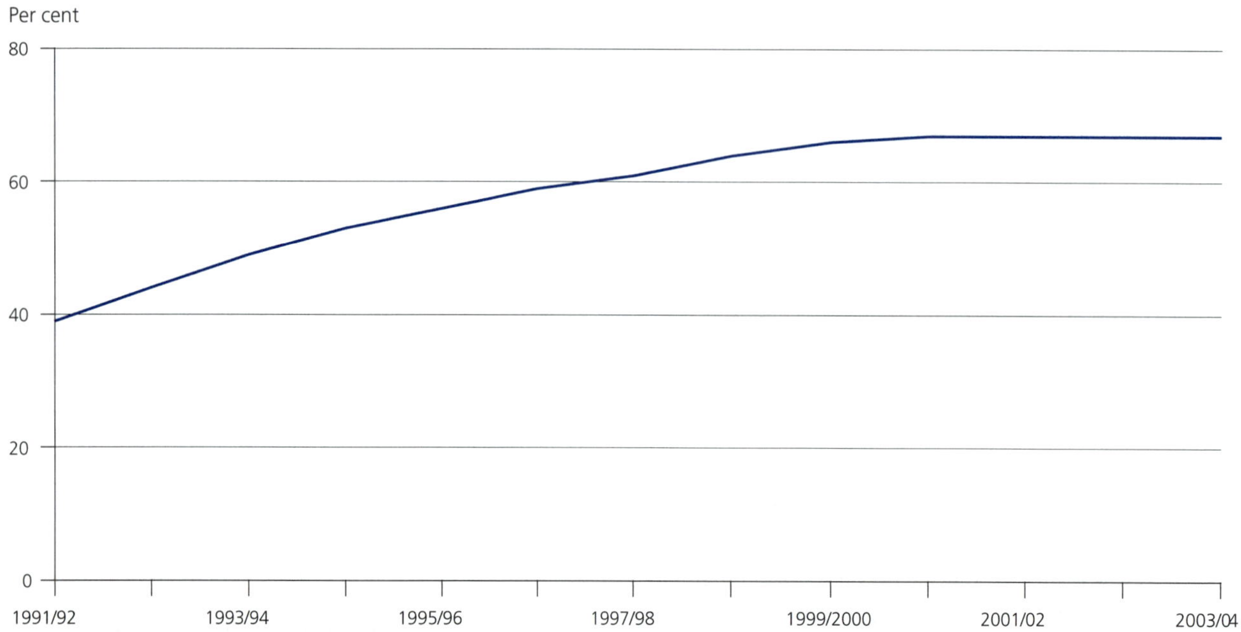

Source: HES, Health and Social Care Information Centre

the average length of stay, the day case rate has been levelling off, albeit slightly later, to around 66 or 67 per cent from the end of the 1990s. This levelling off may be due to some less severe cases being dealt with in outpatient settings or by General Practitioners in primary care.

9.9 The number of day cases performed varies geographically, between 40 and 83 per cent, with only 12 per cent of NHS Trusts reaching the Health Commission's quota of treating 75 per cent of their collection of operations as day cases. Variations between procedures within a single NHS Trust also exist. This wide range in performance leaves considerable scope for improvement (BMJ 2005b), which leaves open the possibility that over time day case rates could continue to rise.

9.10 Increasing the day case rate helps to reduce costs to the NHS, as well as having a part in providing timely treatment; reducing the risk of cross infection; and reducing the number of procedures cancelled (BMJ 2005b). Treatment by day case surgery is also seen to have a positive quality of life aspect for the patient. This is because the procedure is likely to have a shorter waiting time; patients can return home the same day, which means an earlier return to normal activities; and patients can potentially receive care better suited to their needs.

9.11 The increase in elective day case rates since 1991/92 would therefore be consistent with the view that NHS productivity is rising, though again at relatively modest rates in the recent past.

Emergency readmissions

9.12 It is important to look at changes in indicators like average length of stay and day case rates in conjunction with other indicators, such as readmission rates. Emergency readmissions are unlikely to be part of the patient's originally planned treatment and some may be potentially avoidable (NCHOD 2005).

9.13 Readmission rates are often used in health care systems as a measure of the quality of care received by patients (HSJ 2004), but as it is a developing indicator, currently spanning only six years, the results should be interpreted with caution. Various factors could contribute to the quality of care received by the patient, for example, whether or not the treatment takes place in hospital, whether it includes an overnight stay, the length of the overnight stay, the type and level of aftercare, and so on.

9.14 Figure 15 shows that the rate of people readmitted into hospital within 28 days after discharge increased across all age bands between 1998/99 and 2003/04. The age band for people 75 and over has the highest rate for emergency readmissions, and this age group also has the highest rate of increase for this time period. DH is looking into how best to analyse readmission rates, including looking at improving the quality of the indicator itself as well as what could have contributed to this increase in readmission rates.

Figure 15

Emergency readmissions within 28 days of discharge, by age group, 1998/99 to 2003/04

England

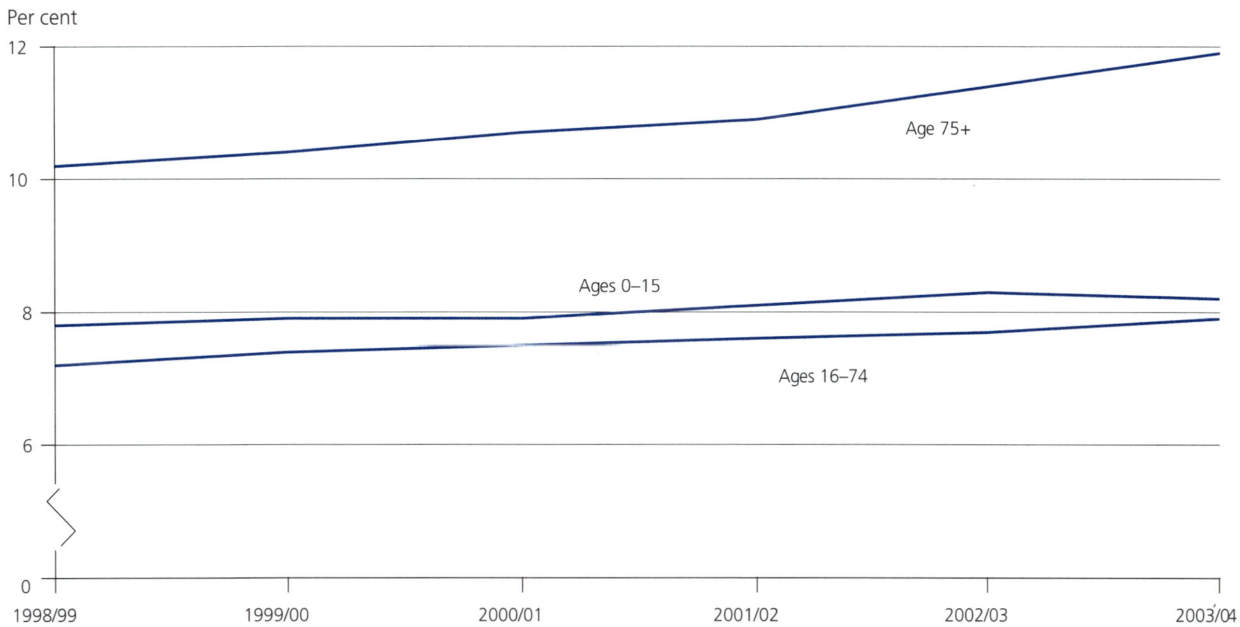

Source: HES, NCHOD

9.15 In general, it is difficult to make a firm judgement on the implications for productivity in the absence of further data. Ideally, in the future, it would be useful to link the data on readmission rates with other indicators, such as those for average length of stay in hospital and elective day case rates.

General public attitudes to health care

9.16 The British Social Attitudes Survey (NatCen 2005a, NatCen 2005b) produces some key findings on public attitudes to health care, with respondents being questioned on how satisfied or dissatisfied they are with the NHS. When interpreting BSAS data it should be noted that unlike patient experience surveys, public attitude surveys are not necessarily linked directly to patient experience and could be affected by public perceptions of the standard of quality expected from the NHS, and the performance of the Government in general. For this reason the comparison between the two different measures should not be overstated.

9.17 Figure 16 illustrates that public satisfaction with the NHS has fluctuated over time, with 1996 showing the highest level of dissatisfaction with the NHS over the period considered. Even so, 'quite satisfied with the NHS' has remained the highest public response. In 2003, when respondents were asked for their overall satisfaction with the NHS, more people were satisfied with the NHS than dissatisfied (44 and 37 per cent respectively). In the same year, the respondents who were satisfied with the NHS were more likely to be those in the older age groups who have had direct personal experience of using NHS services (NatCen 2005a). These figures cannot, of course, be directly compared to those from the National Patient Experience Survey Programme, but they do provide further context.

9.18 This section on triangulation has presented a limited amount of information as context to the productivity estimates. As more evidence becomes available, future productivity articles will be updated in order to paint a wider picture of NHS productivity.

10 Next steps

10.1 This article significantly improves on the methodology and resulting estimates of NHS productivity presented in the first health productivity article published in October 2004, in particular:

- more information is provided on health outcomes;
- NHS output growth has been adjusted to incorporate quality for the first time;
- the methodology to estimate the volume of NHS inputs has been improved;
- a range of NHS productivity estimates are presented, clearly identifying the impact of different estimates of NHS output and inputs; and
- more corroborative information is provided to support productivity estimates.

10.2 To underpin and drive forward further improvement with as wide a professional consensus as possible, ONS will be working with DH in setting up consultation

Figure 16

Trends in public attitudes to health care, 1990 to 2003

Great Britain

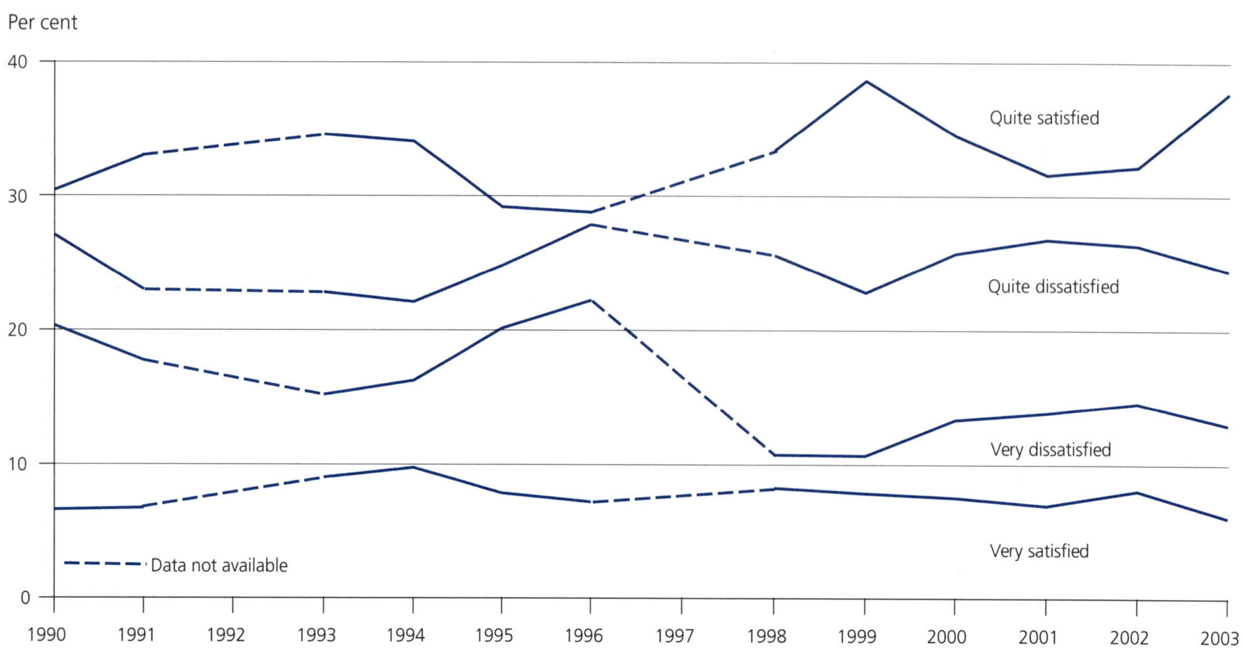

Source: NatCen; British Social Attitudes survey

seminars that will bring together experts in the health field to discuss key issues. For example, wider consultation will be required on: the proposed quality adjustment indicators; using value weights instead of cost weights for statins; and in particular, adjusting the value of health in line with real earnings growth in the economy. A similar process of consultation will be taking place on methodology for measuring productivity in the education sector and for other public services.

10.3 While there has been much progress made in this productivity article, a number of developments are still required. ONS will be working with DH, the Devolved Administrations and other experts to further improve NHS productivity estimates. The development agenda will include the following:

- expanding the coverage of NHS activities used to measure NHS output, factoring in more data from the Devolved Administrations where it is possible to do so;
- improvements in measuring NHS output from primary care using data from computerised General Practitioner research databases;
- treatment of prescription drugs, and what value is added by the NHS;
- consideration of the best source for NHS activity estimates (for example, Reference Costs versus HES) and the best source for unit costs to weight these activity estimates;
- further developments in the quality adjustment of NHS output, taking into account the latest research available;
- further developments in the use of value weights rather than cost weights for NHS activities;
- further advances in measuring NHS inputs, in particular, developing better direct measures of labour input; and
- the use of wider evidence to support estimates of NHS productivity, building in the latest research available.

Notes

1 Writing this article has benefited from the advice of a Quality Assurance Panel, chaired by Professor Peter Smith, University of York. Members of the Board are Richard Willmer, Director of Statistics at the Department of Health; Peter Goldblatt, Director of Health & Care Division at ONS; Joe Grice, Executive Director of the UK Centre for the Measurement of Government Activity at ONS; Graham Jenkinson, a senior member of the National Accounts Group at ONS; Professor Alistair Maguire, London School of Economics; Simon Compton, a senior methodologist in ONS; and, Rhys Herbert and Geoff Tily, Economic Advisors at ONS. ONS gratefully acknowledges this help and assistance, but takes final responsibility for the contents of this article.

2 QRESEARCH is now one of the largest aggregated general practice databases in the world. Version 8 of the database has over 30 million person years of observation from 489 practices spread throughout the UK with representation in every Strategic Health Authority. The database is updated every quarter.

References

Atkinson (2005) *Atkinson Review of measurement of government output and productivity for the National Accounts: Interim Report,* July 2004, available via www.statistics.gov.uk/about/methodology_by_theme/atkinson/

BMJ (1994) Chouillet A, Bell C M J and Hiscox J *Management of breast cancer in South East England* Journal 308 available at www.bmj.bmjjournals.com

BMJ (2000) Blanks R G, Moss S M, McGahan C, Quinn M J and Babb P J *Effect of NHS breast screening programme on mortality from breast cancer in England and Wales, 1990 -8: comparison of observed with predicted mortality* Journal 321 available at www.bmj.bmjjournals.com

BMJ (2005a) Unal B, Critchley J A and Capewell S *Modelling the decline in coronary heart disease deaths in England and Wales, 1981 – 2000: comparing contributions from primary prevention and secondary prevention* Journal 331 available at www.bmj.bmjjournals.com

BMJ (2005b) Dr Foster *Trends in day surgery rates* British Medical Journal 10 November 2005

Cancer Research UK (2002) *Fact sheet: Specific cancer: lung cancer*

DfES (2005), *Measuring government education output in the National Accounts,* DfES, October 2005, available at www.dfes.gov.uk/research/data/uploadfiles/RW45.pdf

DH (2000) *The NHS Plan,* Department of Health, July 2000, available at www.dh.gov.uk/assetRoot/04/05/57/83/04055783.pdf

DH (2005a) *Healthcare output and productivity: Accounting for quality change* Department of Health, December 2005, available at www.dh.gov.uk/assetRoot/04/12/42/67/04124267.pdf

DH (2005b) Technical paper 2: Use of statins and calculation of value weight, available at www.dh.gov.uk/assetRoot/04/12/42/69/04124269.pdf

DH (2005c) Technical paper 3: Using the GP contract quality and outcomes framework for quality adjustment, available at www.dh.gov.uk/assetRoot/04/12/42/70/04124270.pdf

DH (2005d) Technical paper 7: Quality adjustment based on patient experience surveys, available at www.dh.gov.uk/assetRoot/04/12/42/74/04124274.pdf

Eurostat (2001) *Handbook on price and volume measures in national accounts* Office for Official Publications of the European Communities, May 2001, available at www.epp.eurostat.cec.eu.int/cache/ITY_OFFPUB/KS-41-01-543/EN/KS-41-01-543-EN.PDF

Gravelle (2001) *Discounting for health effects in cost-benefit and cost-effectiveness analysis,* Health Economics, volume 10, pp 19-28

HSJ (2004) Dr Foster *Readmission rates: Understanding readmission patterns helps pinpoint why patients return to hospital'* Health Service Journal 19 September 2004

HSJ (2005) *Day-case rates,* Health Service Journal 29 September 2005

MacFarlane A and Mugford M (2000) *Birth Counts: statistics of pregnancy and childbirth. Second edition* TSO: London

NatCen (2005a) *Trends in Attitudes to Healthcare 1983 to 2003* Report based on results from the British Social Attitudes survey

NatCen (2005b) *British social attitudes* Two terms of New Labour: the public's reaction

NCHOD (2005) *Compendium Indicators: Emergency readmission rate within 28 days of discharge from hospital* available at www.nchod.nhs.uk

OECD (2001) *Measuring Productivity* Organisation for Economic Co-operation and Development, 2001, available at www.oecd.org/dataoecd/59/29/2352458.pdf

ONS (2003) Clare Griffiths and Anita Brock *Twentieth Century Mortality Trends in England and Wales* HSQ 18 available at www.statistics.gov.uk/cci/article.asp?ID=500

ONS (2004a) *Public Service Productivity: Health,* Office for National Statistics, October 2004, available at www.statistics.gov.uk/CCI/article.asp?ID=1030&Pos=2&ColRank=1&Rank=224

ONS (2004b) *Cigarette smoking* available at www.statistics.gov.uk/cci/nugget.asp?id=866

ONS (2004c) *Public Service Productivity: Education,* Office for National Statistics, October 2005, available at www.statistics.gov.uk/articles/nojournal/PSProductivityEducation.pdf

ONS (2005a) *United Kingdom National Accounts The Blue Book 2005,* Office for National Statistics, various years to 2004, available at www.statistics.gov.uk/downloads/theme_economy/BB2005.pdf

ONS (2005b) *Estimates of the volume of capital services* Office for National Statistics, November 2005, available at www.statistics.gov.uk/articles/economic_trends/ET624_Wallis.pdf

ONS (2006) *Sources and methods for Public Service Productivity: Health article,* Office for National Statistics, February 2005, available at www.statistics.gov.uk/about/data/methodology/specific/publicsector/output/health.asp

OPCS (1995) *The health of our children – Decennial supplement series DS no 11*

York (2005) *Developing new approaches to measuring NHS output and productivity,* York University and National Institute of Economic and Social Research, available at www.york.ac.uk/inst/che/publications/rp.htm

Glossary

Blue Book (BB): The short name for the annual publication United Kingdom National Accounts
The Blue Book.

Capital: Capital assets are those which contribute to the productive process over periods longer than a year.

CHD: Coronary heart disease.

CHE: Centre for Health Economics, at the University of York.

Devolved Administrations (DA): Scottish Executive for Scotland, the Welsh Assembly Government for Wales and the Northern Ireland Civil Service.

Deflation: The technique used to change figures from nominal terms (current prices) into real terms (constant prices or volume terms).

DH: Department of Health.

Healthy life expectancy: Partitions total life expectancy into years free of health-related problems or good health.

Hospital episode statistics (HES): The national statistical data warehouse for England of the care provided by NHS hospitals and for NHS hospital patients treated elsewhere.

Inputs: Resources used by the NHS.

Intermediate consumption: The consumption of goods and services in the production process.

Labour: The people employed or otherwise contracted to work (in the NHS).

Life expectancy: Provides an estimation of longevity.

Myocardial infarction: Heart attack

National Accounts (NA): The economic accounts of the nation. They detail the production processes, the sector accounts showing, for example, the income, expenditure, saving and financial transactions and balance sheets of each sector, and estimates of gross domestic product.

NHS: National Health Service.

NIESR: National Institute for Economic and Social Research.

Productivity: Defined as the ratio of a volume measure of output to a volume measure of input.

Primary prevention: An apparently healthy person reduces the risk of being diagnosed with a health condition by reducing the risk factors associated with the condition e.g. reducing the risk factors associated with coronary heart disease prior to being diagnosed with it.

Public Service Agreement (PSA): An agreement between a government department and the Treasury, as part of the Spending Review, including objectives and targets.

ONS: Office for National Statistics.

Output: What is produced (by the NHS) in combining various inputs to achieve overall outcomes.

QA Panel: Quality Assurance Panels set up to review UKCeMGA's productivity articles.

Reference Costs: Libraries of unit costs for a broad range of NHS treatments and clinical procedures since 1998.

Secondary prevention: A person who has been diagnosed with a health condition reduces the chances of the condition worsening by reducing the risk factors associated with the condition.

Statins: Drugs designed to reduce cholestrol, which can block arteries, and so reduce the risk of heart attacks.

First findings from the UK Innovation Survey, 2005

Stephanie Robson and Laurent Ortmans
Department of Trade and Industry

Initial analysis of the 2005 UK Innovation Survey shows that:

- In the three-year period 2002–04, 25 per cent of enterprises with ten or more employees were product (goods and services) innovators, 16 per cent were process innovators, while 57 per cent of enterprises in the UK were active in developing or implementing innovations.
- The most frequently reported impact of businesses' innovation activities was on the quality of goods and services produced or supplied, cited by a third of enterprises.
- Information to enable innovation came most often from sources within the business and from market partners. Technical and other formal standards were also important sources.
- Compared with the 2001 UK Innovation Survey, the proportion of firms engaged in innovation activity has increased by some 14 percentage points.

Introduction

This article presents the first findings from the UK Innovation Survey 2005, covering the three-year period from 2002 to 2004. This is the UK contribution to a fourth Europe-wide Community Innovation Survey (CIS).

The 2005 survey is the largest innovation survey so far conducted, sent to 28,000 UK enterprises with ten or more employees and achieving a 58 per cent response rate. The Department of Trade and Industry (DTI) would like to thank all those businesses that completed the survey form.

Business innovation is a vital ingredient in raising growth potential and quality of life. Encouraging innovation is part of DTI's mission to create the conditions for business success and to help the UK adjust to globalisation. Measuring the level of innovation activity in the UK, and thus identifying where policy measures might be required and have some impact, contributes to this mission. The UK Innovation Survey complements other indicators of innovation by providing a periodic snapshot of the spectrum of innovation inputs and outputs and the constraints faced by UK businesses in their innovation efforts, across the entire range of UK industries and business enterprises. It has the additional benefit of providing the basis for some comparisons with other European countries.

The majority of the survey is concerned with innovation through new and improved products and processes and with the investments that develop and implement them. Firstly, the article describes the patterns of innovation activity in these areas. It then discusses the impact of innovation on businesses, the barriers to innovation and the methods used by firms to protect the value of innovations. The article then considers a broader range of innovations in business practices and organisation, such as the introduction of new management techniques. It concludes with a comparison between the 2005 survey and its predecessor from 2001.

Innovation activity

Innovation takes place through a wide variety of business practices and a range of indicators can be used to measure its level within the enterprise or in the economy as a whole. These include the levels of effort employed (measured through resources allocated to innovation) and of achievement (the introduction of new or improved products and processes). This section reports on the types and levels of innovation activity over the three-year period, 2002 to 2004.[1]

We define innovation activity here as where enterprises were engaged in any of the following:

- introduction of new or significantly improved products (goods or services) or processes
- engagement in innovation projects not yet complete or abandoned
- expenditure in areas such as internal research and development, training, acquisition of external knowledge or machinery and equipment linked to innovation activities

Table 1
Enterprises who were innovation active, by type of activity, 2002–04

Percentage of all enterprises

	Size of enterprise: employees		
	10–250	250+	All 10+
Innovation active	*57*	*72*	*57*
Product innovator (share with new to market products)	*25 (56)*	*39 (59)*	*25 (56)*
Process innovator (share with new to industry processes)	*15 (30)*	*31 (31)*	*16 (30)*
Ongoing or abandoned activities	*10*	*21*	*10*
Innovation-related expenditure	*54*	*68*	*54*
Both product and process innovators	*10*	*22*	*11*
Either product or process innovators	*30*	*48*	*30*

Overall, 57 per cent of enterprises were classed as being innovation active during this period. Large enterprises with more than 250 employees were more likely to engage in some sort of innovation activity (72 per cent) than smaller enterprises (57 per cent).

In total, 25 per cent of enterprises had introduced new or significantly improved goods or services in the sample period, of which over half were new to market, and 16 per cent had introduced a new or improved process for production or delivery, with nearly a third of these processes being new to the industry in question. The level of product (goods and services) and process innovation is considerably greater in larger enterprises.

The proportion of enterprises with some innovation-related expenditure (54 per cent) shows that firms recognise the need to allocate resources to innovation. The most commonly reported items of innovation expenditure were machinery and equipment for innovation and in-house research and development.

Co-operation agreements

Twelve per cent of enterprises had co-operation arrangements on innovation activities and, of these, 69 per cent had agreements that operated at a national level. The most frequent partners for co-operation, as shown in Table 2, were suppliers (76 per cent of enterprises with co-operation agreements) followed by clients or customers (at 74 per cent). Around one third of collaborators included universities among their partners.

Table 2
Partners for innovation co-operation

Percentage of those enterprises with co-operation arrangements

	Geography of co-operation				
Type of partner	Local/ regional	UK	Other Europe	All other countries	Any
Suppliers	*34*	*42*	*16*	*12*	*76*
Clients or customers	*37*	*42*	*15*	*12*	*74*
Other enterprises within enterprise group	*24*	*18*	*10*	*11*	*50*
Competitors	*19*	*23*	*7*	*5*	*44*
Consultants	*20*	*23*	*6*	*4*	*42*
Universities/higher education institutes	*20*	*16*	*4*	*2*	*33*
Government research organisations	*16*	*17*	*2*	*2*	*31*
Any	*65*	*69*	*32*	*25*	*100*

Industrial and regional variation

Figure 1 shows the distribution of innovation-active businesses across the countries and regions of the UK. There is very little variation in the proportion, ranging from 55 per cent in Eastern England and the West Midlands to 60 per cent in South East England.

Figure 1
Regional innovation patterns

Mean percentages

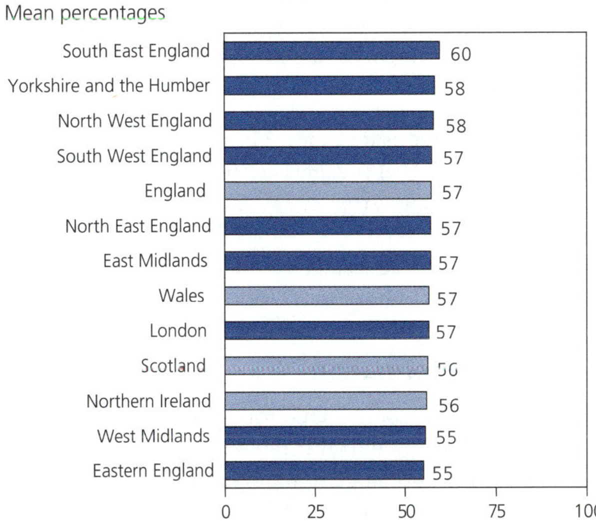

Figure 2
Innovation activity by industry
Percentages

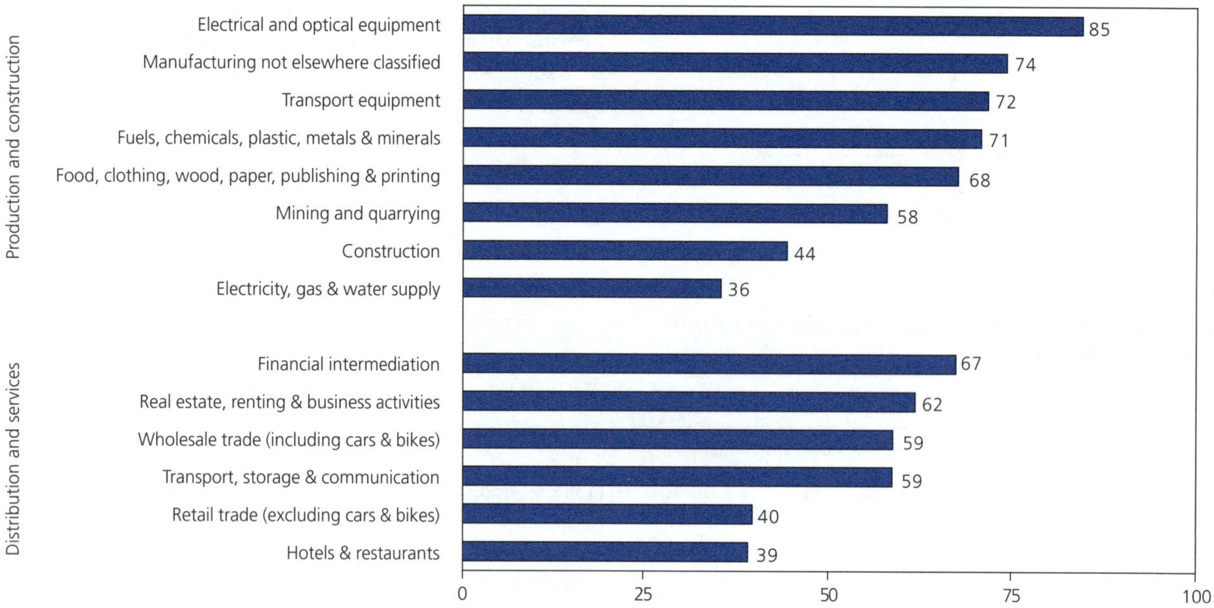

The percentage of firms reported to be innovation active varied considerably across industrial and commercial sectors as shown in Figure 2. In the production and construction sector, 85 per cent of electrical and precision engineering enterprises were innovation active, against just 36 per cent of enterprises supplying electricity, gas, and water. In distribution and services, financial intermediation had the highest share of innovation active businesses (67 per cent) against just 39 per cent of hotels and restaurants.

Effects of innovation on businesses

The survey sought information about the direct and indirect effects of innovation. Respondents were asked to rank a number of effects from innovating on a scale from 'no impact', through 'low', 'medium' or 'high'. The proportion of innovation-active respondents who answered 'high' in each category is shown in Table 3.

Product-related effects were more often cited than process (cost) effects, with quality enhancements most commonly reported, confirming a strongly customer-focused approach to innovation. The effects of meeting regulatory requirements and increasing value added in the business were also widely reported.

Sources of information

It is important to know how enterprises relate to external sources of technology and other innovation-related knowledge and information, as innovation is increasingly complex, requiring the co-ordination of multiple inputs. Firms can gain guidance, advice or even inspiration for their prospective innovation projects from a variety of both public and private sources.

Table 3
Enterprises rating effects of innovation as 'high'
Percentage of innovation-active respondents

Effect	Size of enterprise: employees		
	10–250	250+	All 10+
Product-orientated			
Improved quality of goods or services	*34*	*44*	*34*
Entered new market or increased market share	*25*	*37*	*26*
Increased range of goods or services	*25*	*27*	*25*
Process-orientated			
Reduced costs per unit produced or provided	*21*	*35*	*22*
Improved flexibility of production or service provision	*18*	*27*	*18*
Increased capacity for production or service provision	*18*	*26*	*18*
Other			
Increased value added	*27*	*39*	*28*
Met regulatory requirement	*26*	*36*	*27*
Reduced environmental impacts or improved health and safety	*16*	*20*	*16*

Respondents were asked to rank a number of potential information sources on a scale from 'no relationship' to 'high importance'. The proportion who answered 'high' in each category is shown in Table 4. These sources are:

- *internal*: from within the enterprise itself or other enterprises within the enterprise group
- *market*: from suppliers, customers, clients, consultants, competitors, commercial laboratories or research and development enterprises
- *institutional*: from the public sector such as government research organisations and universities or private research institutes

Table 4
Enterprises rating information sources as of 'high' importance

Percentage of respondents

	Size of enterprise: employees		
	10–250	250+	All 10+
Internal			
Within your enterprise group	21	39	22
Market			
Clients or customers	27	39	27
Suppliers of equipment	15	21	15
Competitors or other enterprises within your industry	9	18	10
Consultants, commercial labs or private R&D institutes	3	5	3
Institutional			
Universities or other higher education institutes	2	2	2
Government or public research institutes	1	2	1
Other sources			
Technical, industry or service standards	7	12	7
Professional and industry associations	5	8	5
Conferences, trade fairs, exhibitions	5	7	5
Scientific journals and trade/technical publications	4	5	4

- *other*: from conferences, trade fairs and exhibitions; scientific journals, trade/technical publications; professional and industry associations; technical, industry or service standards

Both larger and smaller enterprises reported internal and market sources as most important for information on innovation. This suggests that enterprises tend to rely on their own experience and knowledge coupled with information from suppliers, customers and clients. The least frequently cited sources were institutional sources. However, knowledge derived from these sources published in scholarly and trade journals was accessed by a higher proportion of businesses.

Barriers to innovation

Successful and evidence-based policy interventions require an understanding of the barriers to business innovation. These barriers can be internal obstacles that the enterprise encounters while carrying out innovation activities as well as external factors preventing innovation.

The survey asked about a range of constraining factors and their effect on the ability to innovate. Table 5 shows the proportions of respondents who gave a 'high' rating to each category of constraint.

Costs were most commonly regarded as significant barriers to innovation, including the direct resource costs of innovation activities, their perceived economic risk and the costs of acquiring finance. The impact of UK and EU regulations were also thought to be a barrier to innovation, particularly for smaller enterprises. Fewer enterprises felt constrained by a lack of knowledge, although the lack of qualified personnel was viewed as one of the more important constraining factors by smaller businesses.

Table 5
Enterprises regarding potential barriers to innovation as 'high'

Percentage of respondents

	Size of enterprise: employees		
	10–250	250+	All 10+
Cost factors			
Direct innovation costs too high	15	16	15
Excessive perceived economic risk	13	15	13
Cost of finance	12	9	12
Availability of finance	11	9	11
Knowledge factors			
Lack of qualified personnel	8	6	8
Lack of information on technology	3	2	3
Lack of information on markets	3	3	3
Market factors			
Dominated by established enterprises	9	8	9
Uncertain demand	8	8	8
Other factors			
UK regulations	12	9	12
EU regulations	10	7	10

It should be noted that, across all these categories, those enterprises engaged in innovation activity were more likely to perceive barriers than businesses who did not attempt to innovate. This suggests that businesses 'learn' about barriers to innovation as a result of their attempts to innovate.

Methods to protect the value of innovations

Successful innovations tend to generate intellectual property that businesses will try to protect. This can be done in numerous ways depending upon the knowledge generated and the business and market context. This may or may not involve attempts to exercise intellectual property rights.

The survey collected data on business perceptions of the relative importance of different means of protecting innovations, reported in Table 6. These included formal intellectual property rights as well as strategic mechanisms

Table 6
Enterprises rating different methods for protecting innovation as 'high' importance

Percentage of respondents

	Size of enterprise: employees		
	10–250	250+	All 10+
Formal			
Confidentiality agreements	11	22	11
Trademarks	6	16	6
Copyright	6	10	6
Patents	5	13	5
Registration of design	4	11	4
Strategic			
Lead-time advantage on competitors	9	17	10
Secrecy	8	19	9
Complexity of design	5	9	5

such as being first to market. The data show that similar proportions of enterprises rated strategic and formal methods as being of high importance. Larger enterprises attached greater importance than smaller enterprises to all methods for protecting intellectual property. It is not possible to determine from this survey if this is because large businesses have more intellectual property to protect or whether it is because large businesses have a greater awareness of intellectual property issues.

Wider forms of innovation

Innovation is not wholly about the development or use of technology or other forms of product (goods and services) and process change. Enterprises can also change their behaviour or business strategies to make themselves more competitive, often in conjunction with product or process innovation but also as independent means of improving competitiveness.

Table 7
Enterprises that introduced wider forms of innovation

Percentage of respondents

	Size of enterprise: employees		
	10–250	250+	All 10+
Wider innovator (any of changes below)	*32*	*58*	*33*
Change in marketing strategy	*18*	*35*	*20*
New organisational structures	*16*	*39*	*17*
Change in corporate strategy	*16*	*30*	*17*
Advanced management techniques	*13*	*29*	*14*

Enterprises were asked whether they had made major changes to their business structure and practices in the three-year period 2002 to 2004. Some of the findings are summarised in Table 7. As would be expected, a far greater proportion of large firms engaged in one or more of these changes. A change in marketing strategy was most commonly reported, with the introduction of advanced management techniques least reported. Small enterprises were less than half as likely to have introduced a major organisational change as large enterprises.

Comparisons with the 2001 UK Innovation Survey

Comparisons can be made with the 2001 UK Innovation Survey, which measured innovation over the period 1998–2000. The sectoral coverage of the Innovation Survey in 2005 was widened considerably to include a larger portion of the service sector. The estimates presented below adjust for this by excluding data from the additional sectors introduced in the 2005 survey.[2]

Innovation activity

Using this more restricted but comparable sector coverage, the proportion of innovation active enterprises in the 2005 survey is around 62 per cent, an increase of 14 percentage points on the previous survey. This includes a 15 percentage point increase for enterprises with fewer than 250 employees and an eight percentage point increase to 75 per cent for larger enterprises. The proportion of enterprises reporting product innovation increased by 11 percentage points and the proportion reporting process innovation increased by four percentage points.

Figure 3 compares results for the two surveys, including broader concepts of innovation activity.

Interestingly, using a definition of innovation that covers investment in, and implementation of, product and process innovation or some form of wider innovation ('broader innovator'), shows a smaller rate of increase between 2001 and 2005 (up from 61 per cent of enterprises in 2001 to 66 per cent of enterprises in 2005). However, the distribution by type of innovation is different between the surveys. The 2001 survey found lower proportions of innovation-active firms, but with more engaging in wider innovation. The 2005 survey indicates that a larger proportion are innovation active but with relatively less emphasis on wider (marketing and managerial) innovation.

Figure 3
Comparisons of 2001 and 2005 UK Innovation Surveys: proportions of innovating enterprises

Percentages

Figure 4

Proportion of enterprises rating information sources as of 'high' importance

Percentages

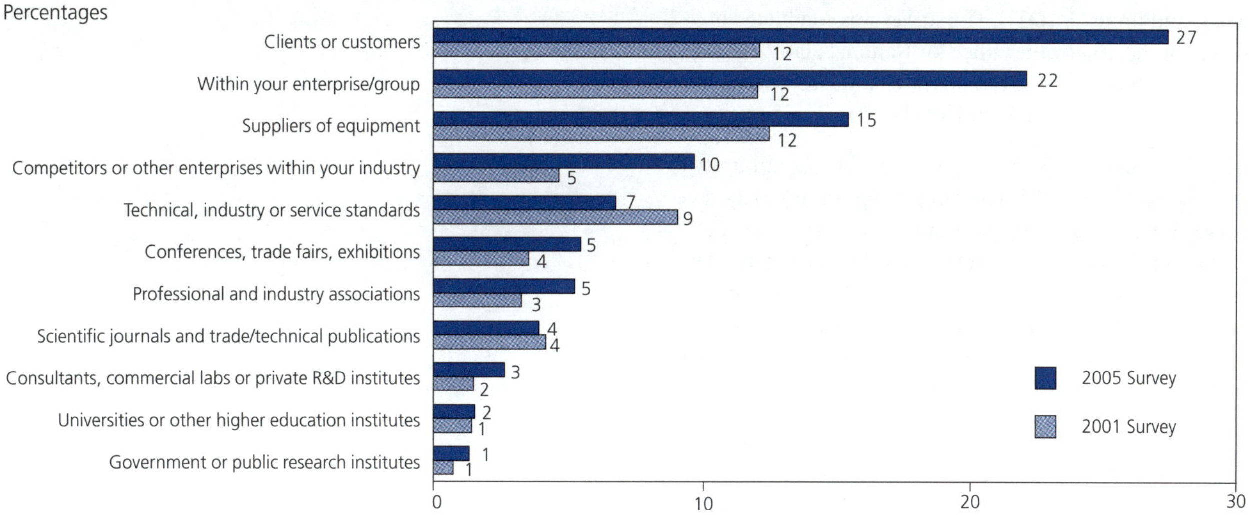

Information sources

Figure 4 makes a 'like for like' comparison between the 2001 and 2005 surveys to examine changes in the relative importance of information sources. In general, higher proportions of enterprises rated information sources of 'high' importance in 2005, especially commercial sources such as clients or customers. The perceived importance of other external sources, such as universities, changed less between the two surveys.

Conclusions and next steps

- This short article has reported just a few of the results of the latest innovation survey and on some dimensions of the changes in innovation behaviour in the UK relative to the previous survey in 2001.
- The DTI will publish more extensive reports on the detailed survey results over the next few months as well as applying the innovation indicators to policy analysis and monitoring purposes.
- The reports will include industrial and regional analyses that will enable the business community to benchmark their own innovation performance.
- The survey represents a major source of data for the research community. We expect a substantial body of further research using the survey results to be undertaken and published in various forms over the next few years.

Contact

DTI, Bay 294, 151 Buckingham Palace Road, London SW1W 9SS E-mail: stephanie.robson@dti.gsi.gov.uk

Notes

1. All results are grossed up to the business population.
2. These are: sale, maintenance and repair of motor vehicles, retail trade, hotels and restaurants. Other differences between the surveys, such as in the sample design and weighting methodology, are not accounted for.

Appendix – methodology

The UK Innovation Survey is funded by the Department of Trade and Industry (DTI). The survey was conducted on behalf of the DTI by the Office for National Statistics (ONS), with assistance from the Northern Ireland Department of Enterprise, Trade and Investment (DETI).

The UK Innovation Survey is part of a wider Community Innovation Survey (CIS) covering European countries. The survey is based on a core questionnaire developed by the European Commission (Eurostat) and Member States. This is the fourth iteration of the survey (CIS 4) – CIS 3, covering the period 1998 to 2000, was carried out in 2001 and the results form part of various EU benchmarking exercises (see www.cordis.lu/innovation-smes/scoreboard/home.htm).

The UK Innovation Survey 2005 sampled over 28,000 UK enterprises. The survey was voluntary and conducted by means of a postal questionnaire. A copy of the questionnaire used can be found at www.dti.gov.uk/iese/cis4quest.htm

Coverage and sampling

The survey covered enterprises with 10 or more employees in sections C to K of the Standard Industrial Classification (SIC) 2003. The 2005 survey included additional sector: Sale, maintenance and repair of motor vehicles (SIC 50), Retail trade (SIC 52) and Hotels and restaurants (SIC 55) excluded from the 2001 survey.

The sample was drawn from the ONS Inter-Departmental Business Register (IDBR) in December 2004. Details can be found at www.dti.gov.uk/iese/cis4sample.htm

Response and weighting

The questionnaires from the initial survey were distributed on 31 March 2005.

Valid responses were received from 16,446 enterprises to give a response rate of 58 per cent.

The results in this article are based on weighted data in order to be representative of the population of firms. The responses were weighted back to the population using the inverse sampling proportion in each stratum, that is, the weight attributed to each enterprises was the number of enterprises in the population divided by the number of responses in that stratum. On average each respondent represents 11 enterprises in the population.

Internet spending: measurement and recent trends[1]

Gavin Wallis
Office for National Statistics

This article considers the coverage of Internet spending in economic statistics, doing so in the context of a review of the available statistical sources and recent trends. It concludes that there is good coverage of the main channels of Internet spending in the statistics, but that it is not always possible (or necessary) to identify them separately. It also identifies some areas of Internet spending which require further investigation.

Overview

Use of the Internet by both consumers and businesses has expanded rapidly in recent years. For example, the latest National Statistics Omnibus Survey shows that in July 2005 over 60 per cent of adults in Great Britain used the Internet, and results from the e-commerce survey show that in 2004 over 64 per cent of all UK businesses had Internet access. Together with this expansion in Internet use, there has been an increase in spending over the Internet. This expansion presents a challenge for the measurement of consumer spending, business spending and prices.

The challenge for measurement comes as a result of the impact that the Internet has on the way business is conducted in the UK, and internationally, and also the extra choices it provides to consumers when making purchasing decisions.

This article provides an overview of the type, extent and recent trends of Internet use and Internet spending by households and businesses, using results from a range of Office for National Statistics (ONS) surveys and also from the Internet industry itself. It goes on to describe how Internet spending is measured in the National Accounts in terms of household consumption, business spending and price measurement. This includes a discussion of how Internet spending is captured in ONS business surveys and how Internet spending is captured in National Accounts aggregate results.

Key findings are as follows:

- Fifty five per cent of households in Great Britain had access to the Internet from home in July 2005, up from 32 per cent in July 2000.
- Internet spending is growing rapidly, with results from the ONS e-commerce survey showing Internet sales of goods and services to households in 2004 of £18.1 billion, with growth since 2003 of over 67 per cent.
- Household Internet spending in 2004, while growing rapidly, was still a small part of total household spending, accounting for only around 2.5 per cent of the total.
- The majority of the expansion in Internet spending is captured within the National Accounts, including both household and business Internet spending.
- The main channels of household Internet spending are included in the Retail Sales Index.
- The way in which information on Internet spending is captured in the National Accounts means that it cannot always be identified as a separate component.
- However, the e-commerce survey provides estimates of the value of Internet sales.
- Household spending on some items, such as gaming subscriptions, online gambling and software downloads, needs investigation, as does how well Internet purchases from abroad are captured in trade data.

- Business Internet spending on goods and services is covered by the Annual Business Inquiry. This ensures good quality estimates feed into the Input-Output Supply and Use Tables framework, which is used to set the annual level of UK GDP, and that GDP is not under-recorded due to the increase in Internet spending.
- For the purposes of calculating price indices, such as the Consumer Prices Index and Retail Prices Index, ONS has been expanding the scope of price collection to account for the increase in the number of goods and services bought and sold on the Internet.

Internet spending

Spending on the Internet is widespread and occurs in a broad variety of formats. The most notable, in terms of the publicity it has received, is consumer spending through specialist Internet retailers, such as Amazon, and auction sites, such as eBay. Sources such as the e-commerce survey, however, confirm that Internet spending extends well beyond these two well-known sites, with many high street retailers and businesses now making significant sales over the Internet. Households are increasingly using the Internet to buy both goods and services and in some cases are buying directly from manufacturers or wholesalers, or from overseas providers rather than using traditional retail channels. Not only are households embracing the Internet, but also businesses are increasingly selling their goods and services via the Internet and some are also using the Internet to make purchases.

The Internet is not only an expanding channel for household and business spending, but it is also a driver for productivity growth. ONS work has shown the importance of business use of the Internet and of other Information and Communication Technologies (ICT). For example:

- Criscuolo and Waldron (2003) show how the use of e-commerce is changing the performance of firms and the behaviour of markets. In particular they show significant productivity gains associated with the use of electronic procurement systems.
- Goodridge and Clayton (2004) extended this work to look at broader use of electronic business processes, including use of the Internet by employees, and again show positive productivity impacts.
- Farooqui (2005) looks in more detail at the effects on productivity associated with measures of ICT use, such as the use of computers and the Internet by employees and the use of electronic trading. His results show that the impact of ICT use on productivity differs across sectors with the strongest gains in the services industry.

In addition, ONS publishes a range of statistics covering ICT, consistent with the National Accounts and based on the annual Input-Output Supply and Use Tables, in the UK *Input-Output Analyses* publication. The 2005 edition covers the years 1992 to 2003.

A wide range of ONS sources capture Internet use and Internet spending by households and businesses. They include:

- National Statistics Omnibus Survey
- e-commerce survey
- Retail Sales Index
- Annual Business Inquiry
- Expenditure and Food Survey

Information on these sources is given elsewhere in this article. The article also draws on information from the Internet-industry trade body Interactive Media in Retail Group.

Household Internet spending

Table 1 below lists the types of household Internet spending that can be identified, including, where possible, some well known examples of the businesses and/or industries from which households make purchases.

The latest National Statistics Omnibus Survey[2] shows that 55 per cent of households (12.9 million households) in Great Britain had access to the Internet from home in July 2005. This compares with just 32 per cent in July 2000, the first year for which comparable figures are available. This expansion in Internet access is shown in Figure 1.

In addition to the expansion of Internet access there has been an increase in the number of people using the Internet to buy or order goods, tickets and services. Figure 2 shows household use of the Internet by purpose of access.

Figure 2 shows that 55 per cent of adults who used the Internet in July 2005 bought or ordered goods, tickets or services. In July 2001 the figure was 39 per cent. Figure 2 also

Table 1
Types of household Internet spending

Type of Internet spending	Example(s)
Spending on goods from specialist Internet retailers	Amazon
Spending on goods from store-based retailers	Tesco, Comet, Next, PC World, Argos
Spending on goods from catalogue-based mail order retailers	Freemans
Spending on goods bought direct from manufacturers	Apple
Spending on goods bought direct from wholesalers	Dell *, Avon
Spending on goods bought from the service sector	Vodafone
Spending on services bought from the service sector	easyJet, Betfair, Banking, Gambling
Spending on services bought from retailers	Sainsbury's Bank
Consumer-to-consumer transactions	eBay, eBid, Totalbids

** Dell is shown as a wholesaler as they do not manufacture in the UK but act as a wholesaler*

shows an increase in the number of people using the Internet for personal banking and financial services. Using e-mail and finding out information about goods and services continue to be the main reason for households accessing the Internet.

Figure 1
Household Internet access

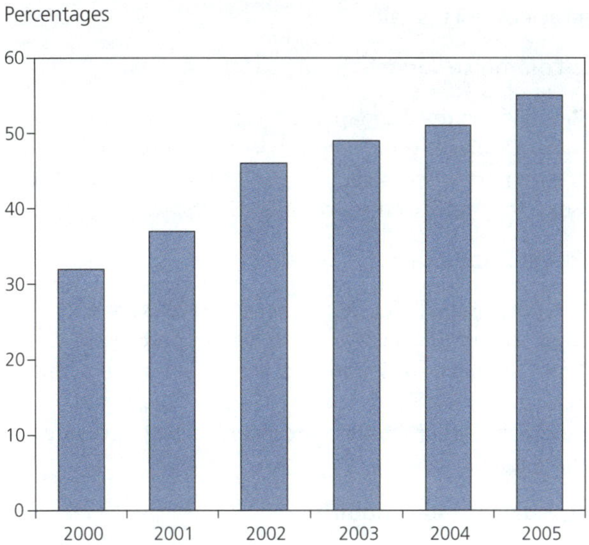

Note: data relate to July interviews of the Omnibus Survey and cover Great Britain only.

Source: National Statistics Omnibus Survey

Figure 2
Internet use: by purpose of access

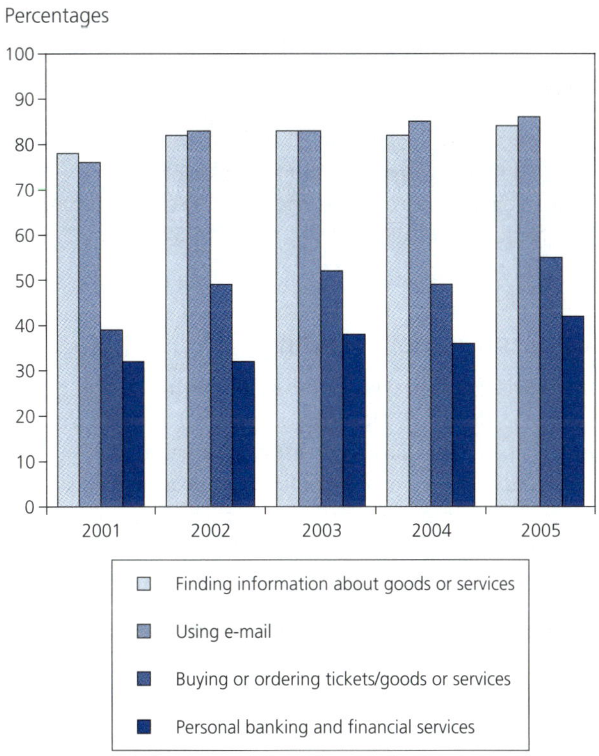

Note: the figures presented are restricted to those who have used the Internet in the last three months for 'personal' and 'private' use. The data relate to July interviews of the Omnibus Survey.

Source: National Statistics Omnibus Survey

Clearly it would be expected that the expansion in household access to the Internet and the increasing proportion of Internet users buying or ordering goods, tickets or services would lead to an increase in Internet spending. One good source of data on the amount of Internet spending by households (and businesses) is the ONS e-commerce survey. Box 2 provides a description of the survey and a brief overview of the data it collects.

Figure 3 shows the rapid growth in Internet sales of goods and services to households over recent years, as recorded by the e-commerce survey. The survey indicates that in 2001 Internet sales to households from the UK non-financial sector stood at £4 billion; by 2004 these had increased to over £18 billion. The growth in Internet sales from 2003 to 2004, as measured by the e-commerce survey, is over 67 per cent, showing a very rapid expansion in the value of Internet sales.

Figure 3
Sales over the Internet to households

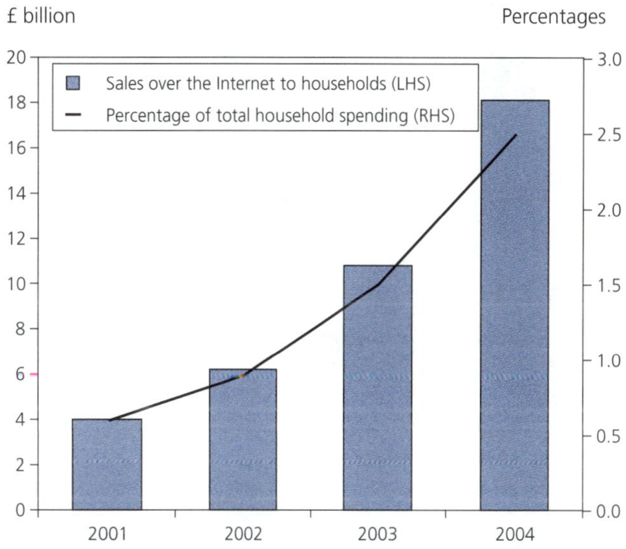

Note: the percentages of total household spending are the e-commerce figure for Internet sales of goods and services as a share of household final consumption expenditure from the latest Blue Book.

Source: e-commerce survey; Blue Book 2005

To put these figures in context, the total value of retail sales in Great Britain in 2004, as measured by the Retail Sales Index, was £247 billion, with growth from 2003 of 4.6 per cent. Household final consumption expenditure in the UK in 2004 was £732 billion,[3] with growth from 2003 of 4.9 per cent. This shows that, in the context of household spending, Internet spending is a small part, accounting for around 2.5 per cent of the total; but also that it is growing much more rapidly than household spending in general. Figure 3 also shows Internet sales of goods and services as a percentage of total household final consumption expenditure.[4]

Figure 4 shows sales over the Internet to households by broad industrial group. Wholesale, Retail, Catering and Travel as a broad industrial group dominates Internet sales to households, accounting for £10.7 billion of the £18.1 billion total Internet sales in 2004. This corresponds to £59 out of every £100 sold over the Internet to households. The largest relative increase by an industrial group in 2004 was in the Post and Telecommunications industries, which increased fourfold, albeit from a very low base.

Figure 4
Sales over the Internet to households: by broad industrial group

£ billion

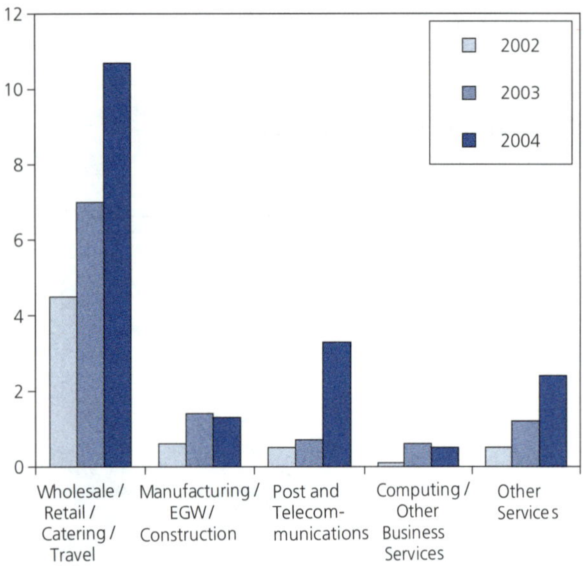

Note: EGW = Electricity, Gas and Water Supply.
Coverage: UK non-financial sector.
Source: e-commerce survey

The value of household Internet spending

The e-commerce survey is not the only source available for estimates of the value of household Internet spending. Various other sources also exist and some of these sources are discussed in more detail below. Box 1 provides an overview of the sources discussed in this article in relation to both household use of the Internet and Internet spending. The Box identifies whether or not the sources provide an estimate of the value of Internet spending and also whether the estimate refers to the purchase of goods and services, or just goods. In cases where the source does provide an estimate of the value of Internet spending, estimates for 2004 are provided for comparison. As with all statistics, care should be taken when comparing estimates across different sources.

Box 1: Sources for household Internet use and spending

National Statistics Omnibus Survey

The National Statistics Omnibus Survey covers areas such as Internet access and purpose of use. Footnote 2 provides more detail.

e-commerce survey

Results from the e-commerce survey give estimates of Internet sales of goods and services to households, from the UK non-financial sector, of £18.1 billion in 2004. See Box 2 for details of the e-commerce survey.

Retail Sales Index

The Retail Sales Index measures total retail sales and does not distinguish between means of purchase. Internet sales by all kinds of retailer, that is store-based retailers, specialist Internet retailers and catalogue-based mail order retailers, are included. Box 3 provides more detail.

Annual Business Inquiry

A special exercise from Annual Business Inquiry (ABI) provisional results has given a rough estimate of Internet retail sales for 2004. This estimate is around £8 billion.

Expenditure and Food Survey

The Expenditure and Food Survey (EFS) allows the identification of some types of Internet spending by households but only certain items of expenditure are split between Internet and non-Internet purchases. See footnote 9 for background on the survey.

IMRG

The trade body Interactive Media in Retail Group (IMRG) produces estimates of the value of Internet sales, covering both goods and services. Their estimate for total online shopping in 2004 is £14.5 billion.

Business Internet spending

Table 2 lists the main types of business Internet spending that can be identified. The types of spending are all business-to-business transactions. In recent years, auction sites have opened up the possibility of consumer-to-business transactions, but these are believed to still be quite rare and so will not be discussed further.

Table 2
Types of business Internet spending

Type of Internet spending
Spending on goods and services bought from manufacturers
Spending on goods bought from wholesalers
Spending on goods and services bought from retailers
Spending on goods and services bought from the service sector

The e-commerce survey provides a wide range of data on business use of the Internet. The most recent survey results show that over 64 per cent of all UK businesses had Internet access in 2004. In 2004, 6.7 per cent of businesses sold over the Internet while 35.3 per cent made purchases over the Internet. The corresponding figures for 2002 are 4.4 per cent and 12.9 per cent. The increase in the value of Internet purchases has also been rapid, as can be seen in Figure 5.[5]

Box 2: e-commerce survey

The e-commerce survey is an annual survey of UK business that asks about use of the Internet and e-commerce. ONS launched the survey in January 2001 as part of a European Union (EU) initiative to provide EU-comparable data on e-commerce. The UK component began as a survey of 9,000 businesses randomly sampled from the Inter-departmental Business Register (stratified by employment size). The sampling methodology ensures wide coverage of the UK economy and the estimates produced cover all sectors, except agriculture, fishing, mining and the public sector. The financial sector is included for ICT usage but not for buying and selling over the Internet. Businesses with employment of ten or more have been sampled every year since the survey began. Businesses with employment of nine or less were included in the sample for the 2001 to 2004 surveys but will not be included in the 2005 survey.

The e-commerce survey is a business inquiry but it covers both household and business Internet spending. It covers the value of Internet sales by businesses to household by various categories, including broad industrial sector, and covers, among other things, sales to other businesses over the Internet, purchases over the Internet by businesses, business Internet access and business use of ICT.

As the annual e-commerce survey is a relatively new survey and is still developing it has been designated as experimental. The National Statistics' Code of Practice Protocol on Dissemination permits this status where National Statistics are developing and undergoing evaluation.

The e-commerce survey is a good source for measuring Internet spending. However, it is not a timely indicator of such spending; results for 2004 were not published until 4 November 2005.

For more detail on coverage and methodology see ONS (2005a).

Results from the e-commerce survey show that Internet purchases represented nearly 4.4 per cent of the total purchases of non-financial businesses in 2004, compared with just under 2.8 per cent in 2003 and just over 1.3 per cent in 2002. This corresponds to businesses purchasing £62.4 billion worth of products and services over the Internet in 2004. From Figure 5 it can be seen that physical products dominate online purchasing, accounting for 74 per cent of the total value of purchases in 2004, with services accounting for 17 per cent and digitised products for 9 per cent.[6]

Figure 5:
Value of purchases over the Internet by UK non-financial sector businesses: by type of product

£ billion

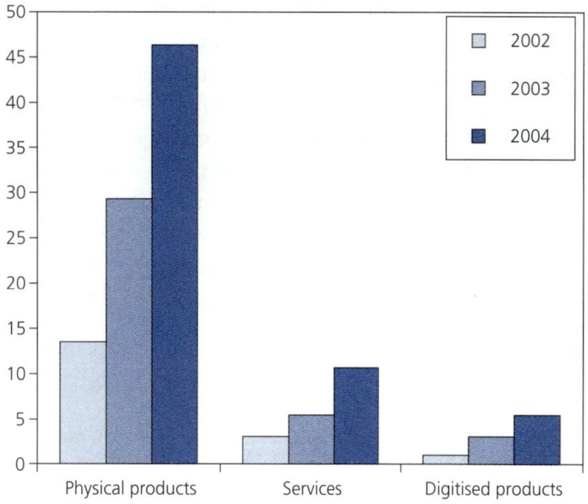

Source: e-commerce survey

Figure 6:
Value of purchases over the Internet by UK non-financial sector businesses: by broad industrial group

£ billion

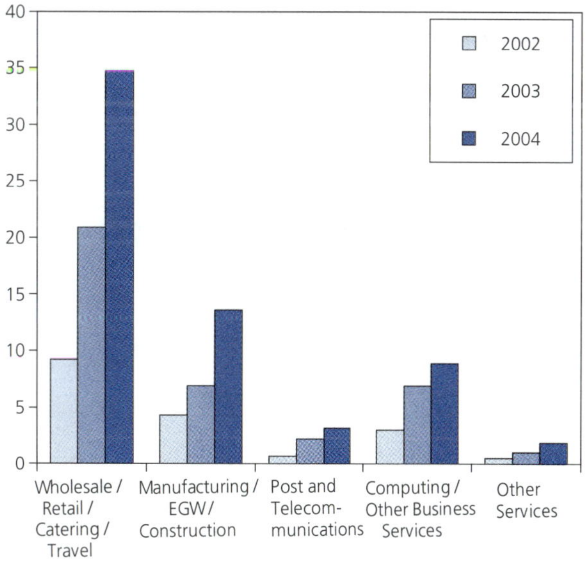

Note: EGW = Electricity, Gas and Water Supply

Source: e-commerce survey

As with household spending, Wholesale, Retail, Catering and Travel dominates Internet purchases by business, accounting for nearly £56 of every £100 spent in 2004. Manufacturing accounted for nearly £22 of every £100 and showed the largest percentage increase year on year in 2004 at 97 per cent. Figure 6 shows the value of purchases over the internet by UK non-financial sector businesses, by broad industrial group.

How Internet spending is measured in the Retail Sales Index and the National Accounts

The expansion of Internet spending has implications for the measurement of consumer spending, business spending and prices. This section describes how Internet spending is captured in the Retail Sales Index (RSI) and the National Accounts. It will be shown that the majority of the expansion in Internet spending is captured within the National Accounts. The way in which Internet spending is picked up in the National Accounts does, however, mean that Internet spending cannot always be identified as a separate component. Internet spending can be separately identified using results from the e-commerce survey, but as noted above this does not provide short-term estimates of the value of Internet sales.

Retail Sales Index

The monthly RSI measures *sales* by retail businesses; household expenditure in the National Accounts measures *purchases* by households. The RSI is often used as an early indicator of consumer spending. However, it should be borne in mind that the RSI only covers spending on goods bought from retailers and this accounts for around one third of total consumer spending, as measured by household final consumption expenditure (HHFCE) in the National Accounts.[7]

Results from sources such as the e-commerce survey suggest that the majority of household Internet spending is on goods rather than services. Therefore, it is important to understand what types of household Internet spending are captured by the RSI. Box 3 provides an overview of the RSI and the types of Internet purchases that are covered by the index.

Figure 7:
The RSI and the comparable component of household consumer spending

Percentage change in volume, quarter on corresponding quarter a year earlier

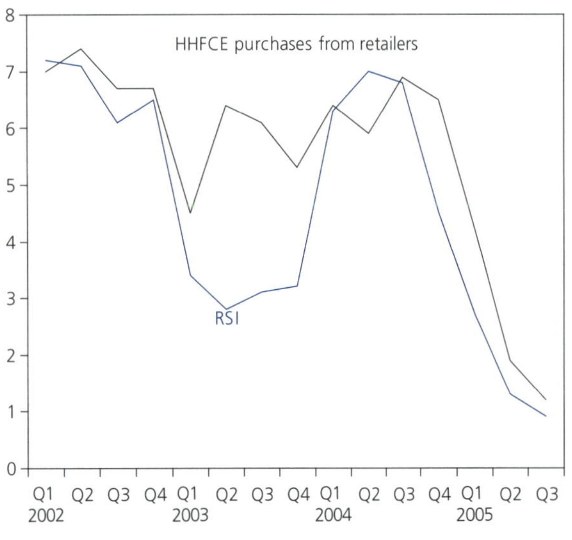

The main points from Box 3 are that the RSI is designed to capture the purchase of goods from the retail sector, so covers the first three types of Internet spending identified in Table 1. The method of data collection for the RSI does, however, mean that Internet sales by retailers cannot be separately identified from total sales.

Box 3: The Retail Sales Index and Internet spending[8]

The RSI is constructed from a monthly inquiry into retail sales carried out by ONS on 5,000 businesses in Great Britain. The sample is representative of the whole retail sector and includes all large retailers and a representative panel of smaller businesses. The achieved response rate each month represents 85 to 90 per cent of total retail sales. The monthly inquiry collects one figure from each sampled business, total retail sales for the month in question, and respondents receive specific instructions to include Internet sales in the total sales figures they provide.

The RSI only covers sales from businesses registered as retailers. Technically this means that the scope of the RSI is defined in terms of the Standard Industrial Classification (SIC), which is an internationally agreed convention for classifying industries. The retail sector is Division 52 of the SIC 2003. This means that the RSI includes all Internet businesses whose primary function is retailing and also covers Internet sales by other retailers in Great Britain, such as online sales by supermarkets, department stores and catalogue companies. Thus, the RSI covers the first three types of household Internet spending identified in Table 1, repeated below, but not the other types of household Internet spending:

- spending on goods from specialist Internet retailers
- spending on goods by store-based retailers
- spending on goods by catalogue-based mail order retailers

The e-commerce survey suggests that these three types of household Internet spending, combined, make up a large proportion of total household Internet spending.

The RSI sample is subject to monthly reviews to ensure that it remains representative of the whole retail sector. This also ensures that growth areas in retailing, such as that for specialist internet retailers, are reflected in the RSI results.

The RSI does not cover household spending on services bought from the retail sector as it is designed only to cover goods. Respondents are asked to separate out the non-goods elements of their sales, for example, income from cafeterias. Consequently on-line sales of services by retailers, such as car insurance, would also be excluded.

Retailers specialising in providing material for downloading over the Internet, such as music and mobile phone ringtones, are covered by the RSI if they are purely retailers only and are not also involved in the production or processing of such material. Sales of downloads by store-based retailers would be included in their total sales figures.

One thing to note is that because the monthly inquiry only collects data on total retail sales, but is not broken down by type of sales outlet, Internet spending cannot be separately identified. For example, the inquiry would collect total retail sales for Tesco but the Internet and non-Internet elements would not be collected separately. Some large businesses do report figures for Internet sales in their publicly available published reports. For instance, Tesco publicly reported Internet sales in the UK of £719 million in the financial year 2004–05.

In terms of published RSI results, Internet sales by retailers are included in the relevant store category. For example, online sales by supermarkets would be included in the 'predominantly food stores' category, while sales by specialist Internet retailers are included in the 'non-store retailing and repair' category along with sales by catalogue-based retailers.

The RSI therefore has good coverage of household spending on the Internet from specialist Internet retailers, such as Amazon, and from established store-based retailers, such as Tesco, which have been expanding their Internet business. The increased use of the Internet to purchase goods is reflected in the RSI as long as the goods are being purchased from a retailer.

Household final consumption expenditure

Household final consumption expenditure (HHFCE) is the largest single component of the expenditure measure of GDP, accounting for about 50 per cent of spending. Accurate measurement of its composition and growth over time is therefore vital to understanding the UK economy. Clearly, accurate measurement includes taking full account of the growth in Internet spending on goods and services which, although still a small part of total final consumption expenditure, is growing rapidly. This section explains how Internet spending is captured in the estimates of HHFCE.

Table 3 shows the data sources used to compile HHFCE estimates, the components of HHFCE that the source is being used to measure, and also the approximate weight of each component. The Table also demonstrates that around 50 per cent of consumer spending is on services and 50 per cent is on goods.

Results from the e-commerce survey show that Internet spending is much more prominent in terms of purchasing goods than purchasing services, so the main focus of this section will be on how Internet purchase of goods are captured. However, the section starts with a discussion of how Internet purchases of services are captured.

Internet purchases of services, rows 7 and 8 of Table 1, are covered either by the EFS[9] or by supply-side estimates.[10] The EFS covers all expenditure by households regardless of whether the spending occurs over the Internet or not. This means that the EFS should provide full coverage of Internet purchases of the services for which it is used as the source. Some services are more difficult to measure, such as gambling, and cannot be measured accurately or reliably by the EFS. In these cases supply-side estimates are used instead.

Some of the listed sub-components in Table 3 cover areas where direct measurement of HHFCE is difficult or supply-side estimates are more reliable. Some of these relate to the purchase of goods, such as vehicles, where supply-side data are used. For services that are more difficult to measure, supply-side estimates are used, based on the Index of Services.

Table 3 shows that the main source for household consumption of goods is the RSI. The other main source for expenditure on goods is the EFS, which is used for estimating spending on food, which makes up around 10 per cent of all household expenditure. The RSI is not used for food as it is industry-based and estimates that are commodity-based are needed for measuring consumption of food. The EFS covers all expenditure on food items regardless of whether the purchase was made over the Internet or not and so should provide full coverage of Internet purchases of food.

Purchases of alcohol, tobacco and vehicles are obtained from administrative data on excise duty receipts and therefore cover all types of purchase, Internet or otherwise.

Therefore, the RSI and EFS together cover the first three

Table 3
Sources for HHFCE

Source	Sub-component of HHFCE	Weight in aggregate (per cent)
Expenditure and Food Survey (EFS)	Food	*10*
	Services excluding on-trade in alcohol	*20*
Retail Sales Index	Goods excluding food, drink, tobacco and vehicles	*20*
Local Authorities and EFS	Rent	*13*
HM Revenue and Customs	Alcohol	*6*
HM Revenue and Customs	Tobacco	*2*
Motor trades, HM Revenue and Customs	Vehicles	*6*
Department of Trade and Industry (DTI)	Energy, motor fuels	*5*
International Passenger Survey	Air and sea transport – tourist expenditure	*3*
Financial Inquiries	Insurance, banking, etc.	*5*
Various – such as data from regulators	Water, rail and bus, telecom (part), gambling, etc.	*10*

types of household Internet spending in Table 1. However, household Internet spending on goods bought direct from manufacturers and direct from wholesalers is not measured using these sources. As explained in Box 3 the RSI only covers the retail sector and so does not cover such purchases. The EFS is used only for food and services. These two areas of Internet spending are captured by adding estimates from the Index of Production (IoP) for household Internet spending on goods bought direct from manufacturers and from the Index of Service (IoS) for household Internet spending on goods bought direct from wholesalers.

Household spending on goods bought from the service sector is a small component of total household expenditure and cannot be estimated accurately from the demand side. Once again the IoS is used here.

The remaining element of household Internet spending identified in Table 1 is consumer-to-consumer transactions. Box 4 describes how Internet auction sites are treated in the National Accounts in terms of household consumption.

To summarise how household Internet spending is measured in the National Accounts, Table 4 repeats Table 1 but with an indication of how the Internet spending is captured.

Box 4: Internet auction sites[11]

When people think about online auctions they typically think of eBay. Just like traditional auction companies, eBay does not actually sell goods, it merely facilitates the process of listing and displaying goods, bidding on items up for auction, and paying for them. eBay acts as a marketplace for both individuals and businesses to auction goods and in some cases services.

Launched in the UK in October 1999, eBay.co.uk is the UK's largest online marketplace with over 10 million registered users. eBay's published reports for 2004 state that gross merchandise volume, the value of all successfully closed listings on eBay.co.uk, reached a record £3.7 billion. eBay, as with other auction sites, makes its money from listing and final value fees collected from registered users who trade their goods on eBay.

The *transfer* of goods between households/consumers does not contribute to GDP as it does not generate any value added. What matters for National Accounts purposes is not gross sales or turnover but the fees and commissions generated by Internet auction companies, such as eBay, for facilitating the sale and purchase of goods, as is the case for traditional auction companies. In terms of household consumption expenditure, consumer-to-consumer transactions do not generate final demand or value added, except in terms of the fees and commissions paid by households. These fees and commissions are regarded as household final consumption expenditure and need to be included as part of value added when estimating GDP.

Fees and commissions of Internet auction houses are captured in the monthly services inquiry, which feeds into the Index of Services. They are not picked up by the Retail Sales Index as they would return a value of zero. They have no retail sales, as they do not actually sell any goods.

Table 4
How different types of household Internet spending are captured in HHFCE

Type of Internet spending	Covered by
Spending on goods from specialist Internet retailers	Retail Sales Inquiry
Spending on goods by store-based retailers	Retail Sales Inquiry and EFS
Spending on goods by catalogue-based mail order retailers	Retail Sales Inquiry
Spending on goods bought direct from manufacturers	Index of Production
Spending on goods bought direct from wholesalers	Index of Services
Spending on goods bought from the service sector	Index of Services
Spending on services bought from the service sector	Index of Services and EFS
Spending on services bought from retailers	EFS
Consumer-to-consumer transactions	Index of Services

Table 4 shows that coverage of Internet spending is good, although current sources mean that this Internet purchasing cannot be separately identified as a single item and hence short-term estimates of household Internet spending are not available. However, estimates of the value of Internet sales can be obtained from the e-commerce survey.

Although Table 4 shows that coverage of Internet spending is good, there are some areas where future work is needed to ensure coverage is as good as possible. The most important area is the increasing use of the Internet to make purchases from abroad. Traditional trade data may not be covering all areas where Internet purchasing is taking place and this needs further investigation. Other areas include looking more closely at how downloads of ringtones and music are captured. These markets are still quite small but are beginning to grow rapidly. Gaming subscriptions, online gambling, software downloads and purchasing of adult material are other areas that will need to be considered. All of these areas are complicated by the global nature of such online activity and purchasing.

As noted in Box 1, the ABI provides a source for household internet spending. Results from the ABI feed into estimates of HHFCE through their use in benchmarking short-term surveys, such as the RSI. However, due to the time lag in its availability, the ABI does not feed into early estimates of consumption expenditure.

Short-term estimates of the value of Internet sales

As noted above, ONS does not produce short-term estimates of the value of Internet sales. However, the trade body Interactive Media in Retail Group (IMRG) does. IMRG produce an e-Retail Sales Index that estimates total UK Internet sales to households on a monthly basis. The index includes both goods and services and is not restricted to retailers, as defined by the SIC (2003). IMRG's estimate for total online shopping in 2004 is £14.5 billion.[12] ONS and IMRG are currently liaising to explore the extent to which our respective sets of statistics on Internet spending can be of mutual benefit. IMRG have kindly allowed us to show their e-Retail Sales Index in this article and the Index up until November 2005 is shown in Figure 8.

Business Internet spending

When estimating the sales or output of a firm or industry, it is clear that we want to include all sales or output of a firm regardless of whether the goods or services were sold online or not. There is also a need for accurately capturing intermediate consumption, of which business Internet spending is a part, for the calculation of Gross Value Added (GVA).

GVA measures the contribution to the economy of each individual producer, industry or sector in the UK and is used in the estimation of Gross Domestic Product (GDP).[13] Annual estimates of GVA for each industry are measured in basic prices as:

GVA = Total output *less* intermediate consumption

Intermediate consumption reflects the goods and services used up in order to make the output, and will include business-to-business Internet spending, so needs to be recorded in order to accurately measure GVA.

The ABI captures both business output and business spending

Figure 8
IMRG index for UK e-retail market
Index, April 2000 = 100

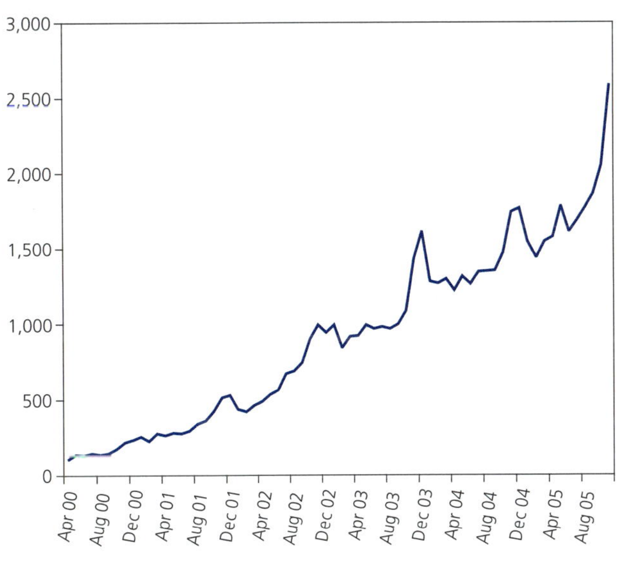

on goods and services (intermediate consumption), regardless of whether the output is sold or the spending is Internet-based or not. The ABI therefore covers all the relevant types of Internet spending in Table 2. Sales are also captured by the ABI regardless of the channel of purchase.

The ABI is the largest single data source used in compiling the Input-Output Supply and Use Tables which are used to set the annual level of UK GDP. In these tables, estimates of industries' inputs, outputs and GVA are produced for 123 industries across the whole economy. The industries' outputs together with imports of goods and services form the supply, which are matched with the demands, including intermediate demand, and final demands such as HHFCE, capital formation and exports.

Through this process, GDP is balanced ensuring consistent underlying components for the production, income and expenditure approaches to estimating GDP. This process equally helps to ensure that GDP is not being under-recorded due to the increase in Internet spending.

Quarterly GDP is primarily based on the movements in the production/output-based approach to GDP, which is mainly based on the IoP and GDP(O) estimates. These estimates are in volume terms and assume that movements in turnover are similar to GVA in the short-term. The estimates of turnover from the short-term inquiries to businesses, like the ABI, will include all sales whether or not sold over the Internet.

Price measurement

The expansion in Internet spending clearly has implications for both consumer and producer prices. The level and rate of change of the prices of Internet purchases may not coincide with that of non-Internet purchases, even if the item being bought is the same. For price collection it is important therefore to cover purchases over the Internet and weight these prices accordingly, in order to ensure the statistical integrity of price indices and that the price effects of the expansion in online purchasing are captured. This section gives an overview of the way in which ONS has been expanding the scope of price collection to ensure that goods and services purchased over the Internet are incorporated into price measurement.

Consumer prices

The Consumer Prices Index (CPI) and Retail Prices Index (RPI) can be viewed as the changing cost of a large 'shopping basket' containing the goods and services bought by a typical household in the course of a year. Since it is impossible to price all of the products bought by every household, a specific selection of representative items is chosen, which should give a reliable estimate of inflation for a broad range of similar goods and services. The expansion of household Internet spending means that many of these representative items are now being purchased over the Internet. It is also important that the RPI reflects the impact on prices due to the expansion of Internet spending because components of the RPI are used to deflate the RSI onto a volume basis and also to deflate elements of HHFCE.

The prices for some goods have been explicitly included from Internet sources, along with traditional sources, for a few years, such as books, CD-ROMs and some supermarket goods. As household Internet spending has increased, so have the number of goods covered by Internet price collection. For example, Internet purchases of DVDs entered the RPI and CPI basket in February 2005. The prices of Internet purchases of services are also used when constructing the CPI and RPI.

In some cases, goods can be bought at the same price on the Internet as from traditional stores, and in these instances the Internet is used as a convenient source of price data.

Collection of Internet prices is not the whole story. In order that collected prices are included with the correct relative importance when constructing the CPI and RPI, appropriate weights are needed. The EFS is the main source used to obtain these weights. From April 2001, the EFS has collected information on purchases over the Internet and this information, supplemented by detailed analyses of trends presented by market research companies, trade journals and in press reports, is used to calculate the weights given to Internet prices.

Producer prices

The Producer Price Index (PPI) is a monthly survey that measures the price changes of goods bought and sold by UK manufacturers. The PPI is based on representative price quotes obtained from sellers and so captures Internet prices in instances where the representative price for a firm is the online price the firm charges.

Business-to-business service prices

The Corporate Services Price Index (CSPI) is a quarterly survey of prices charged for services provided by UK businesses to other UK businesses and government. Industry-specific series, covering about half the total corporate services sector, are currently published as experimental statistics. The 'experimental' status means the indices are still under development. Price indices for industries not yet covered, such as computer services, are being developed and added progressively to the published series. Due to the diversity of types of services available, the CSPI uses a variety of methods to obtain data and calculate the industry-specific indices and these are too detailed to cover here.[14] However, as with the PPI, the use of representative price quotes obtained from sellers is quite common and so in these instances it is clear that the CSPI captures Internet prices in the instances where the representative price for a firm is the online price the firm charges for services. Where price quotes are not used, the methods are designed to best reflect the structure of the industry.

Conclusions

Internet spending has expanded rapidly and occurs in a wide variety of forms throughout the UK economy. Both households and businesses have increased their use of the Internet, including making online purchases.

The expansion in Internet spending is being picked up within the National Accounts, with the main areas of both household and business Internet spending that can be identified being captured by existing ONS surveys. The way in which Internet spending is picked up in the National Accounts does, however, mean that it cannot be identified as a separate component and so the National Accounts do not provide a separate estimate of the value of Internet sales. However, National Accounts aggregates, such as GDP and household final consumption expenditure as well as measures of prices, do incorporate good measurement of Internet purchases.

Household spending on some items, such as gaming subscriptions, online gambling and software downloads, does need additional investigation, as does how well Internet purchases from abroad are captured in trade data.

The e-commerce survey provides estimates of the value of Internet sales and the main channels of household Internet spending are included in the Retail Sales Index.

All spending on goods and services by UK businesses is captured by the Annual Business Inquiry and so all types of UK business Internet spending are covered. The Annual Business Inquiry also captures all sales by UK businesses.

The annual level of UK GDP is determined through the production of Input-Output Supply and Use Tables, which rely on data sources such as the Annual Business Inquiry and other surveys. Data captured through these sources and balancing GDP through this process ensures GDP is not under-recorded as a result of increasing Internet spending.

In terms of the effect of the expanding use of the Internet on price measurement, ONS has been expanding the scope of price collection to incorporate goods and services sold on the Internet into the CPI and RPI. The data collection methods for the PPI and CSPI also ensure that the increased use of the Internet by businesses to make purchases is reflected in the indices.

Acknowledgements

The author is grateful to ONS colleagues for comments and assistance with this article, in particular Tony Clayton, Christina Forrest, Ian Knowles, Sanjiv Mahajan, Colin Mowl, Nicholas Palmer, Cecil Prescott and Geoff Tily.

Notes

1. Data supplied to ONS by individual businesses is treated as strictly confidential and is protected by the National Statistics Code of Practice and the Statistics of Trade Act. All figures quoted in this article regarding individual businesses are from publicly available sources and not from confidential ONS surveys. Examples are used for illustrative purposes and are not indicative of inclusion in ONS surveys.
2. The National Statistics Omnibus Survey is a multi-purpose monthly survey based on interviews with a sample of about 1,900 adults per survey month, with one adult selected from each household. The Survey is a vehicle for providing quick results from a relatively short and simple set of questions. Questions on particular topics can be added for one month or longer if required. The Survey covers Great Britain and data are available at standard regional level.
3. *Blue Book* 2005 www.statistics.gov.uk/StatBase/Product.asp?vlnk=1143
4. It should be noted that the data sources used are not specifically designed for combining in this way. However, the calculation does provide a reasonably good estimate of Internet sales of goods and services as a percentage of total household final consumption expenditure.
5. For more results from the e-commerce survey see ONS (2005a).
6. Digitised products are products that are ordered and delivered (downloaded) on-line in digitised form. For example, reports and software.
7. See also Dolling, Herbert and Skipper (2005) for more detail.
8. Figures quoted for Tesco can be found at: http://81.19.58.74/annualreview05/downloads/retailing_services.pdf
9. The EFS took over from the Family Expenditure Survey (FES) and the National Food Survey (NTS) in April 2001. It is a continuous survey of household expenditure, food consumption and income. Its primary uses are to provide information about spending patterns for the Retail Prices Index and about food consumption. As with the FES previously, it feeds into estimates of consumer expenditure in the National Accounts. The target sample is 7,850 households. For more details see www.statistics.gov.uk/ssd/surveys/expenditure_food_survey.asp
10. Supply-side estimates refer to situations when sources such as business surveys or administrative data are used to obtain estimates of household expenditure.
11. Figures quoted for eBay can be found at http://pages.ebay.co.uk/aboutebay.html
12. For more information on the IMRG e-Retail Sales Index see www.imrg.org/
13. GVA + taxes on products – subsidies on products = GDP.
14. For more information on the CSPI see www.statistics.gov.uk/cspi

References

Dolling M, Herbert R and Skipper H (2005) Early estimates of consumer spending.

www.statistics.gov.uk/articles/nojournal/Early_estimates_of_consumer_spend.pdf

Goodridge P and Clayton T (2004) E-business and labour productivity in manufacturing and services. *Economic Trends* No. 609, pp 47–53. www.statistics.gov.uk/articles/economic_trends/ET609Good.pdf

Criscuolo C and Waldron K (2003) E-commerce and productivity. *Economic Trends* No. 600, pp 52–57. www.statistics.gov.uk/articles/economic_trends/ETNov03Criscuolo.pdf

Farooqui S (2005) Information and Communication Technology use and productivity. *Economic Trends* No. 625, pp 65–73. www.statistics.gov.uk/articles/economic_trends/ET625_Farooqui.pdf

Fenwick D, Brueton A and Ball A. (2003) Internet retail channels in Price Indices: the challenges involved in including non-traditional retailers in the UK Retail Prices Index. Paper prepared for the 7th meeting of the Ottawa Group. Available at www.insee.fr/en/nom_def_met/colloques/ottawa/pdf/paper_fenwick.pdf

Mahajan S (2004) Information, communications and technology, 1992-2001. *Economic Trends* No. 603, pp 54–62. www.statistics.gov.uk/articles/economic_trends/ET603mahajan.pdf

Sadun R (2005) The role of IT in firm productivity; evidence from UK micro data. *Economic Trends* No. 625, pp 55–64. www.statistics.gov.uk/articles/economic_trends/ET625_Sadun.pdf

Office for National Statistics (2005a) *Information and Communication Technology (ICT): Activity of UK Businesses*, 2004. www.statistics.gov.uk/downloads/theme_economy/ecommerce_report_2004.pdf

Office for National Statistics (2005b) *United Kingdom Input-Output Analyses*, 2005 Edition. Available at www.statistics.gov.uk/inputoutput

Internet Access – Household and Individuals survey results are available from www.statistics.gov.uk/statbase/Product.asp?vlnk=5672

Tables

1. Summary

2. UK Economic Accounts

3. Prices

4. Labour market

5. Selected output and demand indicators

6. Selected financial statistics

Notes to tables

Identification codes

The four-letter identification code at the top of each data column is the ONS reference for this series of data on our database. Please quote the relevant code if you contact us requiring any further information about the data.

Currency of data

All data in the tables and accompanying charts are current, as far as possible, to 1 March 2006.

Some data, particularly for the latest time period, are provisional and may be subject to revision in later editions.

Geographic coverage

Statistics relate mainly to the United Kingdom. Where figures are for Great Britain only, this is shown on the table.

Seasonal adjustments

Almost all quarterly data are seaonally adjusted; those not seasonally adjusted are indicated by the abbreviation NSA.

Money

There is no single correct definition of money. The most widely used measures are:

M0
This is the narrowest measure and consists of notes and coins in circulation outside the Bank of England and bankers' operational deposits at the Bank.

M4
This comprises notes and coin in circulation with the public, together with all sterling deposits (including certificates of deposit) held with UK banks and building societies by the rest of the private sector.

The Bank of England also publish data for liquid assets outside M4.

Conventions

Rounding may lead to inconsistencies between the constituent parts and the total in some tables.

A horizontal line between two consecutive figures indicates that the figures above and below the line have been compiled on different bases and are not strictly comparable. Footnotes explain the differences.

Billion denotes one thousand million.

Symbols used

.. not available

- nil or less than half the final digit shown

+ a series for which measures of variability are given on page 157

† data have been revised since the last edition; the period marked is the earliest in the table to have been revised

* average (or total) of five weeks

National Statistics Online

www.statistics.gov.uk

Users can download time series, cross-sectional data and metadata from across the Government Statistical Service (GSS), using the site search and index functions from the homepage. Many datasets can be downloaded, in whole or in part, and directory information for all GSS statistical resources can be consulted, including censuses, surveys, journals and enquiry services. Information is posted as PDF electronic documents, or in XLS and CSV formats, compatible with most spreadsheet packages.

Time Series Data

The time series data facility on the website provide access to around 40,000 time series, of primarily macro-economic data, drawn from the main tables in our major economic and labour market publications. Users can download complete releases or view and download customised selections of individual time series.

Complete copies of *Economic Trends* can be downloaded from the following webpage:

http://www.statistics.gov.uk/statbase/product.asp?vlnk=308

1.1 Selected monthly indicators[1]

Seasonally adjusted unless otherwise stated

		2004	2005	2005 Q1	2005 Q2	2005 Q3	2005 Q4	2005 Jul	2005 Aug	2005 Sep	2005 Oct	2005 Nov	2005 Dec	2006 Jan
Output - chained volume measures (CVM) (2002 = 100 unless otherwise stated)														
Gross value added at basic prices *(2.1, 2.8)*	CGCE	105.6	107.5	106.7	107.2	107.7	108.3	..	..	..	..	..	..	..
Industrial production *(2.8, 5.1)*	CKYW	100.3	98.6	99.3	99.0	98.4	97.6	98.9	97.9	98.4	97.1	97.8	98.0	..
Oil and gas extraction	CKZO	86.2	77.8	81.4	81.5	74.1	74.1	77.0	69.1	76.1	74.3	73.7	74.2	..
Manufacturing *(2.8, 5.1)*	CKYY	101.9	101.1	101.5	101.1	101.4	100.4	101.7	101.6	101.0	100.0	100.5	100.7	..
Construction *(2.8)*	GDQB	108.7	110.3	109.8	110.1	110.6	110.8	..	..	..	..	..	..	..
Car production (thousands) *(5.3)*	FFAO	137.2	133.9	138.4	131.7	138.9	126.8	134.7	146.0	136.0	125.1	130.7	124.5	120.7
Domestic demand														
Retail sales volume (2000 = 100) *(5.8)*	EAPS	123.5	125.9	124.9	125.3	125.8	127.8	125.4	125.6	126.3	126.8	128.0	128.5	126.9
GB new registrations of cars ('000s)[2] *(5.8)*	BCGT	2 598.8	2 443.3	697.9	594.4	677.1	473.9	175.3	84.2	417.6	153.9	160.8	159.2	154.0
Manufacturing: change in inventories (£m CVM, reference year 2002) *(5.6)*	DHBM	–873	894	514	–162	57	485	..	..	..	..	..	..	..
Prices (12 monthly % change) and earnings (3 month average)														
Consumer prices index[2] *(3.1)*	D7G7	1.3	2.1	1.7	2.0	2.4	2.1	2.3	2.4	2.5	2.3	2.1	1.9	1.9
Retail prices index[2] *(3.1)*	CZBH	3.0	2.8	3.2	3.0	2.8	2.4	2.9	2.8	2.7	2.5	2.4	2.2	2.4
Retail prices index[2] (less MIPS)[3] *(3.1)*	CDKQ	2.2	2.3	2.2	2.2	2.4	2.3	2.4	2.3	2.5	2.4	2.3	2.0	2.3
Producer output prices (less FBTP)[4]	EUAA	1.9	2.1	2.5	2.4	2.2	1.4	2.3	2.0	2.1	1.3	1.3	1.6	..
Producer input prices[5]	EUAB	3.9	11.7	10.6	9.9	12.8	13.1	14.4	13.3	10.9	9.1	13.4	17.2	..
GB average earnings -whole economy[6] *(4.6)*	LNNC	..	..	4.5	4.1	4.1	3.6	4.2	4.2	4.1	3.6	3.4	3.6	..
Foreign trade[7] (2002 = 100 volumes unless otherwise stated)														
UK balance on trade in goods (£ million) *(2.13)*	BOKI	–60 414	–65 520	–15 623	–15 488	–17 235	–17 174	–5 365	–6 086	–5 784	–5 105	–6 008	–6 061	..
Non EU balance on trade in goods (£ million)	LGDT	–29 590	–31 041	–7 640	–6 796	–8 117	–8 488	–2 501	–3 011	–2 605	–2 329	–2 964	–3 195	..
Non EU exports of goods (excl oil & erratics)	SHDJ	113.2	129.0	116.3	130.5	133.0	136.2	124.6	133.5	140.8	137.8	134.3	136.4	..
Non EU imports of goods (excl oil & erratics)	SHED	116.4	120.8	117.1	121.9	120.2	124.0	116.7	121.8	122.1	119.4	122.5	130.2	..
Non EU imports price index (excl oil)[8]	LKWQ	94.7	98.3	95.9	97.2	99.3	100.9	100.3	98.8	98.7	100.4	101.3	100.9	..
Non EU exports price index (excl oil)[8]	LKVX	96.4	98.0	97.1	97.6	98.3	99.1	98.8	98.2	98.0	99.0	99.2	99.2	..
Labour market and productivity (2002 = 100 unless otherwise stated)														
UK claimant unemployment (thousands) *(4.4)*	BCJD	853.6	861.1	820.9	853.8	870.0	899.9	864.6	867.3	878.0	891.5	901.9	906.2	904.2
UK employees in manufacturing (thousands) *(4.4)*	YEJA	3 255	3 132	3 168	3 132	3 106	3 085	3 118	3 109	3 106	3 094	3 089	3 085	..
Whole economy productivity[9] *(4.7)*	LNNN	103.8	..	104.2	104.5	104.6	..	..	..	..	..	..	..	..
Manufacturing productivity[9] *(4.7)*	LNNX	111.0	114.1	113.0	113.7	115.1	114.8	115.3	115.3	114.7	114.0	114.9	115.5	..
Unit wage costs - whole economy *(4.7)*	LNNK	103.5	..	105.9	106.1	106.5	..	..	..	..	..	..	..	..
Unit wage costs - manufacturing *(4.7)*	LNNQ	96.7	97.5	97.3	96.7	97.8	98.6	96.4	97.1	98.1	99.0	98.4	98.4	..
Financial markets[2]														
Sterling ERI (1990=100) *(6.1)*	AGBG	104.1	103.3	102.9	104.3	102.9	103.2	102.1	102.8	103.9	103.1	103.2	103.3	102.7
Average exchange rate /US $ *(6.1)*	AUSS	1.8320	1.8197	1.8904	1.8559	1.7844	1.7481	1.7509	1.7943	1.8081	1.7640	1.7341	1.7462	1.7678
Average exchange rate /Euro[10] *(6.1)*	THAP	1.4739	1.4629	1.4424	1.4744	1.4635	1.4706	1.4547	1.4592	1.4761	1.4674	1.4719	1.4725	1.4582
3 month inter-bank rate[11] *(6.8)*	HSAJ	4.81	4.57	4.90	4.69	4.52	4.57	4.54	4.52	4.52	4.54	4.55	4.57	4.52
3 month interest on US Treasury bills[12]	LUST	2.18	3.92	2.73	3.06	3.47	3.92	3.35	3.44	3.47	3.89	3.86	3.92	4.38
Monetary conditions/government finances														
M0 (year on year percentage growth)	VQMX	6.0	5.1	5.5	4.3	5.4	5.1	4.8	6.1	5.4	5.3	5.5	4.6	..
M4 (year on year percentage growth)	VQJW	8.6	11.3	10.6	10.6	11.4	12.5	11.0	9.9	11.2	11.5	12.0	12.6	..
Public sector net borrowing (£ million)[2] *(6.5)*	ANNX	–38 406	–43 548	–1 220	–16 349	–8 319	–17 660	3 923	–5 652	–6 590	640	–9 469	–8 831	12 556
Net lending to consumers (£ million)(broader) *(5.8)*	RLMH	23 030	16 783	5 821	4 515	3 395	3 052	1 036	1 365	1 202	1 261	892	931	1 319

		2005 Jan	2005 Feb	2005 Mar	2005 Apr	2005 May	2005 Jun	2005 Jul	2005 Aug	2005 Sep	2005 Oct	2005 Nov	2005 Dec	2006 Jan
Activity and expectations														
CBI output expectations balance[2]	ETCU	10	19	9	5	–1	–5	6	3	6	2	–4	–4	1
CBI optimism balance[2]	ETBV	–22	..	..	–15	..	..	–16	..	..	–21	..	..	–14
CBI price expectations balance	ETDQ	12	10	12	3	–3	–5	–9	–7	–6	–3	–1	–1	5
New engineering orders (2000 = 100) *(5.2)*	JIQH	79.6	77.7	77.0	76.7	79.8	78.9	78.1	86.3	79.3	77.3	77.9	74.2	..

1 Numbers in brackets after titles of series refer to tables in which they appear.
2 Not seasonally adjusted.
3 MIPS: mortgage interest payments.
4 FBTP: food, beverages, tobacco and petroleum.
5 Includes the climate change levy introduced in April 2001, and the aggregates levy introduced in April 2002.
6 The 3 month average is the percentage change in the average seasonally adjusted indices for the latest 3 months compared with the same period a year earlier.
7 All non-EU figures exclude Austria, Finland and Sweden.
8 12 monthly percentage change.
9 Output per filled job.
10 Before January 1999, a synthetic Euro has been calculated by geometrically averaging the bilateral exchange rate of the 11 Euro-area countries using "internal weights" based on each country's share of the extra Euro-area trade.
11 Last Friday of the period.
12 Last working day.

2.1 National accounts aggregates

	£ million		Indices (2002 = 100)						
	At current prices		Value indices at current prices		Chained volume indices			Implied deflators[3]	
	Gross domestic product at market prices	Gross value added (GVA) at basic prices	Gross domestic product at market prices[1]	Gross value added (GVA) at basic prices	Gross domestic product at market prices	Gross value added (GVA) at basic prices+	Gross national disposable income at market prices[2]	GDP at market prices	GVA at basic prices
	YBHA	ABML	YBEU	YBEX	YBEZ	CGCE	YBFP	YBGB	CGBV
2001	996 758	883 412	95.1	94.9	98.0	98.3	96.4	97.0	96.5
2002	1 048 456	930 796	100.0	100.0	100.0	100.0	100.0	100.0	100.0
2003	1 105 919	981 732	105.5	105.5	102.5	102.5	102.6	102.9	102.9
2004	1 164 941	1 033 573	111.1	111.0	105.8	105.6	106.0	105.0	105.2
2005	1 211 240	1 073 995	115.5	115.4	107.7	107.5	..	107.3	107.4
2001 Q1	245 674	217 424	93.7	93.4	97.5	97.9	95.6	96.2	95.4
Q2	248 157	219 709	94.7	94.4	97.8	98.2	96.0	96.8	96.1
Q3	249 239	221 127	95.1	95.0	98.2	98.4	96.9	96.9	96.5
Q4	253 688	225 152	96.8	96.8	98.7	98.8	97.2	98.1	97.9
2002 Q1	257 004	227 916	98.1	97.9	99.2	99.3	98.7	98.9	98.7
Q2	261 090	232 002	99.6	99.7	99.7	99.7	99.2	99.9	100.0
Q3	264 065	234 484	100.7	100.8	100.4	100.3	101.0	100.4	100.4
Q4	266 297	236 394	101.6	101.6	100.7	100.7	101.1	100.9	100.9
2003 Q1	270 583	240 537	103.2	103.4	101.4	101.4	102.3	101.8	102.0
Q2	274 053	243 452	104.6	104.6	101.9	101.8	101.6	102.6	102.7
Q3	278 966	247 512	106.4	106.4	102.9	102.9	102.8	103.4	103.4
Q4	282 317	250 231	107.7	107.5	103.9	103.9	103.9	103.7	103.5
2004 Q1	285 467	252 721	108.9	108.6	104.8	104.7	104.7	103.9	103.7
Q2	289 569	256 760	110.5	110.3	105.7	105.5	105.9	104.5	104.6
Q3	292 511	259 740	111.6	111.6	106.0	105.8	105.2	105.2	105.5
Q4	297 394	264 352	113.5	113.6	106.6	106.4	108.1	106.4	106.8
2005 Q1	297 985†	264 574†	113.7†	113.7†	106.9	106.7†	106.8	106.3	106.5
Q2	301 728	267 695	115.1	115.0	107.4	107.2	108.6	107.2†	107.3†
Q3	303 246	268 448	115.7	115.4	108.0†	107.7	106.7	107.2	107.1
Q4	308 281	273 278	117.6	117.4	108.6	108.3	..	108.3	108.5
Percentage change, quarter on corresponding quarter of previous year[4]									
2001 Q1	*4.6*	*4.9*	*4.6*	*4.9*	*2.6*	*2.6*	*2.9*	*2.0*	*2.1*
Q2	*5.0*	*5.5*	*5.0*	*5.5*	*2.3*	*2.2*	*3.1*	*2.7*	*3.2*
Q3	*4.1*	*4.6*	*4.1*	*4.6*	*2.0*	*1.5*	*2.6*	*2.1*	*3.0*
Q4	*4.5*	*4.9*	*4.5*	*4.9*	*2.1*	*1.6*	*3.8*	*2.5*	*3.3*
2002 Q1	*4.6*	*4.8*	*4.6*	*4.8*	*1.7*	*1.4*	*3.2*	*2.8*	*3.5*
Q2	*5.2*	*5.6*	*5.2*	*5.6*	*1.9*	*1.5*	*3.3*	*3.2*	*4.1*
Q3	*5.9*	*6.0*	*5.9*	*6.0*	*2.2*	*1.9*	*4.2*	*3.6*	*4.0*
Q4	*5.0*	*5.0*	*5.0*	*5.0*	*2.0*	*1.9*	*4.0*	*2.9*	*3.1*
2003 Q1	*5.3*	*5.5*	*5.3*	*5.5*	*2.2*	*2.1*	*3.6*	*2.9*	*3.3*
Q2	*5.0*	*4.9*	*5.0*	*4.9*	*2.2*	*2.2*	*2.4*	*2.7*	*2.7*
Q3	*5.6*	*5.6*	*5.6*	*5.6*	*2.5*	*2.5*	*1.8*	*3.0*	*3.0*
Q4	*6.0*	*5.9*	*6.0*	*5.9*	*3.2*	*3.1*	*2.8*	*2.8*	*2.6*
2004 Q1	*5.5*	*5.1*	*5.5*	*5.1*	*3.4*	*3.2*	*2.3*	*2.1*	*1.7*
Q2	*5.7*	*5.5*	*5.7*	*5.5*	*3.7*	*3.6*	*4.2*	*1.9*	*1.9*
Q3	*4.9*	*4.9*	*4.9*	*4.9*	*3.0*	*2.8*	*2.3*	*1.7*	*2.0*
Q4	*5.3*	*5.6*	*5.3*	*5.6*	*2.6*	*2.4*	*4.0*	*2.6*	*3.2*
2005 Q1	*4.4†*	*4.7†*	*4.4†*	*4.7†*	*2.0*	*2.0†*	*2.0*	*2.3*	*2.7*
Q2	*4.2*	*4.3*	*4.2*	*4.3*	*1.6*	*1.6*	*2.5*	*2.6†*	*2.6†*
Q3	*3.7*	*3.4*	*3.7*	*3.4*	*1.9†*	*1.8*	*1.4*	*1.9*	*1.5*
Q4	*3.7*	*3.4*	*3.7*	*3.4*	*1.9*	*1.8*	..	*1.8*	*1.6*

1 "Money GDP".
2 This series is only updated once a quarter, in line with the full quarterly national accounts dataset.
3 Based on chained volume measures and current price estimates of expenditure components of GDP.
4 These estimates of change are based in some cases on less rounded figures than those shown in the table.

Source: Office for National Statistics; Enquiries 020 7533 6031

National accounts aggregates

Indices, 2002=100 seasonally adjusted

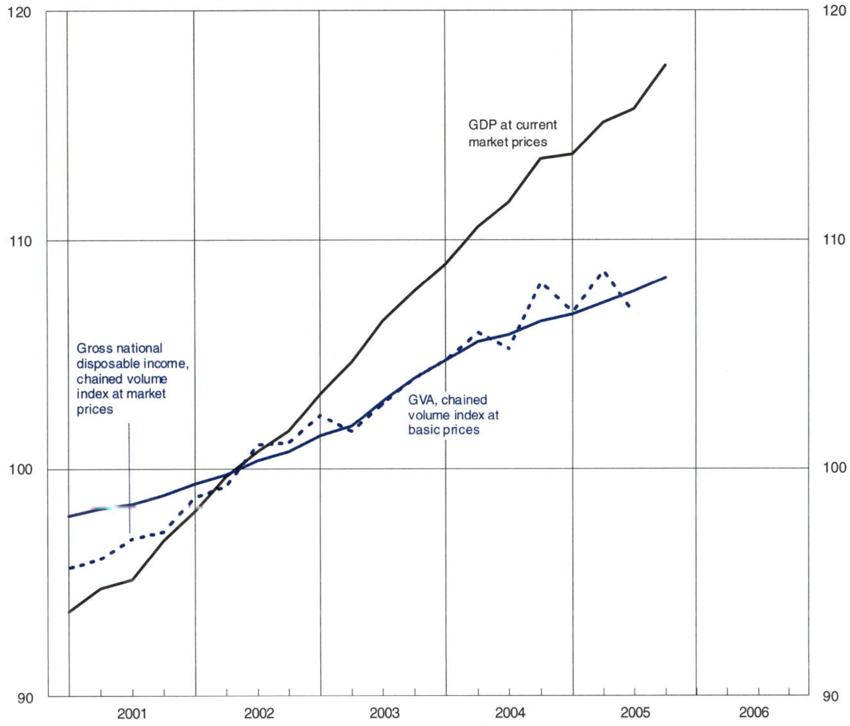

National accounts aggregates

Percentage change on a year earlier

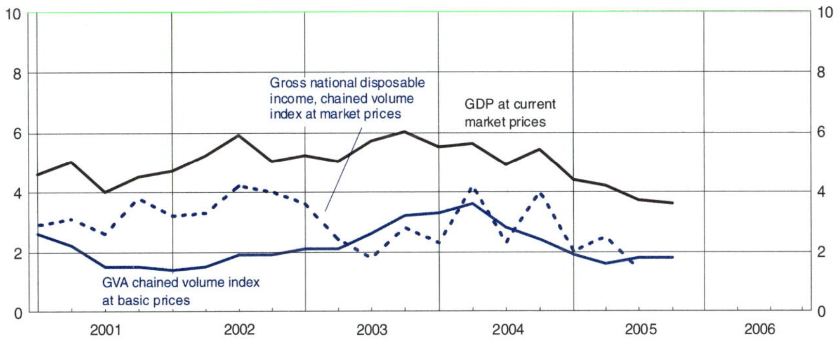

2.2 Gross domestic product: by category of expenditure
Chained volume measures[1]

Reference year 2002, £ million

	Domestic expenditure on goods and services at market prices											
	Final consumption expenditure			Gross capital formation								
	Households	Non-profit institutions[2]	General government	Gross fixed capital formation+	Changes in inventories[3]	Acquisitions less disposals of valuables	Total	Exports of goods and services+	Gross final expenditure	*less* Imports of goods and services+	Statistical discrepancy (expenditure)	Gross domestic product at market prices
	ABJR	HAYO	NMRY	NPQT	CAFU	NPJR	YBIM	IKBK	ABMG	IKBL	GIXS	ABMI
2001	644 895	25 247	201 996	167 563	6 196	373	1 046 424	274 274	1 320 810	293 213	–	1 027 905
2002	667 361	25 998	210 967	172 558	2 909	214	1 080 007	274 945	1 354 952	306 496	–	1 048 456
2003	684 841	26 229	220 449	172 573	4 602	–6	1 108 689	278 159	1 386 848	311 990	–	1 074 858
2004	709 702	26 761	227 424	181 506	5 933	–11	1 151 316	290 989	1 442 305	332 953	–207	1 109 145
2005	722 866	27 026	232 094	187 539	2 683	–314	1 171 895	305 991	1 477 886	348 914	263	1 129 235†
2001 Q1	159 089	6 402	50 036	42 007	1 040	–18	258 590	70 148	328 833	73 449	–	255 459
Q2	160 258	6 323	49 827	42 160	1 375	210	260 275	69 408	329 749	73 368	–	256 450
Q3	162 141	6 280	50 701	42 249	1 662	38	263 114	67 325	330 410	73 187	–	257 301
Q4	163 407	6 242	51 432	41 147	2 119	143	264 445	67 393	331 818	73 209	–	258 695
2002 Q1	165 301	6 321	52 654	41 651	1 177	74	267 140	67 640	334 760	74 838	–	259 971
Q2	166 424	6 425	52 249	42 936	394	56	268 495	70 380	338 897	77 479	–	261 381
Q3	167 273	6 587	52 864	43 562	480	70	270 855	69 894	340 768	77 678	–	263 060
Q4	168 363	6 665	53 200	44 409	858	14	273 517	67 031	340 527	76 501	–	264 044
2003 Q1	169 079	6 557	53 929	43 232	103	–	272 901	71 403	344 304	78 620	–	265 684
Q2	171 108	6 553	54 618	42 843	–387	102	274 837	68 719	343 556	76 406	–	267 150
Q3	171 946	6 564	55 464	42 459	2 339	–60	278 712	68 495	347 207	77 429	–	269 778
Q4	172 708	6 555	56 438	44 039	2 547	–48	282 239	69 542	351 781	79 535	–	272 246
2004 Q1	174 705	6 665	56 639	44 435	1 338	117	283 898	71 440	355 339	80 581	–77	274 681
Q2	177 015	6 663	56 738	45 657	1 230	–81	287 222	72 539	359 760	82 718	–73	276 969
Q3	178 582	6 697	56 916	45 510	1 088	–86	288 707	73 158	361 865	83 849	–49	277 967
Q4	179 400	6 736	57 131	45 904	2 277	39	291 489	73 852	365 341	85 805	–8	279 528
2005 Q1	179 446†	6 711†	57 375†	46 269†	988†	–145†	290 644†	74 143†	364 787†	84 647†	65†	280 205†
Q2	179 929	6 739	57 764	46 339	686	90	291 547	76 653	368 200	86 780	65	281 485
Q3	181 077	6 767	58 238	47 655	801	–187	294 351	77 154	371 504	88 604	66	282 967
Q4	182 414	6 809	58 717	47 276	208	–72	295 353	78 041	373 395	88 883	67	284 578
Percentage change, quarter on corresponding quarter of previous year												
2001 Q1	*2.1*	*4.1*	*1.9*	*4.9*			*2.7*	*9.4*	*4.1*	*9.6*		*2.6*
Q2	*2.8*	*0.8*	*–0.3*	*5.4*			*2.8*	*4.5*	*3.2*	*5.9*		*2.4*
Q3	*3.4*	*–1.8*	*1.5*	*2.8*			*2.8*	*0.5*	*2.3*	*3.5*		*1.9*
Q4	*4.3*	*–3.3*	*3.8*	*–3.3*			*2.9*	*–2.3*	*1.7*	*0.6*		*2.0*
2002 Q1	*3.9*	*–1.3*	*5.2*	*–0.8*			*3.3*	*–3.6*	*1.8*	*1.9*		*1.8*
Q2	*3.8*	*1.6*	*4.9*	*1.8*			*3.2*	*1.4*	*2.8*	*5.6*		*1.9*
Q3	*3.2*	*4.9*	*4.3*	*3.1*			*2.9*	*3.8*	*3.1*	*6.1*		*2.2*
Q4	*3.0*	*6.8*	*3.4*	*7.9*			*3.4*	*–0.5*	*2.6*	*4.5*		*2.1*
2003 Q1	*2.3*	*3.7*	*2.4*	*3.8*			*2.2*	*5.6*	*2.9*	*5.1*		*2.2*
Q2	*2.8*	*2.0*	*4.5*	*–0.2*			*2.4*	*–2.4*	*1.4*	*–1.4*		*2.2*
Q3	*2.8*	*–0.3*	*4.9*	*–2.5*			*2.9*	*–2.0*	*1.9*	*–0.3*		*2.6*
Q4	*2.6*	*–1.7*	*6.1*	*–0.8*			*3.2*	*3.7*	*3.3*	*4.0*		*3.1*
2004 Q1	*3.3*	*1.6*	*5.0*	*2.8*			*4.0*	*0.1*	*3.2*	*2.5*		*3.4*
Q2	*3.5*	*1.7*	*3.9*	*6.6*			*4.5*	*5.6*	*4.7*	*8.3*		*3.7*
Q3	*3.9*	*2.0*	*2.6*	*7.2*			*3.6*	*6.8*	*4.2*	*8.3*		*3.0*
Q4	*3.9*	*2.8*	*1.2*	*4.2*			*3.3*	*6.2*	*3.9*	*7.9*		*2.7*
2005 Q1	*2.7†*	*0.7†*	*1.3†*	*4.1†*			*2.4†*	*3.8†*	*2.7†*	*5.0†*		*2.0*
Q2	*1.6*	*1.1*	*1.8*	*1.5*			*1.5*	*5.7*	*2.3*	*4.9*		*1.6*
Q3	*1.4*	*1.0*	*2.3*	*4.7*			*2.0*	*5.5*	*2.7*	*5.7*		*1.8†*
Q4	*1.7*	*1.1*	*2.8*	*3.0*			*1.3*	*5.7*	*2.2*	*3.6*		*1.8*

1 Estimates are given to the nearest £ million but cannot be regarded as accurate to this degree.
2 Non-profit making institutions serving households (NPISH).
3 Quarterly alignment adjustment is included in this series.

Source: Office for National Statistics; Enquiries 020 7533 6031

Gross domestic product: by category of expenditure

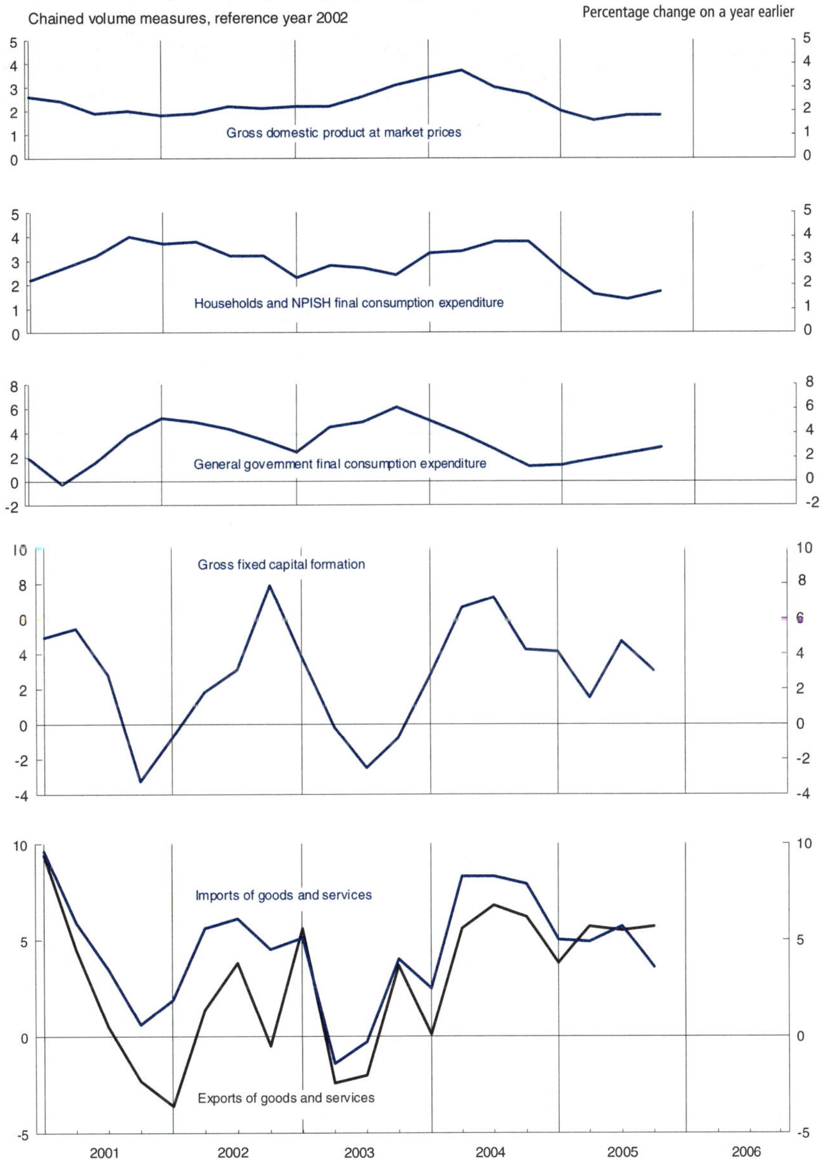

2.3 Gross domestic product and shares of income and expenditure

	Gross domestic product at market prices (£ million)[1]	Gross final expenditure (£ million)	Percentage share of gross final expenditure: Final consumption expenditure: Household and NPISH	General govern -ment	Gross capital formation	Exports of goods and services	Percentage share of GDP by category of income: Gross operating surplus: Corporat-ions[2]	Other[3]	Compen-sation of employees	Mixed income	Taxes on production and imports
	YBHA	ABMF	IHXI	IHXJ	IHXK	IHXL	IHXM	IHXO	IHXP	IHXQ	IHXR
2002	1 048 456	1 354 952	51.2	15.6	13.0	20.3	21.7	3.0	56.1	6.3	12.9
2003	1 105 919	1 419 132	51.1	16.3	12.7	19.9	22.1	2.9	55.8	6.3	12.8
2004	1 164 941	1 498 084	50.8	16.5	13.1	19.6	22.5	2.8	55.7	6.3	12.8
2005	1 211 240	1 572 596	..	..	..	..	..	..	..	..	..
2002 Q1	257 004	332 338	51.4	15.4	12.8	20.4	21.8	2.8	56.0	6.3	13.0
Q2	261 090	339 079	50.9	15.4	12.8	20.9	21.2	3.7	56.1	6.3	12.8
Q3	264 065	341 177	51.0	15.6	13.0	20.4	21.9	2.8	56.1	6.3	12.8
Q4	266 297	342 358	51.4	15.8	13.3	19.4	21.8	2.7	56.3	6.3	12.8
2003 Q1	270 583	349 262	51.0	16.0	12.3	20.7	22.4	2.5	56.0	6.3	12.7
Q2	274 053	350 763	51.4	16.3	12.3	19.9	22.1	3.0	55.8	6.3	12.7
Q3	278 966	356 950	51.1	16.4	12.9	19.6	22.3	2.7	55.9	6.3	12.8
Q4	282 317	362 157	50.8	16.6	13.2	19.4	21.8	3.4	55.7	6.3	12.9
2004 Q1	285 467	365 105	51.1	16.5	12.9	19.5	21.9	2.9	55.9	6.3	13.0
Q2	289 569	371 963	50.9	16.4	13.2	19.5	22.7	2.6	55.6	6.3	12.8
Q3	292 511	376 763	50.8	16.5	13.0	19.6	22.6	2.9	55.6	6.3	12.7
Q4	297 394	384 253	50.4	16.6	13.3	19.8	22.9	2.6	55.7	6.2	12.6
2005 Q1	297 985†	384 331†	50.7	16.8	12.8	19.7	22.0	2.8	56.5	6.3	12.5
Q2	301 728	390 669	50.3	16.7	12.8	20.2	22.2	2.8	56.3	6.2	12.6
Q3	303 246	395 697	50.3	16.7	13.4	19.6	21.2	3.1	56.7	6.3	12.8
Q4	308 281	401 899	..	..	..	..	..	..	..	..	..

1 "Money GDP".
2 Non-financial and financial corporations.
3 Gross operating surplus of general government, and households and NPISH *plus* the adjustment for financial services.

Source: Office for National Statistics; Enquiries 020 7533 6031

2.4 Income, product and spending per head

£

	At current prices: Gross national income at market prices	Gross domestic product at market prices	Household and NPISH final consumption expenditure	Households' gross disposable income	Chained volume measures (reference year 2002): Gross domestic product at market prices	Household and NPISH final consumption expenditure	Real households' disposable income
	IHXS	IHXT	IHXU	IHXV	IHXW	IHXX	IHXZ
2002	18 041	17 674	11 687	11 971	17 675	11 688	11 971
2003	18 959	18 570	12 174	12 499	18 049	11 941	12 260
2004	19 985	19 554	12 771	12 934	18 617	12 361	12 521
2002 Q1	4 409	4 338	2 886	2 945	4 389	2 897	2 956
Q2	4 468	4 404	2 911	2 994	4 409	2 915	2 999
Q3	4 564	4 450	2 929	3 006	4 433	2 930	3 006
Q4	4 600	4 482	2 961	3 026	4 444	2 946	3 010
2003 Q1	4 682	4 549	2 992	3 065	4 466	2 953	3 026
Q2	4 677	4 603	3 030	3 134	4 487	2 984	3 086
Q3	4 762	4 682	3 064	3 126	4 528	2 996	3 057
Q4	4 838	4 736	3 088	3 174	4 568	3 008	3 091
2004 Q1	4 890	4 789	3 131	3 185	4 608	3 043	3 096
Q2	4 967	4 859	3 176	3 219	4 648	3 082	3 124
Q3	4 973	4 911	3 214	3 258	4 666	3 110	3 153
Q4	5 155	4 995	3 250	3 272	4 695	3 126	3 148
2005 Q1	5 116	4 996	3 266	3 308	4 701	3 127	3 167
Q2	5 252	5 071	3 293	3 374	4 724	3 134	3 211
Q3	5 200	5 088	3 329	3 400	4 743	3 151	3 218

Source: Office for National Statistics; Enquiries 020 7533 6031

Shares of income and expenditure

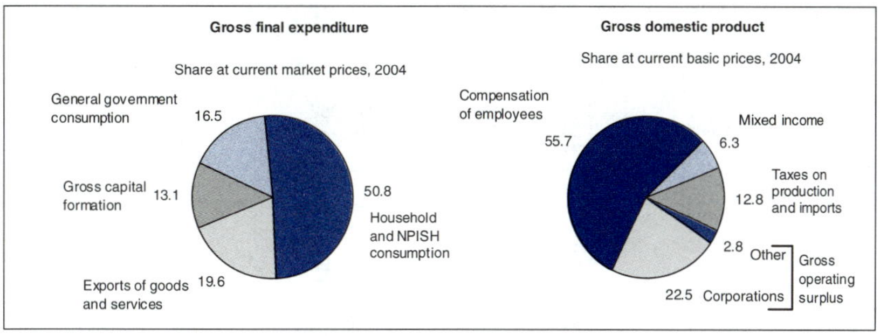

Income, product and spending per head

Chained volume measures, reference year 2002

Percentage change on a year earlier

2.5 Households'[1] disposable income and consumption

	£ million, current prices							£ million, chained volume measures (reference year 2002)		
	Households' income before tax									
	Total	*of which:* Wages and salaries	Gross households' disposable income[2]	Adjustment for the change in net equity of households in pension funds	Total available households' resources	Households' final consumption expenditure	Households' saving ratio[3] (per cent)+	Real households' disposable income[4] +	Household final consumption expenditure+	Real households' disposable income (index 2002=100)
	RPHP	ROYJ	RPHQ	RPQJ	RPQK	RPQM	NRJS	NRJR	NPSP	OSXS
2003	1 067 223	526 949	744 428	21 586	766 014	725 012	*5.4*	730 113	711 070	102.8
2004	1 114 521	551 327	770 529	25 046	795 575	760 762	*4.4*	745 918	736 463	105.1
2005	..	..	..	..	..	791 087	..	..	749 892	..
2003 Q1	260 418	130 003	182 347	5 196	187 543	177 952	*5.1*	179 973	175 636	101.4
Q2	266 472	131 002	186 601	4 046	190 647	180 420	*5.4*	183 746	177 661	103.5
Q3	268 773	132 597	186 289	6 211	192 500	182 562	*5.2*	182 153	178 510	102.6
Q4	271 560	133 347	189 191	6 133	195 324	184 078	*5.8*	184 241	179 263	103.8
2004 Q1	273 420	135 508	189 844	6 478	196 322	186 600	*5.0*	184 520	181 370	103.9
Q2	276 732	136 873	191 800	5 792	197 592	189 248	*4.2*	186 152	183 678	104.9
Q3	280 778	138 352	194 051	5 877	199 928	191 422	*4.3*	187 821	185 279	105.8
Q4	283 591	140 594	194 834	6 899	201 733	193 492	*4.1*	187 425	186 136	105.6
2005 Q1	287 847	142 566	197 116	7 087	204 203	194 620†	*4.7*	188 734	186 157†	106.3
Q2	294 105	143 722	201 070	6 864	207 934	196 419	*5.6*	191 342	186 668	107.8
Q3	297 966	144 844	202 594	7 315	209 909	198 916	*5.5*	191 799	187 844	108.0
Q4	..	..	..	..	..	201 132	..	..	189 223	..

1 All households series also include non-profit institutions serving households (NPISH).
2 Total household income *less* payments of income tax and other taxes, social contributions and other current transfers.
3 Households' saving as a percentage of total available households' resources.
4 Gross household disposable income revalued by the implied household and NPISH final consumption expenditure deflator (2002 = 100).

Sources: Office for National Statistics; Enquiries Column 1 020 7533 6005; Columns 2-5,7,8,10 020 7533 6027; Columns 6,9 020 7533 5999

2.6 Household final consumption expenditure[1,2]

Chained volume measures

Reference year 2002, £ million

	UK national[3]														
			UK domestic[4]												
	Total	Net tourism	Total	Food and drink	Alcohol and tobacco	Clothing and footwear	Housing	Household goods and services	Health	Transport	Communication	Recreation and culture	Education	Restaurants and hotels	Miscellaneous
COICOP[5]	-	-	0	01	02	03	04	05	06	07	08	09	10	11	12
	ABJR	ABTH	ZAKW	ZWUN	ZAKY	ZALA	ZAVO	ZAVW	ZAWC	ZAWM	ZAWW	ZAXA	ZWUT	ZAXS	ZAYG
2003	684 841	10 638	674 203	61 883	26 364	41 993	122 325	42 745	11 292	102 055	15 464	87 734	8 870	76 422	77 056
2004	709 702	11 142	698 560	63 237	26 618	45 865	124 968	45 255	11 619	103 998	16 365	95 647	8 831	78 258	77 899
2005	722 866	..	..	..	..	..	..	..	..	..	..	..	..	..	..
2003 Q1	169 079	2 821	166 258	15 339	6 538	10 066	30 405	10 514	2 767	25 372	3 746	21 055	2 222	18 881	19 353
Q2	171 108	2 745	168 363	15 881	6 556	10 412	30 476	10 803	2 796	25 633	3 846	21 592	2 211	18 927	19 230
Q3	171 946	2 639	169 307	15 412	6 627	10 741	30 567	10 604	2 834	25 558	3 924	22 323	2 216	19 333	19 168
Q4	172 708	2 433	170 275	15 251	6 643	10 774	30 877	10 824	2 895	25 492	3 948	22 764	2 221	19 281	19 305
2004 Q1	174 705	2 725	171 980	15 915	6 666	11 026	31 044	10 861	2 854	25 642	3 998	22 987	2 219	19 431	19 337
Q2	177 015	2 756	174 259	15 596	6 674	11 421	31 264	11 236	2 915	25 773	3 979	24 152	2 210	19 573	19 466
Q3	178 582	2 956	175 626	15 762	6 627	11 630	31 259	11 645	2 909	26 168	4 163	24 225	2 205	19 608	19 425
Q4	179 400	2 705	176 695	15 964	6 651	11 788	31 401	11 513	2 941	26 415	4 225	24 283	2 197	19 646	19 671
2005 Q1	179 446†	2 839†	176 607†	16 001	6 617†	11 788†	31 292†	11 585†	2 939†	26 236†	4 327	24 490†	2 194†	19 956†	19 182†
Q2	179 929	2 480	177 449	16 060†	6 575	11 866	31 468	11 379	2 942	26 464	4 364†	24 837	2 177	20 091	19 226
Q3	181 077	2 815	178 262	15 976	6 564	11 917	31 456	11 266	2 965	26 319	4 468	25 601	2 178	20 042	19 510
Q4	182 414	..	..	..	..	..	..	..	..	..	..	..	..	..	..

1 Estimates are given to the nearest £ million but cannot be regarded as accurate to this degree.
2 More detailed estimates, expressed in both current prices and chained volume measures, both unadjusted and seasonally adjusted, appear in the ONS publication *Consumer Trends.*
3 Final consumption expenditure by UK households in the UK and abroad.
4 Final consumption expenditure in the UK by UK and foreign households.
5 ESA 95 Classification of Individual Consumption by Purpose.

Source: Office for National Statistics; Enquiries 020 7533 5999

Households' disposable income and consumption

Proportion of households' income before tax (current prices), percentages

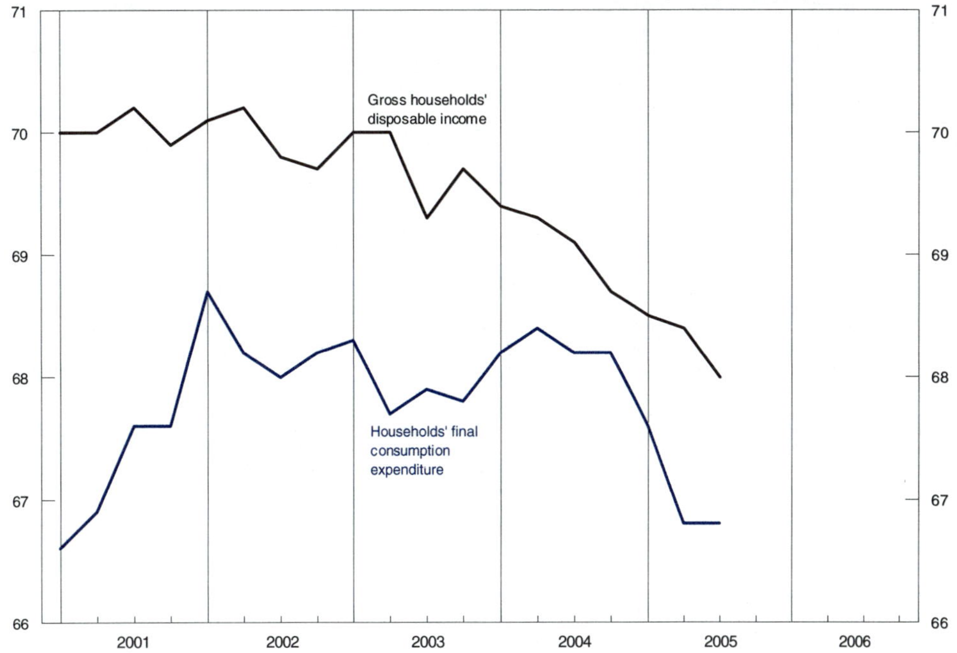

Household final consumption expenditure – component categories

Chained volume measures, reference year 2002, £ billion

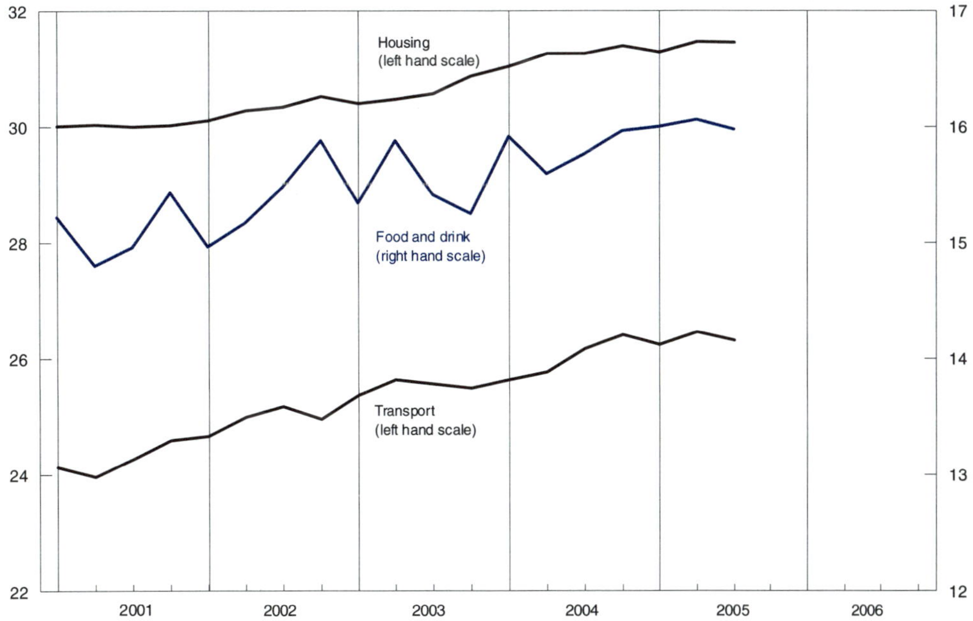

2.7 Gross fixed capital formation
Chained volume measures

Reference year 2002, £ million

	Analysis by sector						Analysis by asset				
			Public corporations[2]	Private sector							
	Business investment[1]	General government	Transfer costs of non-produced assets	Dwellings	Transfer costs of non-produced assets	Total+	Transport equipment	Other machinery and equipment	Dwellings	Other building and structures[3]	Intangible fixed assets
	NPEL	DLWF	DLWH	DFEA	DLWI	NPQT	DLWL	DLWO	DFEG	DLWT	EQDO
2001	109 792	13 954	67	29 195	14 343	167 563	14 786	57 545	32 006	57 928	5 047
2002	110 166	15 580	–41	31 455	15 398	172 558	16 214	56 421	34 499	59 836	5 588
2003	107 747	18 244	–234	32 474	14 342	172 573	14 669	54 104	36 056	61 934	5 810
2004	111 351	20 562	–266	35 547	14 312	181 506	14 257	57 512	38 879	64 662	6 196
2005	113 096	..	..	..	..	187 539	..	..	..	..	..
2001 Q1	27 875	2 985	35	7 312	3 734	42 007	3 303	14 720	7 911	14 686	1 261
Q2	27 726	3 618	28	7 155	3 539	42 160	3 881	14 262	7 891	14 830	1 251
Q3	27 586	3 648	3	7 522	3 427	42 249	3 884	14 460	8 252	14 343	1 265
Q4	26 605	3 703	1	7 206	3 643	41 147	3 718	14 103	7 952	14 069	1 270
2002 Q1	27 145	3 726	4	7 295	3 440	41 651	4 045	13 697	8 006	14 602	1 306
Q2	27 421	3 832	10	7 759	3 924	42 936	4 009	14 394	8 396	14 704	1 404
Q3	27 325	4 029	–25	8 104	4 177	43 562	4 137	14 279	8 829	14 896	1 411
Q4	28 275	3 993	–30	8 297	3 857	44 409	4 023	14 051	9 268	15 634	1 467
2003 Q1	26 670	4 747	–13	7 831	3 997	43 232	3 871	13 766	8 824	15 347	1 424
Q2	27 231	4 079	–49	8 031	3 551	42 843	3 454	13 043	8 835	16 074	1 437
Q3	26 424	4 487	–98	8 237	3 409	42 459	3 633	13 317	9 165	14 885	1 459
Q4	27 422	4 931	–74	8 375	3 385	44 039	3 711	13 978	9 232	15 628	1 490
2004 Q1	27 346	4 871	–58	8 751	3 525	44 435	3 492	14 217	9 510	15 708	1 508
Q2	27 681	5 519	–75	8 877	3 655	45 657	3 754	14 407	9 754	16 205	1 537
Q3	28 186	4 978	–83	8 919	3 510	45 510	3 566	14 360	9 783	16 239	1 562
Q4	28 138	5 194	–50	9 000	3 622	45 904	3 445	14 528	9 832	16 510	1 589
2005 Q1	28 047†	6 197†	–106†	8 879†	3 252†	46 269†	3 484†	14 447†	9 645†	17 095†	1 599
Q2	28 339	5 416	–86	8 856	3 814	46 339	3 488	14 437	9 695	17 104	1 615
Q3	28 497	6 510	–65	8 816	3 897	47 655	3 618	14 864	9 851	17 697	1 625†
Q4	28 213	..	..	..	..	47 276	..	..	..	..	..
Percentage change, quarter on corresponding quarter of previous year											
2001 Q1	*7.3*	*7.2*		*–2.3*	*–8.7*	*4.9*	*–0.6*	*10.6*	*–0.2*	*1.9*	*2.2*
Q2	*5.8*	*22.6*		*–3.5*	*2.2*	*5.4*	*17.7*	*3.9*	*0.3*	*7.3*	*–2.7*
Q3	*0.9*	*26.4*		*3.6*	*–2.8*	*2.8*	*18.3*	*–0.4*	*7.0*	*1.3*	*–0.9*
Q4	*–7.2*	*9.3*		*6.4*	*7.5*	*–3.3*	*3.8*	*–7.7*	*9.1*	*–5.0*	*–1.9*
2002 Q1	*–2.6*	*24.8*		*–0.2*	*–7.9*	*–0.8*	*22.5*	*–6.9*	*1.2*	*–0.6*	*3.6*
Q2	*–1.1*	*5.9*		*8.4*	*10.9*	*1.8*	*3.3*	*0.9*	*6.4*	*–0.8*	*12.2*
Q3	*–0.9*	*10.4*		*7.7*	*21.9*	*3.1*	*6.5*	*–1.3*	*7.0*	*3.9*	*11.5*
Q4	*6.3*	*7.8*		*15.1*	*5.9*	*7.9*	*8.2*	*–0.4*	*16.5*	*11.1*	*15.5*
2003 Q1	*–1.7*	*27.4*		*7.3*	*16.2*	*3.8*	*–4.3*	*0.5*	*10.2*	*5.1*	*9.0*
Q2	*–0.7*	*6.4*		*3.5*	*–9.5*	*–0.2*	*–13.8*	*–9.4*	*5.2*	*9.3*	*2.4*
Q3	*–3.3*	*11.4*		*1.6*	*–18.4*	*–2.5*	*–12.2*	*–6.7*	*3.8*	*–0.1*	*3.4*
Q4	*–3.0*	*23.5*		*0.9*	*–12.2*	*–0.8*	*–7.8*	*–0.5*	*–0.4*	*0.0*	*1.6*
2004 Q1	*2.5*	*2.6*		*11.7*	*–11.8*	*2.8*	*–9.8*	*3.3*	*7.8*	*2.4*	*5.9*
Q2	*1.7*	*35.3*		*10.5*	*2.9*	*6.6*	*8.7*	*10.5*	*10.4*	*0.8*	*7.0*
Q3	*6.7*	*10.9*		*8.3*	*3.0*	*7.2*	*–1.8*	*7.8*	*6.7*	*9.1*	*7.1*
Q4	*2.6*	*5.3*		*7.5*	*7.0*	*4.2*	*–7.2*	*3.9*	*6.5*	*5.6*	*6.6*
2005 Q1	*2.6†*	*27.2†*		*1.5*	*–7.7†*	*4.1†*	*–0.2†*	*1.6†*	*1.4†*	*8.8†*	*6.0*
Q2	*2.4*	*–1.9*		*–0.2†*	*4.4*	*1.5*	*–7.1*	*0.2*	*–0.6*	*5.5*	*5.1*
Q3	*1.1*	*30.8*		*–1.2*	*11.0*	*4.7*	*1.5*	*3.5*	*0.7*	*9.0*	*4.0†*
Q4	*0.3*	..		..	..	*3.0*	..	..	..	..	..

1 Excluding dwellings and costs associated with the transfer of ownership of non-produced assets.
2 Remaining investment by public non-financial corporations is included under business investment.
3 Including costs associated with transfer of ownership of non-produced assets.

Source: Office for National Statistics; Enquiries 020 7533 6010

Gross fixed capital formation – by sector

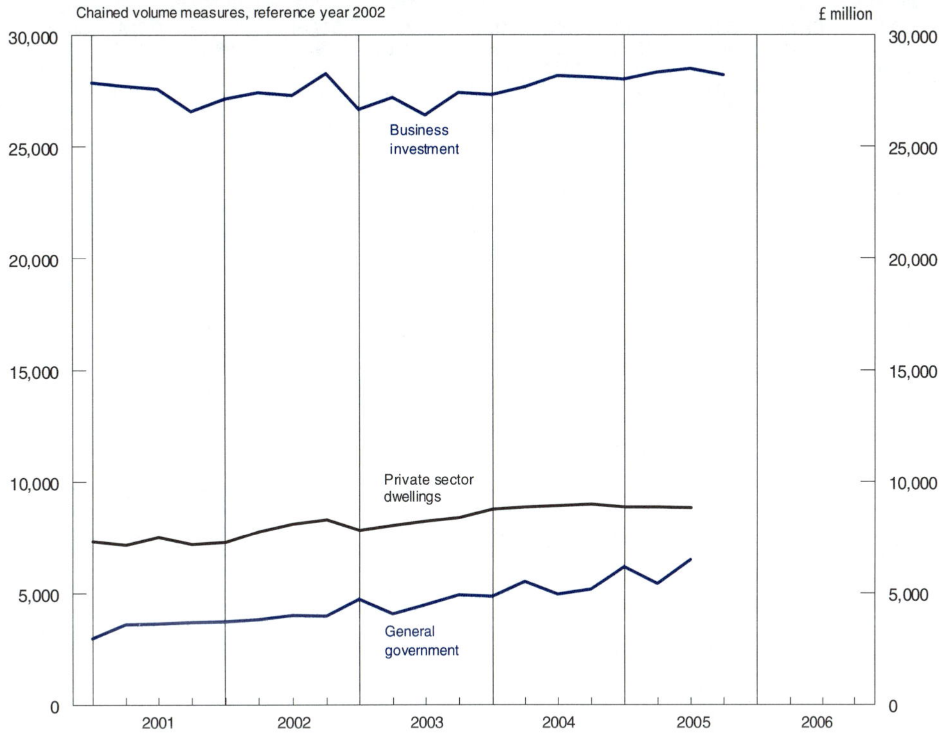

Gross fixed capital formation – by asset

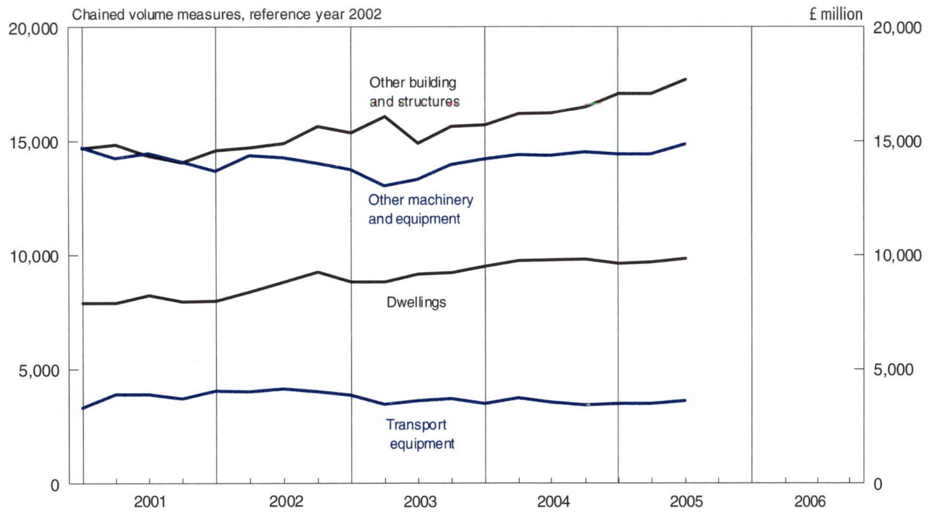

2.8 Gross value added chained volume indices at basic prices, by category of output[1,2]

2002 = 100

	Production						Service industries						
	Agriculture, forestry, and fishing	Mining and quarrying including oil and gas extraction	Manufacturing	Electricity gas and water supply	Total	Construction	Distribution hotels and catering; repairs	Transport storage and communication	Business services and finance	Government and other services	Total	Gross value added at basic prices	Gross value added excluding oil
2002 Weights[3]	*10*	*24*	*159*	*18*	*201*	*59*	*157*	*80*	*264*	*229*	*730*	*1000*	*979*
	GDQA	CKYX	CKYY	CKYZ	CKYW	GDQB	GDQE	GDQH	GDQN	GDQU	GDQS	CGCE	JUNT
2001	89.1	100.3	103.2	100.5	102.6	96.3	95.6	97.8	98.4	97.5	97.4	98.3	98.3
2002	100.0	100.0	100.0	100.0	100.0	100.0	100.0	100.0	100.0	100.0	100.0	100.0	100.0
2003	98.3	94.9	100.1	101.2	99.5	105.2	103.5	102.6	102.8	102.1	102.7	102.5	102.7
2004	99.3	87.2	101.9	103.3	100.3	108.7	108.7	105.3	107.0	104.5	106.4	105.6	106.0
2005	98.5†	79.6†	101.1†	102.2†	98.6†	110.3	109.7	109.0	110.6†	107.3	109.2	107.5	108.1
2001 Q1	89.8	99.3	105.5	102.1	104.5	95.5	94.7	97.7	96.6	96.5	96.3	97.9	97.8
Q2	88.2	101.9	103.2	101.1	102.9	95.8	95.1	98.0	98.4	97.1	97.2	98.2	98.1
Q3	88.0	100.8	103.0	99.9	102.4	96.4	95.7	97.4	98.7	97.7	97.6	98.4	98.4
Q4	90.2	99.2	100.9	98.8	100.4	97.6	97.0	98.0	99.8	98.6	98.6	98.8	98.8
2002 Q1	98.4	100.1	100.2	98.2	100.0	99.2	98.6	99.6	99.1	99.2	99.1	99.3	99.3
Q2	100.6	104.3	99.7	99.4	100.3	98.8	99.3	99.0	99.7	99.8	99.6	99.7	99.6
Q3	101.0	95.6	100.7	101.2	100.1	100.4	100.4	100.1	100.6	100.2	100.4	100.3	100.4
Q4	100.1	100.0	99.3	101.3	99.6	101.7	101.7	101.2	100.6	100.7	101.0	100.7	100.7
2003 Q1	97.9	99.6	99.4	99.3	99.4	102.0	101.7	101.5	101.8	101.0	101.5	101.4	101.4
Q2	97.8	95.2	99.5	100.2	99.1	104.0	103.0	102.3	101.8	101.6	102.0	101.8	102.0
Q3	98.7	93.5	100.2	101.6	99.5	107.1	104.1	103.1	102.9	102.5	103.1	102.9	103.1
Q4	98.8	91.1	101.1	103.5	100.1	107.7	105.3	103.4	104.8	103.4	104.3	103.9	104.2
2004 Q1	99.6	89.5	101.5	104.0	100.3	108.0	107.2	103.5	105.8	103.8	105.2	104.7	105.0
Q2	98.7	89.9	102.3	102.7	100.8	108.2	108.7	105.1	106.3	104.6	106.1	105.5	105.8
Q3	99.6	85.9	101.5	103.5	99.8	109.0	109.4	105.8	107.4	104.6	106.8	105.8	106.3
Q4	99.2	83.3	102.4	103.0	100.2	109.7	109.4	106.9	108.3	105.2	107.4	106.4	106.9
2005 Q1	97.9†	82.9†	101.5	101.8†	99.3†	109.8	109.1†	108.2†	109.2	106.1	108.1	106.7†	107.3†
Q2	99.5	83.0	101.1†	102.8	99.0	110.1	109.4	108.5	109.9†	106.9†	108.7	107.2	107.8
Q3	98.5	76.1	101.4	102.0	98.4	110.6	109.6	109.1	111.0	107.9	109.5	107.7	108.4
Q4	98.0	76.4	100.4	102.1	97.6	110.8†	110.7	110.4	112.2	108.4	110.5	108.3	109.0
Percentage change, quarter on corresponding quarter of previous year													
2001 Q1	-8.9	-9.9	1.6	5.4	0.7	-1.4	2.4	7.1	5.0	2.0	3.7	2.6	2.9
Q2	-10.0	-6.3	-1.1	1.9	-1.4	1.3	2.1	5.0	5.7	1.9	3.6	2.2	2.4
Q3	-11.4	-4.0	-1.5	1.8	-1.6	3.7	1.5	2.1	4.1	1.8	2.6	1.5	1.8
Q4	-5.9	-1.6	-4.4	0.3	-3.9	3.8	3.2	1.7	4.3	2.7	3.2	1.5	1.8
2002 Q1	9.6	0.8	-5.0	-3.8	-4.3	3.9	4.1	1.9	2.6	2.8	2.9	1.4	1.5
Q2	14.1	2.4	-3.4	-1.7	-2.5	3.1	4.4	1.0	1.3	2.8	2.5	1.5	1.5
Q3	14.8	-5.2	-2.2	1.3	-2.2	4.1	4.9	2.8	1.9	2.6	2.9	1.9	2.0
Q4	11.0	0.8	-1.6	2.5	-0.8	4.2	4.8	3.3	0.8	2.1	2.4	1.9	1.9
2003 Q1	-0.5	-0.5	-0.8	1.1	-0.6	2.8	3.1	1.9	2.7	1.8	2.4	2.1	2.1
Q2	-2.8	-8.7	-0.2	0.8	-1.2	5.3	3.7	3.3	2.1	1.8	2.4	2.1	2.4
Q3	-2.3	-2.2	-0.5	0.4	-0.6	6.7	3.7	3.0	2.3	2.3	2.7	2.6	2.7
Q4	-1.3	-8.9	1.8	2.2	0.5	5.9	3.5	2.2	4.2	2.7	3.3	3.2	3.5
2004 Q1	1.7	-10.1	2.1	4.7	0.9	5.9	5.4	2.0	3.9	2.8	3.6	3.3	3.6
Q2	0.9	-5.6	2.8	2.5	1.7	4.0	5.5	2.7	4.4	3.0	4.0	3.6	3.7
Q3	0.9	-8.1	1.3	1.9	0.3	1.8	5.1	2.6	4.4	2.0	3.6	2.8	3.1
Q4	0.4	-8.6	1.3	-0.5	0.1	1.9	3.9	3.4	3.3	1.7	3.0	2.4	2.6
2005 Q1	-1.7†	-7.4†	0.0	-2.1†	-1.0†	1.7	1.8†	4.5†	3.2	2.2	2.8	1.9†	2.2†
Q2	0.8	-7.7	-1.2†	0.1	-1.8	1.8	0.6	3.2	3.4†	2.2†	2.5	1.6	1.9
Q3	-1.1	-11.4	-0.1	-1.4	-1.4	1.5	0.2	3.1	3.4	3.2	2.5	1.8	2.0
Q4	-1.2	-8.3	-2.0	-0.9	-2.6	1.0†	1.2	3.3	3.6	3.0	2.9	1.8	2.0

1 Estimates cannot be regarded as accurate to the last digit shown.
2 Components of output are valued at basic prices, which exclude taxes and subsidies on production.
3 Weights may not sum to totals due to rounding. The weights shown are in proportion to total gross value added (GVA) in 2002, and are used to combine the industry output indices to calculate the totals for 2003 and 2004. For 2002 and earlier, totals are calculated using the equivalent weights for the previous year (e.g. totals for 2002 use 2001 weights).

Sources: Office for National Statistics; Enquiries Columns 1-11 01633 813126; Columns 12-13 020 7533 6031

Gross value added chained volume measures at basic prices, by category of output

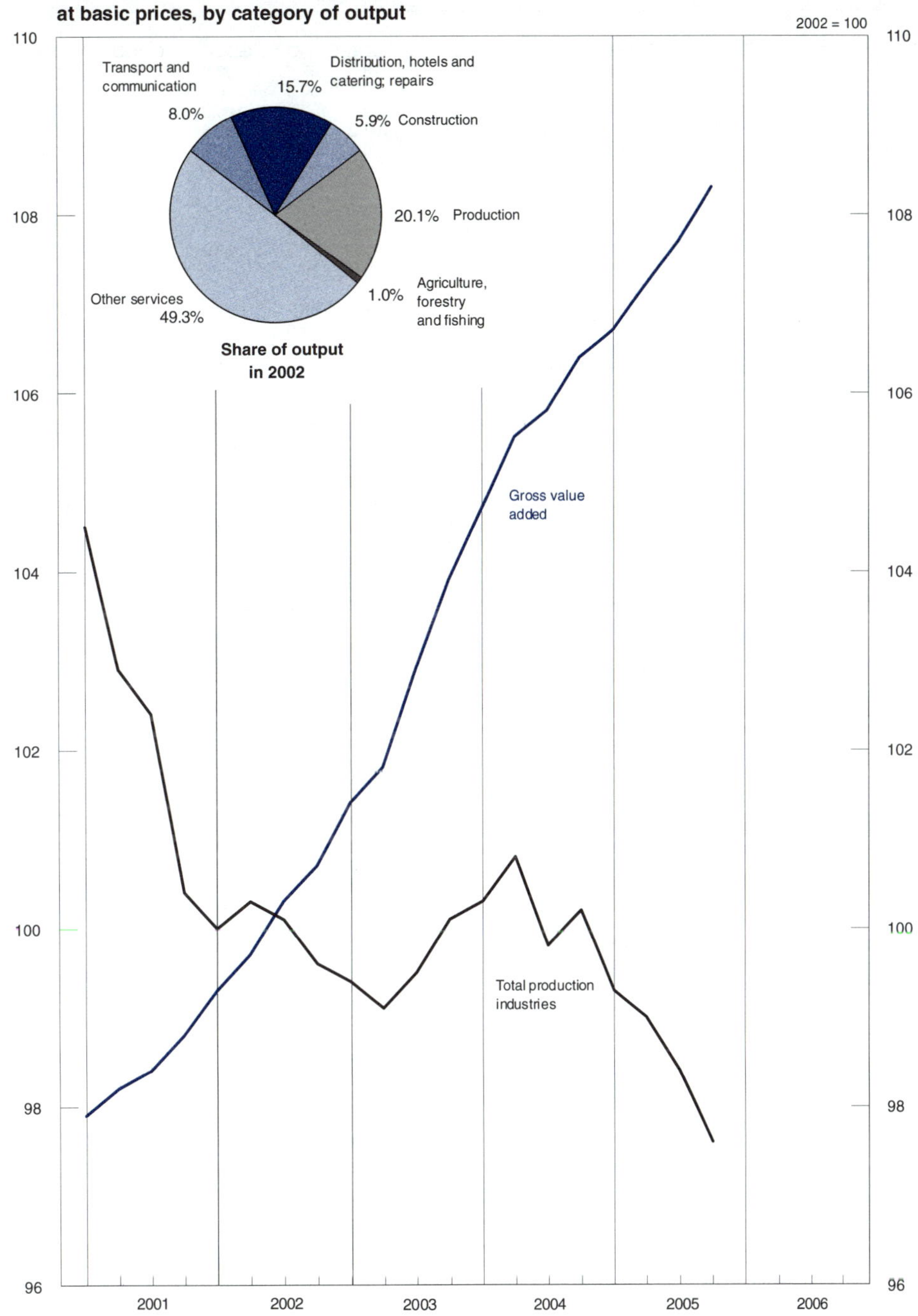

2.9 Gross value added chained volume indices at basic prices, by category of output: service industries

2002 = 100

	Distribution hotels and catering; repairs		Transport, storage and communication		Business services and finance		Government and other services						
	Motor trades; wholesale and retail trade; repairs	Hotels and restaurants	Transport and storage	Post and telecommunication	Financial intermediation[1]	Real estate, renting and business activities	Ownership of dwellings	PAD[2]	Education	Health and social work	Other services[3]	Adjustment for financial services[4]	Total services
2002 weights[5]	*124*	*34*	*48*	*31*	*68*	*162*	*78*	*50*	*60*	*67*	*52*	*-44*	*730*
	GDQC	GDQD	GDQF	GDQG	GDQI	GDQK	GDQL	GDQO	GDQP	GDQQ	GDQR	GDQJ	GDQS
2001	95.2	97.4	97.3	98.5	100.9	97.2	98.8	97.5	98.6	96.6	97.1	97.2	97.4
2002	100.0	100.0	100.0	100.0	100.0	100.0	100.0	100.0	100.0	100.0	100.0	100.0	100.0
2003	102.9	105.9	100.8	105.4	101.8	105.7	102.2	103.5	100.5	103.2	101.2	110.8	102.7
2004	108.0	111.2	104.4	106.7	105.7	113.8	104.2	105.3	100.5	107.4	104.7	125.3	106.4
2005	108.8	113.1	108.4	110.0	111.0	119.8	106.0	106.9	101.7	110.7	109.8	136.9	109.2
2001 Q1	94.2	97.0	96.8	99.1	99.2	95.5	98.1	97.0	97.8	95.4	95.8	97.7	96.3
Q2	94.5	97.1	97.6	98.7	101.2	97.0	98.7	97.4	98.4	96.4	96.1	96.5	97.2
Q3	95.2	97.9	97.4	97.4	100.7	97.5	99.2	97.3	98.9	96.8	97.8	97.1	97.6
Q4	96.8	97.8	97.5	98.8	102.4	98.7	99.3	98.4	99.3	98.0	98.8	97.4	98.6
2002 Q1	98.7	98.3	99.3	100.1	99.5	98.3	99.4	98.9	99.9	98.2	100.2	97.4	99.1
Q2	99.5	98.5	99.3	98.6	98.9	99.8	99.7	99.8	99.9	100.1	99.5	99.0	99.6
Q3	100.4	100.3	100.5	99.5	100.9	100.8	100.0	100.2	100.0	100.7	99.8	100.4	100.4
Q4	101.4	102.8	100.9	101.8	100.8	101.1	100.8	101.1	100.2	101.0	100.6	103.2	101.0
2003 Q1	101.0	104.2	99.7	104.4	101.2	103.1	101.5	102.2	100.3	101.7	99.6	105.3	101.5
Q2	102.2	106.0	99.5	106.6	101.7	104.1	101.8	103.1	100.5	102.1	100.5	110.1	102.0
Q3	103.6	106.1	101.8	105.0	101.6	106.2	102.3	104.3	100.5	103.5	101.6	111.9	103.1
Q4	104.8	107.2	102.1	105.5	102.6	109.5	103.2	104.5	100.5	105.4	102.9	115.8	104.3
2004 Q1	106.7	109.1	102.2	105.4	105.3	111.2	103.7	105.2	100.4	107.0	102.1	120.9	105.2
Q2	107.9	111.3	104.4	106.0	104.0	112.9	104.0	105.1	100.4	106.6	106.4	123.0	106.1
Q3	108.7	111.8	104.5	107.7	105.9	114.7	104.2	105.3	100.6	107.5	104.7	126.2	106.8
Q4	108.5	112.7	106.3	107.8	107.8	116.4	104.8	105.7	100.7	108.4	105.7	131.1	107.4
2005 Q1	108.2†	112.3†	108.0†	108.4†	109.5†	117.7†	105.2	106.1†	101.2	109.3	107.4†	133.8†	108.1
Q2	108.3	113.5	107.9	109.4	110.6	118.6	105.7	106.8	101.7	110.3†	108.5	135.4	108.7
Q3	108.7	112.6	108.1	110.7	111.5	120.5	106.3	107.0	101.8†	111.2	111.3	138.5	109.5
Q4	109.8	113.8	109.6	111.5	112.4	122.4	106.7	107.5	102.0	111.8	112.2	139.9	110.5
Percentage change, quarter on corresponding quarter of previous year													
2001 Q1	*3.7*	*−2.5*	*3.1*	*13.6*	*4.9*	*7.2*	*2.9*	*1.9*	*0.0*	*3.2*	*2.8*	*9.4*	*3.7*
Q2	*2.7*	*−0.5*	*1.8*	*10.4*	*6.0*	*6.0*	*3.9*	*1.5*	*0.5*	*2.6*	*2.8*	*4.0*	*3.6*
Q3	*2.0*	*−0.4*	*0.2*	*5.0*	*4.8*	*4.4*	*3.0*	*0.4*	*1.0*	*2.4*	*3.4*	*4.2*	*2.6*
Q4	*3.8*	*1.3*	*1.8*	*1.5*	*5.6*	*4.7*	*1.5*	*1.2*	*1.6*	*3.4*	*4.7*	*2.0*	*3.2*
2002 Q1	*4.8*	*1.3*	*2.6*	*1.0*	*0.3*	*2.9*	*1.3*	*2.0*	*2.1*	*2.9*	*4.6*	*−0.3*	*2.9*
Q2	*5.3*	*1.4*	*1.7*	*−0.1*	*−2.3*	*2.9*	*1.0*	*2.5*	*1.5*	*3.8*	*3.5*	*2.6*	*2.5*
Q3	*5.5*	*2.5*	*3.2*	*2.2*	*0.2*	*3.4*	*0.8*	*3.0*	*1.1*	*4.0*	*2.0*	*3.4*	*2.9*
Q4	*4.8*	*5.1*	*3.5*	*3.0*	*−1.6*	*2.4*	*1.5*	*2.7*	*0.9*	*3.1*	*1.8*	*6.0*	*2.4*
2003 Q1	*2.3*	*6.0*	*0.4*	*4.3*	*1.7*	*4.9*	*2.1*	*3.3*	*0.4*	*3.6*	*−0.6*	*8.1*	*2.4*
Q2	*2.7*	*7.6*	*0.2*	*8.1*	*2.8*	*4.3*	*2.1*	*3.3*	*0.6*	*2.0*	*1.0*	*11.2*	*2.4*
Q3	*3.2*	*5.8*	*1.3*	*5.5*	*0.7*	*5.4*	*2.3*	*4.1*	*0.5*	*2.8*	*1.8*	*11.5*	*2.7*
Q4	*3.4*	*4.3*	*1.2*	*3.6*	*1.8*	*8.3*	*2.4*	*3.4*	*0.3*	*4.4*	*2.3*	*12.2*	*3.3*
2004 Q1	*5.6*	*4.7*	*2.5*	*1.0*	*4.1*	*7.9*	*2.2*	*2.9*	*0.1*	*5.2*	*2.5*	*14.8*	*3.6*
Q2	*5.6*	*5.0*	*4.9*	*−0.6*	*2.3*	*8.5*	*2.2*	*1.9*	*−0.1*	*4.4*	*5.9*	*11.7*	*4.0*
Q3	*4.9*	*5.4*	*2.7*	*2.6*	*4.2*	*8.0*	*1.9*	*1.0*	*0.1*	*3.9*	*3.1*	*12.8*	*3.6*
Q4	*3.5*	*5.1*	*4.1*	*2.2*	*5.1*	*6.3*	*1.6*	*1.1*	*0.2*	*2.8*	*2.7*	*13.2*	*3.0*
2005 Q1	*1.4†*	*2.9†*	*5.7†*	*2.8†*	*4.0†*	*5.8†*	*1.4*	*0.9†*	*0.8*	*2.1*	*5.2†*	*10.7†*	*2.8*
Q2	*0.4*	*2.0*	*3.4*	*3.2*	*6.3*	*5.0*	*1.6*	*1.6*	*1.3*	*3.5†*	*2.0*	*10.1*	*2.5*
Q3	*0.0*	*0.7*	*3.4*	*2.8*	*5.3*	*5.1*	*2.0*	*1.6*	*1.2†*	*3.4*	*6.3*	*9.7*	*2.5*
Q4	*1.2*	*1.0*	*3.1*	*3.4*	*4.3*	*5.2*	*1.8*	*1.7*	*1.3*	*3.1*	*6.1*	*6.7*	*2.9*

1 Comprises section J of the SIC(92). This covers activities of institutions such as banks, building societies, securities dealers, insurance companies and pension funds. It also covers institutions whose activities are closely related to financial intermediation: for example fund managers and insurance brokers.

2 Public administration and national defence; compulsory social security.

3 Comprising sections O, and P of the SIC(92).

4 The weight and proxy series for financial intermediation are calculated before the deduction of interest receipts and payments to provide a better indication of the underlying activity for this section (see note 1). However, this overstates the contribution to GDP because interest flows should be treated as transfer payments rather than final consumption. The financial services adjustment, which has a negative weight, corrects for this.

5 See footnote 3 on Table 2.8

Source: Office for National Statistics; Enquiries 01633 813126

Gross value added chained volume indices at basic prices, by category of output: service industries

2002 = 100

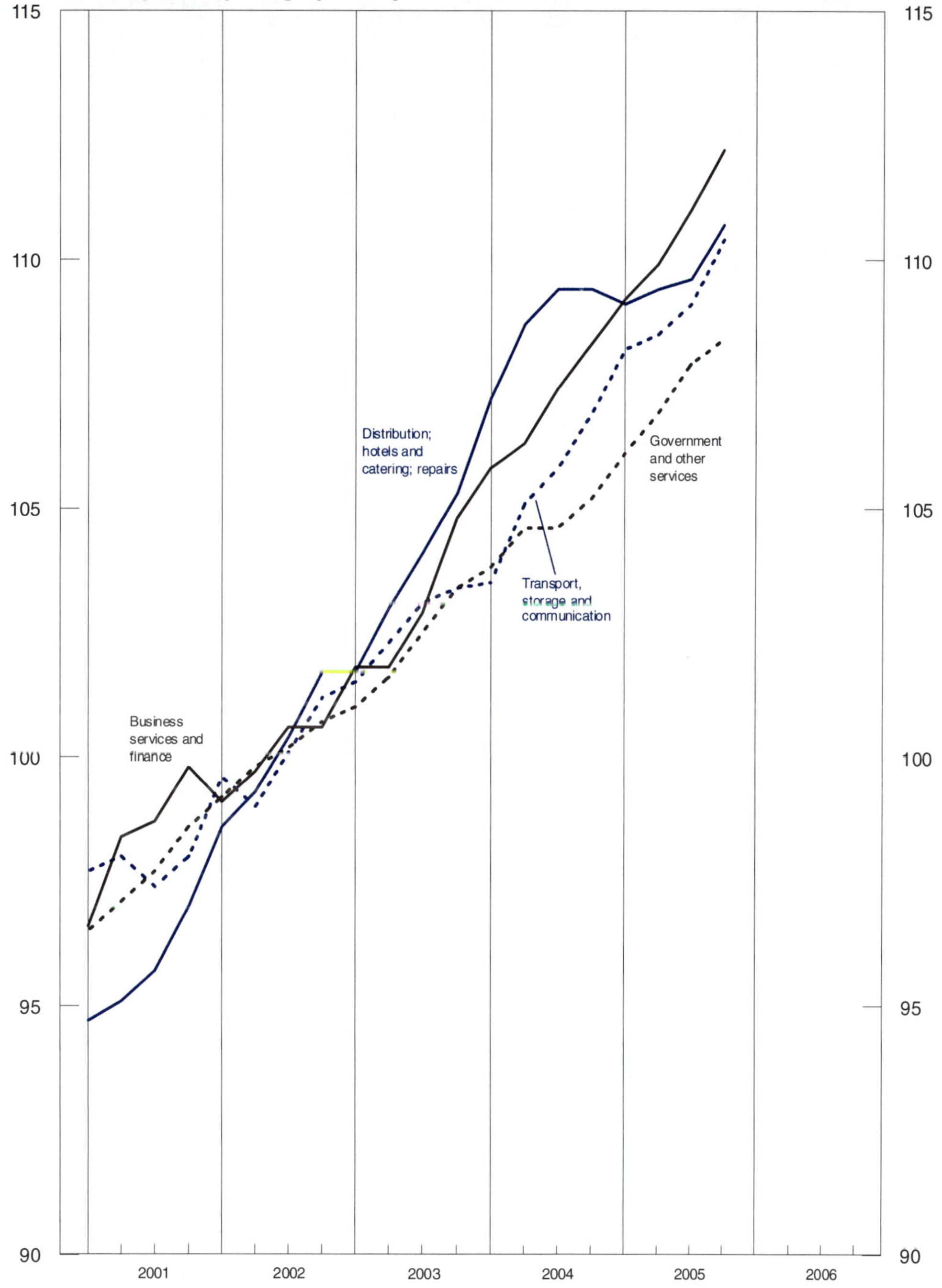

Source : see data on Table 2.8

2.10 Summary capital accounts and net lending/net borrowing

£ million

	Non-financial corporations				Financial corporations				General government			
	Gross saving[1]	Capital transfers (net receipts)	Gross capital formation[2]	Net acquisition of non-financial assets	Gross saving[1]	Capital transfers (net receipts)	Gross capital formation[2]	Net acquisition of non-financial assets	Gross saving[1]	Capital transfers (net receipts)	Gross capital formation[2]	Net acquisition of non-financial assets
	RPJV	GZQW	RQBZ	RQAX	RPPS	GZQE	RPYP	RPYO	RPQC	GZQU	RPZF	RPZE
2001	89 893	2 661	103 976	1 208	-9 450	–	7 300	–43	25 272	–4 081	13 929	–916
2002	107 576	2 098	99 453	1 431	15 325	–	6 732	–36	1 602	–3 674	15 602	–1 087
2003	116 527	3 316	99 413	1 241	19 671	–	3 452	–3	–13 036	–5 525	18 244	–957
2004	124 790	3 396	105 921	1 672	26 074	–	3 844	–6	–12 496	–5 227	21 165	–1 071
2001 Q1	22 815	599	25 568	271	–5 721	–	2 368	–9	8 635	–749	2 966	–222
Q2	21 835	627	26 171	305	–1 717	–	2 239	–11	6 420	–1 229	3 621	–221
Q3	23 676	719	26 324	331	–2 789	–	1 342	–11	6 372	–1 152	3 617	–234
Q4	21 567	716	25 913	301	777	–	1 351	–12	3 845	–951	3 725	–239
2002 Q1	25 584	517	25 016	379	2 755	–	843	–11	1 880	–1 054	3 803	–284
Q2	26 944	350	24 705	330	2 068	–	1 196	–10	192	–647	3 900	–233
Q3	27 663	561	24 418	358	4 060	–	3 068	–9	1 026	–971	4 019	–238
Q4	27 385	670	25 314	364	6 442	–	1 625	–6	–1 496	–1 002	3 880	–332
2003 Q1	28 957	729	22 061	282	6 395	–	2 120	–3	–2 338	–1 560	4 546	–205
Q2	27 167	947	24 024	332	4 004	–	876	–	–2 911	–1 468	4 190	–256
Q3	29 360	850	25 990	364	4 356	–	148	1	–2 803	–1 304	4 573	–252
Q4	31 043	790	27 338	263	4 916	–	308	–1	–4 984	–1 193	4 935	–244
2004 Q1	31 270	882	26 273	368	4 533	–	275	–	–3 473	–1 195	4 521	–251
Q2	30 694	906	26 114	418	6 650	–	697	–2	–2 019	–1 427	5 671	–273
Q3	27 818	856	26 281	447	7 376	–	1 327	–2	–3 549	–1 418	5 226	–277
Q4	35 008	752	27 253	439	7 515	–	1 545	–2	–3 455	–1 187	5 747	–270
2005 Q1	28 797	1 550	26 540	399	7 001	–	–623	–2	–2 392	–1 721	6 329	–268
Q2	35 317	1 096	25 102	409	5 192	–	2 600	–1	–2 907	–1 313	5 791	–282
Q3	31 912	803	27 816	418	812	–	436	–	–1 120	–1 271	6 396	–287

	Households and NPISH				Net lending(+)/net borrowing(-)[3]					
	Gross saving[1]	Capital transfers (net receipts)	Gross capital formation[2]	Net acquisition of non-financial assets	Non-financial corporations	Financial corporations	General government	Households and NPISH	Rest of the world[4]	Statistical discrepancy
	RPQL	GZQI	RPZV	RPZU	RQAW	RPYN	RPZD	RPZT	RQCH	DJDS
2001	44 352	3 023	43 996	–152	–15 981	–16 707	8 178	3 531	20 979	–
2002	34 691	2 876	50 268	–176	4 864	8 629	–16 587	–12 525	15 619	–
2003	41 002	3 876	55 475	–210	15 361	16 222	–35 848	–10 387	14 652	–
2004	34 813	4 322	62 592	–276	17 426	22 236	–37 817	–23 181	21 311	25
2001 Q1	12 161	418	10 881	–25	–3 363	–8 080	5 142	1 723	4 578	–
Q2	11 344	1 266	10 540	–36	–4 867	–3 945	1 791	2 106	4 915	–
Q3	10 640	747	11 628	–44	–3 009	–4 120	1 837	–197	5 489	–
Q4	10 207	592	10 947	–47	–4 742	–562	–592	–101	5 997	–
2002 Q1	7 468	787	12 028	–47	–68	1 923	–2 693	–3 726	4 564	–
Q2	9 218	556	12 968	–45	1 543	882	–4 122	–3 149	4 846	–
Q3	9 278	697	12 149	–43	2 713	1 001	–3 726	–2 131	2 143	–
Q4	8 727	836	13 123	–41	676	4 823	–6 046	–3 519	4 066	–
2003 Q1	9 591	1 156	13 018	–46	5 968	4 278	–8 239	–2 225	217	–
Q2	10 227	779	13 255	–49	2 862	3 128	–8 313	–2 200	4 522	–
Q3	9 938	863	14 525	–55	3 018	4 207	–8 428	–3 669	4 872	–
Q4	11 246	1 078	14 677	–60	3 513	4 609	–10 868	–2 293	5 041	–
2004 Q1	9 722	1 120	15 163	–64	4 696	4 258	–8 938	–4 257	4 161	80
Q2	8 344	1 227	15 959	–68	4 255	5 955	–8 844	–6 320	4 902	52
Q3	8 506	954	15 630	–71	1 184	6 051	–9 916	–6 099	8 788	–8
Q4	8 241	1 021	15 840	–73	7 291	5 972	–10 119	–6 505	3 460	–99
2005 Q1	9 562	1 807	16 495	–76	2 036	7 626	–10 174	–5 050	5 943	–382
Q2	11 676	1 001	15 845	–79	10 006	2 593	–9 729	–3 089	701	–482
Q3	11 529	927	17 393	–81	3 645	376	–8 500	–4 856	9 883	–547

1 Before providing for depreciation, inventory holding gains.

2 Comprises gross fixed capital formation and changes in inventories and acquisitions *less* disposals of valuables.

3 This balance is equal to gross saving *plus* capital transfers *less* gross fixed capital formation, *less* net acquisition of non-financial assets, *less* changes in inventories.

4 Equals the current balance of payments accounts, *plus* capital transfers.

Sources: Office for National Statistics;
Enquiries Part 1 (Upper) Columns 1,3-5,7-9,11,12 020 7533 6031;
Columns 2,6,10 020 7533 5985;
Part 2 (Lower) Columns 1, 3-10 020 7533 6031; Column 2 020 7533 5985

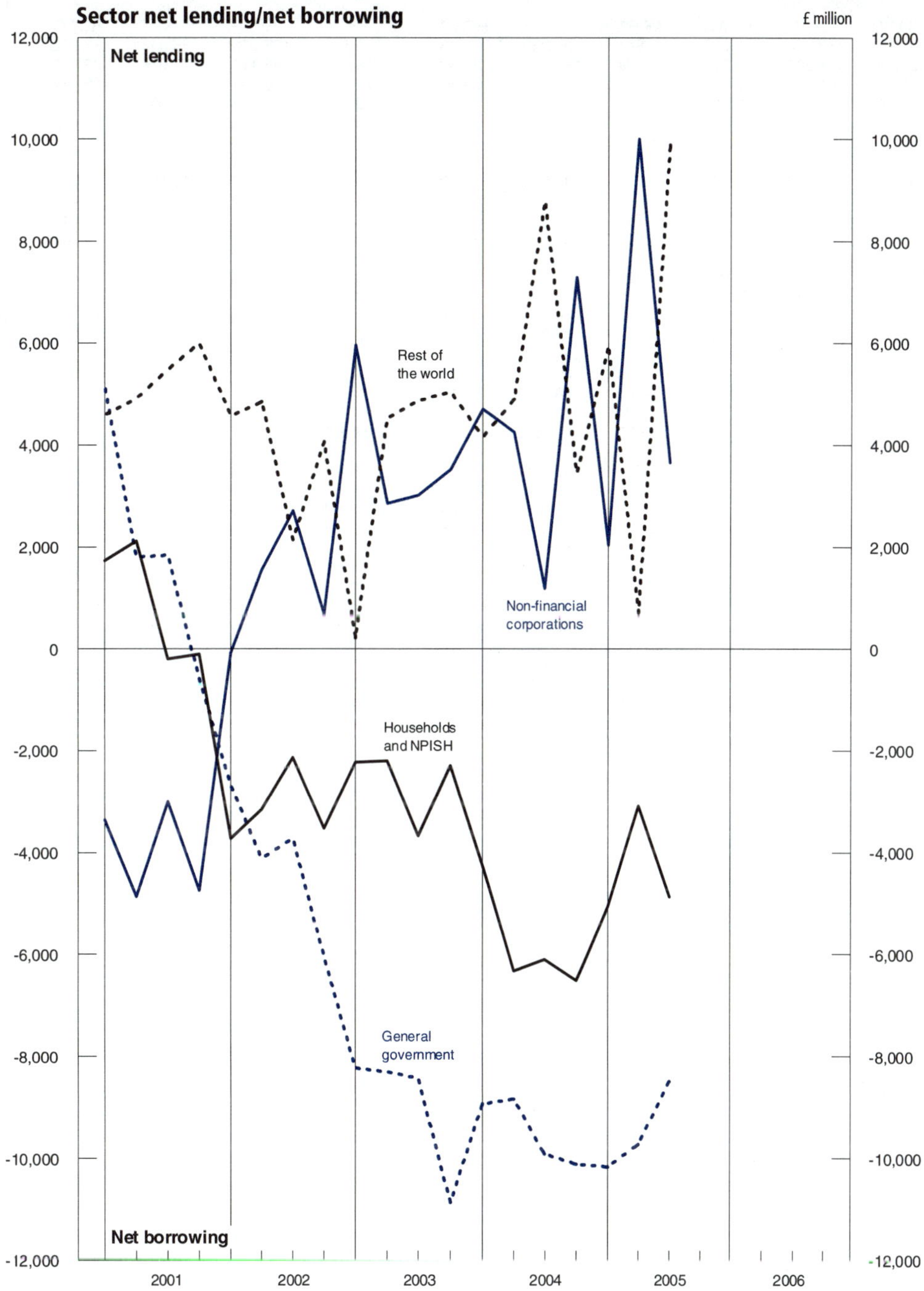
Sector net lending/net borrowing
£ million
Net lending
Net borrowing
12,000
10,000
8,000
6,000
4,000
2,000
0
-2,000
-4,000
-6,000
-8,000
-10,000
-12,000
Rest of the world
Non-financial corporations
Households and NPISH
General government
2001
2002
2003
2004
2005
2006

2.11 Private non-financial corporations: allocation of primary income account

£ million

	Resources: Gross operating surplus: Gross trading profits: Continental shelf companies	Others[1]	Rental of buildings	*less* Inventory holding gains	Gross operating surplus[1] +	Property income receipts	Total resources[1,2]	Uses: Property income payments: Total payments	*of which* Dividends	*of which* Interest	Gross balance of primary incomes[1]	Share of gross national income[1] (per cent)
	CAGD	CAED	DTWR	-DLRA	CAER	RPBM	RPBN	RPBP	RVFT	ROCG	RPBO	NRJL
2000	20 936	156 678	11 657	−2 941	186 330	60 525	246 855	128 508	55 846	37 912	118 347	*12.4*
2001	19 696	154 292	12 304	434	186 726	72 749	259 475	145 111	77 516	39 419	114 364	*11.4*
2002	19 132	161 586	12 885	−2 856	190 747	66 330	257 077	126 455	61 580	36 459	130 622	*12.2*
2003	18 631	172 608	13 652	−4 148	200 743	71 495	272 238	134 465	71 096	35 697	137 773	*12.2*
2004	18 932	186 208	14 225	−4 113	215 252	78 890	294 142	145 276	72 509	41 452	148 866	*12.5*
2000 Q1	4 626	38 558	2 801	−702	45 649	14 310	59 959	32 410	15 181	8 844	27 549	*11.7*
Q2	5 134	38 494	2 875	−830	46 057	14 446	60 503	30 455	12 370	9 405	30 048	*12.7*
Q3	5 407	38 882	2 953	−799	45 922	15 138	61 060	31 071	12 127	9 615	29 989	*12.5*
Q4	5 769	40 744	3 028	−610	48 702	16 631	65 333	34 572	16 168	10 048	30 761	*12.7*
2001 Q1	5 450	36 936	3 039	329	46 265	17 627	63 892	34 961	15 759	10 406	28 931	*11.7*
Q2	5 348	36 862	3 071	5	45 747	18 820	64 567	36 530	19 491	9 929	28 037	*11.2*
Q3	4 697	39 808	3 093	−52	46 904	21 158	68 062	38 796	21 835	10 107	29 266	*11.6*
Q4	4 201	40 686	3 101	152	47 810	15 144	62 954	34 824	20 431	8 977	28 130	*11.0*
2002 Q1	4 329	41 071	3 181	−733	47 848	17 375	65 223	34 242	18 302	9 077	30 981	*11.9*
Q2	4 774	41 177	3 193	−762	48 382	16 111	64 493	31 588	15 336	9 123	32 905	*12.4*
Q3	4 771	39 943	3 232	−384	47 562	16 242	63 804	30 462	14 917	9 083	33 342	*12.3*
Q4	5 258	39 395	3 279	−977	46 955	16 602	63 557	30 163	13 025	9 176	33 394	*12.2*
2003 Q1	5 116	41 381	3 337	−761	49 073	17 108	66 181	31 637	15 800	9 065	34 544	*12.4*
Q2	4 047	42 817	3 393	−1 286	48 971	18 890	67 861	35 847	19 645	8 771	32 014	*11.5*
Q3	4 951	44 101	3 442	−912	51 582	18 459	70 041	34 983	19 372	8 825	35 058	*12.4*
Q4	4 517	44 309	3 480	−1 189	51 117	17 038	68 155	31 998	16 279	9 036	36 157	*12.5*
2004 Q1	4 737	44 876	3 507	−908	52 212	18 008	70 220	33 516	16 647	9 514	36 704	*12.6*
Q2	4 773	46 013	3 534	−799	53 521	18 427	71 948	34 678	17 244	10 213	37 270	*12.6*
Q3	4 842	47 113	3 570	−1 051	54 474	20 308	74 782	40 924	21 861	10 691	33 858	*11.4*
Q4	4 580	48 206	3 614	−1 355	55 045	22 147	77 192	36 158	16 757	11 034	41 034	*13.4*
2005 Q1	4 897	46 650	3 651	−954	54 244	22 894	77 138	41 307	21 699	11 697	35 831	*11.8*
Q2	5 346	47 574	3 687	101	56 708	25 498	82 206	39 209	18 475	12 338	42 997	*13.7*
Q3	5 563	48 512	3 729	−1 039	56 765	26 705	83 470	43 668	23 115	12 648	39 802	*12.8*
Percentage change, quarter on corresponding quarter of previous year												
2000 Q1	*77.7*	*−0.9*	*8.1*		*3.7*	*79.4*	*15.3*	*72.8*	+	*18.5*	*−17.1*	
Q2	*70.1*	*−4.2*	*8.6*		*0.8*	*2.4*	*1.2*	*−17.6*	*−47.3*	*26.9*	*31.5*	
Q3	*36.7*	*0.4*	*8.8*		*3.4*	*34.0*	*9.6*	*3.8*	*−16.9*	*23.2*	*16.4*	
Q4	*40.9*	*3.7*	*8.6*		*6.7*	*13.4*	*8.4*	*6.0*	*4.0*	*20.6*	*11.2*	
2001 Q1	*17.8*	*−4.2*	*8.5*		*1.3*	*23.2*	*6.6*	*7.9*	*3.8*	*17.7*	*5.0*	
Q2	*4.2*	*−4.2*	*6.8*		*−0.7*	*30.3*	*6.7*	*19.9*	*57.6*	*5.6*	*−6.7*	
Q3	*−13.1*	*2.4*	*4.7*		*2.1*	*39.8*	*11.5*	*24.9*	*80.1*	*5.1*	*−2.4*	
Q4	*−27.2*	*−0.1*	*2.4*		*−1.8*	*−8.9*	*−3.6*	*0.7*	*26.4*	*−10.7*	*−8.6*	
2002 Q1	*−20.6*	*11.2*	*4.7*		*3.4*	*−1.4*	*2.1*	*−2.1*	*16.1*	*−12.8*	*7.1*	
Q2	*−10.7*	*11.7*	*4.0*		*5.8*	*−14.4*	*−0.1*	*−13.5*	*−21.3*	*−8.1*	*17.4*	
Q3	*1.6*	*0.3*	*4.5*		*1.4*	*−23.2*	*−6.3*	*−21.5*	*−31.7*	*−10.1*	*13.9*	
Q4	*25.2*	*−3.2*	*5.7*		*−1.8*	*9.6*	*1.0*	*−13.4*	*−36.2*	*2.2*	*18.7*	
2003 Q1	*18.2*	*0.8*	*4.9*		*2.6*	*−1.5*	*1.5*	*−7.6*	*−13.7*	*−0.1*	*11.5*	
Q2	*−15.2*	*4.0*	*6.3*		*1.2*	*17.2*	*5.2*	*13.5*	*28.1*	*−3.9*	*−2.7*	
Q3	*3.8*	*10.4*	*6.5*		*8.5*	*13.6*	*9.8*	*14.8*	*29.9*	*−2.8*	*5.1*	
Q4	*−14.1*	*12.5*	*6.1*		*8.9*	*2.6*	*7.2*	*6.1*	*25.0*	*−1.5*	*8.3*	
2004 Q1	*−7.4*	*8.4*	*5.1*		*6.4*	*5.3*	*6.1*	*5.9*	*5.4*	*5.0*	*6.3*	
Q2	*17.9*	*7.5*	*4.2*		*9.3*	*−2.5*	*6.0*	*−3.3*	*−12.2*	*16.4*	*16.4*	
Q3	*−2.2*	*6.8*	*3.7*		*5.6*	*10.0*	*6.8*	*17.0*	*12.8*	*21.1*	*−3.4*	
Q4	*1.4*	*8.8*	*3.9*		*7.7*	*30.0*	*13.3*	*13.0*	*2.9*	*22.1*	*13.5*	
2005 Q1	*3.4*	*4.0*	*4.1*		*3.9*	*27.1*	*9.9*	*23.2*	*30.3*	*22.9*	*−2.4*	
Q2	*12.0*	*3.4*	*4.3*		*6.0*	*38.4*	*14.3*	*13.1*	*7.1*	*20.8*	*15.4*	
Q3	*14.9*	*3.0*	*4.5*		*4.2*	*31.5*	*11.6*	*6.7*	*5.7*	*18.3*	*17.6*	

1 Quarterly alignment adjustment is included in this series.
2 Total resources equal total uses.

Source: Office for National Statistics; Enquiries 020 7533 6014

Private non-financial corporations: allocation of primary income account

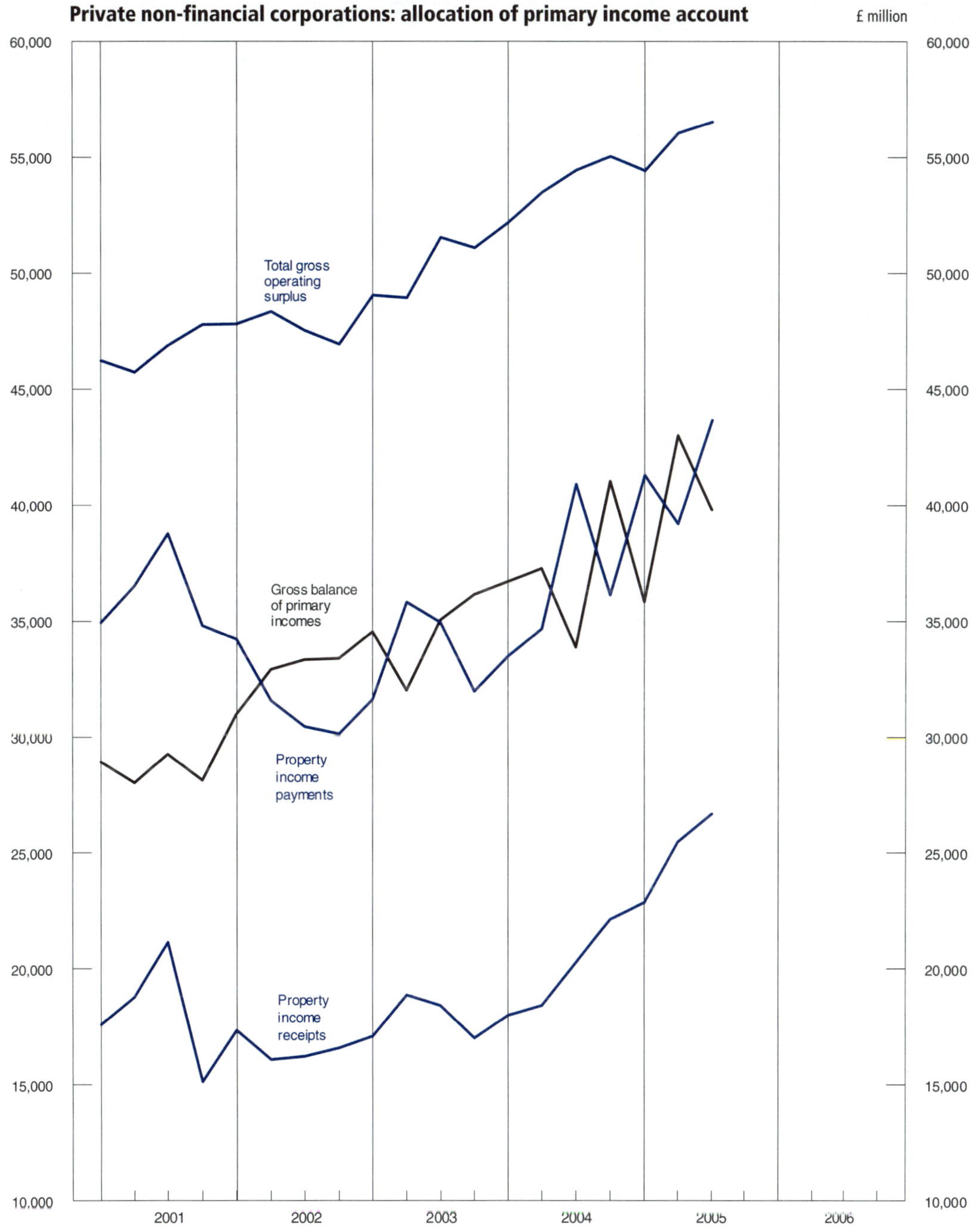

2.12 Private non-financial corporations: secondary distribution of income account and capital account

£ million

	Secondary distribution of income account						Capital account					
	Resources			Uses			Changes in liabilities and net worth		Changes in assets			
	Gross balance of primary incomes [1]	Other resources [2]	Total [1,3]	Taxes on income	Other uses [4]	Gross disposable income [1,5]	Net capital transfer receipts	Total [1]	Gross fixed capital formation	Changes in inventories [1]	Other changes in assets [6]	Net lending (+) or borrowing (-) [1,7]
	RPBO	NROQ	RPKY	RPLA	NROO	RPKZ	NROP	RPXH	ROAW	DLQY	NRON	RQBV
2000	118 347	9 990	128 337	26 188	10 403	91 746	405	92 151	96 873	5 512	776	−11 010
2001	114 364	9 229	123 593	26 061	9 640	87 892	1 621	89 513	98 035	5 941	1 138	−15 601
2002	130 622	9 889	140 511	24 432	10 311	105 768	1 093	106 861	96 819	2 677	1 212	6 153
2003	137 773	10 199	147 972	23 461	10 633	113 878	2 692	116 570	95 556	3 954	862	16 198
2004	148 866	10 172	159 038	26 621	10 618	121 799	2 861	124 660	100 383	5 637	1 227	17 413
2000 Q1	27 549	2 475	30 024	7 059	2 592	20 373	315	20 688	23 769	1 358	193	−4 632
Q2	30 048	2 429	32 477	6 410	2 526	23 541	20	23 561	23 549	1 123	157	−1 268
Q3	29 989	2 734	32 723	6 491	2 833	23 399	34	23 433	24 256	1 481	158	−2 462
Q4	30 761	2 352	33 113	6 228	2 452	24 433	36	24 469	25 299	1 550	268	−2 648
2001 Q1	28 931	2 253	31 184	6 489	2 354	22 341	200	22 541	24 862	734	238	−3 293
Q2	28 037	2 377	30 414	6 591	2 480	21 343	439	21 782	24 713	1 424	326	−4 681
Q3	29 266	2 262	31 528	6 011	2 365	23 152	485	23 637	24 730	1 606	297	−2 996
Q4	28 130	2 337	30 467	6 970	2 441	21 056	497	21 553	23 730	2 177	277	−4 631
2002 Q1	30 981	2 392	33 373	5 709	2 496	25 168	333	25 501	24 196	828	336	141
Q2	32 905	2 396	35 301	6 282	2 501	26 518	300	26 818	24 183	529	282	1 824
Q3	33 342	2 501	35 843	6 108	2 607	27 128	392	27 520	24 017	406	306	2 791
Q4	33 394	2 600	35 994	6 333	2 707	26 954	68	27 022	24 423	914	288	1 397
2003 Q1	34 544	2 562	37 106	6 110	2 669	28 327	541	28 868	22 504	−419	197	6 586
Q2	32 014	2 616	34 630	5 313	2 724	26 593	653	27 246	24 478	−454	264	2 958
Q3	35 058	2 602	37 660	6 308	2 711	28 641	786	29 427	23 775	2 251	254	3 147
Q4	36 157	2 419	38 576	5 730	2 529	30 317	712	31 029	24 799	2 576	147	3 507
2004 Q1	36 704	2 575	39 279	6 005	2 685	30 589	825	31 414	25 148	1 125	287	4 854
Q2	37 270	2 627	39 897	7 215	2 738	29 944	745	30 689	24 891	1 261	296	4 241
Q3	33 858	2 533	36 391	6 641	2 645	27 105	697	27 802	25 281	1 043	316	1 162
Q4	41 034	2 437	43 471	6 760	2 550	34 161	594	34 755	25 063	2 208	328	7 156
2005 Q1	35 831	2 557	38 388	7 633	2 700	28 055	1 402	29 457	25 522	1 074	245	2 616
Q2	42 997	2 893	45 890	7 974	3 007	34 909	938	35 847	24 660	444	303	10 440
Q3	39 802	2 769	42 571	8 331	2 884	31 356	658	32 014	26 269	1 613	242	3 890
Percentage change, quarter on corresponding quarter of previous year												
2000 Q1	*−17.1*	*21.5*	*−14.9*	*27.3*	*14.5*	*−25.8*	*−8.4*	*−25.6*	*2.0*			
Q2	*31.5*	*26.2*	*31.1*	*32.4*	*23.9*	*31.5*	*−89.9*	*30.2*	*2.2*			
Q3	*16.4*	*70.0*	*19.6*	*10.6*	*64.5*	*18.3*	*−84.3*	*17.2*	*0.7*			
Q4	*11.2*	*2.0*	*10.5*	*−2.0*	*1.3*	*15.2*	*−81.9*	*14.3*	*5.3*			
2001 Q1	*5.0*	*−9.0*	*3.9*	*−8.1*	*−9.2*	*9.7*	*−36.5*	*9.0*	*4.6*			
Q2	*−6.7*	*−2.1*	*−6.4*	*2.8*	*−1.8*	*−9.3*	+	*−7.6*	*4.9*			
Q3	*−2.4*	*−17.3*	*−3.7*	*−7.4*	*−16.5*	*−1.1*	+	*0.9*	*2.0*			
Q4	*−8.6*	*−0.6*	*−8.0*	*11.9*	*−0.4*	*−13.8*	+	*−11.9*	*−6.2*			
2002 Q1	*7.1*	*6.2*	*7.0*	*−12.0*	*6.0*	*12.7*	*66.5*	*13.1*	*−2.7*			
Q2	*17.4*	*0.8*	*16.1*	*−4.7*	*0.8*	*24.2*	*−31.7*	*23.1*	*−2.1*			
Q3	*13.9*	*10.6*	*13.7*	*1.6*	*10.2*	*17.2*	*−19.2*	*16.4*	*−2.9*			
Q4	*18.7*	*11.3*	*18.1*	*−9.1*	*10.9*	*28.0*	*−86.3*	*25.4*	*2.9*			
2003 Q1	*11.5*	*7.1*	*11.2*	*7.0*	*6.9*	*12.6*	*62.5*	*13.2*	*−7.0*			
Q2	*−2.7*	*9.2*	*−1.9*	*−15.4*	*8.9*	*0.3*	+	*1.6*	*1.2*			
Q3	*5.1*	*4.0*	*5.1*	*3.3*	*4.0*	*5.6*	+	*6.9*	*−1.0*			
Q4	*8.3*	*−7.0*	*7.2*	*−9.5*	*−6.6*	*12.5*	+	*14.8*	*1.5*			
2004 Q1	*6.3*	*0.5*	*5.9*	*−1.7*	*0.6*	*8.0*	*52.5*	*8.8*	*11.7*			
Q2	*16.4*	*0.4*	*15.2*	*35.8*	*0.5*	*12.6*	*14.1*	*12.6*	*1.7*			
Q3	*−3.4*	*−2.7*	*−3.4*	*5.3*	*−2.4*	*−5.4*	*−11.3*	*−5.5*	*6.3*			
Q4	*13.5*	*0.7*	*12.7*	*18.0*	*0.8*	*12.7*	*−16.6*	*12.0*	*1.1*			
2005 Q1	*−2.4*	*−0.7*	*−2.3*	*27.1*	*0.6*	*−8.3*	*69.9*	*−6.2*	*1.5*			
Q2	*15.4*	*10.1*	*15.0*	*10.5*	*9.8*	*16.6*	*25.9*	*16.8*	*−0.9*			
Q3	*17.6*	*9.3*	*17.0*	*25.4*	*9.0*	*15.7*	*−5.6*	*15.1*	*3.9*			

1 Quarterly alignment adjustment is included in this series.
2 Social contributions and other current transfers.
3 Total resources equal total uses.
4 Social benefits and other current transfers.
5 Also known as gross saving.
6 Acquisitions *less* disposals of valuables and non-produced non-financial assets.
7 Gross of fixed capital consumption.

Source: Office for National Statistics; Enquiries 020 7533 6014

Private non-financial corporations: secondary distribution of income account

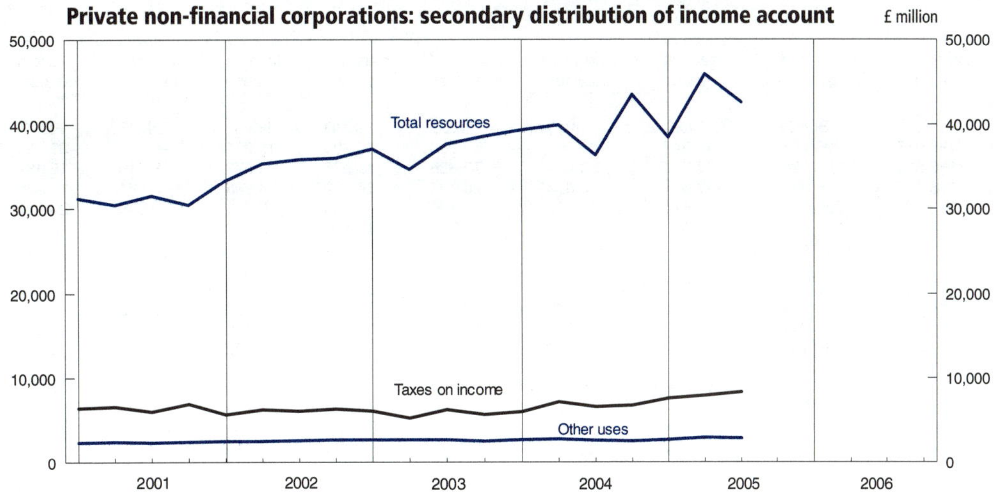

Private non-financial corporations: capital account

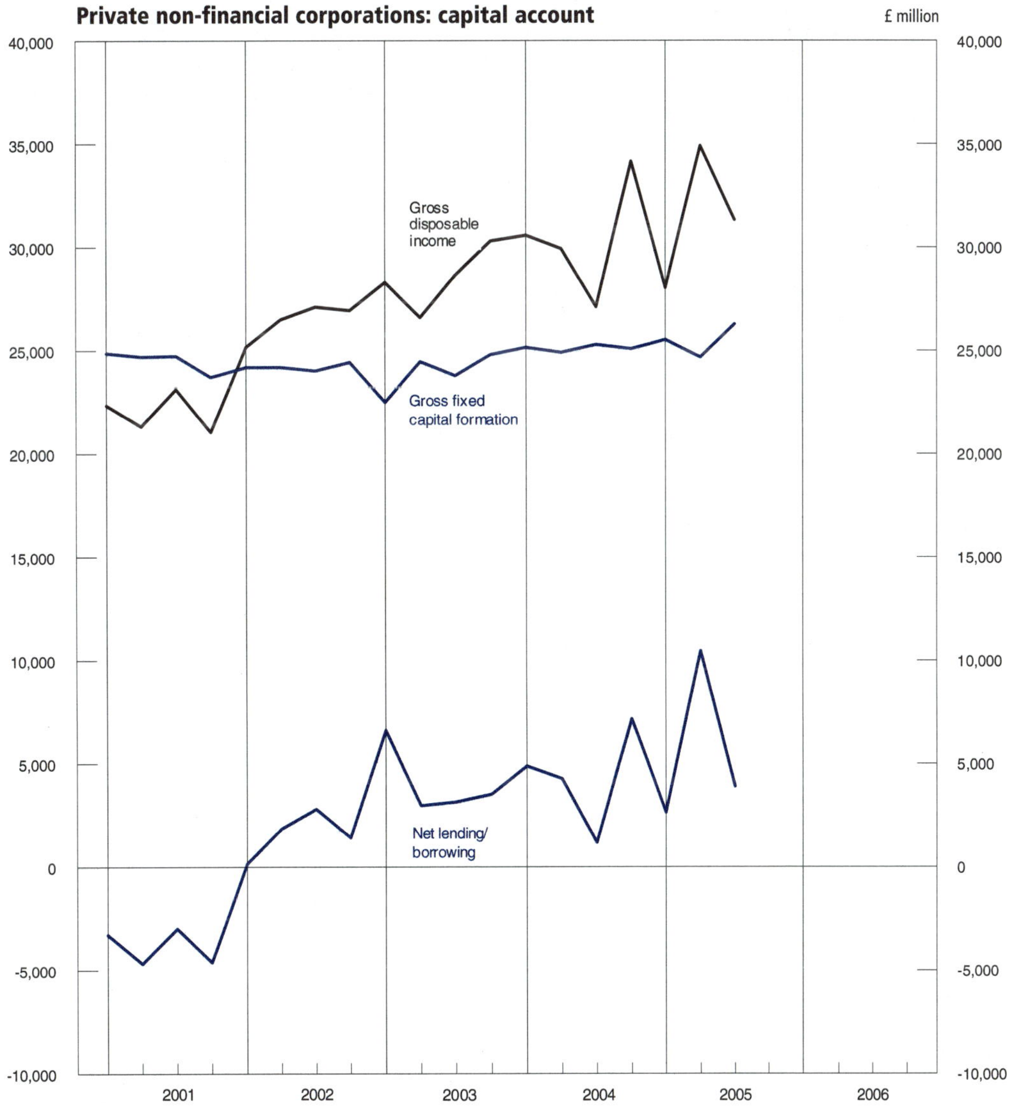

2.13 Balance of payments: current account

£ million

	Trade in goods and services									
	Exports of goods+	Imports of goods+	Balance of trade in goods	Exports of services	Imports of services	Services balance	Income balance	Current transfers balance	Current balance	Current balance as percentage of GDP[1]
	BOKG	BOKH	BOKI	IKBB	IKBC	IKBD	HBOJ	IKBP	HBOP	AA6H
2001	190 055	230 703	–40 648	83 061	69 358	13 703	11 371	–6 611	–22 185	*–2.2*
2002	186 511	233 598	–47 087	88 434	72 898	15 536	23 679	–8 615	–16 487	*–1.6*
2003	188 615	236 479	–47 864	93 616	76 734	16 882	24 995	–9 961	–15 948	*–1.4*
2004	190 933	251 347	–60 414	103 016	81 580	21 436	26 721	–10 940	–23 197	*–2.0*
2005	209 308	274 828	–65 520	105 318	86 810	18 508	..	..	..	..
2001 Q1	49 523	58 884	–9 361	21 764	17 534	4 230	2 182	–1 807	–4 756	*–1.9*
Q2	48 329	58 774	–10 445	21 922	17 464	4 458	3 202	–2 682	–5 467	*–2.2*
Q3	46 561	56 911	–10 350	18 775	17 495	1 280	3 355	29	–5 686	*–2.3*
Q4	45 642	56 134	–10 492	20 600	16 865	3 735	2 632	–2 151	–6 276	*–2.5*
2002 Q1	46 192	57 437	–11 245	21 716	17 897	3 819	4 993	–2 269	–4 702	*–1.8*
Q2	49 273	59 820	–10 547	21 475	18 169	3 306	4 649	–2 396	–4 988	*–1.9*
Q3	46 772	58 663	–11 891	22 936	18 449	4 487	6 521	–1 404	–2 287	*–0.9*
Q4	44 274	57 678	–13 404	22 307	18 383	3 924	7 516	–2 546	–4 510	*–1.7*
2003 Q1	49 034	59 686	–10 652	23 179	18 993	4 186	8 264	–2 237	–439	*–0.2*
Q2	46 813	57 856	–11 043	23 082	18 854	4 228	5 035	–2 898	–4 678	*–1.7*
Q3	46 302	58 602	–12 300	23 635	19 382	4 253	5 400	–2 501	–5 148	*–1.8*
Q4	46 466	60 335	–13 869	23 720	19 505	4 215	6 296	–2 325	–5 683	*–2.0*
2004 Q1	46 185	59 874	–13 689	25 022	19 684	5 338	6 273	–2 762	–4 840	*–1.7*
Q2	47 135	62 219	–15 084	25 573	20 099	5 474	6 592	–2 444	–5 462	*–1.9*
Q3	48 207	63 611	–15 404	25 787	20 589	5 198	3 995	–2 802	–9 013	*–3.1*
Q4	49 406	65 643	–16 237	26 634	21 208	5 426	9 861	–2 932	–3 882	*–1.3*
2005 Q1	49 331†	64 954†	–15 623†	26 572†	21 461†	5 111†	7 498	–3 572	–6 676	*–2.2*
Q2	51 810	67 298	–15 488	26 644	21 713	4 931	10 952	–2 565	–1 360	*–0.5*
Q3	53 451	70 686	–17 235	24 660	21 836	2 824	6 928	–3 024	–10 215	*–3.4*
Q4	54 716	71 890	–17 174	27 442	21 800	5 642	..	..	..	..
2003 Jan	16 537	20 055	–3 518	7 605	6 299	1 306	..	..	..	..
Feb	16 460	19 594	–3 134	7 762	6 335	1 427	..	..	..	..
Mar	16 037	20 037	–4 000	7 812	6 359	1 453	..	..	..	..
Apr	16 545	19 139	–2 594	7 669	6 193	1 476	..	..	..	..
May	15 293	19 405	–4 112	7 712	6 349	1 363	..	..	..	..
Jun	14 975	19 312	–4 337	7 701	6 312	1 389	..	..	..	..
Jul	15 675	19 479	–3 804	7 792	6 440	1 352	..	..	..	..
Aug	15 441	19 037	–3 596	7 921	6 489	1 432	..	..	..	..
Sep	15 186	20 086	–4 900	7 922	6 453	1 469	..	..	..	..
Oct	15 729	20 174	–4 445	7 852	6 275	1 577	..	..	..	..
Nov	15 110	19 919	–4 809	7 867	6 501	1 366	..	..	..	..
Dec	15 627	20 242	–4 615	8 001	6 729	1 272	..	..	..	..
2004 Jan	15 058	20 337	–5 279	8 170	6 588	1 582	..	..	..	..
Feb	15 278	19 482	–4 204	8 401	6 618	1 783	..	..	..	..
Mar	15 849	20 055	–4 206	8 451	6 478	1 973	..	..	..	..
Apr	15 731	20 785	–5 054	8 583	6 699	1 884	..	..	..	..
May	15 518	20 517	–4 999	8 503	6 692	1 811	..	..	..	..
Jun	15 886	20 917	–5 031	8 487	6 708	1 779	..	..	..	..
Jul	15 938	21 212	–5 274	8 498	6 750	1 748	..	..	..	..
Aug	15 881	21 109	–5 228	8 623	6 860	1 763	..	..	..	..
Sep	16 388	21 290	–4 902	8 666	6 979	1 687	..	..	..	..
Oct	16 139	21 794	–5 655	8 842	7 036	1 806	..	..	..	..
Nov	16 497	21 796	–5 299	8 904	7 066	1 838	..	..	..	..
Dec	16 770	22 053	–5 283	8 888	7 106	1 782	..	..	..	..
2005 Jan	16 378†	21 679†	–5 301†	8 787	7 084	1 703	..	..	..	..
Feb	16 050	21 642	–5 592	8 766	7 010	1 756	..	..	..	..
Mar	16 903	21 633	–4 730	8 659	6 974	1 685	..	..	..	..
Apr	16 966	22 587	–5 621	8 792	7 022	1 770	..	..	..	..
May	16 865	22 079	–5 214	8 842	7 193	1 649	..	..	..	..
Jun	17 979	22 632	–4 653	8 628	7 047	1 581	..	..	..	..
Jul	17 397	22 762	–5 365	8 709	7 084	1 625	..	..	..	..
Aug	17 839	23 925	–6 086	6 784	7 026	–242	..	..	..	..
Sep	18 215	23 999	–5 784	8 605	7 121	1 484	..	..	..	..
Oct	18 221	23 326	–5 105	8 736	7 065	1 671	..	..	..	..
Nov	17 938	23 946	–6 008	8 663	7 182	1 481	..	..	..	..
Dec	18 557	24 618	–6 061	8 748	7 040	1 708	..	..	..	..

1 Using series YBHA: GDP at current market prices

Sources: Office for National Statistics;
Enquiries Columns 1-3 020 7533 6064; Columns 4-6 & 8 020 7533 6090;
Columns 7, 9 & 10 020 7533 6078.

Balance of payments: current account

Balance of trade in goods

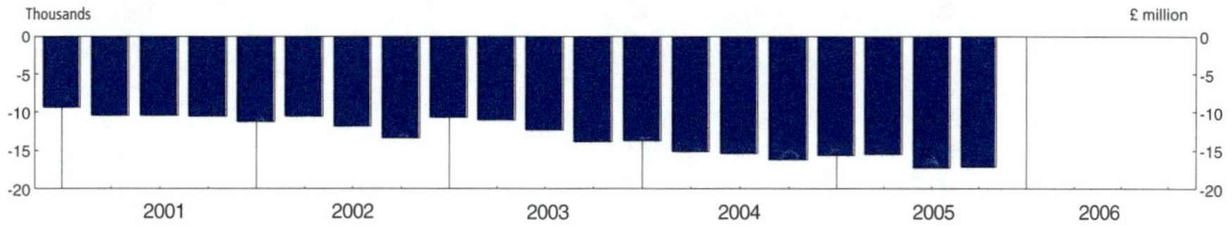

Services balance

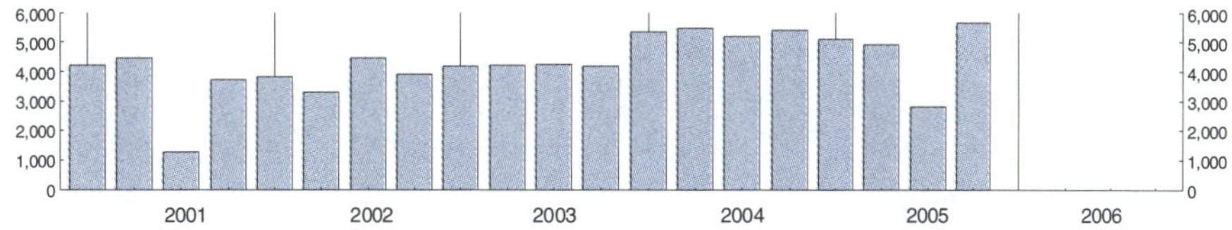

Income balance

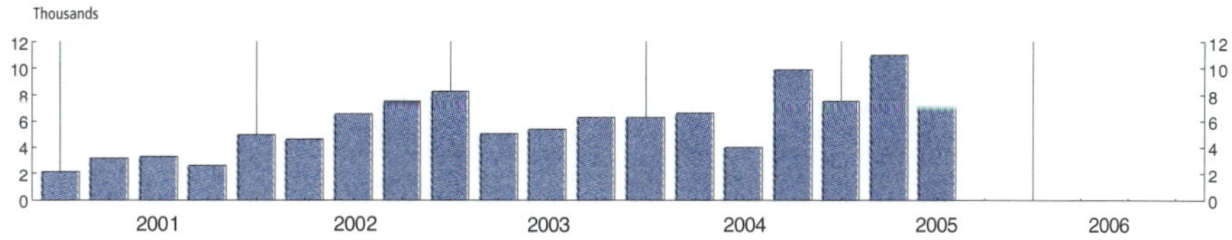

Current transfers balance

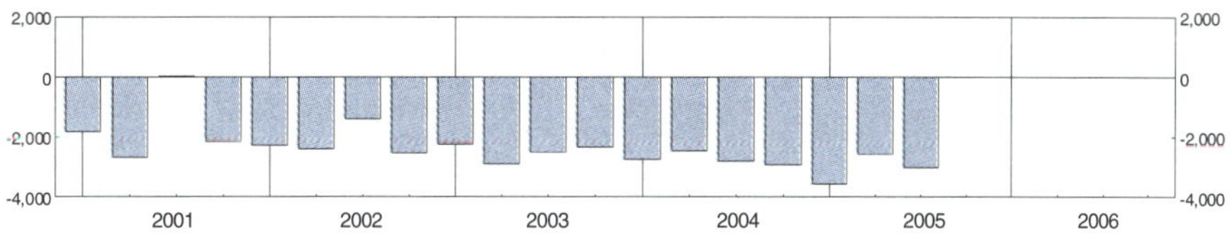

Current balance

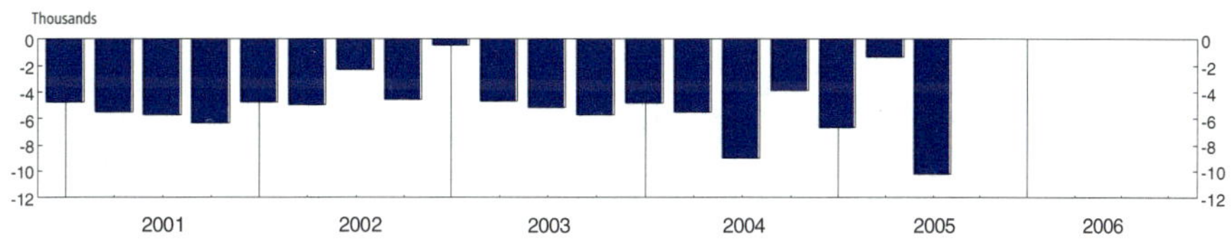

2.14 Trade in goods (on a balance of payments basis)

2002 = 100

	Volume indices (SA)		Price indices (NSA)		
	Exports	Imports	Exports	Imports	Terms of trade[1]
	BQKU	BQKV	BQKR	BQKS	BQKT
2001	101.7	95.9	100.0	102.6	97.5
2002	100.0	100.0	100.0	100.0	100.0
2003	99.7	102.0	101.8	99.3	102.5
2004	101.0	108.6	102.0	98.7	103.3
2005	108.6	114.6	106.3	102.7	103.5
2001 Q1	104.2	95.9	101.6	104.7	97.0
Q2	101.8	95.8	101.8	104.6	97.3
Q3	100.9	95.4	99.3	101.7	97.6
Q4	100.0	96.4	97.4	99.5	97.9
2002 Q1	98.9	97.2	100.2	100.9	99.3
Q2	104.9	101.6	101.1	100.8	100.3
Q3	100.6	101.3	99.9	99.5	100.4
Q4	95.6	99.9	98.8	98.9	99.9
2003 Q1	103.5	102.9	101.8	99.5	102.3
Q2	99.0	99.7	102.2	99.2	103.0
Q3	97.6	100.9	102.2	99.6	102.6
Q4	98.9	104.4	101.1	98.8	102.3
2004 Q1	99.6	105.1	99.6	97.0	102.7
Q2	100.5	108.0	101.2	98.3	103.0
Q3	101.7	109.3	102.8	99.6	103.2
Q4	102.4	112.0	104.5	99.9	104.6
2005 Q1	102.8†	110.0†	104.2†	100.7	103.5†
Q2	108.5	113.7	104.9	101.3†	103.6
Q3	110.5	117.0	107.9	104.1	103.7
Q4	112.4	117.8	108.2	104.8	103.2
2003 Jan	105.9	103.9	100.4	98.7	101.7
Feb	104.1	101.9	101.5	99.2	102.3
Mar	100.4	102.9	103.4	100.5	102.9
Apr	104.8	98.4	102.0	99.8	102.2
May	96.8	100.4	102.9	99.3	103.6
Jun	95.4	100.3	101.8	98.5	103.4
Jul	99.3	100.7	101.9	99.1	102.8
Aug	97.3	98.2	102.8	99.8	103.0
Sep	96.3	103.8	102.0	99.8	102.2
Oct	100.5	104.2	101.6	99.3	102.3
Nov	96.1	103.5	100.9	98.9	102.0
Dec	100.0	105.5	100.7	98.3	102.4
2004 Jan	97.0	107.2	99.7	97.2	102.6
Feb	99.4	103.2	98.7	96.0	102.8
Mar	102.3	105.0	100.4	97.7	102.8
Apr	101.0	108.6	100.9	97.8	103.2
May	98.9	106.4	102.1	99.0	103.1
Jun	101.7	109.1	100.7	98.1	102.7
Jul	102.1	110.5	101.0	98.3	102.7
Aug	100.4	109.0	102.9	99.8	103.1
Sep	102.5	108.4	104.4	100.6	103.8
Oct	99.8	111.1	106.2	101.3	104.8
Nov	101.8	110.8	104.8	100.1	104.7
Dec	105.7	114.1	102.5	98.4	104.2
2005 Jan	102.6†	110.7†	103.5†	100.3	103.2†
Feb	100.8	108.8	103.7	100.5	103.2
Mar	104.9	110.5	105.5	101.3†	104.1
Apr	106.3	114.9	104.8	100.8	104.0
May	105.9	112.2	104.9	101.2	103.7
Jun	113.4	114.0	104.9	101.8	103.0
Jul	107.3	113.1	107.7	104.3	103.3
Aug	111.0	119.0	108.3	104.1	104.0
Sep	113.3	118.9	107.8	103.8	103.9
Oct	112.2	115.0	108.5	104.7	103.6
Nov	111.2	117.5	108.1	105.1	102.9
Dec	113.8	120.8	107.9	104.7	103.1

1 Price index for exports expressed as a percentage of price index for imports.

Source: Office for National Statistics; Enquiries 020 7533 6064

Trade in goods (on a balance of payments basis)

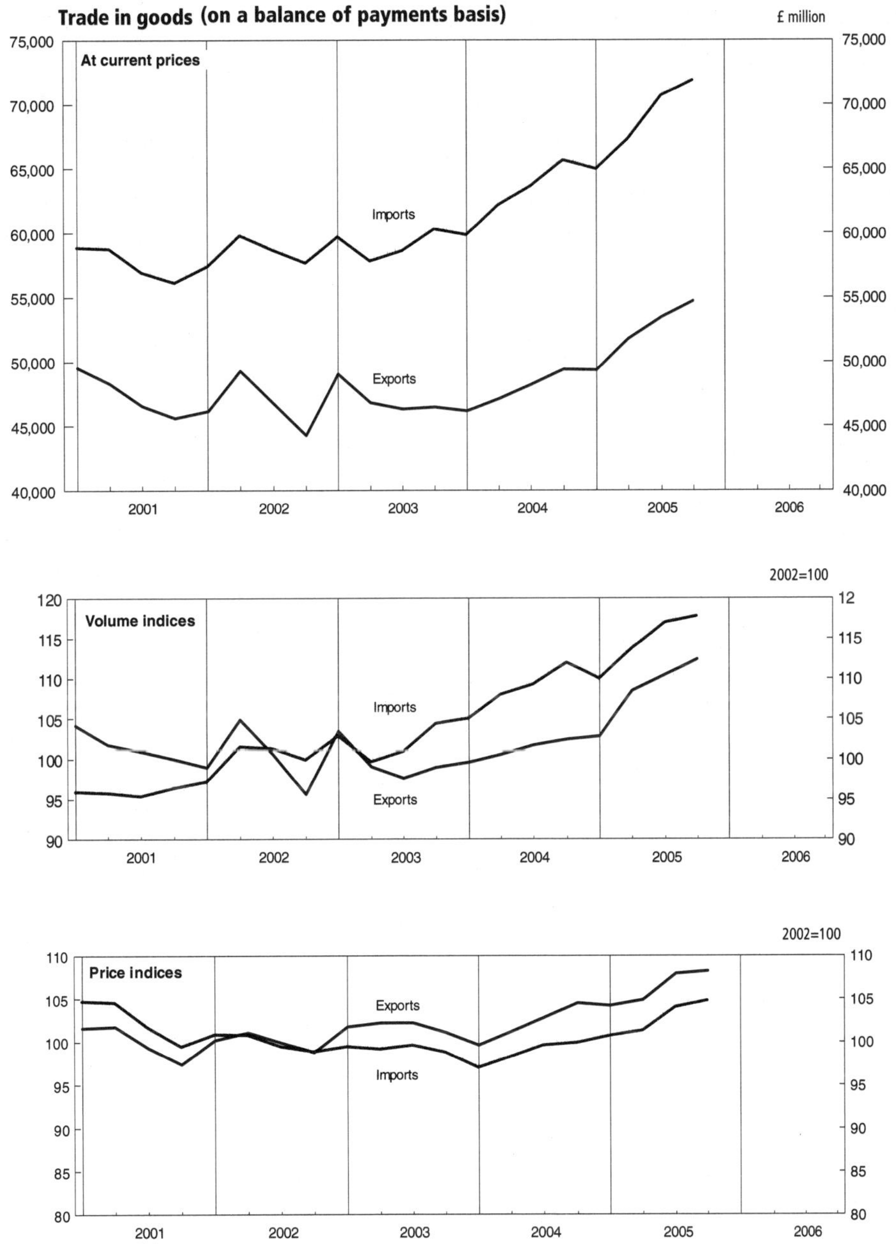

2.15 Measures of UK competitiveness in trade in manufactures

1995=100

	Summary measures						Export unit value index[1,6]				
	Relative export prices[6]	Relative wholesale prices[5] (1990=100)	IMF index of relative unit labour costs[6] Actual	IMF index of relative unit labour costs[6] Normalised	Import price competitiveness[2,4]	Relative profitability of exports[2,4]	United Kingdom	United States	Japan	France	Germany[3]
	CTPC	CTPD	CTPE	CTPF	BBKM	BBKN	CTPI	CTPJ	CTPK	CTPL	CTPM
1997	111.4	114.7	130.4	123.6	105.9	97.4	98.7	101.2	83.8	86.0	80.3
1998	111.4	..	141.2	131.5	109.2	95.8	97.7	101.2	78.1	86.0	80.5
1999	114.2	..	141.7	133.9	109.7	94.4	97.4	101.1	82.7	81.4	76.7
2000	118.2	..	147.8	141.6	106.9	93.7	94.9	102.3	86.5	71.3	66.7
2001	117.0	..	143.9	141.4	105.6	95.8	90.7	102.3	78.3	69.5	64.7
2002	..	..	..	..	109.0	96.0	..	..	..	..	..
2000 Q1	119.4	..	149.4	142.1	108.7	92.0	99.3	102.1	86.2	76.0	71.5
Q2	118.2	..	148.9	141.2	108.6	93.2	95.8	102.5	86.2	72.1	67.5
Q3	116.7	..	146.2	140.2	107.0	94.6	93.0	102.6	87.2	70.1	65.4
Q4	117.9	..	146.8	142.7	105.4	94.9	91.4	102.3	86.5	67.6	62.8
2001 Q1	115.5	..	142.2	138.8	105.0	95.3	92.6	102.0	84.4	72.2	66.7
Q2	117.4	..	144.3	141.9	104.8	95.5	90.7	101.9	82.4	68.5	63.0
Q3	117.6	..	144.2	142.1	107.1	95.6	92.3	101.8	84.2	70.1	64.2
Q4	117.7	..	144.8	142.7	108.0	94.8	92.9	101.7	84.2	70.8	64.7
2002 Q1	..	..	..	..	109.2	95.9	..	..	..	..	..
Q2	..	..	..	..	109.4	96.8	..	..	..	..	..
Q3	..	..	..	..	108.0	95.7	..	..	..	..	..
Q4	..	..	..	..	109.3	94.6	..	..	..	..	..
2003 Q1	..	..	..	..	109.4	96.7	..	..	..	..	..
Percentage change, quarter on corresponding quarter of previous year											
2001 Q2	*–0.7*	..	*–3.1*	*0.5*	*–3.5*	*2.5*	*–5.3*	*–0.6*	*–4.4*	*–5.0*	*–6.7*
Q3	*0.8*	..	*–1.4*	*1.4*	*0.1*	*1.1*	*–0.8*	*–0.8*	*–3.4*	*0.0*	*–1.8*
Q4	*–0.2*	..	*–1.4*	*0.0*	*2.5*	*–0.1*	*1.6*	*–0.6*	*–2.7*	*4.7*	*3.0*
2002 Q1	..	..	..	..	*4.0*	*0.6*	..	..	..	..	..
Q2	..	..	..	..	*4.4*	*1.4*	..	..	..	..	..
Q3	..	..	..	..	*0.8*	*0.1*	..	..	..	..	..
Q4	..	..	..	..	*1.2*	*–0.2*	..	..	..	..	..
2003 Q1	..	..	..	..	*0.2*	*0.8*	..	..	..	..	..

	Wholesale price index[1] (1990=100)					Unit labour costs index[1,6]				
	United Kingdom	United States	Japan	France	Germany[3]	United Kingdom	United States	Japan	France	Germany[3]
	CTPN	CTPO	CTPP	CTPQ	CTPR	CTPS	CTPT	CTPU	CTPV	CTPW
1998	116.5	106.8	102.7	..	..	118.6	95.6	70.5	82.8	77.1
1999	115.1	108.4	114.1	..	..	116.2	95.1	77.9	79.3	73.7
2000	..	..	..	..	..	108.0	94.9	77.5	68.2	61.6
2001	..	..	..	..	..	103.3	100.8	71.1	66.4	59.5
1999 Q4	116.8	109.7	123.4	..	..	116.8	94.6	82.2	77.1	70.5
2000 Q1	..	..	..	..	..	115.6	94.0	81.3	73.1	67.2
Q2	..	..	..	..	..	109.8	94.1	78.8	69.0	62.9
Q3	..	..	..	..	..	104.6	94.9	76.1	66.8	59.5
Q4	..	..	..	..	..	102.2	96.5	74.0	64.3	57.5
2001 Q1	..	..	..	..	..	104.3	99.2	72.5	68.5	61.5
Q2	..	..	..	..	..	101.6	100.8	70.7	64.8	58.0
Q3	..	..	..	..	..	103.2	101.4	71.3	66.1	59.1
Q4	..	..	..	..	..	104.2	101.7	70.1	66.4	59.5
Percentage change, quarter on corresponding quarter of previous year										
1999 Q4	*–0.6*	*2.7*	*12.2*	..	..	*–3.6*	*–1.0*	*5.8*	*–12.0*	*–15.3*
2000 Q1	..	..	..	..	..	*–2.3*	*–1.1*	*3.4*	*–12.6*	*–14.8*
Q2	..	..	..	..	..	*–5.3*	*–1.3*	*5.8*	*–12.3*	*–17.2*
Q3	..	..	..	..	..	*–8.3*	*–0.7*	*–0.8*	*–14.4*	*–16.8*
Q4	..	..	..	..	..	*–12.5*	*2.0*	*–10.0*	*–16.6*	*–18.4*
2001 Q1	..	..	..	..	..	*–9.8*	*5.5*	*–10.8*	*–6.3*	*–8.5*
Q2	..	..	..	..	..	*–7.5*	*7.1*	*–10.3*	*–6.1*	*–7.8*
Q3	..	..	..	..	..	*–1.3*	*6.8*	*–6.3*	*–1.0*	*–0.7*
Q4	..	..	..	..	..	*2.0*	*5.4*	*–5.3*	*3.3*	*3.5*

1 All the indices are based on data expressed in US dollars.
2 Excludes erratics (ships, North sea installations, aircraft, precious stones and silver bullion).
3 Includes the former German Democratic Republic as from 1991 Q1.
4 These series are on a SIC 92 basis.
5 This series is calculated using UK producer prices. All other country indices are wholesale price indices.
6 Quarterly data have been obtained by interpolating the annuals.

Sources: International Monetary Fund; Office for National Statistics; Enquiries 020 7533 5914

Measures of UK trade competitiveness

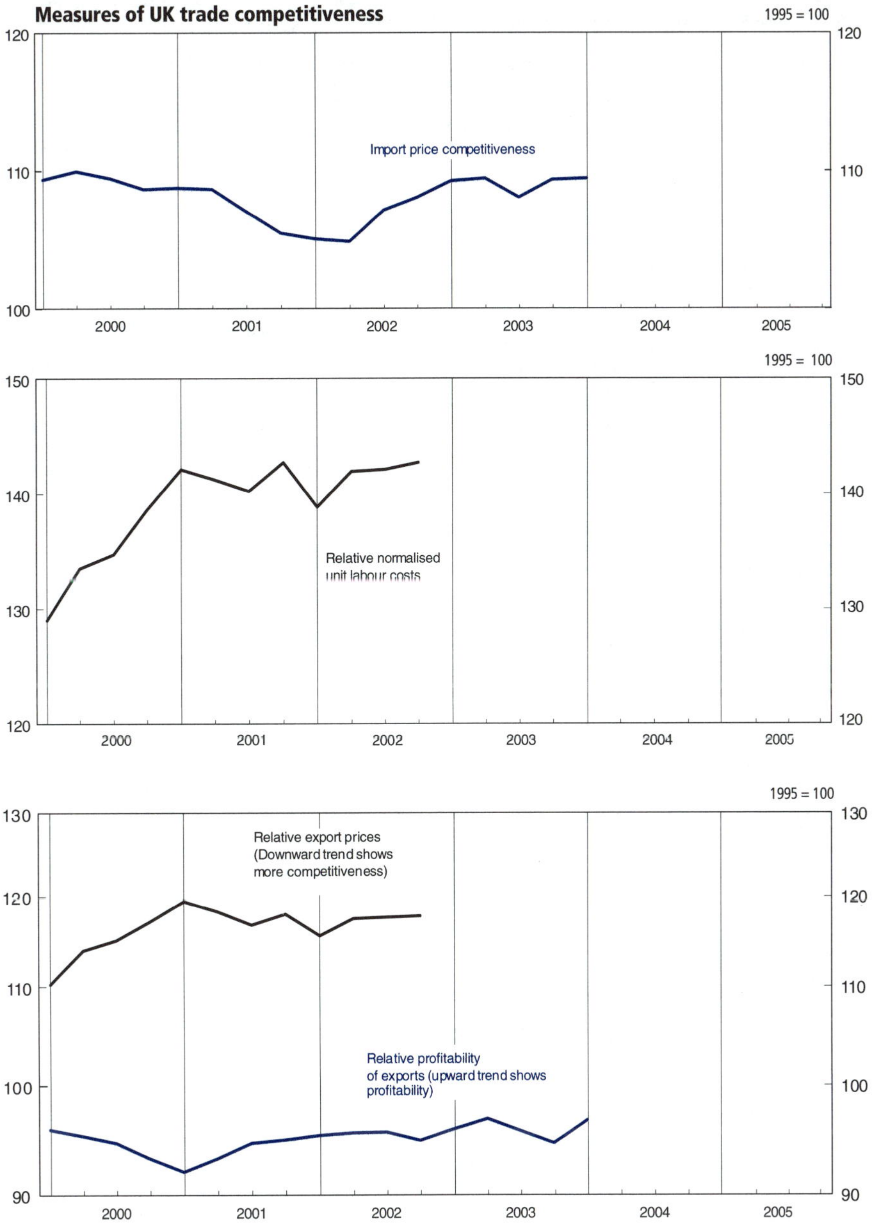

3.1 Prices

Not seasonally adjusted except series RNPE

	Producer price index (2000=100)		Consumer prices index[2,3] (2005=100)		Retail prices index (13 January 1987=100)						Pensioner price index[5] (13 January 1987=100)		
			All items		All items (RPI)		All items excluding mortgage interest payments (RPIX)		All items excluding mortgage interest payments and indirect taxes (RPIY)[4]				
	Materials and fuel purchased by manufacturing industry (SA)[1]	Output: all manufactured products: home sales	Index	Percentage change on a year earlier	Index	Percentage change on a year earlier	Index	Percentage change on a year earlier	Index	Percentage change on a year earlier	One-person household	Two-person household	Purchasing power of the pound[6] (NSA) (1985=100)
	RNPE	PLLU	D7BT	D7G7	CHAW	CZBH	CHMK	CDKQ	CBZW	CBZX	CZIF	CZIU	FJAK
2001	98.8	99.7	94.2	*1.2*	173.3	*1.8*	171.3	*2.1*	163.7	*2.4*	152.7	158.5	55
2002	94.4	99.8	95.4	*1.3*	176.2	*1.7*	175.1	*2.2*	167.5	*2.3*	155.3	160.9	54
2003	95.7	101.3	96.7	*1.4*	181.3	*2.9*	180.0	*2.8*	172.0	*2.7*	158.1	163.8	52
2004	99.4	103.8	98.0	*1.3*	186.7	*3.0*	184.0	*2.2*	175.5	*2.0*	160.9	166.4	51
2005	111.2†	106.7	100.0	*2.1*	192.0	*2.8*	188.2	*2.3*	179.4	*2.2*	165.1	170.0	49
2001 Q1	100.9	99.7	93.1	*0.9*	171.8	*2.6*	168.9	*1.9*	161.1	*1.6*	150.6	156.5	55
Q2	101.8	100.1	94.5	*1.5*	173.9	*1.9*	171.8	*2.3*	164.1	*2.6*	153.3	159.3	54
Q3	98.2	99.8	94.5	*1.5*	174.0	*1.8*	172.1	*2.4*	164.6	*2.8*	153.0	158.9	54
Q4	94.2	99.3	94.6	*1.0*	173.8	*1.0*	172.4	*2.0*	165.0	*2.4*	153.9	159.3	55
2002 Q1	94.2	99.2	94.6	*1.5*	173.9	*1.2*	172.9	*2.4*	165.5	*2.7*	154.7	160.1	54
Q2	95.2	99.8	95.4	*0.9*	176.0	*1.2*	175.0	*1.9*	167.1	*1.8*	155.3	161.0	54
Q3	94.2	99.9	95.5	*1.0*	176.6	*1.5*	175.5	*2.0*	167.8	*1.9*	155.0	160.7	54
Q4	93.9	100.1	96.0	*1.5*	178.2	*2.5*	176.9	*2.6*	169.5	*2.7*	156.1	161.7	53
2003 Q1	95.9	100.9	96.0	*1.5*	179.2	*3.0*	177.9	*2.9*	170.6	*3.1*	156.7	162.6	53
Q2	94.8	101.1	96.6	*1.3*	181.3	*3.0*	180.1	*2.9*	171.8	*2.8*	157.9	163.7	52
Q3	95.4	101.3	96.8	*1.4*	181.8	*2.9*	180.5	*2.8*	172.3	*2.7*	158.3	164.0	52
Q4	96.7	101.7	97.3	*1.3*	182.9	*2.6*	181.5	*2.6*	173.2	*2.2*	159.4	165.0	52
2004 Q1	95.7	102.4	97.2	*1.3*	183.8	*2.6*	182.0	*2.3*	173.8	*1.9*	159.7	165.4	51
Q2	98.6	103.4	98.0	*1.4*	186.3	*2.8*	184.0	*2.2*	175.4	*2.1*	160.9	166.6	51
Q3	100.5	104.2	98.0	*1.3*	187.4	*3.1*	184.3	*2.1*	175.6	*1.9*	160.5	166.1	50
Q4	102.9	105.1	98.7	*1.4*	189.2	*3.4*	185.6	*2.3*	177.1	*2.3*	162.3	167.6	50
2005 Q1	105.8	105.2	98.9	*1.7*	189.7	*3.2*	186.0	*2.2*	177.5	*2.1*	163.4	168.3	50
Q2	108.4	106.3	99.9	*2.0*	191.9	*3.0*	188.1	*2.2*	179.3	*2.2*	164.8	169.8	49
Q3	113.5r†	107.4	100.4	*2.4*	192.6	*2.8*	188.7	*2.4*	179.9	*2.4*	165.1	170.1	49
Q4	117.0p	107.6p	100.8	*2.1*	193.7	*2.4*	189.8	*2.3*	181.0	*2.2*	167.1	171.7	49
2004 Jan	95.6	102.1	97.0	*1.4*	183.1	*2.6*	181.4	*2.4*	173.2	*2.0*	..	..	52
Feb	94.9	102.3	97.2	*1.3*	183.8	*2.5*	182.0	*2.3*	173.9	*1.9*	..	..	51
Mar	96.6	102.8	97.4	*1.1*	184.6	*2.6*	182.5	*2.1*	174.3	*1.7*	..	..	51
Apr	97.6	103.1	97.8	*1.1*	185.7	*2.5*	183.6	*2.0*	174.9	*1.8*	..	..	51
May	99.9	103.5	98.1	*1.5*	186.5	*2.8*	184.3	*2.3*	175.6	*2.2*	..	..	51
Jun	98.4	103.6	98.1	*1.6*	186.8	*3.0*	184.2	*2.3*	175.6	*2.3*	..	..	51
Jul	99.1	103.8	97.8	*1.4*	186.8	*3.0*	183.8	*2.2*	175.1	*2.0*	..	..	51
Aug	100.2	104.2	98.1	*1.3*	187.4	*3.2*	184.3	*2.2*	175.7	*2.0*	..	..	50
Sep	102.3	104.5	98.2	*1.1*	188.1	*3.1*	184.7	*1.9*	176.1	*1.7*	..	..	50
Oct	105.0	105.2	98.4	*1.2*	188.6	*3.3*	185.1	*2.1*	176.6	*2.0*	..	..	50
Nov	103.0	105.3	98.6	*1.5*	189.0	*3.4*	185.4	*2.2*	176.9	*2.2*	..	..	50
Dec	100.6	104.9	99.1	*1.7*	189.9	*3.5*	186.4	*2.5*	177.9	*2.5*	..	..	50
2005 Jan	105.0	104.8	98.6	*1.6*	188.9	*3.2*	185.2	*2.1*	176.7	*2.0*	..	..	50
Feb	105.3	105.1	98.8	*1.7*	189.6	*3.2*	185.9	*2.1*	177.4	*2.0*	..	..	50
Mar	107.2	105.8	99.3	*1.9*	190.5	*3.2*	186.8	*2.4*	178.3	*2.3*	..	..	50
Apr	107.6	106.5	99.7	*1.9*	191.6	*3.2*	187.8	*2.3*	179.0	*2.3*	..	..	49
May	107.5	106.3	100.0	*1.9*	192.0	*2.9*	188.2	*2.1*	179.4	*2.2*	..	..	49
Jun	110.1	106.2	100.0	*2.0*	192.2	*2.9*	188.3	*2.2*	179.5	*2.2*	..	..	49
Jul	113.4	107.0	100.1	*2.3*	192.2	*2.9*	188.3	*2.4*	179.5	*2.5*	..	..	49
Aug	113.5	107.3	100.4	*2.4*	192.6	*2.8*	188.6	*2.3*	179.8	*2.3*	..	..	49
Sep	113.5r†	108.0	100.6	*2.5*	193.1	*2.7*	189.3	*2.5*	180.5	*2.5*	..	..	49
Oct	114.9	107.9	100.7	*2.3*	193.3	*2.5*	189.5	*2.4*	180.7	*2.3*	..	..	49
Nov	117.2	107.6	100.7	*2.1*	193.6	*2.4*	189.7	*2.3*	180.9	*2.3*	..	..	49
Dec	119.0p	107.4p	101.0	*1.9*	194.1	*2.2*	190.2	*2.0*	181.5	*2.0*	..	..	49
2006 Jan	121.2p	107.8p	100.5	*1.9*	193.4	*2.4*	189.4	*2.3*	180.7	*2.3*	..	..	49

Note: Figures marked with a 'p' are provisional.

1 Includes the Climate Change Levy introduced in April 2001 and the Aggregates Levy introduced in April 2002.

2 Rebased from 1996=100 with effect from the January 2006 CPI release. Inflation rates prior to 1997 and index levels prior to 1996 are estimated. Further details are given in *Economic Trends* No.541 December 1998.

3 Prior to 10 December 2003, the consumer prices index (CPI) was published in the UK as the harmonised index of consumer prices (HICP).

4 The taxes excluded are council tax, VAT, duties, vehicle excise duty, insurance tax and airport passenger duty.

5 Pensioner price indices exclude housing costs, as these are often atypical for a pensioner household, based on RPI.

6 Movements in the purchasing power of the pound are based on movements in the retail prices index.

Sources: Office for National Statistics;
Enquiries Columns 1-2 01633 812106; Columns 3-13 020 7533 5853.

Prices

1987 = 100 not seasonally adjusted
percentage change on a year earlier

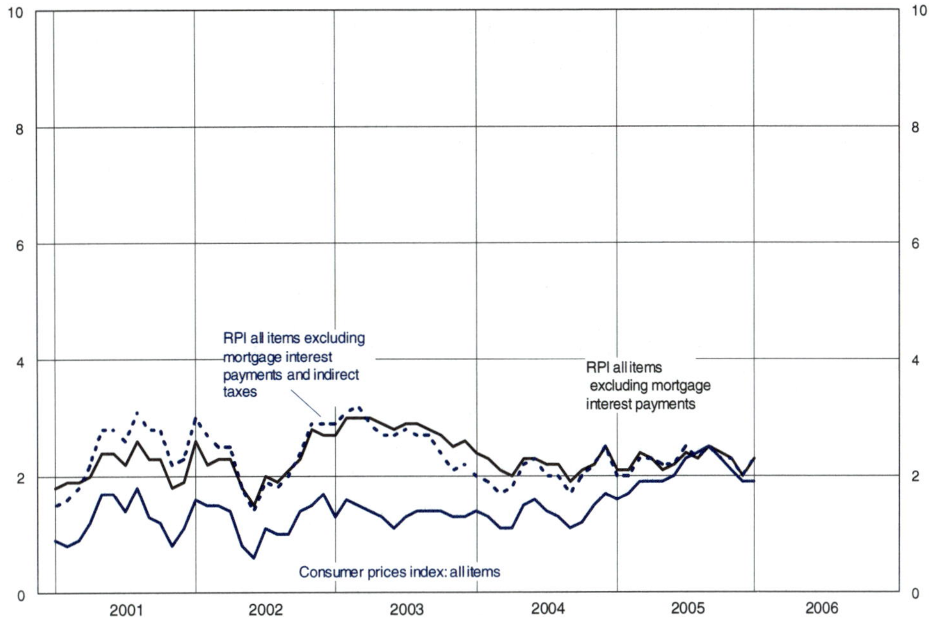

Not seasonally adjusted
percentage change on a year earlier

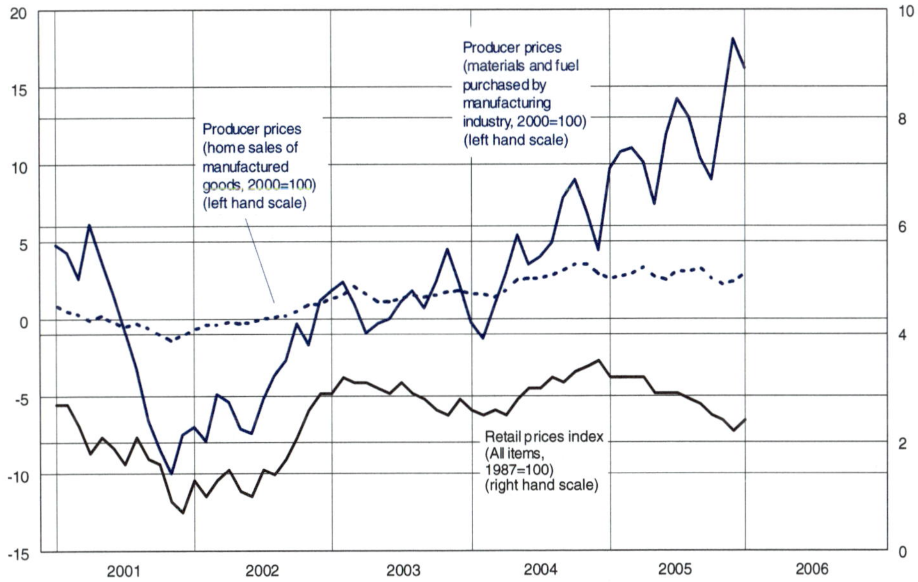

4.1 Labour market activity[1]

United Kingdom

Thousands, seasonally adjusted[2]

	Employment categories									
	Employees	Self-employed	Unpaid family workers	Government training and employment programmes	Total in employment	Unemployed	Total economically active	Economically inactive	Total aged 16 and over	Employment rate: age 16-59/64[3]
Total										
	MGRN	MGRQ	MGRT	MGRW	MGRZ	MGSC	MGSF	MGSI	MGSL	MGSU
2002 Q1	24 247	3 321	97	112	27 777	1 511	29 288	17 369	46 657	74.3
Q2	24 365	3 336	97	106	27 905	1 515	29 420	17 306	46 727	74.5
Q3	24 366	3 355	94	97	27 912	1 561	29 473	17 325	46 798	74.4
Q4	24 521	3 363	94	96	28 074	1 514	29 588	17 284	46 872	74.7
2003 Q1	24 452	3 435	83	94	28 065	1 524	29 588	17 358	46 946	74.6
Q2	24 456	3 555	88	93	28 191	1 463	29 654	17 366	47 020	74.8
Q3	24 360	3 647	108	107	28 222	1 499	29 721	17 377	47 098	74.6
Q4	24 388	3 659	99	108	28 254	1 458	29 712	17 470	47 183	74.6
2004 Q1	24 550	3 628	103	116	28 398	1 432	29 830	17 438	47 268	74.8
Q2	24 518	3 670	98	125	28 410	1 434	29 844	17 509	47 352	74.7
Q3	24 662	3 586	91	128	28 467	1 392	29 859	17 585	47 444	74.7
Q4	24 720	3 644	97	126	28 586	1 418	30 004	17 546	47 550	74.9
2005 Q1	24 819	3 630	104	126	28 679	1 409	30 087	17 569	47 656	74.9
Q2	24 860	3 621	101	116	28 698	1 435	30 132	17 629	47 762	74.7
Q3	24 965	3 660	93	107	28 825	1 434	30 259	17 605	47 863	74.9
Q4	24 869	3 700	90	109	28 769	1 541	30 310	17 647	47 957	74.5
Males										
	MGRO	MGRR	MGRU	MGRX	MGSA	MGSD	MGSG	MGSJ	MGSM	MGSV
2002 Q1	12 467	2 449	30	70	15 016	919	15 935	6 587	22 522	78.9
Q2	12 535	2 442	31	61	15 068	910	15 978	6 586	22 564	79.0
Q3	12 517	2 457	36	60	15 070	945	16 015	6 591	22 606	78.9
Q4	12 671	2 460	34	61	15 226	891	16 117	6 533	22 650	79.5
2003 Q1	12 594	2 505	26	56	15 181	926	16 107	6 586	22 694	79.1
Q2	12 602	2 604	32	53	15 291	886	16 177	6 560	22 738	79.5
Q3	12 512	2 672	41	61	15 285	896	16 180	6 602	22 783	79.3
Q4	12 482	2 680	38	60	15 261	879	16 140	6 691	22 830	79.0
2004 Q1	12 581	2 657	42	68	15 348	841	16 190	6 688	22 878	79.4
Q2	12 544	2 695	41	73	15 353	841	16 195	6 731	22 926	79.2
Q3	12 630	2 653	35	75	15 393	815	16 208	6 769	22 977	79.3
Q4	12 651	2 686	37	75	15 450	834	16 284	6 753	23 037	79.3
2005 Q1	12 709	2 668	41	70	15 488	830	16 318	6 778	23 096	79.3
Q2	12 710	2 662	38	71	15 481	834	16 316	6 839	23 155	79.1
Q3	12 751	2 678	34	63	15 526	849	16 376	6 837	23 213	79.1
Q4	12 721	2 718	30	62	15 531	910	16 441	6 825	23 266	78.8
Females										
	MGRP	MGRS	MGRV	MGRY	MGSB	MGSE	MGSH	MGSK	MGSN	MGSW
2002 Q1	11 780	872	66	42	12 760	593	13 353	10 782	24 135	69.4
Q2	11 831	895	65	45	12 837	606	13 443	10 720	24 163	69.7
Q3	11 850	898	58	37	12 843	615	13 458	10 734	24 192	69.7
Q4	11 850	903	60	35	12 848	623	13 471	10 751	24 222	69.6
2003 Q1	11 858	930	57	38	12 883	598	13 481	10 771	24 252	69.7
Q2	11 853	951	56	40	12 900	578	13 477	10 805	24 283	69.7
Q3	11 848	975	67	46	12 937	603	13 541	10 775	24 315	69.7
Q4	11 906	979	61	47	12 993	579	13 572	10 780	24 352	69.8
2004 Q1	11 969	971	61	48	13 049	591	13 640	10 749	24 390	70.0
Q2	11 974	975	57	52	13 057	592	13 649	10 778	24 427	69.8
Q3	12 033	933	55	53	13 074	577	13 651	10 816	24 467	69.9
Q4	12 068	959	59	50	13 136	584	13 721	10 793	24 514	70.1
2005 Q1	12 110	962	63	55	13 191	579	13 769	10 791	24 560	70.1
Q2	12 150	959	63	44	13 216	600	13 817	10 790	24 606	70.1
Q3	12 214	982	59	44	13 299	584	13 883	10 768	24 651	70.4
Q4	12 148	982	60	48	13 238	632	13 869	10 822	24 691	69.8

1 Data are from the Labour Force Survey which uses the definitions recommended by the International Labour Organisation (ILO), an agency of the United Nations. For details see the *Guide to Labour Market Statistics Releases.*

2 Seasonally adjusted estimates are revised in September each year.

3 The employment rate equals those in employment aged 16-64 (male) and 16-59 (female), as a percentage of all in these age groups. The underlying data are available on request.

Source: Office for National Statistics; Enquiries 020 7533 6094

4.2 Labour market activity[1]

United Kingdom

Thousands, not seasonally adjusted

	Employment categories									
	Employees	Self-employed	Unpaid family workers	Government training and employment programmes	Total in employment	Unemployed	Total economically active	Economically inactive	Total aged 16 and over	Employment rate: age 16-59/64[2]
Total										
	MGTA	MGTD	MGTG	MGTJ	MGTM	MGTP	MGTS	MGTV	MGSL	MGUH
2002 Q1	24 146	3 315	95	117	27 672	1 517	29 189	17 468	46 657	74.0
Q2	24 321	3 326	95	105	27 847	1 468	29 315	17 411	46 727	74.4
Q3	24 458	3 377	97	90	28 022	1 633	29 656	17 142	46 798	74.7
Q4	24 576	3 363	95	99	28 133	1 476	29 609	17 263	46 872	74.9
2003 Q1	24 363	3 426	83	99	27 971	1 525	29 497	17 450	46 946	74.3
Q2	24 412	3 545	86	91	28 134	1 416	29 550	17 470	47 020	74.6
Q3	24 441	3 670	110	101	28 321	1 572	29 892	17 202	47 098	74.9
Q4	24 433	3 660	100	110	28 303	1 422	29 724	17 445	47 183	74.7
2004 Q1	24 463	3 615	104	121	28 302	1 429	29 731	17 513	47 268	74.6
Q2	24 454	3 659	96	121	28 330	1 387	29 717	17 601	47 352	74.5
Q3	24 741	3 607	91	123	28 562	1 466	30 029	17 416	47 444	75.0
Q4	24 768	3 649	97	128	28 642	1 383	30 025	17 525	47 550	75.0
2005 Q1	24 752	3 616	106	130	28 604	1 405	30 009	17 647	47 656	74.6
Q2	24 809	3 613	98	112	28 633	1 392	30 025	17 737	47 762	74.5
Q3	25 041	3 686	92	102	28 920	1 509	30 429	17 434	47 863	75.2
Q4	24 891	3 715	89	111	28 807	1 525	30 332	17 625	47 957	74.6
Males										
	MGTB	MGTE	MGTH	MGTK	MGTN	MGTQ	MGTT	MGTW	MGSM	MGUI
2002 Q1	12 388	2 446	31	73	14 938	932	15 870	6 652	22 522	78.5
Q2	12 508	2 431	30	60	15 030	888	15 918	6 646	22 564	78.8
Q3	12 598	2 470	36	57	15 161	971	16 132	6 475	22 606	79.4
Q4	12 696	2 467	34	63	15 260	867	16 127	6 523	22 650	79.7
2003 Q1	12 521	2 499	27	59	15 107	938	16 045	6 649	22 694	78.7
Q2	12 576	2 594	31	52	15 253	864	16 116	6 621	22 738	79.3
Q3	12 587	2 685	41	58	15 371	921	16 292	6 489	22 783	79.8
Q4	12 502	2 689	38	62	15 291	855	16 146	6 679	22 830	79.2
2004 Q1	12 511	2 647	44	70	15 273	851	16 124	6 745	22 878	79.0
Q2	12 510	2 684	40	71	15 305	819	16 124	6 789	22 926	79.0
Q3	12 704	2 667	35	73	15 478	842	16 320	6 657	22 977	79.7
Q4	12 672	2 697	37	77	15 483	811	16 294	6 742	23 037	79.5
2005 Q1	12 650	2 656	43	72	15 422	839	16 261	6 835	23 096	78.9
Q2	12 680	2 654	37	70	15 440	814	16 254	6 901	23 155	78.8
Q3	12 822	2 695	33	61	15 610	878	16 488	6 724	23 213	79.5
Q4	12 730	2 738	29	63	15 560	900	16 459	6 806	23 266	79.0
Females										
	MGTC	MGTF	MGTI	MGTL	MGTO	MGTR	MGTU	MGTX	MGSN	MGUJ
2002 Q1	11 758	869	64	44	12 735	585	13 319	10 816	24 135	69.2
Q2	11 813	895	65	45	12 818	579	13 397	10 766	24 163	69.6
Q3	11 860	907	60	33	12 862	662	13 524	10 668	24 192	69.8
Q4	11 880	896	61	36	12 873	609	13 482	10 740	24 222	69.8
2003 Q1	11 843	927	55	40	12 865	587	13 452	10 801	24 252	69.6
Q2	11 836	952	55	39	12 881	552	13 434	10 849	24 283	69.6
Q3	11 854	984	69	43	12 950	650	13 600	10 713	24 315	69.7
Q4	11 930	971	62	48	13 011	567	13 578	10 766	24 352	70.0
2004 Q1	11 952	967	60	51	13 029	578	13 608	10 767	24 390	69.9
Q2	11 945	975	56	50	13 025	568	13 593	10 812	24 427	69.7
Q3	12 037	941	56	50	13 084	624	13 708	10 759	24 467	70.0
Q4	12 096	952	60	51	13 159	571	13 730	10 783	24 514	70.2
2005 Q1	12 102	960	62	58	13 183	565	13 748	10 812	24 560	70.0
Q2	12 129	960	62	42	13 193	578	13 771	10 835	24 606	69.9
Q3	12 219	991	59	41	13 310	631	13 941	10 710	24 651	70.5
Q4	12 160	978	60	49	13 247	625	13 872	10 819	24 691	69.9

1 Data are from the Labour Force Survey which uses the definitions recommended by the International Labour Organisation (ILO), an agency of the United Nations. For details see the *Guide to Labour Market Statistics Releases.*

2 The employment rate equals those in employment aged 16-64 (male) and 16-59 (female), as a percentage of all in these age groups. The underlying data are available on request.

Source: Office for National Statistics; Enquiries 020 7533 6094

Employment, not seasonally adjusted:
United Kingdom, population aged 16 and over

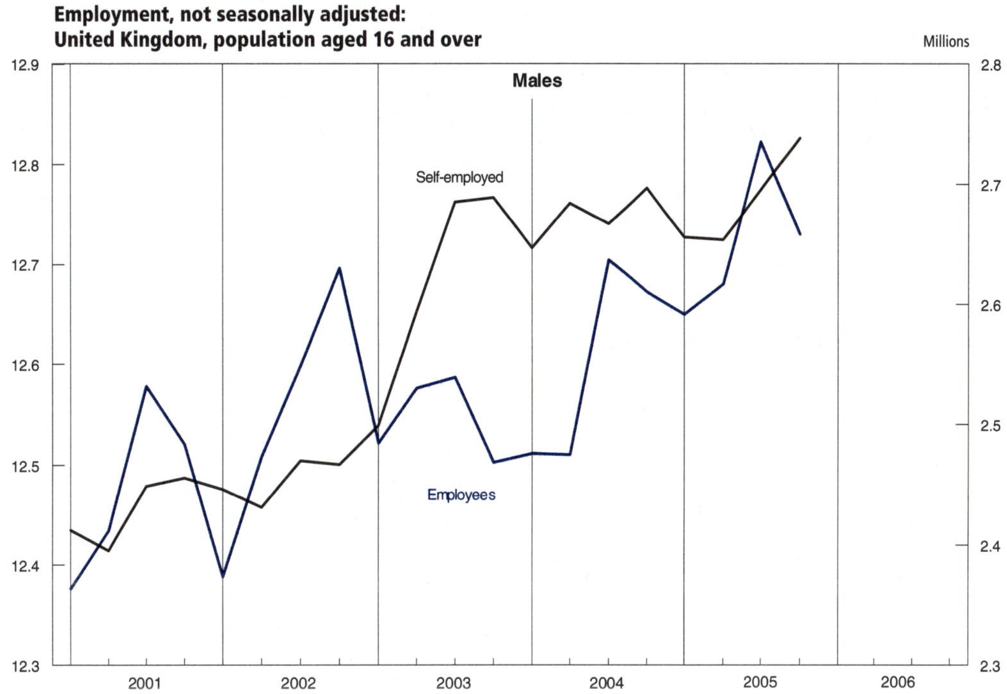

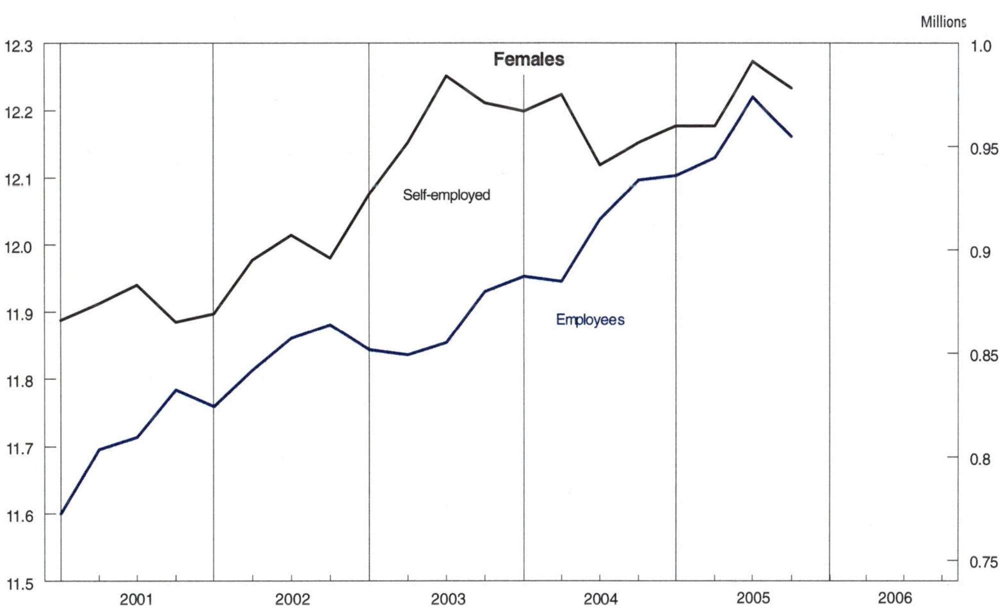

Economically active population *(seasonally adjusted)*

Quarter on previous quarter percentage change

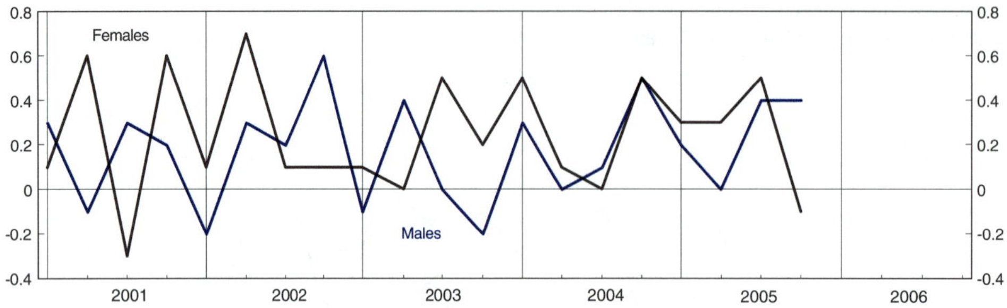

Economic activity rate *(seasonally adjusted)*

Quarter on previous quarter percentage change

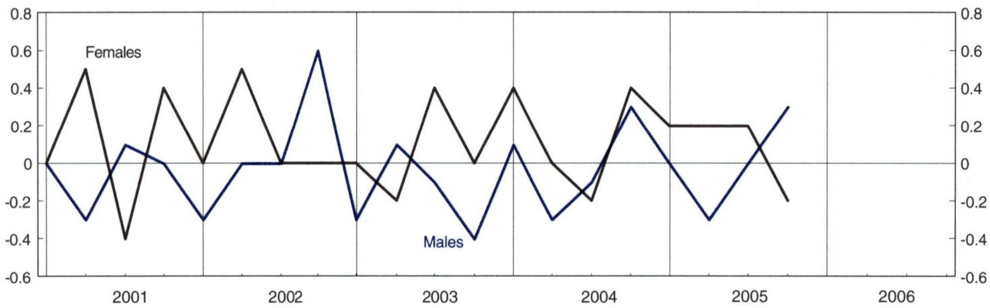

Unemployment *(seasonally adjusted)*

Quarter on previous quarter percentage change

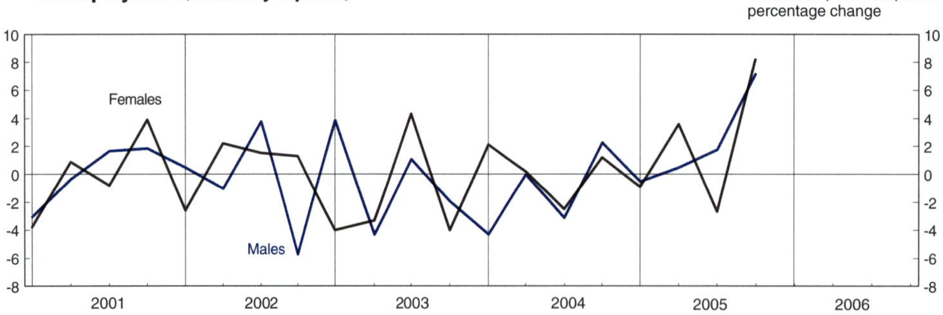

Economically inactive population *(seasonally adjusted)*

Quarter on previous quarter percentage change

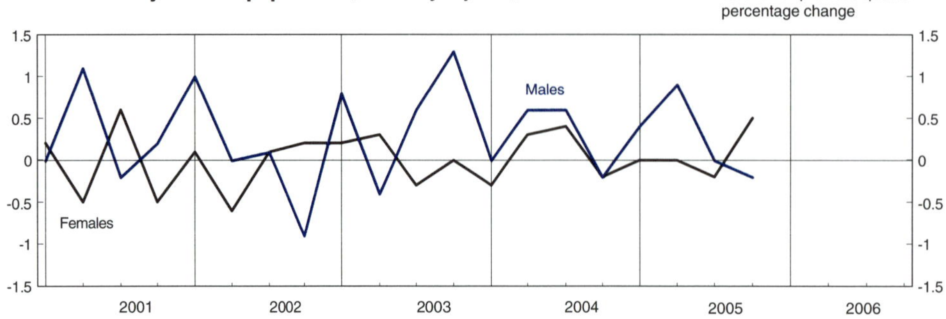

Employees ***(seasonally adjusted)***

Quarter on previous quarter percentage change

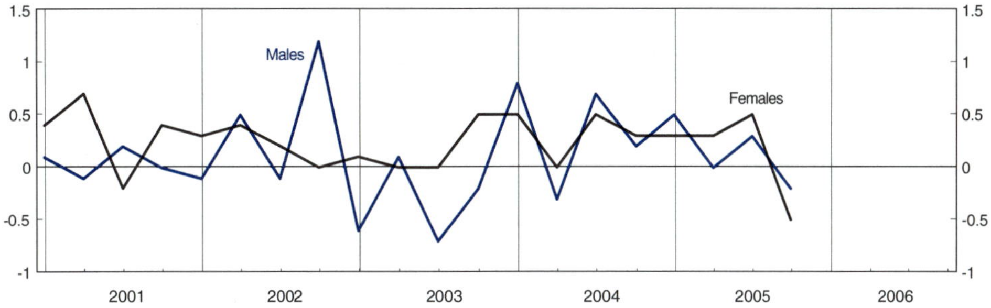

Self-employed ***(seasonally adjusted)***

Quarter on previous quarter percentage change

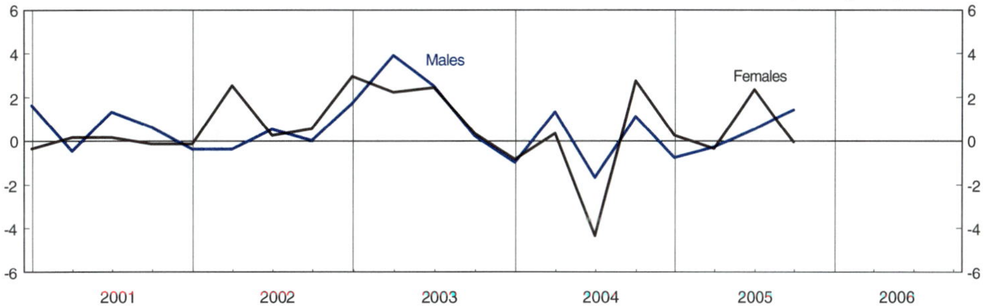

Unemployment Rate ***(seasonally adjusted)***

Percentage

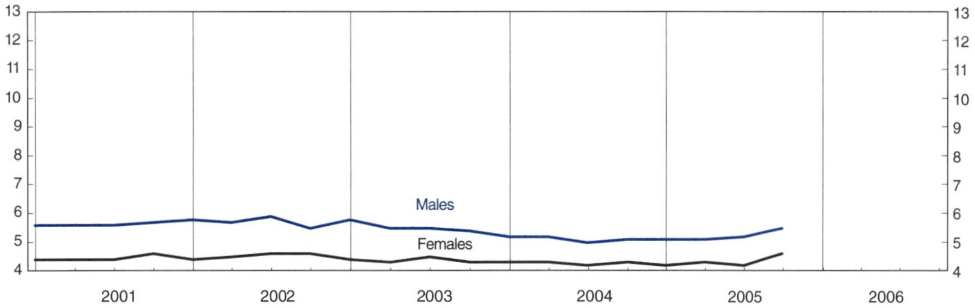

Total employment ***(seasonally adjusted)***

Quarter on previous quarter percentage change

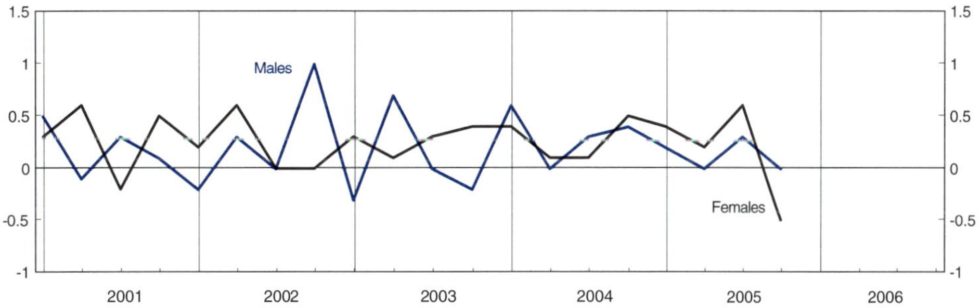

4.3 Labour market activity by age[1]

United Kingdom

Thousands, seasonally adjusted[2]

	Total aged 16 and over			Age groups[3]							
				16-24		25-49		50-59/64		60/65 and over	
	Total	Males	Females	Males	Females	Males	Females	Males	Females	Males	Females
In employment											
	MGRZ	MGSA	MGSB	MGUR	MGUS	MGUU	MGUV	MGUX	MGUY	MGVA	MGVB
2003 Q4	28 254	15 261	12 993	2 124	1 983	9 113	7 833	3 691	2 535	332	643
2004 Q1	28 398	15 348	13 049	2 151	2 011	9 149	7 828	3 714	2 558	334	651
Q2	28 410	15 353	13 057	2 166	1 978	9 127	7 856	3 721	2 554	340	669
Q3	28 467	15 393	13 074	2 157	1 987	9 161	7 872	3 736	2 561	338	653
Q4	28 586	15 450	13 136	2 156	1 994	9 189	7 889	3 759	2 588	345	666
2005 Q1	28 679	15 488	13 191	2 171	1 986	9 189	7 927	3 773	2 586	356	692
Q2	28 698	15 481	13 216	2 158	1 979	9 195	7 943	3 774	2 592	354	703
Q3	28 825	15 526	13 299	2 148	1 973	9 215	8 010	3 800	2 610	363	707
Q4	28 769	15 531	13 238	2 115	1 931	9 218	7 981	3 815	2 591	383	734
Unemployed											
	MGSC	MGSD	MGSE	MGVG	MGVH	MGVJ	MGVK	MGVM	MGVN	MGVP	MGVQ
2003 Q4	1 458	879	579	331	221	399	284	139	65	10	..
2004 Q1	1 432	841	591	329	233	370	285	133	64	10	..
Q2	1 434	841	592	328	246	368	281	136	56	..	..
Q3	1 392	815	577	342	248	332	262	133	59	..	..
Q4	1 418	834	584	350	248	343	269	131	60	11	..
2005 Q1	1 409	830	579	341	231	346	278	134	60	..	..
Q2	1 435	834	600	362	249	342	278	123	64	..	10
Q3	1 434	849	584	370	237	336	270	133	63	10	14
Q4	1 541	910	632	392	262	370	294	137	66	11	10
Economically inactive											
	MGSI	MGSJ	MGSK	MGVV	MGVW	MGVY	MGVZ	MGWB	MGWC	MGWE	MGWF
2003 Q4	17 470	6 691	10 780	932	1 119	832	2 446	1 325	1 206	3 602	6 008
2004 Q1	17 438	6 688	10 749	929	1 095	827	2 453	1 318	1 188	3 614	6 014
Q2	17 509	6 731	10 778	936	1 132	853	2 432	1 320	1 203	3 622	6 010
Q3	17 585	6 769	10 816	950	1 136	864	2 443	1 318	1 197	3 637	6 041
Q4	17 546	6 753	10 793	960	1 142	842	2 434	1 310	1 171	3 641	6 046
2005 Q1	17 569	6 778	10 791	971	1 180	856	2 401	1 306	1 176	3 645	6 034
Q2	17 629	6 839	10 790	979	1 182	871	2 400	1 327	1 168	3 661	6 040
Q3	17 605	6 837	10 768	997	1 211	872	2 354	1 305	1 154	3 663	6 049
Q4	17 647	6 825	10 822	1 021	1 237	847	2 370	1 304	1 173	3 652	6 042
Economic activity rate (per cent)[4]											
	MGWG	MGWH	MGWI	MGWK	MGWL	MGWN	MGWO	MGWQ	MGWR	MGWT	MGWU
2003 Q4	63.0	70.7	55.7	72.5	66.3	92.0	76.8	74.3	68.3	8.7	9.8
2004 Q1	63.1	70.8	55.9	72.7	67.2	92.0	76.8	74.5	68.8	8.7	9.9
Q2	63.0	70.6	55.9	72.7	66.3	91.8	77.0	74.5	68.4	8.8	10.1
Q3	62.9	70.5	55.8	72.5	66.3	91.7	76.9	74.6	68.6	8.7	9.9
Q4	63.1	70.7	56.0	72.3	66.2	91.9	77.0	74.8	69.3	8.9	10.0
2005 Q1	63.1	70.7	56.1	72.1	65.3	91.8	77.4	74.9	69.2	9.1	10.4
Q2	63.1	70.5	56.2	72.0	65.3	91.6	77.4	74.6	69.4	9.0	10.6
Q3	63.2	70.5	56.3	71.6	64.6	91.6	77.9	75.1	69.8	9.2	10.6
Q4	63.2	70.7	56.2	71.1	63.9	91.9	77.7	75.2	69.4	9.7	11.0
Unemployment rate (per cent)[5]											
	MGSX	MGSY	MGSZ	MGWZ	MGXA	MGXC	MGXD	MGXF	MGXG	MGXI	MGXJ
2003 Q4	4.9	5.4	4.3	13.5	10.0	4.2	3.5	3.6	2.5	3.0	..
2004 Q1	4.8	5.2	4.3	13.3	10.4	3.9	3.5	3.5	2.4	2.8	..
Q2	4.8	5.2	4.3	13.2	11.1	3.9	3.5	3.5	2.2	..	..
Q3	4.7	5.0	4.2	13.7	11.1	3.5	3.2	3.4	2.2	..	..
Q4	4.7	5.1	4.3	14.0	11.1	3.6	3.3	3.4	2.3	3.0	..
2005 Q1	4.7	5.1	4.2	13.6	10.4	3.6	3.4	3.4	2.3	..	..
Q2	4.8	5.1	4.3	14.4	11.2	3.6	3.4	3.2	2.4	..	1.3
Q3	4.7	5.2	4.2	14.7	10.7	3.5	3.3	3.4	2.4	2.7	1.9
Q4	5.1	5.5	4.6	15.6	11.9	3.9	3.6	3.5	2.5	2.8	1.4

1 Data are from the Labour Force Survey which uses the definitions recommended by the International Labour Organisation (ILO), an agency of the United Nations. For details see the *Guide to Labour Market Statistics Releases.*
2 Seasonally adjusted estimates are revised in September each year.
3 Data for more detailed age groups are published in *Labour Market Trends.*
4 The activity rate is the percentage of people in each age group who are economically active.
5 Unemployment rate is the percentage of economically active people who are unemployed on the ILO measure.

Source: Office for National Statistics; Enquiries 020 7533 6094

4.4 Jobs and claimant count
United Kingdom

Thousands

	Jobs[1]					Claimant count[5,6,7]			Vacancies: average for three months ending in month shown[9]
		Employee jobs[3,4]							
	Workforce jobs[2,3,4]	All industries	Manufacturing industries	Production industries	Service industries	Total	Percentage of workforce jobs and claimant count[8]	Total not seasonally adjusted	
	DYDC	BCAJ	YEJA	YEJF	YEID	BCJD	BCJE	BCJA	AP2Y
2002	29 985	26 107	3 599	3 800	20 904	946.7†	*3.1*	958.8	..
2003	30 283	26 175	3 411	3 598	21 202	933.3	*3.0*	945.9	..
2004	30 572	26 381	3 255	3 424	21 557	853.6	*2.7*	866.1	..
2005	30 810	26 650	3 132	3 293	21 916	861.1	*2.8*	874.4	..
2002 Q1	29 974	26 154	3 647	3 852	20 863	952.5	*3.1*	1 014.6	..
Q2	29 985	26 107	3 599	3 800	20 904	950.6	*3.1*	958.1	..
Q3	30 029	26 103	3 554	3 749	20 975	946.5	*3.1*	951.8	..
Q4	30 122	26 182	3 513	3 703	21 108	937.0	*3.0*	910.6	..
2003 Q1	30 168	26 133	3 465	3 652	21 115	939.0	*3.0*	1 001.1	..
Q2	30 283	26 175	3 411	3 598	21 202	945.3	*3.0*	954.3	..
Q3	30 384	26 172	3 365	3 546	21 232	934.6	*3.0*	939.0	..
Q4	30 489	26 284	3 325	3 500	21 397	914.2	*2.9*	889.2	..
2004 Q1	30 524	26 334	3 284	3 458	21 480	885.8	*2.8*	947.2	..
Q2	30 572	26 381	3 255	3 424	21 557	861.3	*2.8*	871.8	..
Q3	30 558	26 396	3 217	3 381	21 614	836.3	*2.7*	839.0	..
Q4	30 747	26 569	3 187	3 346	21 770	831.1	*2.7*	806.7	..
2005 Q1	30 832	26 663	3 168	3 328	21 866	820.9	*2.6*	879.8	..
Q2	30 810	26 650	3 132	3 293	21 916	853.8	*2.8*	865.9	..
Q3	30 819	26 642	3 106	3 267	21 915	870.0	*2.8*	874.4	..
Q4	..	..	3 085	3 248	..	899.9†	*2.9*	877.6	..
2004 Jan	..	..	3 308	3 484	..	893.2	*2.9*	952.4	608.3
Feb	..	..	3 297	3 472	..	884.2	*2.8*	957.0	611.2
Mar	..	26 334	3 284	3 458	21 480	879.9	*2.8*	932.0	616.4
Apr	..	..	3 272	3 444	..	871.5	*2.8*	905.2	623.3
May	..	..	3 263	3 434	..	860.9	*2.8*	869.7	628.4
Jun	..	26 381	3 255	3 424	21 557	851.5	*2.7*	840.5	632.6
Jul	..	..	3 246	3 412	..	838.2	*2.7*	841.5	646.5
Aug	..	..	3 232	3 398	..	834.8	*2.7*	847.6	647.2
Sep	..	26 396	3 217	3 381	21 614	836.0	*2.7*	827.8	643.2
Oct	..	..	3 205	3 368	..	836.4	*2.7*	806.8	638.4
Nov	..	..	3 194	3 356	..	831.9	*2.7*	803.0	641.7
Dec	..	26 569	3 187	3 346	21 770	825.0	*2.6*	810.2	646.9
2005 Jan	..	..	3 182	3 343	..	813.8	*2.6*	872.1	651.0†
Feb	..	..	3 174	3 334	..	817.7	*2.6*	885.0	647.4
Mar	..	26 663	3 168	3 328	21 866	831.3	*2.7*	882.3	636.9
Apr	..	..	3 160	3 319	..	842.1	*2.7*	871.8	632.9
May	..	..	3 145	3 304	..	856.1	*2.7*	867.6	639.1
Jun	..	26 650	3 132	3 293	21 916	863.2	*2.8*	858.2	640.9
Jul	..	..	3 118	3 279	..	864.6	*2.8*	871.0	635.8
Aug	..	..	3 109	3 270	..	867.3	*2.8*	880.7	625.4
Sep	..	26 642	3 106	3 267	21 915	878.0	*2.8*	871.5	619.2
Oct	..	..	3 094	3 256	..	891.5	*2.9*	864.8	604.7
Nov	..	..	3 089	3 251	..	901.9	*2.9*	875.3	601.3
Dec	..	..	3 085	3 248	..	906.2†	*2.9*	892.7	605.8
2006 Jan	..	..	..	..	..	904.2	*2.9*	955.3	616.8

1 Estimates of employee jobs and workforce jobs for Great Britain now use the Annual Business Inquiry as a benchmark on which quarterly movements are based. For further information see Labour Market Statistics First Release, April 2001 which is held on the National Statistics website **www.statistics.gov.uk** The Northern Ireland component of workforce jobs and employee jobs has not changed.
2 Workforce jobs comprise employee jobs, self-employed jobs, HM Forces and participants in work-related government supported training, which includes the Project Work Plan.
3 For all dates, individuals with two jobs as employees of different employers are counted twice.
4 Annual estimates relate to mid-year. Figures for the four quarters relate to March, June, September and December. For claimant count, unlike employment and workforce figures, the annual figure is an annual average.
5 Unadjusted claimant count figures have been affected by changes in the coverage. The seasonally adjusted figures however, as given in this table are estimated on the current basis, allowing for the discontinuities, except for the effect of the Jobseeker's Allowance introduced in October 1996 (see also below).
The seasonally adjusted figures now relate only to claimants aged 18 or over in order to maintain the consistent series, available back to 1971 (1974 for the regions), allowing for the effect of the change in benefit regulations for under 18 year olds from September 1988 (see pages 398-400 of November 1995 *Labour Market Trends*).
6 Claimant count figures do not include students claiming benefit during a vacation who intend to return to full-time education.
7 Quarterly and annual values are now the mean of the monthly and quarterly data respectively.
8 The denominator used to calculate claimant count unemployment rates comprises the workforce jobs plus the claimant count.
9 The ONS Vacancy Survey, a monthly business survey of the number of job vacancies held by employers across the UK economy, has been running since April 2001. The results were adopted as National Statistics in June 2003.

Sources: Office for National Statistics;
Enquiries Columns 1-5 01633 812079; Columns 6-9 020 7533 6094;
also 24 hour recorded headline service on 020 7533 6176

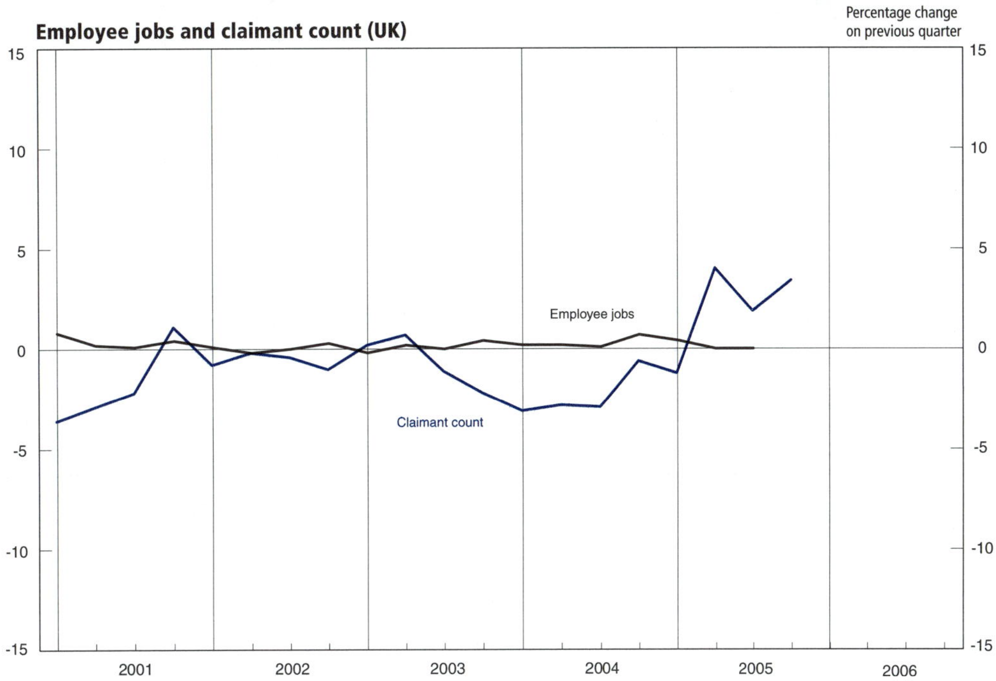
Employee jobs and claimant count (UK)
Percentage change on previous quarter
15
10
5
0
-5
-10
-15
Employee jobs
Claimant count
2001
2002
2003
2004
2005
2006

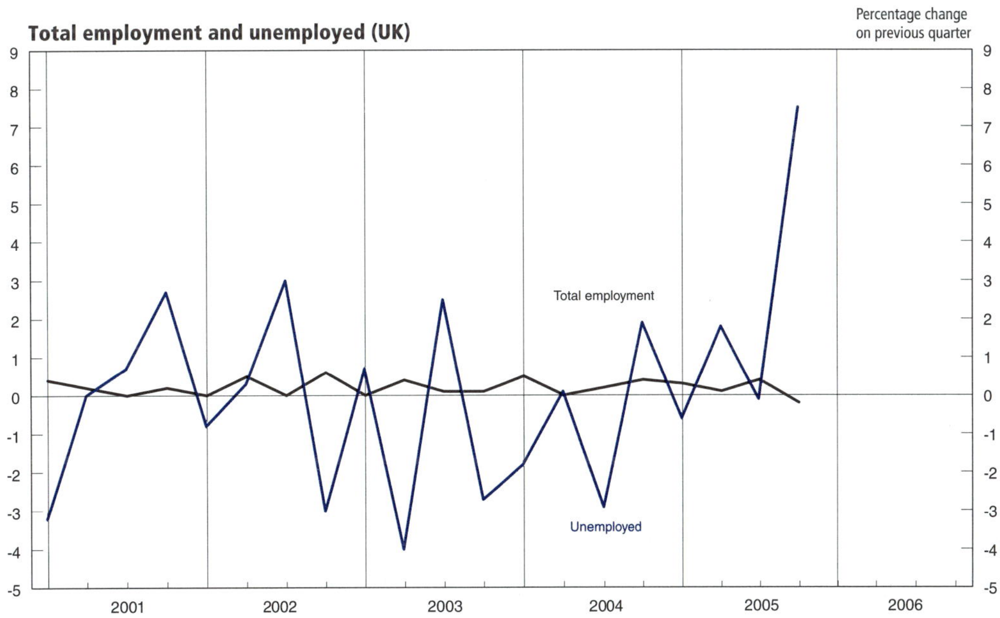
Total employment and unemployed (UK)
Percentage change on previous quarter
9
8
7
6
5
4
3
2
1
0
-1
-2
-3
-4
-5
Total employment
Unemployed
2001
2002
2003
2004
2005
2006

4.5 Regional claimant count rates[1,2]
by Government Office Region

Percentages

	North East	North West[3]	Yorkshire and the Humber	East Midlands	West Midlands	East	London	South East
	DPDM	IBWC	DPBI	DPBJ	DPBN	DPDP	DPDQ	DPDR
2000 Q1	6.6	4.4	4.6	3.5	4.1	2.6	4.0	2.0
Q2	6.4	4.2	4.4	3.4	4.0	2.4	3.8	1.9
Q3	6.2	4.0	4.2	3.3	4.0	2.3	3.6	1.8
Q4	6.0	3.9	4.1	3.3	3.9	2.2	3.5	1.7
2001 Q1	5.9	3.8	4.1	3.2	3.9	2.1	3.3	1.6
Q2	5.6	3.7	4.0	3.1	3.8	2.0	3.2	1.5
Q3	5.5	3.6	3.9	3.0	3.6	2.0	3.2	1.5
Q4	5.5	3.6	3.8	3.0	3.6	2.0	3.5	1.6
2002 Q1	5.3	3.5	3.7	2.9	3.5	2.0	3.5	1.6
Q2	5.2	3.5	3.6	2.8	3.5	2.1	3.6	1.6
Q3	5.1	3.5	3.6	2.8	3.5	2.1	3.6	1.7
Q4	4.8	3.4	3.6	2.8	3.5	2.1	3.6	1.7
2003 Q1	4.7	3.3	3.4	2.8	3.5	2.1	3.6	1.7
Q2	4.6	3.3	3.4	2.9	3.5	2.1	3.7	1.7
Q3	4.5	3.2	3.3	2.9	3.5	2.1	3.7	1.7
Q4	4.4	3.1	3.2	2.8	3.5	2.1	3.6	1.7
2004 Q1	4.2	3.0	3.0	2.7	3.4	2.0	3.6	1.7
Q2	4.1	2.9	2.9	2.5	3.3	2.0	3.5	1.6
Q3	3.9	2.8	2.8	2.5	3.2	1.9	3.4	1.6
Q4	3.9	2.8	2.8	2.5	3.2	1.9	3.4	1.6
2005 Q1	3.8	2.7	2.8	2.4	3.1	1.9	3.4	1.6
Q2	3.9	2.9	3.0	2.6	3.5	2.1	3.4	1.6
Q3	4.1	3.1	3.1	2.7	3.7	2.1	3.5	1.7
Q4	4.1	3.1	3.3†	2.8	3.8†	2.2	3.6	1.8†

	South West	England	Wales	Scotland	Great Britain	Northern Ireland	United Kingdom
	DPBM	VASQ	DPBP	DPBQ	DPAJ	DPBR	BCJE
2000 Q1	2.7	3.6	*4.5*	*4.8*	*3.7*	*5.5*	*3.8*
Q2	2.5	3.4	*4.4*	*4.6*	*3.6*	*5.3*	*3.6*
Q3	2.4	3.3	*4.3*	*4.4*	*3.4*	*5.1*	*3.5*
Q4	2.3	3.2	*4.3*	*4.3*	*3.4*	*5.2*	*3.4*
2001 Q1	2.1	3.1	*4.2*	*4.1*	*3.2*	*5.0*	*3.3*
Q2	2.1	3.0	*4.0*	*4.0*	*3.1*	*4.9*	*3.2*
Q3	2.0	2.9	*3.8*	*3.9*	*3.1*	*4.8*	*3.1*
Q4	2.0	3.0	*3.8*	*4.0*	*3.1*	*4.7*	*3.1*
2002 Q1	2.0	2.9	*3.6*	*3.9*	*3.1*	*4.6*	*3.1*
Q2	2.0	2.9	*3.6*	*3.9*	*3.0*	*4.5*	*3.1*
Q3	1.9	2.9	*3.6*	*3.9*	*3.0*	*4.3*	*3.1*
Q4	1.9	2.9	*3.5*	*3.8*	*3.0*	*4.3*	*3.0*
2003 Q1	1.9	2.9	*3.4*	*3.8*	*3.0*	*4.2*	*3.0*
Q2	1.9	2.9	*3.4*	*3.8*	*3.0*	*4.2*	*3.0*
Q3	1.9	2.9	*3.3*	*3.8*	*3.0*	*4.2*	*3.0*
Q4	1.8	2.8	*3.2*	*3.7*	*2.9*	*4.1*	*2.9*
2004 Q1	1.7	2.7	*3.1*	*3.6*	*2.8*	*3.9*	*2.8*
Q2	1.6	2.6	*3.1*	*3.5*	*2.7*	*3.7*	*2.8*
Q3	1.5	2.6	*3.0*	*3.4*	*2.7*	*3.5*	*2.7*
Q4	1.5	2.5	*3.0*	*3.4*	*2.6*	*3.5*	*2.7*
2005 Q1	1.5	2.5	*2.9*	*3.3*	*2.6*	*3.4*	*2.6*
Q2	1.6	2.7	*3.1*	*3.3*	*2.7*	*3.5*	*2.8*
Q3	1.6	2.8	*3.2*	*3.3*	*2.8*	*3.4*	*2.8*
Q4	1.6	2.8	*3.3*	*3.2*	*2.9*	*3.4*	*2.9*

Note: Quarterly claimant count figures relate to the average of the three months in each quarter.

1 Government Office Regions came into effect in April 1994. It was decided that from May 1997 sub-national data should be published for these areas rather than standard statistical regions (SSRs). Data by standard statistical regions are available on request.

2 The seasonally adjusted figures now relate only to claimants aged 18 or over in order to maintain the consistent series, available back to 1971 for Great Britain, Northern Ireland and the United Kingdom (1974 for Wales and Scotland; 1986 for the Government Office Regions), allowing for the effect of the change in benefit regulations for under 18 year olds from September 1988 (see pages 398-400 of November 1995 *Labour Market Trends*). The denominators used to calculate claimant count rates are the sum of the appropriate mid-year estimates of employee jobs, the self-employed, government-supported trainees, HM Forces and claimants of unemployment-related benefits.

3 Includes Merseyside.

Source: Office for National Statistics; Enquiries 020 7533 6094

Regional claimant count rates

Percentages

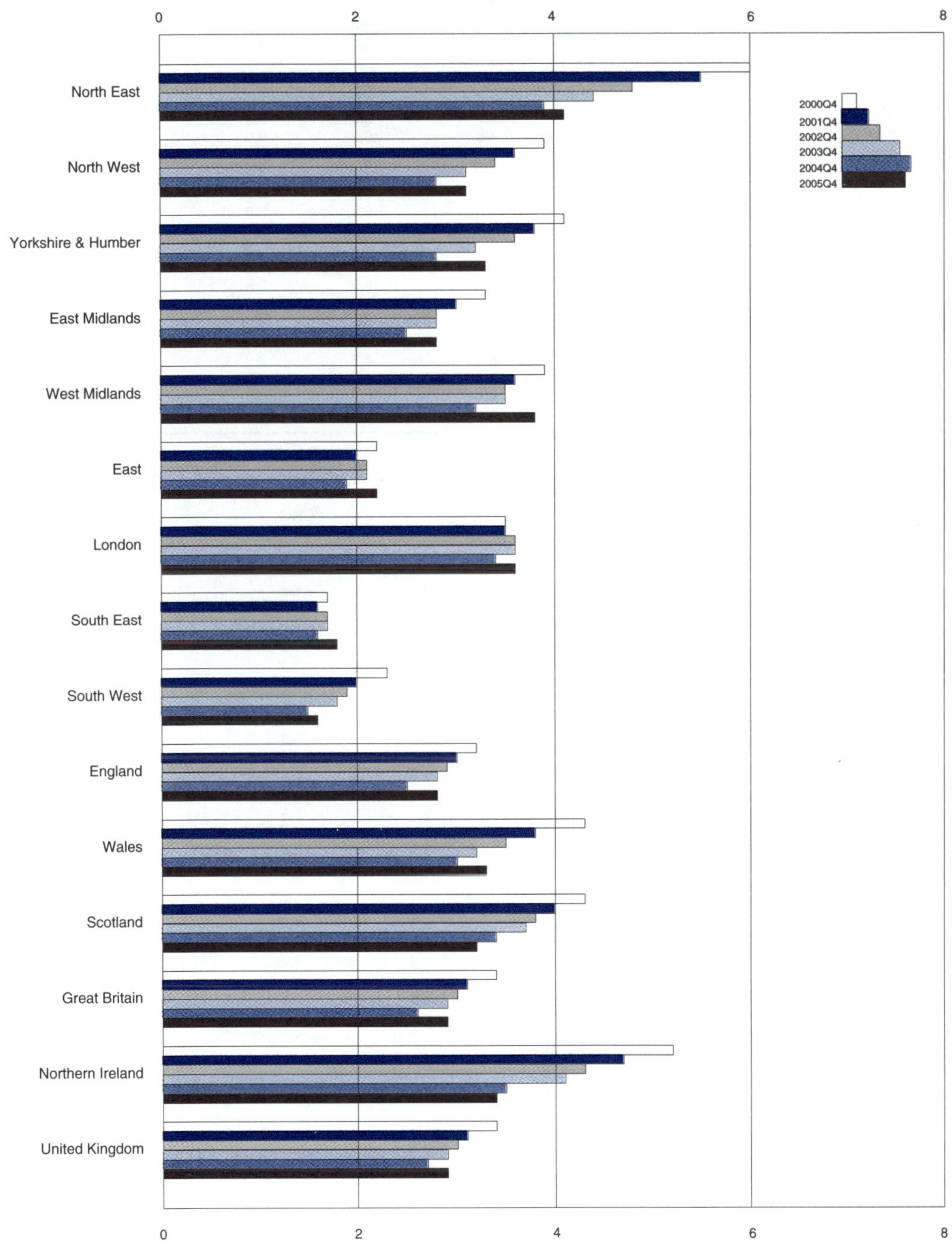

4.5A Unemployment rates[1]
by Government Office Region

Percentages, seasonally adjusted [2]

	North East	North West[3]	Yorkshire and the Humber	East Midlands	West Midlands	East	London	South East
	YCNC	YCND	YCNE	YCNF	YCNG	YCNH	YCNI	YCNJ
2000 Q1	8.8	6.0	6.4	5.1	6.1	3.9	7.6	3.5
Q2	8.9	5.3	6.1	4.8	6.1	3.7	7.4	3.3
Q3	8.9	5.4	5.9	4.8	5.7	3.7	6.9	3.1
Q4	7.7	5.3	6.1	4.7	6.0	3.6	6.8	3.4
2001 Q1	7.6	5.2	5.4	4.7	5.6	3.5	6.5	3.4
Q2	7.4	5.3	5.5	5.0	5.5	3.6	6.2	3.2
Q3	7.1	5.1	5.3	4.6	5.4	4.0	6.6	3.4
Q4	7.2	5.4	5.1	4.5	5.5	3.9	7.4	3.4
2002 Q1	7.3	5.4	5.1	4.7	5.6	3.7	6.9	3.6
Q2	6.5	5.5	5.3	4.6	5.7	3.7	6.8	3.8
Q3	6.2	5.5	5.6	4.7	5.9	3.9	7.1	4.0
Q4	7.3	4.9	5.0	4.8	5.7	4.0	6.6	4.0
2003 Q1	6.6	4.9	5.3	4.0	6.0	4.7	7.0	3.9
Q2	6.1	5.0	5.1	4.4	5.6	3.9	7.2	3.9
Q3	6.6	4.9	4.9	4.6	5.9	3.9	7.2	3.9
Q4	6.3	4.7	5.0	4.4	5.7	3.5	7.0	3.9
2004 Q1	5.6	4.5	4.8	4.7	5.5	3.5	7.0	3.9
Q2	5.5	4.4	4.5	4.3	5.5	3.8	7.0	3.6
Q3	6.0	4.4	4.6	4.0	5.0	3.5	7.2	3.7
Q4	6.4	4.6	4.7	4.2	4.8	3.8	7.2	3.5
2005 Q1	5.7	4.8	4.3	4.3	4.7	3.9	6.7	3.7
Q2	6.8	4.4	4.7	4.4	4.6	3.9	7.1	3.8
Q3	6.6	4.4	4.6	4.4	4.7	4.0	6.7	4.0
Q4	6.5	4.8	5.3	4.5	5.3	4.5	7.3	4.2

	South West	England	Wales	Scotland	Great Britain	Northern Ireland	United Kingdom
	YCNK	YCNL	YCNM	YCNN	YCNO	ZSFB	MGSX
2000 Q1	4.3	5.5	6.7	7.5	5.8	6.5	5.8
Q2	4.3	5.3	6.1	7.1	5.5	6.7	5.5
Q3	4.0	5.1	6.7	6.6	5.3	5.6	5.3
Q4	3.9	5.1	5.8	6.2	5.2	6.1	5.2
2001 Q1	3.9	4.9	6.0	5.9	5.0	6.2	5.1
Q2	3.6	4.8	6.1	6.3	5.0	6.1	5.0
Q3	3.6	4.9	5.5	6.6	5.1	6.0	5.1
Q4	3.6	5.0	5.8	6.7	5.2	5.9	5.2
2002 Q1	3.5	5.0	5.7	6.6	5.1	6.1	5.2
Q2	3.7	5.0	5.7	6.3	5.1	5.6	5.2
Q3	4.0	5.2	5.2	6.4	5.3	6.1	5.3
Q4	4.0	5.0	5.1	6.1	5.1	5.5	5.1
2003 Q1	3.8	5.1	4.8	6.0	5.1	5.3	5.1
Q2	3.4	4.9	4.5	5.3	4.9	5.2	4.9
Q3	3.2	5.0	4.7	5.9	5.0	5.6	5.0
Q4	3.1	4.8	4.8	5.8	4.9	6.3	4.9
2004 Q1	3.0	4.7	4.6	5.8	4.8	5.3	4.8
Q2	3.7	4.7	4.2	6.0	4.8	5.2	4.8
Q3	3.2	4.6	4.9	5.2	4.7	5.0	4.7
Q4	3.4	4.7	4.2	5.6	4.7	4.6	4.7
2005 Q1	3.6	4.6	4.5	5.6	4.7	4.8	4.7
Q2	3.2	4.7	4.6	5.5	4.8	5.0	4.8
Q3	3.6	4.7	4.6	5.4	4.8	4.3	4.7
Q4	4.0	5.1	4.9	5.2	5.1	4.5	5.1

1 Data are from the Labour Force Survey. Unemployment rate is the percentage of economically active people who are unemployed on the ILO measure.
2 Seasonally adjusted estimates are revised in September each year.
3 Includes Merseyside.

Source: Office for National Statistics; Enquiries 020 7533 6094

Unemployment rates

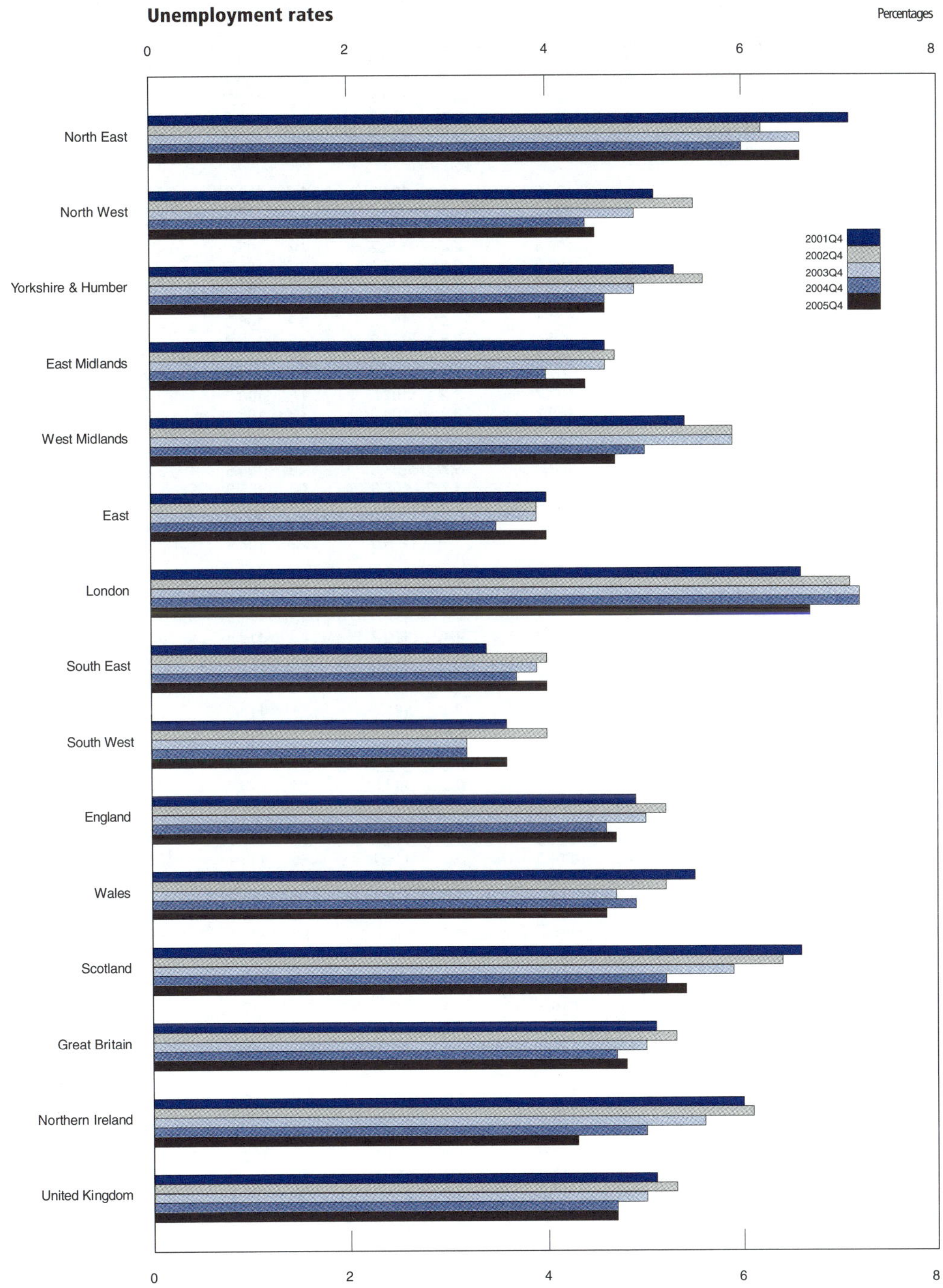

4.6 Average earnings (including bonuses)[1]
Great Britain

2000 = 100

	Whole economy+	3 month average[2]	Private sector	3 month average[2]	Public sector	3 month average[2]	Manufacturing industries[3]	3 month average[2,3]	Production industries	3 month average[2]	Service industries	3 month average[2]	Private sector services	3 month average[2]
	LNMQ		LNKY		LNNJ		LNMR		LNMS		LNMT		JJGH	
2002	108.2		107.9		109.3		108.0		107.9		108.1		107.8	
2003	111.9		111.3		114.8		111.9		111.7		112.0		110.9	
2004	116.7		116.0		119.8		115.9		115.8		116.7		115.7	
2005	121.5		120.6		125.5		120.2		120.0		121.6		120.4	
		LNNC		LNND		LNNE		LNNG		LNNF		LNNH		JJGJ
2001 Jan	103.1	4.5	103.3	4.7	102.3	3.9	102.9	4.6	103.0	4.3	103.3	4.5	103.4	4.7
Feb	103.6	4.7	103.7	4.8	102.7	3.6	103.4	4.8	103.7	4.6	103.7	4.7	103.8	4.9
Mar	103.6	4.7	103.5	4.7	103.3	3.7	102.5	4.5	102.6	4.5	103.7	4.7	103.7	4.7
Apr	103.9	5.0	103.8	5.0	104.6	4.3	104.1	5.0	103.9	4.9	103.8	5.0	103.6	5.0
May	104.0	5.1	103.8	5.1	104.9	5.2	104.1	4.7	103.9	4.7	103.9	5.1	103.6	5.1
Jun	104.3	5.3	104.1	5.3	105.2	5.5	104.3	5.0	104.2	4.9	104.2	5.3	103.9	5.3
Jul	104.4	5.2	104.2	5.1	105.6	5.6	104.5	4.8	104.3	4.6	104.3	5.2	103.9	5.1
Aug	104.9	4.9	104.7	4.8	105.9	5.6	104.9	4.8	104.7	4.6	104.9	4.9	104.5	4.7
Sep	105.1	4.6	104.9	4.4	105.9	5.7	105.3	4.6	105.1	4.4	105.0	4.6	104.7	4.2
Oct	105.3	4.3	105.0	4.0	106.5	5.6	105.4	4.4	105.2	4.3	105.2	4.2	104.8	3.8
Nov	105.6	3.9	105.4	3.7	106.5	5.4	105.3	3.8	105.1	3.7	105.5	3.9	105.2	3.5
Dec	105.8	3.3	105.5	2.9	106.9	5.2	105.5	3.3	105.3	3.2	105.7	3.2	105.5	2.7
2002 Jan	106.0	2.9	105.9	2.5	107.1	4.9	106.1	3.0	106.2	2.9	106.0	2.8	105.5	2.2
Feb	106.8	2.7	106.6	2.3	107.3	4.8	106.1	2.8	105.9	2.6	106.9	2.7	106.7	2.1
Mar	106.4	2.8	105.9	2.6	107.9	4.6	105.8	3.0	106.2	2.9	106.2	2.7	105.7	2.2
Apr	107.9	3.2	108.0	3.1	108.3	4.1	107.0	2.9	106.8	2.8	107.9	3.2	107.8	2.9
May	108.0	3.5	107.8	3.4	108.6	3.8	107.7	3.2	107.5	3.2	108.0	3.4	107.8	3.3
Jun	108.2	3.8	108.1	3.9	108.9	3.5	108.2	3.3	108.0	3.3	108.2	3.9	108.1	4.0
Jul	108.5	3.8	108.3	3.9	109.7	3.6	108.4	3.6	108.2	3.6	108.6	3.9	108.1	4.0
Aug	108.7	3.8	108.6	3.8	109.0	3.4	108.9	3.7	108.8	3.8	108.6	3.8	108.4	3.9
Sep	109.0	3.8	108.8	3.8	110.0	3.6	108.9	3.7	108.9	3.8	108.9	3.8	108.6	3.8
Oct	109.3	3.7	109.0	3.8	110.9	3.7	109.5	3.8	109.4	3.9	109.2	3.7	108.7	3.7
Nov	110.1	4.0	109.7	3.9	111.7	4.3	109.7	3.9	109.6	4.0	110.2	4.0	109.7	3.9
Dec	109.5	3.9	108.6	3.6	112.2	4.7	110.0	4.1	109.9	4.2	108.9	3.8	108.1	3.5
2003 Jan	109.0	3.5	108.6	3.2	112.6	5.0	110.2	4.1	110.2	4.1	108.9	3.4	107.4	2.9
Feb	109.8	3.0	109.0	2.6	112.9	5.1	110.6	4.1	110.3	4.1	109.5	2.7	108.3	1.9
Mar	110.9	3.3	110.1	2.9	113.3	5.1	111.8	4.6	112.0	4.5	110.4	3.0	109.2	2.2
Apr	110.7	3.2	110.0	2.7	113.9	5.1	110.3	4.4	110.2	4.3	110.8	3.0	109.7	2.2
May	111.4	3.3	110.9	2.9	113.6	4.9	111.1	4.0	110.9	4.0	111.6	3.3	111.0	2.7
Jun	111.7	3.0	111.1	2.5	114.7	5.0	111.4	3.1	111.3	3.2	111.9	3.1	110.9	2.5
Jul	112.6	3.4	111.9	3.0	115.6	5.1	111.8	3.1	111.7	3.1	113.0	3.6	111.9	3.0
Aug	112.6	3.5	111.9	3.0	115.5	5.6	112.2	3.0	112.0	3.1	112.8	3.8	111.8	3.1
Sep	113.2	3.7	112.5	3.3	116.0	5.6	112.8	3.2	112.6	3.2	113.2	4.0	112.3	3.4
Oct	113.4	3.7	112.8	3.3	116.1	5.4	113.0	3.3	112.9	3.2	113.4	3.9	112.5	3.4
Nov	113.7	3.6	113.1	3.3	116.4	4.8	113.7	3.5	113.5	3.4	113.7	3.7	112.8	3.3
Dec	114.3	3.8	113.9	3.9	117.0	4.4	113.6	3.4	113.4	3.3	114.5	4.1	113.4	3.7
2004 Jan	115.6	4.6	115.0	4.6	117.2	4.2	114.3	3.5	114.1	3.4	115.7	4.8	115.4	5.0
Feb	113.8	4.7	113.0	4.8	117.8	4.3	114.5	3.5	114.4	3.5	113.4	5.0	111.9	5.2
Mar	115.7	4.7	114.9	4.6	118.3	4.3	115.5	3.5	115.4	3.4	115.7	4.8	114.6	5.2
Apr	115.7	4.2	115.1	4.2	118.5	4.3	115.4	3.8	115.3	3.8	115.6	4.2	114.6	4.2
May	116.1	4.4	115.5	4.4	118.7	4.3	116.0	4.1	115.7	4.0	115.8	4.3	115.0	4.3
Jun	116.4	4.3	115.7	4.3	119.9	4.4	116.0	4.4	115.8	4.3	116.4	4.1	115.3	4.0
Jul	116.4	3.9	115.5	3.8	119.9	4.2	116.1	4.1	115.9	4.0	116.2	3.6	114.8	3.4
Aug	117.2	3.9	116.4	3.8	120.7	4.2	116.0	3.8	115.8	3.7	117.3	3.6	116.1	3.4
Sep	117.7	3.8	116.9	3.7	121.2	4.2	116.2	3.4	116.1	3.4	117.9	3.6	116.8	3.5
Oct	118.6†	4.2	117.9†	4.1	121.7	4.6	116.8†	3.2	116.6	3.2	118.8†	4.3	117.8	4.2
Nov	118.9	4.4†	118.3	4.3†	121.9	4.7	117.0	3.1	117.0†	3.1	119.1	4.5	118.0†	4.4
Dec	118.8	4.4	118.3	4.3	122.2	4.7	117.6	3.3	117.4	3.3	119.2	4.5	118.1	4.5
2005 Jan	120.1	4.2	119.4	4.1	122.7	4.6	117.8	3.2	117.7	3.2†	120.2	4.2	119.6	4.1
Feb	120.2	4.5	119.6	4.5	123.3	4.6	118.6	3.4†	118.5	3.4	120.5	4.8	119.5	4.8†
Mar	120.3	4.5	119.5	4.6	123.3	4.5	120.0	3.5	119.6	3.5	120.7	4.8	119.5	4.9
Apr	120.6	4.6	119.7	4.6	124.3	4.6	118.9	3.5	118.7	3.4	120.8	5.0	119.6	5.1
May	120.8	4.1	119.3	3.8	127.8	5.6	118.2	3.0	118.1	2.9	121.2	4.5	119.4	4.1
Jun	121.1	4.1	120.2	3.7	125.0	5.6	119.3	2.6	119.0	2.6	121.4	4.5	120.1	4.1
Jul	121.6	4.2	120.7	3.9	125.2	5.5	120.1	2.8	119.8	2.7	121.8	4.6	120.6	4.4
Aug	121.9	4.2	121.0	4.1	125.9	4.3	121.0	3.5	120.6	3.5	121.9	4.4	120.8	4.4
Sep	122.1	4.1	121.2	4.1	126.1	4.2	121.6	4.1	121.2	4.0	122.0	4.1	120.7	4.1
Oct	122.3	3.6	121.3	3.5	126.7†	4.1	122.0	4.4	121.7	4.3	122.1	3.4	120.7	3.3
Nov	123.0	3.4	122.0	3.3	127.3	4.2†	122.2	4.5	121.9	4.3	123.0	3.2	121.6	2.9
Dec	123.8	3.6	123.0	3.3	128.0	4.4	122.8	4.4	122.9	4.4	123.9	3.4	122.5	3.0

1 Data for the latest published month are provisional.

2 The 3 month average is the percentage change in the average seasonally adjusted indices for the latest 3 months compared with the same period a year earlier.

3 Owing to an irregularity, these series have been withdrawn for the period 1963-1982.

Source: Office for National Statistics; Enquiries 01633 816024

Earnings, wages, retail prices and output

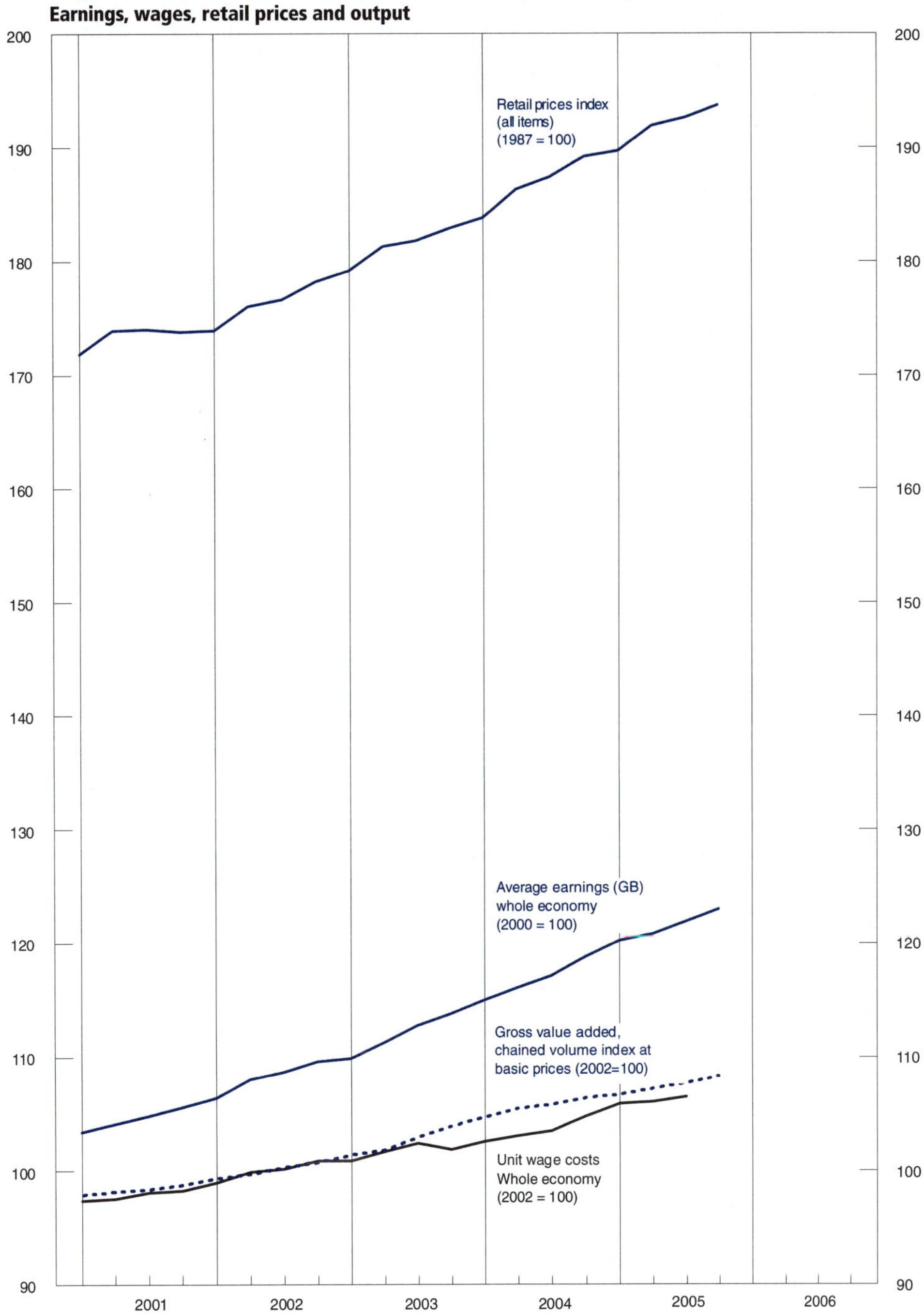

4.7 Productivity and unit wage costs[1]
United Kingdom

2002 = 100

	Productivity jobs: Whole economy	Productivity jobs: Total production industries	Productivity jobs: Manufacturing industries	Output per worker:[2] whole economy	Output per filled job[3]: Whole economy	Output per filled job[3]: Total production industries	Output per filled job[3]: Manufacturing industries	Output per hour worked[4]: Whole economy	Output per hour worked[4]: Total production industries	Output per hour worked[4]: Manufacturing industries	Unit wage costs[5]: Whole economy	Unit wage costs[5]: Manufacturing industries
	LNNM	LNOJ	LNOK	A4YM	LNNN	LNNW	LNNX	LZVB	LZVK	LZVF	LNNK	LNNQ
2003	100.9	95.8	95.8	101.5	101.6	103.9	104.5	102.0	103.5	104.1	101.7	99.1
2004	101.7	91.9	91.8	103.5	103.8	109.1	111.0	104.5	108.0	109.8	103.5	96.7
2005	..	..	88.6	..	..	..	114.1	..	..	..	..	97.5
2002 Q2	99.9	100.8	100.8	99.7	99.8	99.5	98.9	100.1	100.3	99.8	99.9	100.8
Q3	100.1	99.3	99.3	100.3	100.2	100.8	101.4	100.1	101.5	102.1	100.2	99.2
Q4	100.5	98.4	98.4	100.2	100.2	101.2	101.0	100.4	100.4	100.2	100.9	100.6
2003 Q1	100.6	97.7	98.0	100.8	100.8	101.7	101.3	101.2	100.8	100.8	100.9	101.3
Q2	100.8	96.5	96.3	100.8	101.0	102.7	103.3	101.1	102.5	103.0	101.7	99.4
Q3	101.0	95.1	95.0	101.8	101.8	104.6	105.5	102.2	103.8	104.7	102.4	98.5
Q4	101.1	93.8	93.8	102.7	102.8	106.7	107.8	103.7	106.8	107.8	101.9	97.4
2004 Q1	101.4	92.9	92.8	102.9	103.2	107.9	109.3	103.9	107.4	108.6	102.6	97.2
Q2	101.6	92.4	92.3	103.6	103.8	109.1	110.8	104.8	108.1	109.5	103.1	96.7
Q3	101.7	91.5	91.5	103.8	104.0	109.1	110.9	104.9	107.4	109.2	103.5	96.9
Q4	102.0	90.7	90.6	103.9	104.3	110.4	113.1	104.6	109.3	111.9	104.8	95.9
2005 Q1	102.4	90.0	89.9	103.8	104.2	110.3	113.0†	104.5	108.4	111.2	105.9	97.3†
Q2	102.6	89.0	88.9	104.2	104.5	111.4	113.7	105.3	110.1	112.9	106.1	96.7
Q3	102.8	88.4	88.1	104.2	104.6	111.4	115.1	104.9	108.8	112.5	106.5	97.8
Q4	..	..	87.4	..	..	..	114.8	..	..	..	..	98.6
2004 Jul	..	..	92.0	..	..	..	110.0	..	..	..	..	97.7
Aug	..	..	91.5	..	..	..	110.7	..	..	..	..	97.0
Sep	..	..	91.0	..	..	..	112.1	..	..	..	..	95.9
Oct	..	..	90.9	..	..	..	111.7	..	..	..	..	96.7
Nov	..	..	90.5	..	..	..	113.5	..	..	..	..	95.4
Dec	..	..	90.4	..	..	..	113.9	..	..	..	..	95.6†
2005 Jan	..	..	90.2	..	..	..	113.4†	..	..	..	..	96.1
Feb	..	..	89.9	..	..	..	113.5	..	..	..	..	96.7
Mar	..	..	89.5	..	..	..	112.0	..	..	..	..	99.2
Apr	..	..	89.3	..	..	..	112.9	..	..	..	..	97.4
May	..	..	88.8	..	..	..	113.7	..	..	..	..	96.2
Jun	..	..	88.5	..	..	..	114.5	..	..	..	..	96.4
Jul	..	..	88.2	..	..	..	115.3	..	..	..	..	96.4
Aug	..	..	88.1	..	..	..	115.3	..	..	..	..	97.1
Sep	..	..	88.0	..	..	..	114.7	..	..	..	..	98.1
Oct	..	..	87.7	..	..	..	114.0	..	..	..	..	99.0
Nov	..	..	87.5†	..	..	..	114.9	..	..	..	..	98.4
Dec	..	..	87.2	..	..	..	115.5	..	..	..	..	98.4
Percentage change, quarter on corresponding quarter of previous year												
	LNNO	LNNR	LNNS	A4YN	LNNP	LNNT	LNNU	LZVD	LZVM	LZVH	LOJE	LOJF
2003 Q1	*1.0*	*−3.8*	*−3.5*	*1.1*	*1.1*	*3.3*	*2.7*	*1.8*	*3.1*	*2.9*	*1.9*	*1.9*
Q2	*0.9*	*−4.3*	*−4.4*	*1.1*	*1.2*	*3.2*	*4.4*	*1.0*	*2.2*	*3.3*	*1.7*	*−1.4*
Q3	*0.9*	*−4.2*	*−4.3*	*1.4*	*1.6*	*3.8*	*4.0*	*2.1*	*2.3*	*2.6*	*2.1*	*−0.7*
Q4	*0.6*	*−4.7*	*−4.7*	*2.5*	*2.6*	*5.5*	*6.8*	*3.3*	*6.3*	*7.6*	*1.0*	*−3.2*
2004 Q1	*0.8*	*−5.0*	*−5.3*	*2.1*	*2.4*	*6.1*	*7.9*	*2.6*	*6.5*	*7.7*	*1.7*	*−4.1*
Q2	*0.8*	*−4.2*	*−4.1*	*2.8*	*2.8*	*6.3*	*7.2*	*3.6*	*5.4*	*6.3*	*1.4*	*−2.6*
Q3	*0.7*	*−3.8*	*−3.7*	*2.0*	*2.2*	*4.2*	*5.2*	*2.7*	*3.4*	*4.3*	*1.1*	*−1.7*
Q4	*0.9*	*−3.3*	*−3.4*	*1.2*	*1.4*	*3.4*	*4.9†*	*0.9*	*2.3*	*3.8*	*2.8*	*−1.5*
2005 Q1	*0.9*	*−3.2*	*−3.2*	*0.9*	*1.0*	*2.2*	*3.4*	*0.6*	*0.9*	*2.4*	*3.2*	*0.2*
Q2	*1.0*	*−3.6*	*−3.8*	*0.6*	*0.6*	*2.1*	*2.7*	*0.4*	*1.8*	*3.1*	*3.0*	*−0.1†*
Q3	*1.1*	*−3.3*	*−3.7*	*0.4*	*0.6*	*2.2*	*3.7*	*–*	*1.3*	*3.0*	*3.0*	*1.0*

1 The full productivity and unit wage costs data sets with associated articles can be found on the National Statistics web site at **www.statistics.gov.uk/productivity**. Contact the Labour Market Statistics helpline (020 7533 6094) for further information.

2 Output per worker is the ratio of gross value added (GVA) at basic prices to LFS total employment. On 29 July 2004, ONS published details on the National Statistics website of a change in productivity methodology. Output per worker is the new headline measure.

3 Output per filled job is the ratio of gross value added at basic prices to productivity jobs.

4 Output per hour worked is the ratio of gross value added at basic prices to productivity hours.

5 Unit wage costs are calculated as total wages and salaries per job divided by output per job.

Source: Office for National Statistics; Enquiries 01633 812766

Index of output per filled job
(United Kingdom)

2002 = 100

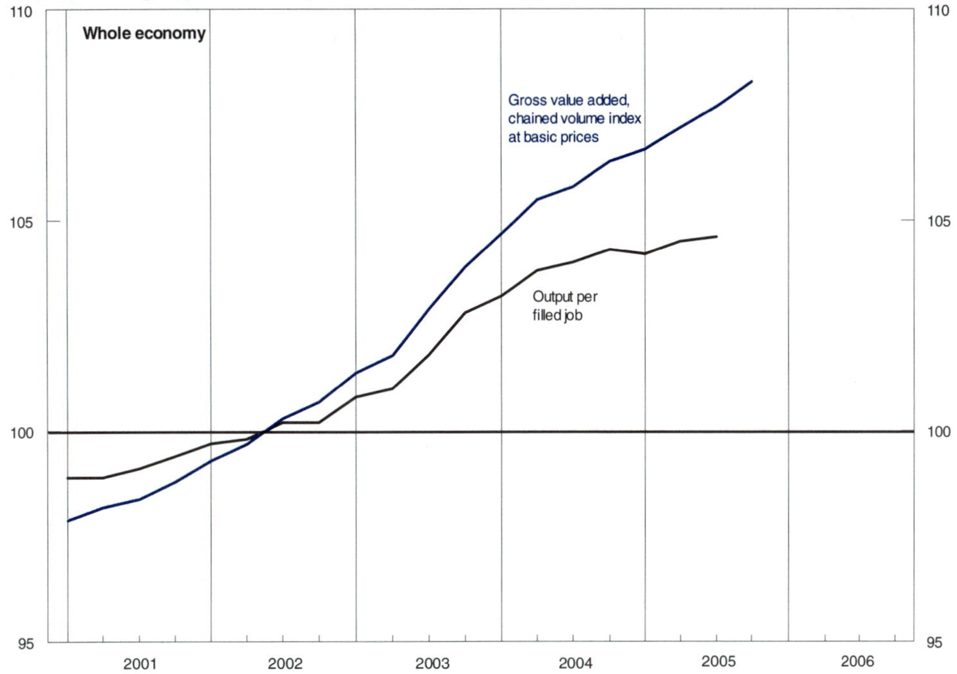

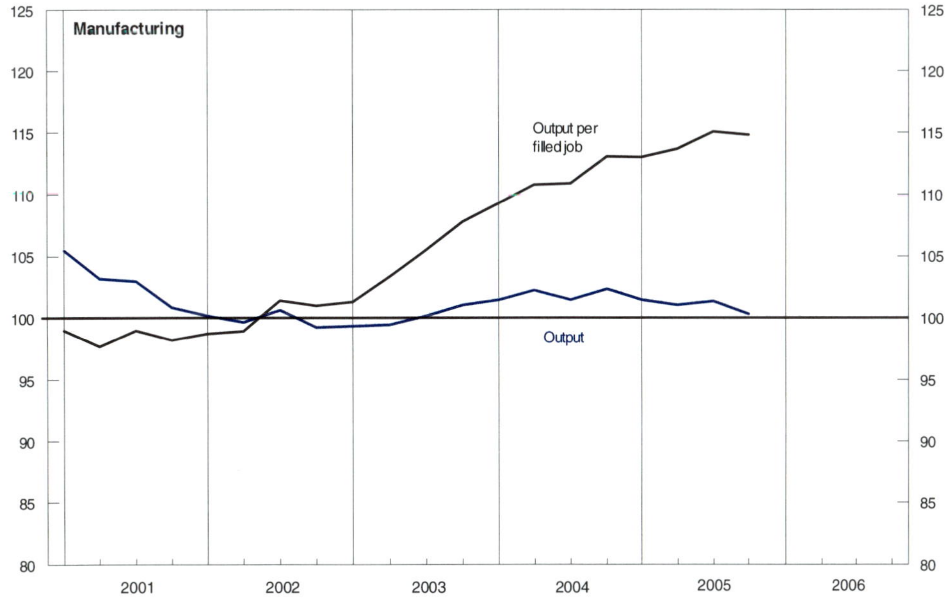

5.1 Output of production industries[1]

2002 = 100

	Broad industry groups				By main industrial groupings			
	Total production industries+	Mining and quarrying	Electricity, gas and water supply	Total manufacturing industries+	Consumer durables	Consumer non-durables	Capital goods	Intermediate goods and energy
2002 weights	*1 000*	*121*	*88*	*790*	*37*	*269*	*213*	*481*
	CKYW	CKYX	CKYZ	CKYY	UFIU	UFJS	UFIL	JMOH
2000	104.2	106.1	98.2	104.6	96.3	98.8	110.2	105.5
2001	102.6	100.3	100.5	103.2	98.7	100.0	108.4	102.0
2002	100.0	100.0	100.0	100.0	100.0	100.0	100.0	100.0
2003	99.5	94.9	101.2	100.1	99.2	100.0	101.4	98.4
2004	100.3	87.2	103.3	101.9	104.7	99.9	105.0	98.0
2005	98.6†	79.6†	102.2†	101.1†	102.7	100.0	104.6	94.8
2000 Q1	103.8	110.2	96.9	103.8	96.6	99.0	108.2	105.3
Q2	104.4	108.7	99.2	104.4	96.2	99.2	109.6	105.9
Q3	104.1	105.0	98.1	104.6	96.0	98.5	110.3	105.5
Q4	104.5	100.8	98.5	105.5	96.3	98.3	112.6	105.3
2001 Q1	104.5	99.3	102.1	105.5	99.6	100.0	113.8	103.6
Q2	102.9	101.9	101.1	103.2	98.2	99.6	108.4	102.8
Q3	102.4	100.8	99.9	103.0	98.1	100.3	108.0	101.8
Q4	100.4	99.2	98.8	100.9	98.9	100.1	103.4	99.7
2002 Q1	100.0	100.1	98.2	100.2	102.0	100.4	99.6	99.9
Q2	100.3	104.3	99.4	99.7	99.1	100.1	99.6	100.8
Q3	100.1	95.6	101.2	100.7	98.8	100.6	101.4	99.4
Q4	99.6	100.0	101.3	99.3	100.1	98.9	99.4	100.0
2003 Q1	99.4	99.6	99.3	99.4	98.3	99.1	99.9	99.4
Q2	99.1	95.2	100.2	99.5	99.0	99.5	100.7	98.1
Q3	99.5	93.5	101.6	100.2	99.2	100.6	101.6	98.1
Q4	100.1	91.1	103.5	101.1	100.3	101.0	103.4	98.1
2004 Q1	100.3	89.5	104.0	101.5	102.0	100.4	103.2	98.7
Q2	100.8	89.9	102.7	102.3	105.0	100.3	104.9	99.0
Q3	99.8	85.9	103.5	101.5	106.7	99.0	105.3	97.3
Q4	100.2	83.3	103.0	102.4	105.0	100.0	106.5	97.0
2005 Q1	99.3†	82.9†	101.8†	101.5	104.6†	100.2†	103.9†	96.4†
Q2	99.0	83.0	102.8	101.1†	102.4	100.0	104.4	95.8
Q3	98.4	76.1	102.0	101.4	101.6	100.0	106.3	93.7
Q4	97.6	76.4	102.1	100.4	102.1	99.8	103.8	93.3
2003 Jul	99.9	94.7	100.7	100.6	100.5	101.1	101.9	98.4
Aug	99.0	93.3	101.5	99.7	97.6	100.2	100.5	97.8
Sep	99.6	92.5	102.5	100.4	99.3	100.4	102.4	98.1
Oct	100.8	93.1	105.0	101.5	99.9	101.9	103.2	99.2
Nov	99.4	90.8	102.0	100.5	101.0	100.1	103.1	97.3
Dec	100.1	89.4	103.6	101.4	99.9	100.9	104.0	97.9
2004 Jan	100.1	90.1	103.0	101.3	100.8	100.5	103.1	98.5
Feb	99.8	88.5	105.0	100.9	101.6	99.8	102.7	98.3
Mar	100.9	89.9	103.9	102.3	103.7	100.8	104.0	99.3
Apr	100.9	89.6	103.0	102.3	104.7	101.3	104.2	98.8
May	100.7	88.9	102.8	102.3	104.4	99.6	105.8	98.8
Jun	100.9	91.2	102.3	102.2	105.9	99.9	104.7	99.4
Jul	100.1	91.1	102.5	101.2	108.0	97.6	105.3	98.6
Aug	99.6	85.7	104.4	101.2	106.3	99.5	104.4	97.1
Sep	99.7	81.0	103.5	102.1	105.9	99.8	106.4	96.2
Oct	99.3	81.9	103.2	101.5	105.7	99.5	105.6	95.9
Nov	100.5	83.5	103.4	102.8	103.3	100.5	107.0	97.4
Dec	100.7	84.6	102.4	103.0	106.0	100.2	106.9	97.8
2005 Jan	99.9†	82.9†	101.3†	102.3†	103.7†	101.2†	104.5†	96.7†
Feb	99.6	82.5	101.8	102.0	106.0	100.6	104.4	96.5
Mar	98.4	83.3	102.5	100.2	104.2	98.6	102.7	95.8
Apr	99.0	83.3	103.5	100.9	104.8	98.9	103.9	96.4
May	99.1	84.5	102.6	101.0	101.8	100.1	104.2	96.1
Jun	99.0	81.1	102.3	101.3	100.6	101.1	105.2	94.9
Jul	98.9	78.4	102.0	101.7	100.6	100.8	106.6	94.3
Aug	97.9	71.6	101.4	101.6	101.4	99.6	106.6	92.9
Sep	98.4	78.2	102.6	101.0	102.9	99.5	105.8	94.1
Oct	97.1	76.4	99.2	100.0	101.7	99.2	103.5	92.7
Nov	97.8	76.1	103.8	100.5	102.2	99.7	104.4	93.5
Dec	98.0	76.5	103.3	100.7	102.3	100.5	103.5	93.9

1 Figures contain, where appropriate, an adjustment for stock changes.

Source: Office for National Statistics; Enquiries 01633 812059

Output of production industries
By broad industry groups

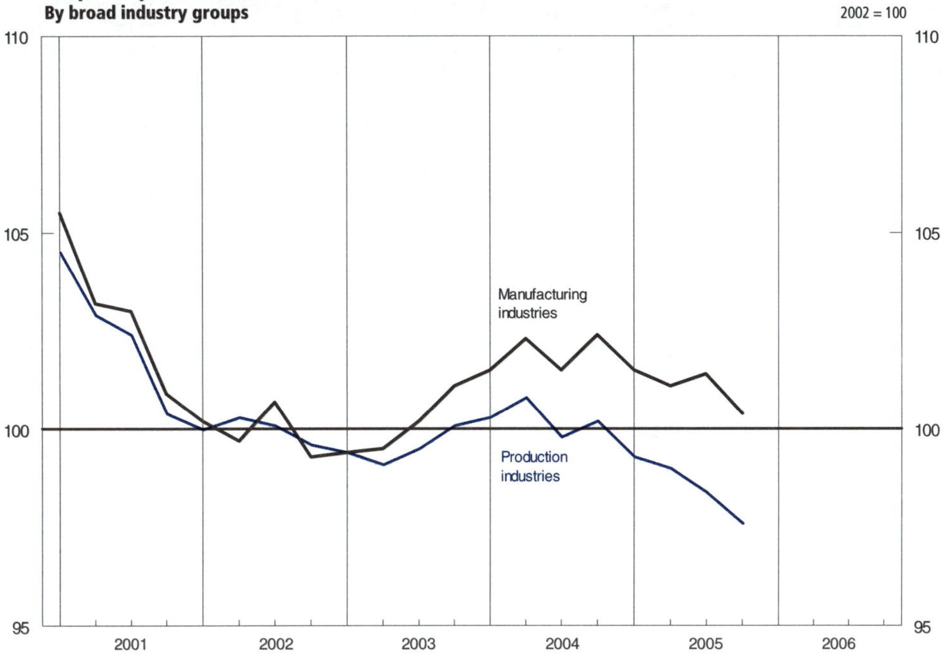

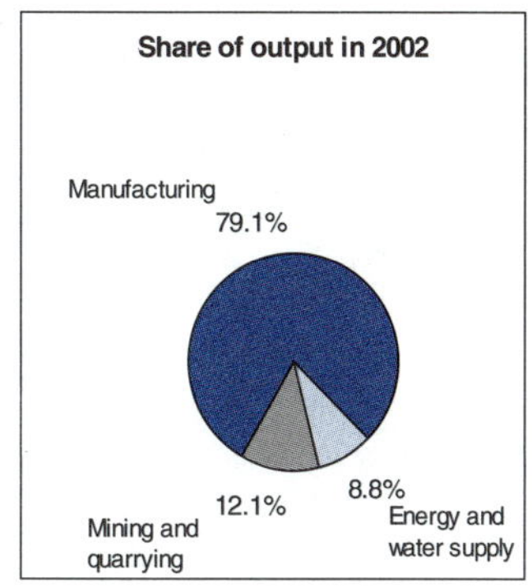

By main industrial groupings

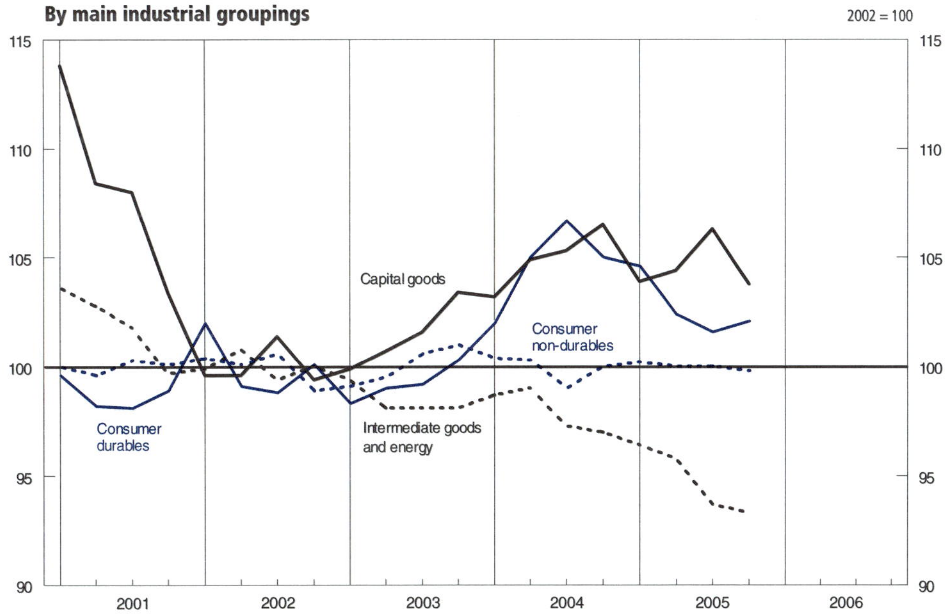

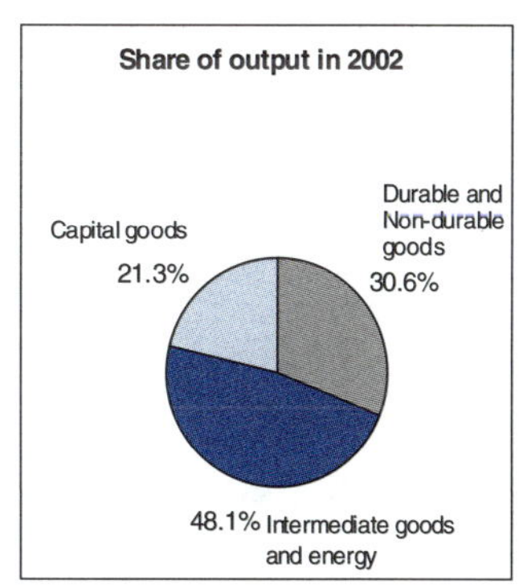

5.2 Engineering and construction: output and orders

Seasonally adjusted index numbers at constant prices[1]

	Engineering (2000 = 100)									Construction (GB) (2000 = 100)	
	Total			Home			Export				
	Orders[2] on hand	New[3] orders	Turnover	Orders[2] on hand	New[3] orders	Turnover	Orders[2] on hand	New[3] orders	Turnover	Gross output[4] +	Orders received
	JIQI	JIQH	JIQJ	JIQC	JIQB	JIQD	JIQF	JIQE	JIQG	SFZX	SGAA
2001	94.4	89.5	95.3	104.6	94.5	98.4	77.2	82.9	91.2	102.0	99.5
2002	92.7	80.8	84.5	104.8	88.0	91.8	72.1	71.2	74.8	106.3	102.5
2003	92.7	78.9	81.6	108.7	87.9	90.2	65.5	66.8	70.3	111.7	97.8
2004	89.3	78.3	82.1	103.2	84.0	89.3	65.8	70.8	72.6	115.2	104.8
2005	91.1	78.6	80.7	102.5	85.4	89.1	71.7	69.4	69.8	..	111.8
2001 Q1	104.4	102.1	104.4	106.2	102.2	104.7	101.3	102.0	104.2	101.2	108.4
Q2	102.0	91.0	97.1	108.2	97.8	99.0	91.3	81.9	94.5	101.3	95.6
Q3	99.9	86.6	92.0	107.6	91.5	96.0	86.9	79.9	86.6	102.1	103.6
Q4	94.4	78.5	87.8	104.6	86.4	93.9	77.2	67.8	79.6	103.5	90.5
2002 Q1	94.9	81.5	85.3	105.0	87.8	92.1	77.9	73.2	76.2	105.3	107.6
Q2	93.6	80.4	84.7	105.4	89.3	92.5	73.8	68.5	74.5	104.7	90.7
Q3	93.8	81.8	84.4	106.4	89.4	91.7	72.6	71.7	74.8	106.8	109.2
Q4	92.7	79.5	83.6	104.8	85.5	91.1	72.1	71.3	73.6	108.5	102.5
2003 Q1	90.9	76.4	81.1	103.4	85.3	90.7	69.8	64.4	68.5	108.7	104.7
Q2	91.7	79.7	81.5	104.9	88.9	90.4	69.3	67.4	69.7	110.4	95.8
Q3	91.5	78.7	81.6	106.0	88.1	90.2	66.8	66.0	70.2	113.5	98.0
Q4	92.7	80.8	82.2	108.7	89.3	89.3	65.5	69.5	72.6	114.4	92.7
2004 Q1	93.7	78.9	80.4	108.7	83.3	86.8	68.4	73.0	72.1	117.1	108.5
Q2	92.7	78.5	82.5	106.5	82.6	88.9	69.3	73.0	73.9	114.2	106.2
Q3	90.3	77.0	82.5	103.7	82.6	89.7	67.5	69.5	73.2	115.1	99.8
Q4	89.3	79.0	82.8	103.2	87.5	91.6	65.8	67.7	71.2	114.3	104.8
2005 Q1	89.5†	78.1†	80.6†	101.1†	83.3†	89.4†	69.9	71.1†	69.0†	113.9	105.0†
Q2	89.7	78.5	81.0	100.4	85.1	89.4	71.5	69.5	69.7	114.5	115.7
Q3	91.8	81.2	81.5	103.1	89.2	89.3	72.6	70.6	71.3	115.0	109.6
Q4	91.1	76.5	79.9	102.5	83.9	88.1	71.7	66.5	69.1	..	114.5
2003 Jul	91.7	79.9	82.8	104.7	87.0	91.6	69.6	70.3	71.0	..	111.1
Aug	91.7	77.7	80.3	106.1	90.5	88.5	67.2	60.5	69.4	..	80.7
Sep	91.5	78.4	81.8	106.0	86.7	90.5	66.8	67.3	70.3	..	102.3
Oct	92.3	82.6	82.5	107.3	92.1	90.7	66.8	69.8	71.6	..	87.3
Nov	94.0	84.6	81.3	110.0	95.5	88.8	66.9	70.0	71.4	..	102.7
Dec	92.7	75.3	82.7	108.7	80.2	88.5	65.5	68.7	74.9	..	88.2
2004 Jan	93.9	81.6	80.2	108.8	84.5	87.3	68.6	77.8	70.8	..	90.2
Feb	91.6	69.2	80.0	106.6	72.6	84.6	66.2	64.7	73.9	..	126.1
Mar	93.7	85.8	81.1	108.7	92.9	88.4	68.4	76.4	71.5	..	109.2
Apr	92.0	72.4	81.1	105.0	69.9	87.3	69.9	75.7	72.9	..	103.4
May	92.9	83.0	82.6	105.7	88.2	89.0	71.1	75.9	74.3	..	111.3
Jun	92.7	80.2	83.7	106.5	89.7	90.5	69.3	67.5	74.6	..	103.9
Jul	93.0	81.8	83.3	107.2	89.5	90.4	69.0	71.3	74.1	..	109.5
Aug	90.9	71.5	81.6	104.5	74.3	87.9	67.8	67.8	73.3	..	100.6
Sep	90.3	77.7	82.7	103.7	83.9	90.7	67.5	69.5	72.2	..	89.2
Oct	89.1	75.3	82.0	102.4	82.2	90.6	66.6	66.0	70.5	..	101.3
Nov	88.7	79.2	83.6	102.1	88.7	93.4	65.8	66.6	70.6	..	107.6
Dec	89.3	82.5	82.9	103.2	91.5	90.9	65.8	70.4	72.4	..	105.5
2005 Jan	89.7†	79.6	81.1†	104.3†	91.8†	90.6†	64.9†	63.3†	68.7†	..	101.6†
Feb	89.5	77.7†	81.1	103.2	82.7	90.6	66.2	71.0	68.6	..	98.3
Mar	89.5	77.0	79.5	101.1	75.4	87.0	69.9	79.0	69.6	..	115.2
Apr	88.8	76.7	81.9	102.2	90.5	89.8	66.2	58.2	71.4	..	106.6
May	89.4	79.8	80.4	101.1	81.1	88.7	69.6	77.9	69.3	..	127.9
Jun	89.7	78.9	80.6	100.4	83.7	89.8	71.5	72.5	68.4	..	112.5
Jul	89.7	78.1	80.6	99.8	83.3	89.1	72.6	71.2	69.5	..	104.8
Aug	91.9	86.3	81.5	103.0	98.3	89.8	73.1	70.3	70.5	..	115.5
Sep	91.8	79.3	82.4	103.1	86.0	89.0	72.6	70.4	73.8	..	108.5
Oct	91.9	77.3	79.4	103.5	86.6	88.6	72.3	64.9	67.3	..	119.4
Nov	92.1	77.9	79.9	103.4	84.3	87.9	73.0	69.4	69.3	..	120.5
Dec	91.1	74.2	80.4	102.5	80.9	87.8	71.7	65.1	70.7	..	111.4

1 The figures shown represent the output of UK-based manufacturers classified to subsections DK and DL of the Standard Industrial Classification (2003).

2 For orders on hand, the annual and quarterly indices represent the value at the end of the period in question, rather than the average value for that period, so the annual value shown for 2000 may not equal 100.

3 Net of cancellations.

4 This index is based on a gross output series which includes repair and maintenance estimates, unrecorded output by self-employed workers and small firms and output by the direct labour departments of the public sector.

Sources: Office for National Statistics; Enquiries Columns 1-9 01633 812540; Department of Trade and Industry; Enquiries Columns 10-11 020 7944 5583

Engineering industries: turnover and orders

Volume indices 2000 = 100

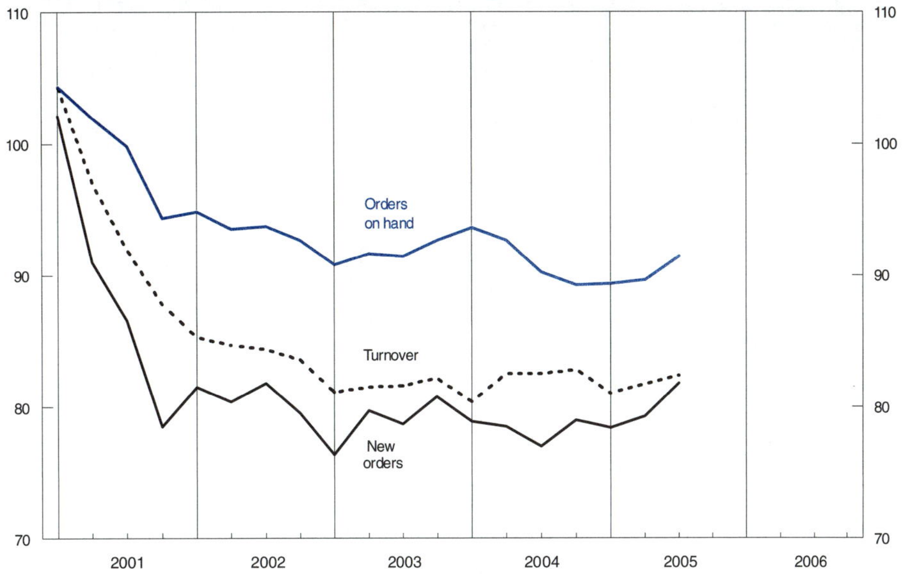

Construction industries (GB): output and orders

Volume indices 2000 = 100

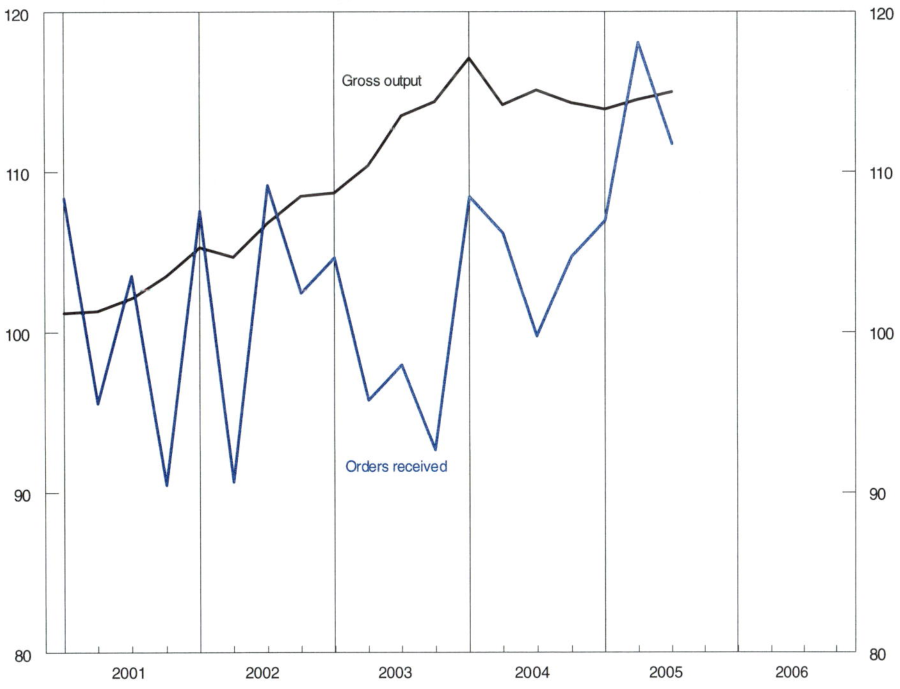

5.3 Motor vehicle and steel production

	Passenger cars[1]				Commercial vehicles[1]				
	Not seasonally adjusted		Seasonally adjusted		Not seasonally adjusted		Seasonally adjusted		
	Total production (thousands)	*of which* for export (thousands)	Total production (thousands)	*of which* for export (thousands)	Total production (thousands)	*of which* for export (thousands)	Total production (thousands)	*of which* for export (thousands)	Crude steel production (NSA)[2] (thousand tonnes)
	FFAA	FFAB	FFAO	FFAP	FFAC	FFAD	FFAQ	FFAR	BCBS
2001	124.4	74.5	124.4	74.5	16.1	8.0	16.1	8.0	13 542.7
2002	135.8†	87.3	135.8	87.3	15.9	9.5	15.9	9.5	11 667.1
2003	138.1	95.3	138.1	95.3	15.7	8.6	15.7	8.6	13 128.4
2004	137.2	98.3	137.2	98.3	17.4	10.7	17.4	10.7	13 765.8
2005	133.0	98.7	133.9†	99.6†	17.2	10.9	17.4†	10.8	13 239.3†
2001 Q1	129.0	75.5	119.5	73.3	17.2	6.6	15.5	6.1	3 651.7
Q2	124.1	76.5	120.1	71.3	16.6	7.7	15.6	7.2	3 729.6
Q3	111.9	61.0	124.8	76.1	14.5	7.4	17.9	9.3	3 205.5
Q4	132.4	85.1	133.1	77.4	16.1	10.3	15.3	9.5	2 955.9
2002 Q1	149.9	85.0	139.4	83.5	16.7	8.4	15.3	8.0	3 046.3
Q2	134.1†	94.0	126.6	84.7	14.8	9.4	14.4	8.9	3 060.0
Q3	130.6	80.7	147.0	97.1	14.9	9.3	17.4	10.8	2 801.9
Q4	128.7	89.3	130.3	83.7	17.3	10.9	16.7	10.3	2 758.9
2003 Q1	141.4	91.5	129.8	86.4	16.5	9.3	15.2	9.0	3 081.0
Q2	144.4	101.3	139.1	94.8	15.5	8.3	15.0	8.0	3 258.7
Q3	130.4	85.8	144.8	101.0	13.4	6.9	15.5	8.1	3 264.3
Q4	136.2	102.7	138.8	99.1	17.6	9.7	17.2	9.2	3 524.4
2004 Q1	148.5	101.2	136.8	96.3	19.3	10.4	17.9	10.1	3 380.7
Q2	142.7	102.3	137.5	96.0	16.9	11.2	16.5	10.7	3 681.4
Q3	126.3	88.3	137.9	100.7	15.6	9.7	18.0	11.1	3 405.2
Q4	131.4	101.5	136.7	100.1	17.9	11.4	17.4	10.8	3 298.5
2005 Q1	144.3	99.1	138.4	99.6	18.4	11.3	17.1	10.7	3 310.9
Q2	138.7	105.3	131.7	97.0	18.2	10.7	18.1	10.4	3 523.8
Q3	125.7	91.5	138.9	104.9	14.9	9.2	17.7	11.0	3 119.3
Q4	123.3	98.9	126.8†	97.0†	17.3	12.2	16.5†	11.3	3 285.3†
2003 Jul	146.3	93.1	144.1	98.3	15.2	7.6	16.6	8.4	1 245.8*
Aug	91.4	57.5	145.0	100.4	7.8	3.8	14.9	7.6	977.8
Sep	153.5	106.8	145.3	104.3	17.1	9.2	15.0	8.3	1 040.7
Oct	153.4	113.8	138.6	96.8	16.8	9.5	15.4	8.6	1 198.0*
Nov	142.9	110.5	134.8	99.3	19.0	9.8	17.2	9.5	1 117.8
Dec	112.4	83.8	142.9	101.1	17.0	9.9	19.0	9.6	1 208.6*
2004 Jan	141.3	96.4	138.7	97.9	20.5	9.6	19.6	11.0	1 009.3
Feb	141.1	93.0	131.9	92.2	17.3	10.0	16.4	9.9	1 024.9
Mar	163.0†	114.3	139.7	98.8	20.2	11.7	17.7	9.3	1 346.5*
Apr	129.6	95.7	136.6	98.1	15.7	10.1	16.0	10.2	1 155.5
May	143.1	102.3	139.3	92.9	16.9	11.9	17.4	11.5	1 160.7
Jun	155.5	108.9	136.7	97.1	18.2	11.6	16.2	10.5	1 365.2*
Jul	140.5	100.5	145.2	107.4	14.9	10.1	16.7	11.3	1 042.6
Aug	83.2	56.7	132.5	97.2	10.2	5.7	18.1	9.8	1 015.8
Sep	155.3	107.6	136.0	97.6	21.7	13.3	19.1	12.2	1 346.8*
Oct	135.1	107.2	134.1	102.0	18.6	12.2	18.1	11.4	1 091.5
Nov	149.3	114.4	140.4	102.1	20.1	12.3	17.0	10.3	1 001.4
Dec	109.7	82.8	135.7	96.3	14.9	9.7	17.0	10.6	1 205.6*
2005 Jan	136.0	89.2	137.0	95.1	17.7	10.7	17.0	11.0	1 033.5
Feb	143.5	98.3	138.8	100.6	18.0	10.7	17.2	10.5	1 016.8
Mar	153.3	109.9	139.4	103.1	19.6	12.6	17.2	10.5	1 260.6*
Apr	139.8	105.1	140.1	100.3	18.9	11.4	20.1	11.9	1 161.8
May	132.0	99.1	130.2	94.3	17.5	10.7	17.9	10.1	1 147.5
Jun	144.3	111.7	124.9	96.5	18.3	10.0	16.3	9.3	1 214.5*
Jul	130.2	93.8	134.7	99.9	14.2	8.5	17.3	10.4	966.4
Aug	97.1	71.8	146.0	114.2	10.8	6.8	18.2	11.2	1 193.5*
Sep	149.9	108.9	136.0	100.6	19.7	12.4	17.5	11.3	959.4
Oct	124.8	99.4	125.1	95.0	18.4	12.4	16.6	10.6	986.2
Nov	149.7	119.4	130.7†	99.9†	20.0	13.8	17.2†	11.8	1 279.5*†
Dec	95.3	77.9	124.5	96.1	13.6	10.3	15.7	11.5	1 019.6
2006 Jan	119.1	86.4	120.7	91.6	18.2	11.8	17.0	11.7	1 043.1[3]

1 Annual and quarterly figures are monthly averages.
2 The totals are for 'usable steel' in accordance with the system used by the EC and the IISI, but in a change from previous publications, figures are actual production totals based on a four or five week period (not seasonally adjusted).
3 Provisional.

Sources: Office for National Statistics; Enquiries Columns 1-8 01633 812810; ISSB Ltd; Enquiries Column 9 020 7343 3900

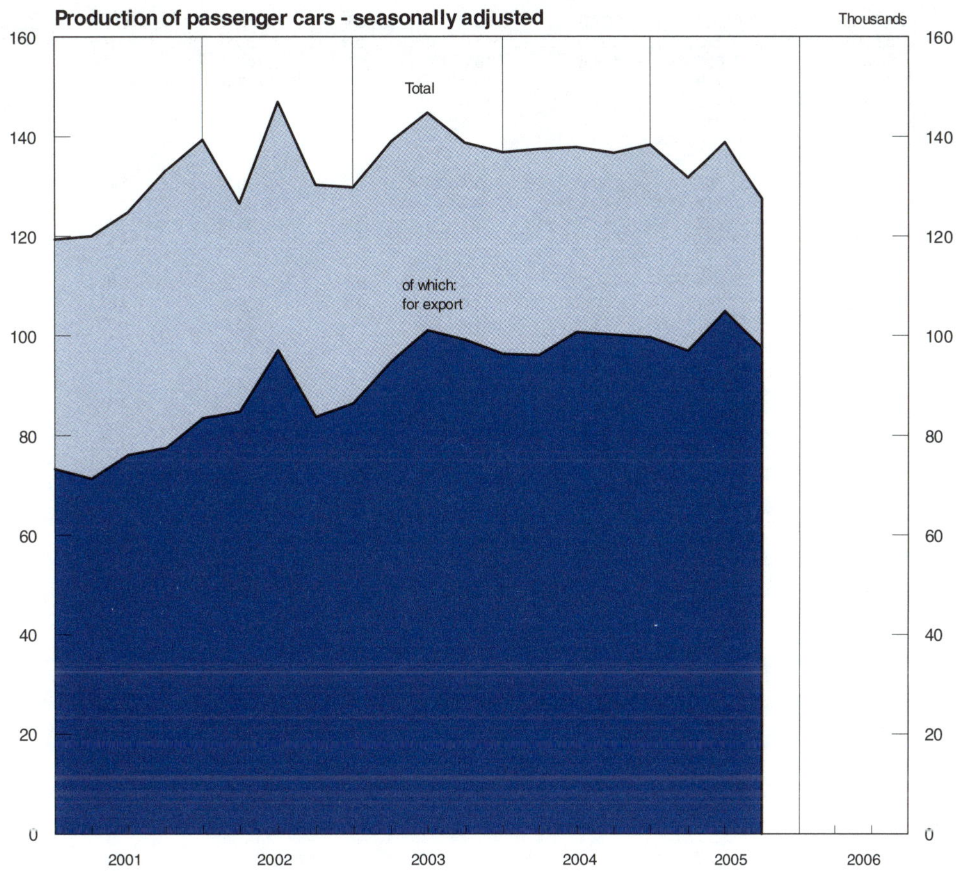
Production of passenger cars - seasonally adjusted
Thousands
160
140
120
100
80
60
40
20
0
Total
of which:
for export
2001
2002
2003
2004
2005
2006

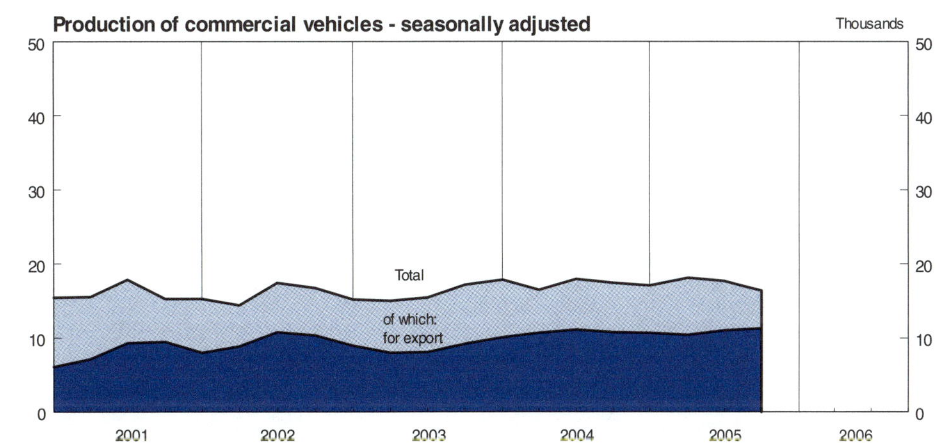
Production of commercial vehicles - seasonally adjusted
Thousands
50
40
30
20
10
0
Total
of which:
for export
2001
2002
2003
2004
2005
2006

5.4 Indicators of fixed investment in dwellings

	Fixed investment in dwellings (£ million, chained volume measures, reference year 2002)	Orders received by contractors for new houses (GB) (£ million, 2000 prices)	Housing starts (NSA)[1] (GB)			Housing completions (NSA)[1] (GB)			Mix-adjusted price of new dwellings at mortgage completion stage (NSA)[3] (£)
			Private enterprise (thousands)	Registered social landlords[2] (thousands)	Local authorities (thousands)	Private enterprise (thousands)	Registered social landlords[2] (thousands)	Local authorities (thousands)	
	DFEG	SGAB	FCAB	CTOR	CTOV	FCAD	CTOT	CTOX	WMPS
2001	32 006	7 122	162.8	16.8	0.3	139.9	20.9	0.3	134 234
2002	34 499	7 805	164.6	16.2	0.2	149.3	19.3	0.2	161 533
2003	36 056	8 219	177.5	16.2	0.3	158.3	17.2	0.3	186 427
2004	38 879	9 472	194.3	19.0	0.2	166.5	20.6	0.1	205 818
2005	..	10 013	..	..	..	..	..	..	218 342
2001 Q1	7 911	1 767	39.2	5.7	0.2	32.5	5.6	0.1	130 771
Q2	7 891	1 772	43.8	4.2	–	34.4	4.7	0.1	130 774
Q3	8 252	1 822	43.5	3.2	–	35.6	4.6	0.1	135 507
Q4	7 952	1 761	36.3	3.7	0.1	37.5	5.9	0.1	137 368
2002 Q1	8 006	1 916	41.7	5.4	0.1	33.6	5.1	–	143 996
Q2	8 396	1 782	42.6	3.8	0.1	36.9	4.6	0.2	157 646
Q3	8 829	2 031	44.0	3.4	–	36.4	4.7	–	164 293
Q4	9 268	2 075	36.3	3.6	–	42.4	4.9	–	173 254
2003 Q1	8 824	2 095	44.2	5.0	0.1	34.7	4.5	0.1	175 947
Q2	8 835	2 108	46.9	4.4	0.2	39.3	4.1	0.1	187 676
Q3	9 165	1 894	45.8	3.8	–	37.5	4.5	–	188 711
Q4	9 232	2 123	40.6	3.0	0.1	46.9	4.1	0.1	193 373
2004 Q1	9 510	2 346	47.0	6.5	–	34.0	5.1	–	194 276
Q2	9 754	2 287	52.1	4.3	0.1	43.1	4.3	0.1	204 679
Q3	9 783	2 488	51.3	3.6	–	43.6	5.3	–	212 505
Q4	9 832	2 351	44.0	4.6	–	45.8	5.8	–	211 812
2005 Q1	9 645†	2 217†	44.5	7.1	0.1	35.7	6.4	–	214 704
Q2	9 695	2 677	..	..	..	..	..	..	216 780
Q3	9 851	2 628	..	..	..	..	..	..	220 477
Q4	..	2 517	..	..	..	..	..	..	221 407
2003 Jul	..	692	..	..	..	..	..	..	186 807
Aug	..	597	..	..	..	..	..	..	191 100
Sep	..	605	..	..	..	..	..	..	188 227
Oct	..	724	..	..	..	..	..	..	195 551
Nov	..	743	..	..	..	..	..	..	189 913
Dec	..	656	..	..	..	..	..	..	194 655
2004 Jan	..	796	..	..	..	..	..	..	195 238
Feb	..	754	..	..	..	..	..	..	192 165
Mar	..	796	..	..	..	..	..	..	195 426
Apr	..	880	..	..	..	..	..	..	201 796
May	..	697	..	..	..	..	..	..	203 015
Jun	..	710	..	..	..	..	..	..	209 225
Jul	..	758	..	..	..	..	..	..	211 663
Aug	..	889	..	..	..	..	..	..	211 314
Sep	..	841	..	..	..	..	..	..	214 537
Oct	..	742	..	..	..	..	..	..	214 509
Nov	..	805	..	..	..	..	..	..	212 354
Dec	..	803	..	..	..	..	..	..	208 574
2005 Jan	..	646†	..	..	..	..	..	..	212 952
Feb	..	770	..	..	..	..	..	..	213 093
Mar	..	801	..	..	..	..	..	..	218 067
Apr	..	955	..	..	..	..	..	..	213 950
May	..	772	..	..	..	..	..	..	217 361
Jun	..	950	..	..	..	..	..	..	219 029
Jul	..	950	..	..	..	..	..	..	221 548
Aug	..	833	..	..	..	..	..	..	220 141
Sep	..	845	..	..	..	..	..	..	219 742
Oct	..	839	..	..	..	..	..	..	223 550†
Nov	..	872	..	..	..	..	..	..	217 427
Dec	..	781	..	..	..	..	..	..	223 244

1 Monthly data collection ceased after March 2003. Seasonally adjusted data for Great Britain are no longer updated. Seasonally adjusted data for England are available from the website of the Office of the Deputy Prime Minister (ODPM): **www.odpm.gov.uk**

2 Includes registered and non-registered social landlords.

3 Series is based on mortgage lending by all financial institutions rather than building societies only, as previously published. This change has been made necessary because of the mergers, takeovers and conversions to plc status affecting the building society sector. The series is based on the ODPM's survey of mortgage lenders (at completion stage), but now includes all mortgage lenders rather than building societies only. From February 2002, monthly data have been obtained from the enlarged survey and quarterly data from 2002Q2 are based on monthly prices. From September 2005, figures are based on the new Regulated Mortgage Survey (CML/BankSearch). Prices have been chain-linked to adjust for the structural change arising from the new survey.

Sources: Office for National Statistics;
Enquiries Column 1 020 7533 6010;
Department of Trade and Industry ; Column 2 020 7944 5583;
Office of the Deputy Prime Minister;
Columns 3-8 0117 372 8055; Column 9 020 7944 3325

Fixed investment in dwellings

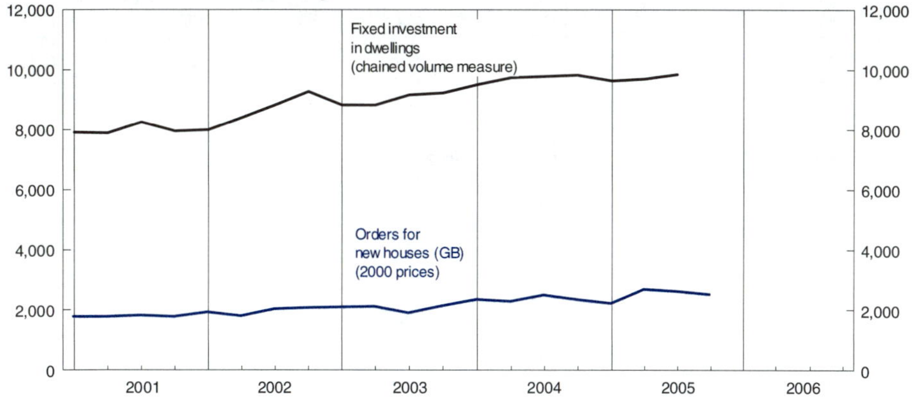

Housing completions (Great Britain, NSA)

Percentage change, quarter on corresponding quarter of previous year

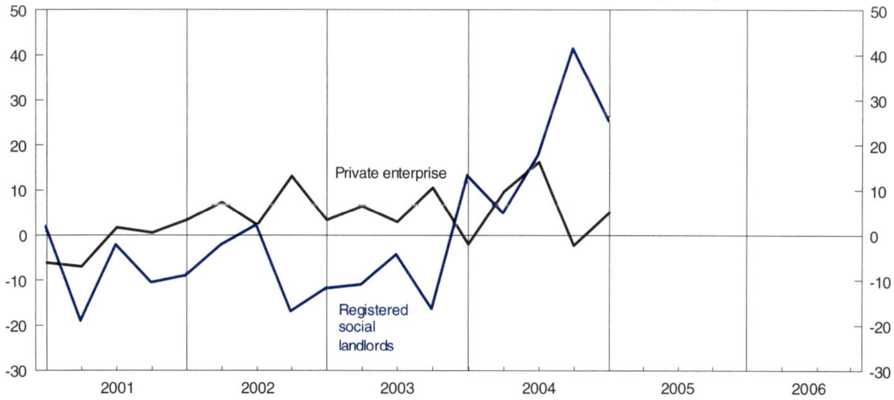

5.5 Number of property transactions[1,2,3,7]

Thousands

	Number of property transactions		
	Not seasonally adjusted England & Wales	Seasonally adjusted England & Wales[4,5]	Not seasonally adjusted England, Wales & N. Ireland
	FTAP		FTAR
2001	1 457		1 497
2002	1 586		1 627
2003	1 345		1 397
2004	1 792		1 848
2005	1 529		1 595
		FTAQ	
2001 Q1	327	347	337
Q2	347	358	359
Q3	396	368	405
Q4	387	384	396
2002 Q1	342	375	351
Q2	395	404	404
Q3	457	415	468
Q4	392	391	404
2003 Q1	340	363	359
Q2	306	317	320
Q3	358	325	369
Q4	340	339	349
2004 Q1	447	477	457
Q2	452	470	463
Q3	494	446	507
Q4	398	398	420
2005 Q1	300	337	329
Q2	352	356	363
Q3	447	404	461
Q4	430	432	443
2001 Jan	123	114	127
Feb	99	117	102
Mar	105	116	108
Apr	101	114	105
May	121	122	126
Jun	125	122	128
Jul	132	121	135
Aug	140	123	143
Sep	124	124	127
Oct	140	126	143
Nov	137	137	141
Dec	110	122	112
2002 Jan	131	124	134
Feb	108	126	110
Mar	104	126	106
Apr	129	135	132
May	137	138	140

	Number of property transactions		
	Not seasonally adjusted England & Wales	Seasonally adjusted England & Wales[4,5]	Not seasonally adjusted England, Wales & N. Ireland
Jun	129	131	132
Jul	152	134	154
Aug	166	149	171
Sep	139	133	144
Oct	147	133	151
Nov	127	131	131
Dec	118	128	122
2003 Jan	131	125	137
Feb	103	119	109
Mar	106	119	113
Apr	101	112	108
May	101	105	105
Jun	103	101	107
Jul	132	116	135
Aug	112	105	116
Sep	114	104	118
Oct	120	108	124
Nov	110	118	113
Dec	111	113	113
2004 Jan	157	155	160
Feb	148	172	152
Mar	142	150	145
Apr	140	156	143
May	145	155	148
Jun	167	159	172
Jul[6]	175	158	179
Aug[6]	159	144	163
Sep	160	145	165
Oct	148	144	142
Nov	123	123	142
Dec	128	132	136
2005 Jan	100	103	109
Feb	102	118	114
Mar	98	116	105
Apr	109	114	112
May	109	117	113
Jun	134	126	138
Jul	132	124	136
Aug	153	133	158
Sep	163	147	167
Oct	140	134	144
Nov	144	145	148
Dec	146	154	150
2006 Jan	131	133	134

1 The figures are based on counts of the relevant administrative forms successfully processed each month. For completions up to and including November 2003 the relevant form was the Particulars Delivered form. Since December 2003 the relevant form is the Land Transaction Return associated with the introduction of Stamp Duty Land Tax (although in December 2003 most forms processed were still Particulars Delivered forms). The count of Land Transaction Return forms is based on the month when the Stamp Duty Land Tax certificate is issued. The figures for the the latest month includes estimates for returns where a certificate has been issued but the form was not captured on the database at the time the count was taken. The figure is therefore subject to revision next month.

2 Because of the change in administrative arrangements associated with the introduction of Stamp Duty Land Tax, the figures from December 2003 onwards may not be comparable with the earlier series. In particular Land Transaction Returns in respect of transactions subject to Stamp Duty Land Tax are being submitted more promptly by conveyancers than Particulars Delivered forms in respect of transactions subject to stamp duty. The overhang of particulars delivered forms into the first quarter of 2004 has boosted the total property transactions processed figures in that quarter. Other reasons for higher figures since the introduction of Stamp Duty Land Tax include (1) there are some types of transaction which require a Land Transaction Return which did not require a Particulars Delivered form and (2) there are higher numbers of registering commercial transactions.

3 Because of the time lags involved, the series above should be lagged by one month to give a broad representation of transactions completed in the month. However this relationship was weaker in the second quarter of 2002, because of the operational pressures in the network of Stamp Offices which delayed the processing of a proportion of property transactions.

4 The Jubilee celebrations meant that the late May bank holiday was taken in June 2002. Seasonal features in the data arising from the May Bank holiday will therefore not automatically be removed by the process of seasonal adjustment. Caution should therefore be taken when interpreting monthly movements involving May or June 2002 data.

5 The sum of seasonally adjusted components does not exactly match the unadjusted (definitive) annual total.

6 On 19 July 2004 the Inland Revenue ended the arrangement under which a Stamp Duty Land Tax certificate could be issued even though some of the information had not been provided (the 'light touch' process). This is likely to have reduced the transaction count for July and August by a few thousand.

7 Seasonally adjusted figures have been revised back to January 2001 and not seasonally adjusted figures back to September 2004 in this edition.

Source: HM Revenue and Customs; Enquiries 020 7147 2941

5.6 Change in inventories
Chained volume measures[1]

Reference year 2002, £ million

		Manufacturing industries					Distributive trades			
	Mining and quarrying	Materials and fuel	Work in progress	Finished goods	Total	Elect-ricity, gas and water supply	Wholesale[2]	Retail[2]	Other industries[3]	Change in inventories
Level of inventories at end-December 2004	*1034*	*16 155*	*15 931*	*19 676*	*51 762*	*1726*	*27 873*	*26 080*	*45 284*	*153 759*
	FAEA	FBNF	FBNG	FBNH	DHBM	FAEB	FAJX	FBYN	DLWX	CAFU
2001 Q1	63	–652	325	–133	–459	–214	566	–130	1 215	1 040
Q2	–45	–200	331	224	354	190	–76	–160	1 112	1 375
Q3	93	352	271	32	656	88	519	229	76	1 662
Q4	–15	93	–413	45	–275	–15	–299	1 076	1 647	2 119
2002 Q1	48	118	36	615	769	–63	13	674	–264	1 177
Q2	–30	–82	–159	–128	–369	140	810	1 112	–1 269	394
Q3	–20	–115	341	–263	–37	–66	431	–74	246	480
Q4	–26	–311	–222	–588	–1 121	–110	–643	–94	2 852	858
2003 Q1	–25	540	137	34	711	67	169	167	–986	103
Q2	53	–385	–130	–215	–730	–5	–583	455	423	–387
Q3	–86	–213	–246	279	–180	–41	275	274	2 097	2 339
Q4	1	–34	–266	–228	–528	–1	369	247	2 459	2 547
2004 Q1	4†	–178†	132†	–607†	–653	166†	–229†	828†	1 222	1 338
Q2	3	–34	–521	469	–86	–188	978	–153	676	1 230
Q3	–42	113	4	157	274	10	–1	544	303	1 088
Q4	–5	–36	–274	–98	–408	–74	515	409	1 840	2 277
2005 Q1	5	254	197	63	514†	–107	75	–630	1 131†	988†
Q2	–29	–179	151	–134	–162	193	560	–846	970	686
Q3	–20	–61	103	15	57	93	256	712	–297	801
Q4	7	–63	412	136	485	406	239	–141	–788	208

1 Estimates are given to the nearest £ million but cannot be regarded as accurate to this degree.
2 Excluding the motor trades.
3 Quarterly alignment adjustment is included in this series. For a description see notes to the *Economic Trends Annual Supplement.* For details of adjustments, see notes section in the Sector and Financial Accounts article in *UK Economic Accounts.*

Sources: Office for National Statistics; Enquiries Columns 1-8 020 7533 6264; Columns 9-10 020 7533 6031

5.7 Inventory ratios

	Manufacturers' inventories[1] to manufacturing production				Retail inventories[1] to retail sales[2]	Total inventories[1,3] to gross value added
	Materials and fuel	Work in progress	Finished goods	Total inventories		
	FAPG	FAPH	FAPI	FAPF	FAPC	FDCA
2000 Q4	101.4	99.0	100.0	100.2	101.2	100
2001 Q1	97.6	101.0	99.3	99.3	98.9	100
Q2	98.6	105.3	102.8	102.3	96.3	101
Q3	100.9	107.1	103.0	103.6	95.6	102
Q4	103.6	106.8	105.5	105.3	99.2	103
2002 Q1	101.8	104.5	106.1	104.2	100.5	103
Q2	101.8	104.0	106.0	104.1	103.5	103
Q3	100.1	105.0	103.6	103.0	102.4	102
Q4	99.7	105.2	102.0	102.3	100.1	103
2003 Q1	102.8	105.9	102.1	103.5	102.0	102
Q2	100.4	105.0	100.9	102.0	102.6	101
Q3	98.4	102.8	101.6	101.0	102.7	102
Q4	97.3	100.2	99.5	99.1	101.7	103
2004 Q1	96.4	100.2	96.1	97.5	104.3	102
Q2	95.1	97.3	97.1	96.5	99.7	102
Q3	96.3	97.4	98.8	97.6	102.1	103
Q4	95.6	95.2	98.0	96.4	103.7	103
2005 Q1	98.7	97.2	99.5	98.5	103.2	104
Q2	99.9	97.3	99.1	98.8	101.9	104
Q3	101.1	97.4	98.6	99.0	100.6	..

1 Chained volume measure: reference year 2002.
2 Classes 64-65 excluding activity headings 6510 and 6520, retail distribution of motor vehicles and parts, and filling stations.
3 Including quarterly alignment adjustment. For details of adjustments see notes section in the Sector and Financial Accounts article in *UK Economic Accounts.*

Source: Office for National Statistics; Enquiries Columns 1-6 020 7533 6264

Inventory ratios

Chained volume measures
Indices, 2002 = 100
seasonally adjusted

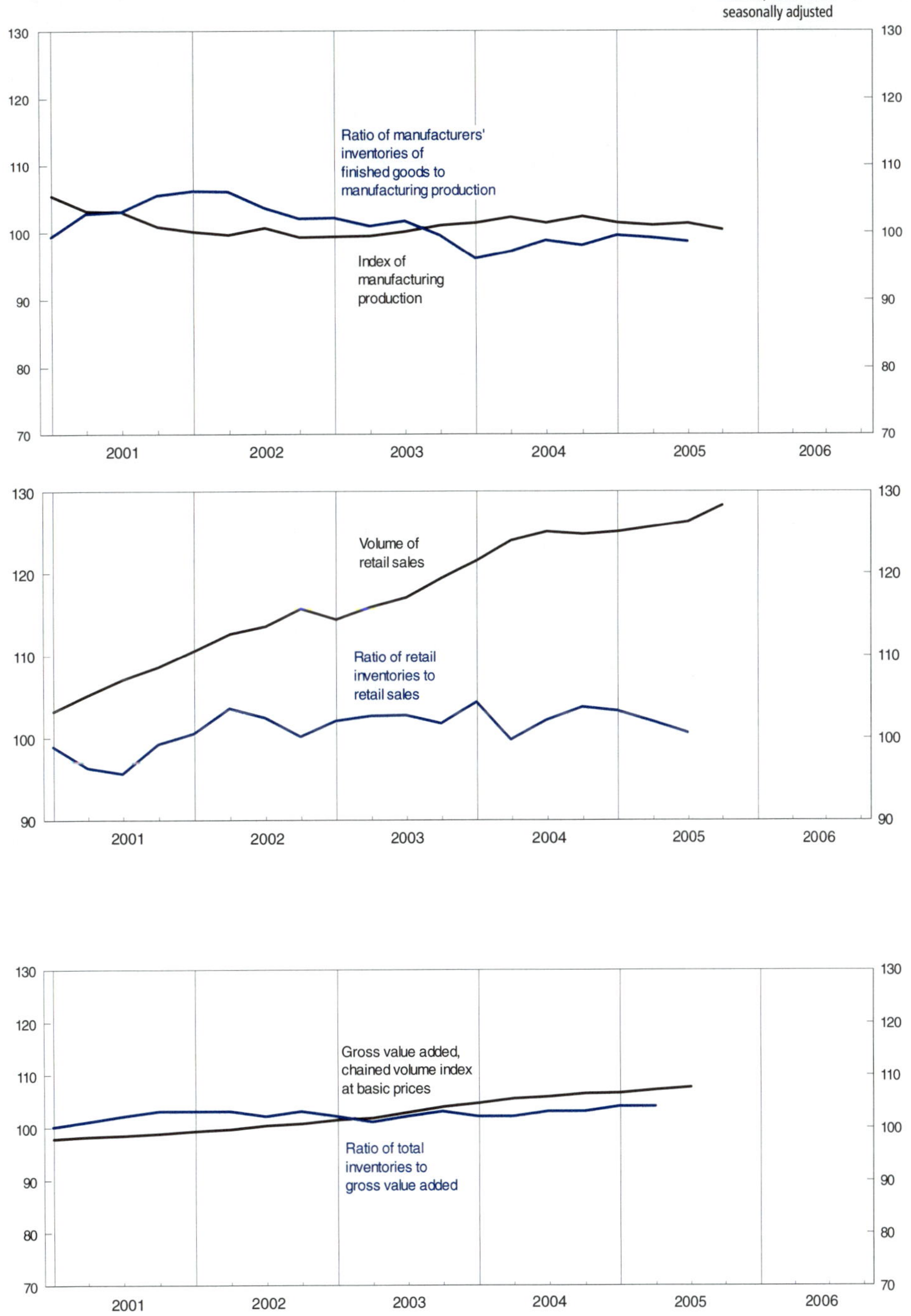

5.8 Retail sales, new registrations of cars and credit business (Great Britain)

	Value of retail sales per week: total (average 2000=100)[1]	Volume of retail sales per week (average 2000=100)[1]								New registrations of cars (NSA, '000s)[2]	Total consumer credit: net lending (£ million)[3,4]	*of which*	
				Predominantly non-food stores									
		All retailers	Predominantly food stores+	Total+	Non-specialist stores	Textile, clothing and footwear stores	Household goods stores	Other stores	Non-store and repair+			Credit cards[5]	Other lending[5]
Sales in 2000, £ million	*207 149*	*207 149*	*89 041*	*106 359*	*18 781*	*27 880*	*27 699*	*31 999*	*11 749*				
	EAQV	EAPS	EAPT	EAPV	EAPU	EAPX	EAPY	EAPW	EAPZ	BCGT	RLMH	VZQX	VZQY
2001	105.9	106.1	104.1	107.8	106.0	109.4	109.8	105.7	106.0	2 577.5	17 590†	6 287†	11 387†
2002	111.1	112.7	108.2	116.4	110.4	121.0	117.9	114.7	113.2	2 682.0	21 303	7 621	13 733
2003	113.9†	116.5†	111.8	121.4†	113.7	128.9	123.0	117.8†	107.5	2 646.2	20 173	8 930	11 423
2004	119.1	123.5	116.4	130.0	117.5†	139.0	131.5	128.3	117.7	2 598.8	23 030	9 997	13 058
2005	120.3	125.9	119.6	132.0	119.0	143.7	132.1†	129.3	118.4†	2 443.3	16 783	6 010	10 807
2001 Q1	102.9	103.2	102.8	103.8	104.4	105.0	105.9	100.5	100.4	704.2	3 320†	1 356	2 156†
Q2	105.4	105.2	103.7	106.5	106.0	107.1	109.6	103.6	105.8	617.7	4 599	1 681	2 848
Q3	107.0	107.1	104.6	108.9	106.7	110.7	110.1	107.7	110.1	725.6	4 059	1 233†	2 838
Q4	108.1	108.6	105.5	111.1	107.5	113.9	112.9	109.1	108.6	530.0	5 612	2 017	3 545
2002 Q1	109.9	110.6	106.7	114.5	108.8	118.4	115.0	114.2	104.7	758.7	5 047	1 952	3 198
Q2	111.1	112.7	108.0	116.7	109.3	120.6	117.1	117.2	111.5	650.0	4 717	1 657	2 988
Q3	111.7	113.6	109.0	116.9	111.5	122.2	118.1	114.4	118.3	744.6	6 099	2 051	4 020
Q4	113.4†	115.6†	111.0	118.8†	112.5†	124.3†	120.2†	116.5†	121.1†	528.7	5 440	1 961	3 527
2003 Q1	112.5	114.5	110.2†	118.8	110.9	126.7	117.9	117.5	107.6	737.6	4 852	2 220	2 692
Q2	113.2	115.8	111.8	120.1	112.5	128.0	121.7	116.4	106.2	642.7	5 474	2 519	2 899
Q3	114.6	117.1	112.7	121.9	114.6	131.2	122.9	117.3	106.5	742.8	5 153	2 183	2 987
Q4	116.1	119.1	113.5	124.8	116.3	132.6	125.7	122.2	110.0	523.1	4 694	2 008	2 845
2004 Q1	118.0	121.6	114.7	128.3	116.0	137.8	128.0	127.4	113.0	762.2	5 962	2 381	3 422
Q2	119.7	123.8	116.3	130.6	118.8	140.2	129.9	129.8	118.4	629.8	5 786	2 475	3 278
Q3	120.3	124.9	117.5	131.9	119.8	140.8	133.1	130.1	119.0	709.9	5 752	2 621	3 165
Q4	119.6	124.5	117.7	130.7	117.3	141.4	131.6	128.6	120.3	496.9	5 530	2 520	3 193
2005 Q1	119.9	124.9	119.0	130.3	120.3	142.0	129.9	126.3	120.5	697.9	5 821	2 260	3 367
Q2	120.1	125.3	119.2	131.0	117.5	144.6	129.2	128.5	121.0	594.4	4 515	1 422	3 074
Q3	120.3	125.8	119.8	132.0	117.8	144.3	129.9	131.4	115.7	677.1	3 395	1 125	2 318
Q4	121.5	127.8	121.2	134.4	120.6	146.9	134.1	131.9	118.1	473.9	3 052	1 203	2 048
2004 Jan	118.1†	121.2†	114.3†	128.1†	115.2†	137.8†	127.3†	127.8†	111.5†	199.6	2 154†	742†	1 412†
Feb	117.7	121.1	114.7	127.5	116.2	136.4	127.6	126.4	111.5	92.3	2 053	590	1 462
Mar	118.2	122.3	115.1	129.0	116.4	139.0	128.8	128.0	115.3	470.3	1 820	1 188	632
Apr	118.9	122.8	115.5	129.7	117.7	140.0	128.7	128.5	115.4	191.1	1 524	803	722
May	119.8	123.9	116.4	130.6	119.8	141.1	129.3	129.0	119.3	197.6	2 105	682	1 423
Jun	120.2	124.5	117.0	131.4	118.9	139.6	131.3	131.5	120.1	241.1	1 999	902	1 096
Jul	119.6	124.0	116.5	130.9	117.9	137.5	133.1	130.8	118.2	188.2	1 923	925	998
Aug	120.2	124.7	117.7	131.6	121.2	142.3	132.0	127.9	116.3	87.3	2 009	938	1 071
Sep	121.0	125.9	118.0	132.9	120.1	142.1	133.9	131.4	121.7	434.4	1 969	849	1 120
Oct	120.4	125.1	118.0	131.7	118.9	142.9	131.6	129.6	119.5	171.8	1 695	749	946
Nov	120.6	125.6	118.2	132.3	119.5	141.8	135.3	128.8	120.6	175.6	1 996	912	1 084
Dec	118.2	123.3	117.1	128.7	114.1	139.8	128.5	127.6	120.8	149.5	1 801	692	1 109
2005 Jan	120.3	125.2	119.5	130.6	120.0	140.8	132.6	126.1	120.6	180.0	2 389	1 085	1 304
Feb	119.6	124.8	118.8	130.0	119.3	142.8	129.2	125.7	123.1	77.5	1 702	715	987
Mar	119.8	124.6	118.6	130.4	121.3	142.4	128.4	127.0	118.3	440.4	1 819	649	1 169
Apr	119.7	125.0	118.8	130.3	117.6	143.9	128.3	127.7	123.2	178.9	1 273	292	982
May	119.4	124.7	118.8	130.2	116.4	143.8	128.7	127.8	119.7	189.2	1 551	696	856
Jun	120.9	126.1	119.8	132.1	118.4	145.8	130.4	129.6	120.4	226.3	1 458	308	1 150
Jul	120.2	126.1	120.0	130.8	115.7	143.3	129.0	130.4	117.4	175.3	1 036	325	711
Aug	120.1	125.6	118.7	132.2	118.5	144.1	129.7	132.0	118.0	84.2	1 365	450	916
Sep	120.4	126.3	120.4	132.8	118.9	145.2	130.7	131.8	112.6	417.6	1 202	409	793
Oct	120.7	126.8	120.8	132.9	119.7	144.2	131.5	132.1	115.8	153.9	1 261	560	701
Nov	121.7	128.0	121.5	134.6	121.4	150.6	131.8	130.9	117.6	160.8	892	339	553
Dec	122.0	128.5	121.4	135.5	120.7	146.1	138.1	132.6	120.2	159.2	931	195	736
2006 Jan	120.6	126.9	120.7	132.8	119.8	143.9	133.9	130.0	120.2	154.0	1 319	733	586

1 Great Britain only, excluding the motor trades. Information for periods earlier than those shown is available from ONS Newport (tel 01633 812509).

2 Seasonally adjusted data are not published in *Economic Trends*. Data up to 1998 are published in the *Economic Trends Annual Supplement*.

3 Net lending equals changes in amounts outstanding adjusted to remove distortions arising from revaluations of debt such as write-offs.

4 Covers all institutions providing finance for consumers, including loans by banks on personal accounts and on bank credit cards and charge cards, by insurance companies, retailers and other specialist lenders, but excluding loans for house purchase.

5 These figures fall outside the scope of National Statistics.

Sources: Office for National Statistics;
Enquiries Columns 1-9 01633 812713; Columns 11-13 01633 812782;
Department for Transport;
Enquiries Column 10 020 7944 3077.

Volume of retail sales (excluding motor trades)
Weekly average 2000 = 100
130
120
110
100
90
Quarterly average
2001
2002
2003
2004
2005
2006

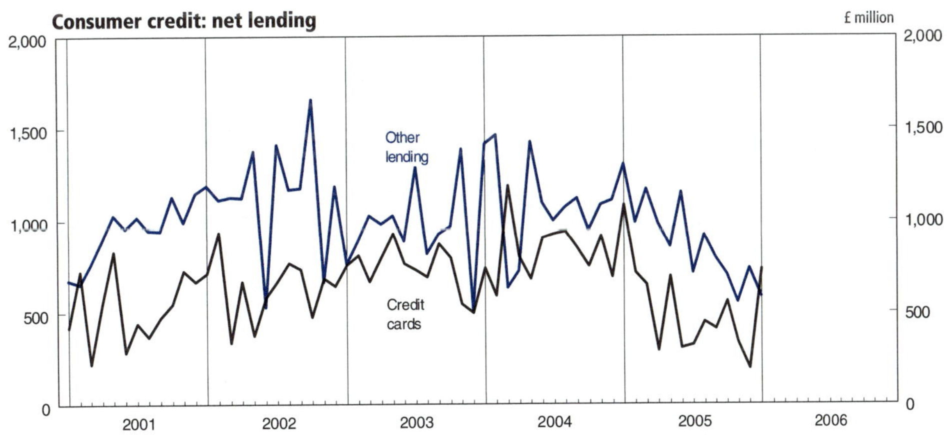
Consumer credit: net lending
£ million
2,000
1,500
1,000
500
0
Other lending
Credit cards
2001
2002
2003
2004
2005
2006

5.9 Inland energy consumption: primary fuel input basis

Million tonnes of oil equivalent

Seasonally adjusted and temperature corrected[1] (annualised rates)

	Coal[2]	Petroleum[3]	Natural gas[4]	Primary electricity[5]: Nuclear	Primary electricity[5]: Wind and natural flow Hydro[6]	Net imports[7]	Total
	FDAI	FDAJ	FDAK	FDAL	FDAM	FDAW	FDAH
2001	43.1	76.6	96.7	20.8	0.4	0.9	238.6
2002	40.0	75.3	98.7	20.0	0.5	0.7	235.3
2003	42.9	74.9	97.7	20.0	0.4	0.2	236.1
2004	42.0	77.4	100.0	18.1	0.6	0.6	238.9
2005	42.5	78.6	95.9	18.6	0.5	0.7	236.8
2000 Q1	38.9	81.3	110.8	20.1	0.6	1.1	252.8
Q2	40.6	74.4	95.3	19.8	0.4	1.3	231.8
Q3	40.2	77.8	85.4	19.4	0.5	1.3	224.5
Q4	40.5	77.6	103.1	19.4	0.5	1.2	242.2
2001 Q1	45.6	75.8	108.8	19.9	0.3	1.1	251.5
Q2	44.6	73.3	93.1	19.0	0.4	0.9	231.3
Q3	42.5	79.4	84.6	21.8	0.5	0.9	229.7
Q4	39.8	77.8	100.6	22.6	0.5	0.7	242.0
2002 Q1	42.1	77.9	108.2	21.2	0.6	0.6	250.6
Q2	35.8	76.3	95.9	20.0	0.7	1.0	229.6
Q3	38.4	76.2	88.3	19.9	0.5	0.2	223.5
Q4	43.6	70.8	102.6	18.9	0.4	1.1	237.4
2003 Q1	42.9	72.7	108.1	21.0	0.3	0.3	245.3
Q2	44.9	78.5	92.7	20.6	0.5	0.1	237.3
Q3	41.9	73.8	85.6	19.7	0.5	–0.1	221.4
Q4	41.8	74.6	104.5	18.6	0.4	0.4	240.3
2004 Q1	43.5	71.0	111.2	20.2	0.5	0.4	246.8
Q2	40.6	79.4	97.2	17.2	0.6	0.6	235.5
Q3	41.0	77.1	86.8	17.9	0.8	0.7	224.4
Q4	42.9	82.1	105.1	17.3	0.6	0.8	248.8
2005 Q1	45.7	75.2†	108.4	19.3	0.5	0.5	249.6†
Q2	40.6	80.8	93.3	18.3	0.6	0.7	234.2
Q3	38.1	77.7	84.0†	19.6	0.5	0.7	220.6
Q4	45.7	80.5	98.0	17.1	0.5	1.0	242.8

Percentage change, quarter on corresponding quarter of previous year

	Coal	Petroleum	Natural gas	Nuclear	Wind and natural flow Hydro	Net imports	Total
	FDAP	FDAQ	FDAR	FDAS	FDAT	FDAX	FDAO
2000 Q1	*3.9*	*–0.2*	*5.4*	*–13.8*	*12.1*	*–10.6*	*1.5*
Q2	*7.7*	*–5.0*	*5.4*	*–14.6*	*–25.9*	*1.9*	*0.2*
Q3	*5.1*	*3.5*	*1.3*	*–9.9*	*–12.3*	*12.9*	*1.6*
Q4	*3.1*	*2.0*	*–0.2*	*–7.7*	*6.2*	*–5.1*	*0.4*
2001 Q1	*17.2*	*–6.7*	*–1.8*	*–1.0*	*–43.8*	–	*–0.5*
Q2	*9.9*	*–1.5*	*–2.3*	*–4.2*	*–9.6*	*–30.3*	*–0.3*
Q3	*5.7*	*2.1*	*–1.0*	*12.8*	*4.7*	*–29.0*	*2.3*
Q4	*–1.6*	*0.3*	*–2.4*	*16.6*	*6.1*	*–45.0*	*–0.1*
2002 Q1	*–7.7*	*2.7*	*–0.5*	*6.8*	*73.8*	*–43.7*	*–0.4*
Q2	*–19.8*	*4.1*	*3.0*	*5.6*	*73.5*	*5.5*	*–0.7*
Q3	*–9.6*	*–4.1*	*4.4*	*–8.8*	*11.4*	*–75.5*	*–2.7*
Q4	*9.4*	*–9.0*	*2.1*	*–16.3*	*–32.7*	*67.6*	*–1.9*
2003 Q1	*1.9*	*–6.7*	–	*–1.3*	*–42.4*	*–56.2*	*–2.1*
Q2	*25.5*	*2.9*	*–3.3*	*2.9*	*–29.6*	*–89.0*	*3.4*
Q3	*9.1*	*–3.1*	*–3.0*	*–0.9*	*–13.6*	–	*–0.9*
Q4	*–4.0*	*5.3*	*1.8*	*–1.6*	*–2.7*	*–59.6*	*1.2*
2004 Q1	*1.5*	*–2.3*	*2.8*	*–3.9*	*58.6*	*61.0*	*0.6*
Q2	*–9.7*	*1.1*	*4.9*	*–16.5*	*16.7*	–	*–0.8*
Q3	*–2.0*	*4.5*	*1.3*	*–9.1*	*66.1*	–	*1.3*
Q4	*2.5*	*10.1*	*0.6*	*–7.3*	*64.6*	*92.5*	*3.5*
2005 Q1	*5.1*	*5.9*†	*–2.5*	*–4.1*	*–7.0*	*8.8*	*1.1*†
Q2	–	*1.7*	*–4.0*	*6.5*	*1.6*	*26.1*	*–0.5*
Q3	*–7.2*	*0.8*	*–3.2*†	*9.3*	*–33.2*	*–5.5*	*–1.7*
Q4	*6.6*	*–1.9*	*–6.7*	*–1.3*	*–18.7*	*15.9*	*–2.4*

1 For details of temperature correction see DTI energy statistics website at **www.dti.gov.uk/energy/inform/dukes/dukes2003/01longterm.pdf**
2 Includes solid renewable sources (wood, straw, waste), and net foreign trade and stock changes in other solid fuels.
3 Excludes non-energy use.
4 Includes gas used during production, colliery methane, landfill gas and sewage gas. Excludes gas flared or re-injected and non energy-use of gas.
5 Not temperature corrected.
6 Includes generation by solar photovoltaics (PV). Excludes generation from pumped storage stations.
7 Not seasonally adjusted.

Source: Department of Trade and Industry; Enquiries 020 7215 2698

Inland energy consumption

Million tonnes of oil equivalent, seasonally adjusted

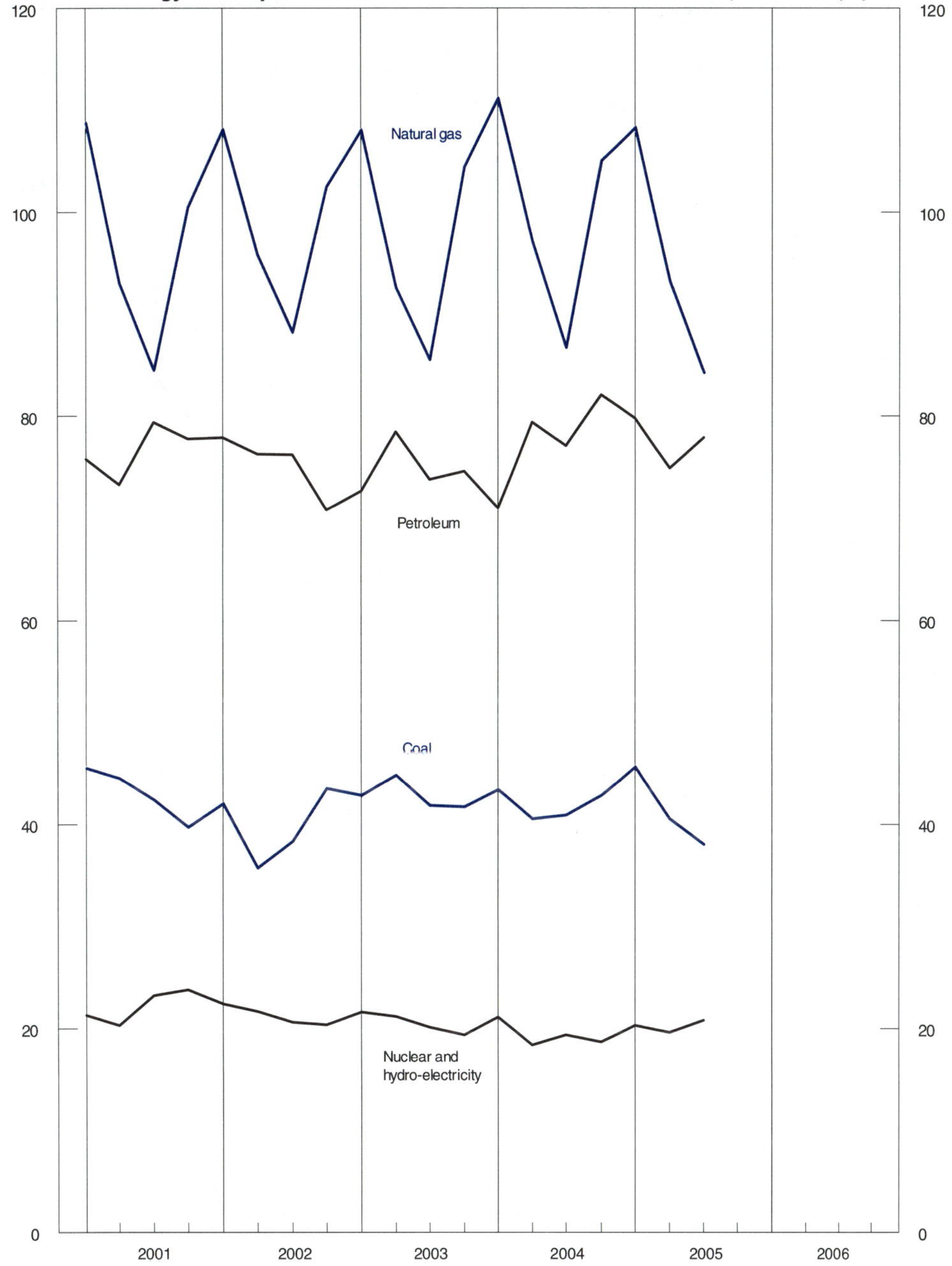

6.1 Sterling exchange rates and UK reserves[1]

Not seasonally adjusted

	Sterling exchange rate against major currencies[2]								UK international reserves[4] at end of period (£ million)	Sterling exchange rate index 1990 = 100
	Japanese yen	US dollar	Swiss franc	Euro[3]	Danish kroner	Norwegian kroner	Swedish kronor	Hong Kong dollar		
	AJFO	AUSS	AJFD	THAP	AJFK	AJFJ	AJFI	AJFU	THFE	AGBG
2001	174.90	1.4400	2.430	1.6087	11.987	12.944	14.886	11.2335	27 773	105.8
2002	187.84	1.5026	2.334	1.5909	11.821	11.953	14.570	11.7265	26 566	106.0
2003	189.34	1.6346	2.197	1.4456	10.742	11.562	13.189	12.7337	25 724	100.2
2004	198.10	1.8320	2.276	1.4739	10.965	12.342	13.453	14.2707	25 908	104.1
2005	200.14	1.8197	2.265	1.4629	10.901	11.718	13.577	14.1477	28 018	103.3
2001 Q1	172.26	1.4584	2.424	1.5814	11.7988	12.965	14.230	11.3765	30 457	104.5
Q2	174.19	1.4208	2.487	1.6280	12.1436	13.039	14.847	11.0866	30 632	106.4
Q3	174.67	1.4380	2.432	1.6152	12.0231	12.928	15.203	11.2092	29 662	106.1
Q4	178.45	1.4428	2.375	1.6111	11.9887	12.845	15.264	11.2548	27 773	106.1
2002 Q1	188.79	1.4260	2.396	1.6263	12.0863	12.700	14.895	11.1230	28 053	106.9
Q2	185.29	1.4630	2.329	1.5923	11.8379	11.956	14.564	11.4015	28 623	105.3
Q3	184.85	1.5495	2.305	1.5747	11.6973	11.662	14.538	12.0871	27 950	105.7
Q4	192.42	1.5720	2.304	1.5716	11.6733	11.494	14.285	12.2547	26 566	106.0
2003 Q1	190.67	1.6017	2.189	1.4937	11.0987	11.313	13.709	12.5030	26 388	102.3
Q2	191.90	1.6194	2.163	1.4256	10.5851	11.344	13.032	12.6352	25 199	99.1
Q3	189.14	1.6108	2.209	1.4300	10.6264	11.794	13.103	12.5605	26 954	99.2
Q4	185.64	1.7065	2.228	1.4334	10.6591	11.796	12.913	13.2305	25 724	100.2
2004 Q1	197.07	1.8391	2.306	1.4708	10.9571	12.703	13.507	14.2983	25 266	104.1
Q2	198.21	1.8052	2.305	1.4992	11.1529	12.387	13.712	14.0831	25 178	105.2
Q3	199.95	1.8189	2.285	1.4877	11.0633	12.478	13.627	14.1861	25 382	104.8
Q4	197.18	1.8648	2.206	1.4388	10.6958	11.798	12.966	14.5080	25 908	102.4
2005 Q1	197.53	1.8904†	2.234	1.4424	10.7362	11.889	13.092	14.7449	25 801	102.9
Q2	199.56	1.8559	2.276	1.4744	10.9788	11.863	13.572	14.4506	26 844	104.3
Q3	198.44	1.7844	2.273	1.4635	10.9160	11.534	13.709	13.8685	26 728	102.9
Q4	205.02	1.7481	2.275	1.4706	10.9687	11.584	13.935	13.5546	28 018	103.2
2003 Jul	192.72	1.6242	2.209	1.4277	10.613	11.828	13.130	12.6671	25 785	99.4
Aug	189.42	1.5950	2.200	1.4286	10.617	11.800	13.186	12.4395	26 550	99.0
Sep	185.29	1.6131	2.219	1.4338	10.649	11.755	12.994	12.5590	26 954	99.2
Oct	183.76	1.6787	2.220	1.4334	10.651	11.807	12.917	12.9962	26 131	99.8
Nov	184.47	1.6901	2.250	1.4426	10.729	11.832	12.973	13.1201	26 617	100.4
Dec	188.70	1.7507	2.214	1.4246	10.602	11.749	12.850	13.5923	25 724	100.3
2004 Jan	193.82	1.8234	2.262	1.4447	10.760	12.425	13.203	14.1598	25 329	102.4
Feb	199.16	1.8673	2.324	1.4774	11.008	12.983	13.566	14.5165	24 689	104.8
Mar	198.22	1.8267	2.332	1.4890	11.092	12.701	13.752	14.2349	25 266	105.0
Apr	194.04	1.8005	2.337	1.5022	11.182	12.458	13.775	14.0381	25 377	105.2
May	200.69	1.7876	2.293	1.4894	11.082	12.222	13.594	13.9374	24 819	104.6
Jun	199.91	1.8275	2.285	1.5050	11.189	12.482	13.767	14.2499	25 178	105.8
Jul	201.66	1.8429	2.294	1.5023	11.170	12.730	13.818	14.3740	24 579	105.9
Aug	200.87	1.8216	2.297	1.4933	11.105	12.437	13.725	14.2077	25 189	105.2
Sep	197.32	1.7922	2.265	1.4676	10.916	12.268	13.337	13.9777	25 382	103.3
Oct	196.54	1.8065	2.229	1.4455	10.751	11.895	13.093	14.0707	25 557	102.2
Nov	194.76	1.8603	2.177	1.4311	10.635	11.658	12.877	14.4662	25 757	101.7
Dec	200.23	1.9275	2.212	1.4401	10.705	11.841	12.928	14.9890	25 908	103.2
2005 Jan	193.97	1.8764	2.217	1.4331	10.664	11.783	12.979	14.6292	25 840	102.1
Feb	198.10	1.8871	2.248	1.4499	10.791	12.064	13.172	14.7185	26 080	103.3
Mar	200.51	1.9078	2.237	1.4440	10.753	11.821	13.126	14.8801	25 801	103.2
Apr	203.34	1.8960	2.267	1.4652	10.916	11.980	13.433	14.7865	26 103	104.4
May	197.70	1.8538	2.258	1.4611	10.877	11.805	13.428	14.4439	26 595	103.6
Jun	197.64	1.8179	2.302	1.4952	11.132	11.805	13.854	14.1362	26 844	104.9
Jul	195.99	1.7509	2.267	1.4547	10.850	11.523	13.717	13.6141	25 950	102.1
Aug	198.48	1.7943	2.266	1.4592	10.885	11.551	13.631	13.9444	25 437	102.8
Sep	200.86	1.8081	2.287	1.4761	11.009	11.527	13.779	14.0356	26 728	103.9
Oct	202.62	1.7640	2.273	1.4674	10.950	11.490	13.835	13.6823	26 435	103.1
Nov	205.41	1.7341	2.274	1.4719	10.980	11.522	14.080	13.4469	27 482	103.2
Dec	207.02	1.7462	2.279	1.4725	10.976	11.740	13.889	13.5390	28 018	103.3
2006 Jan	204.09	1.7678	2.259	1.4582	10.880	11.724	13.568	13.7079	..	102.7

1 These figures fall outside the scope of National Statistics.
2 Average of daily telegraphic transfer rates in London.
3 Prior to January 1999, a synthetic Euro has been calculated by geometrically averaging the bilateral exchange rates of the 11 Euro-area countries using "internal weights" based on each country's share of the extra Euro-area trade.
4 International reserves data are all valued at end-period market prices and exchange rates. They additionally include other reserve assets such as repos (sale and purchase agreements) and derivatives. Full details are shown in Table 1.2I of *Financial Statistics*.

Source: Bank of England: Enquiries 020 7601 4342

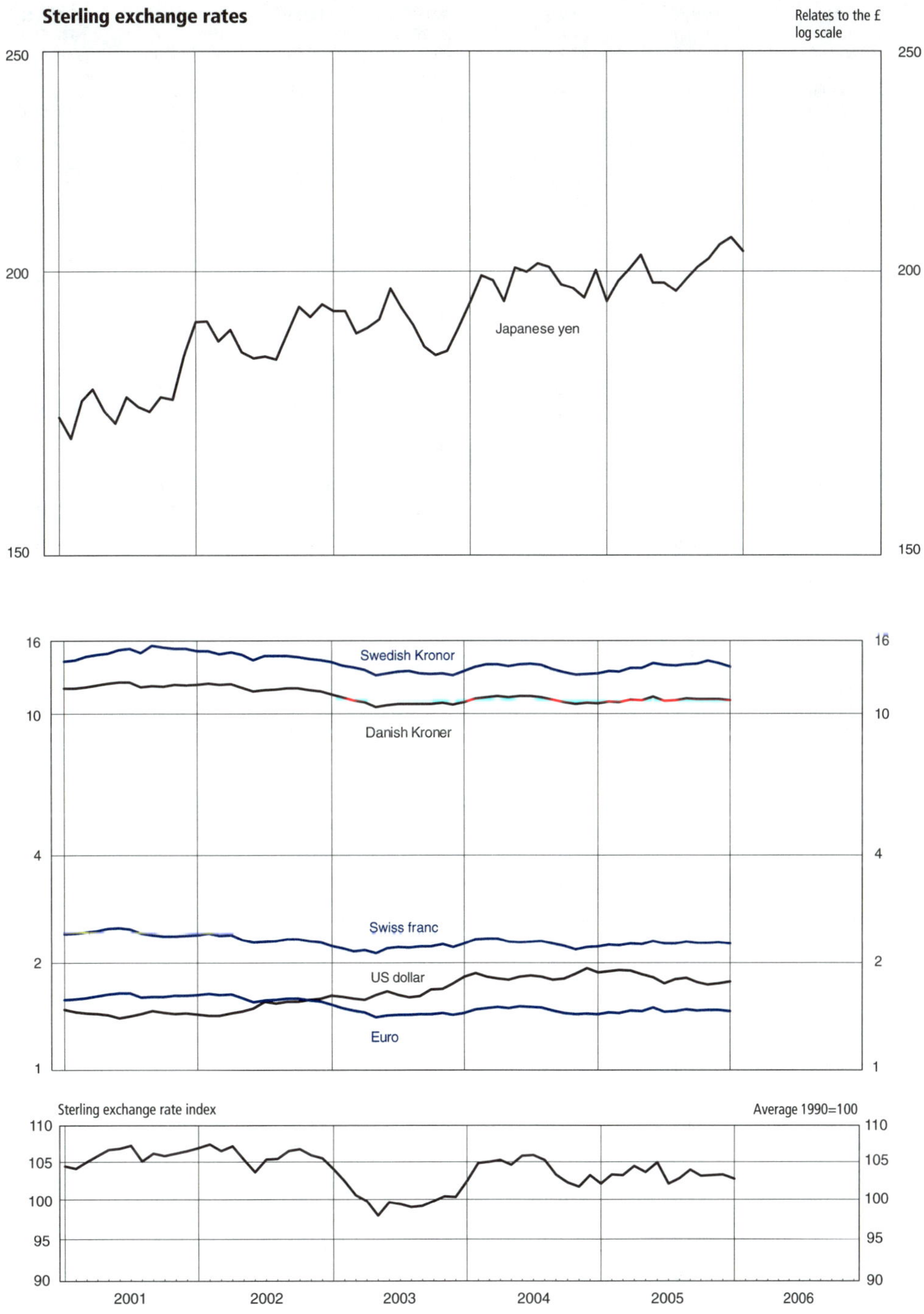
Sterling exchange rates
Relates to the £
log scale
250
200
150
Japanese yen
16
10
4
2
1
Swedish Kronor
Danish Kroner
Swiss franc
US dollar
Euro
Sterling exchange rate index
Average 1990=100
110
105
100
95
90
2001
2002
2003
2004
2005
2006

6.2 Monetary aggregates[1,2]

	M0				M4			
	Amount outstanding[3] (NSA)				Amount outstanding (NSA)			
	£ million	Annual percentage change	Amount outstanding (£ million)+	Velocity of circulation: ratio	£ million	Annual percentage change	Amount outstanding (£ million)+	Velocity of circulation: ratio
	AVAD	VQNB	AVAE	AVAM	AUYM	VQLC	AUYN	AUYU
2001	37 319	8.0	34 995†	29.76	942 433	6.7	943 600†	1.09
2002	39 540	6.0	37 238	28.99	1 008 678	7.3	1 009 634	1.08
2003	42 317	7.0	39 999	28.49	1 081 121	7.3	1 081 889	1.07
2004	44 466	5.1	42 293	28.30	1 179 117	9.3	1 179 666	1.03
2005	47 093	5.9	44 420	..	1 325 278	12.6	1 325 844	..
						VQRY		
2001 Q1	32 489	8.4	33 131†	29.91	905 800	8.3	905 315†	1.10
Q2	32 896	6.5	33 284	30.00	921 571	7.6	917 880	1.10
Q3	33 797	6.2	33 933	29.68	937 071	8.4	940 070	1.08
Q4	37 319	8.0	34 995	29.45†	942 433	6.7	943 600	1.08
2002 Q1	35 157	8.2	35 572	29.08	955 196	5.7	955 087	1.09
Q2	36 225	10.1	36 643	29.11	975 699	6.1	971 201	1.09
Q3	36 511	8.0	36 653	28.96	989 473	5.9	993 162	1.08
Q4	39 540	6.0	37 238	28.80	1 008 678	7.3	1 009 634	1.07
2003 Q1	37 184	5.8	37 926	28.83	1 020 595	7.1	1 020 699	1.07
Q2	38 403	6.0	38 910	28.34	1 047 982	7.9	1 042 722	1.07
Q3	39 348	7.8	39 480	28.43	1 051 120	6.6	1 055 575	1.07
Q4	42 317	7.0	39 999	28.38	1 081 121	7.3	1 081 889	1.06
2004 Q1	39 812	7.1	40 627	28.35	1 101 901	7.9	1 102 087	1.05
Q2	41 109	7.0	41 421	28.27	1 133 485	8.0	1 127 370	1.04
Q3	41 748	6.1	41 756	28.24	1 148 458	9.0	1 154 017	1.03
Q4	44 466	5.1	42 293	28.33	1 179 117	9.3	1 179 666	1.02
2005 Q1	42 395	6.5	42 714	27.99	1 216 988	10.6	1 217 157	1.00
Q2	42 656	3.8	42 985	28.23	1 251 036†	10.6	1 244 003	0.98
Q3	43 969	5.3	44 008	27.84	1 274 893	11.3†	1 281 528	0.97†
Q4	47 093	5.9	44 420	..	1 325 278	12.6	1 325 844	..
						VQLC		
2003 Jul	38 938	8.0	39 175†	..	1 036 608	7.3	1 038 975†	..
Aug	39 579	7.9	39 373	..	1 040 203	6.2	1 039 712	..
Sep	39 348	7.8	39 480	..	1 051 120	6.6	1 051 652	..
Oct	39 416	7.3	39 641	..	1 054 713	6.4	1 054 373	..
Nov	40 149	8.0	40 012	..	1 070 453	7.1	1 068 168	..
Dec	42 317	7.0	39 999	..	1 081 121	7.3	1 079 393	..
2004 Jan	40 222	8.0	40 235	..	1 080 398	8.7	1 089 436	..
Feb	39 448	6.8	40 274	..	1 087 970	8.4	1 095 848	..
Mar	39 812	7.1	40 627	..	1 101 901	7.9	1 098 948	..
Apr	40 799	5.7	40 819	..	1 109 089	7.6	1 105 924	..
May	40 668	4.7	41 075	..	1 121 331	8.3	1 117 716	..
Jun	41 109	7.0	41 421	..	1 133 485	8.1	1 124 858	..
Jul	41 115	5.6	41 340	..	1 133 394	9.2	1 134 157	..
Aug	41 489	4.8	41 360	..	1 143 082	9.8	1 144 573	..
Sep	41 748	6.1	41 756	..	1 148 458	9.0	1 149 231	..
Oct	41 721	5.8	41 933	..	1 158 204	9.6	1 159 257	..
Nov	42 222	5.2	42 000	..	1 166 540	8.9	1 165 606	..
Dec	44 466	5.1	42 293	..	1 179 117	9.3	1 174 132	..
2005 Jan	42 700	6.2	42 498	..	1 177 455	9.2	1 188 904	..
Feb	41 757	5.9	42 654	..	1 189 021	9.5	1 199 385	..
Mar	42 395	6.5	42 714	..	1 216 988	10.6	1 213 043	..
Apr	42 188	3.4	42 767	..	1 223 962†	10.5†	1 221 408	..
May	42 426	4.3	42 836	..	1 242 187	11.1	1 239 208	..
Jun	42 656	3.8	42 985	..	1 251 036	10.6	1 240 759	..
Jul	43 127	4.9	43 339	..	1 255 715	11.0	1 256 203	..
Aug	44 078	6.2	43 873	..	1 253 884	9.9	1 256 148	..
Sep	43 969	5.3	44 008	..	1 274 893	11.3	1 274 326	..
Oct	43 926	5.3	44 127	..	1 285 650	11.3	1 289 371	..
Nov	44 644	5.7	44 230	..	1 303 706	12.0	1 303 330	..
Dec	47 093	5.9	44 420	..	1 325 278	12.6	1 320 016	..

1 A fuller range of monetary aggregates is published monthly in *Financial Statistics*.
2 These figures fall outside the scope of National Statistics.
3 The monthly figures for M0 give the average of the amounts outstanding each Wednesday during the calendar month.

Source: Bank of England; Enquiries 020 7601 5467

Monetary aggregates

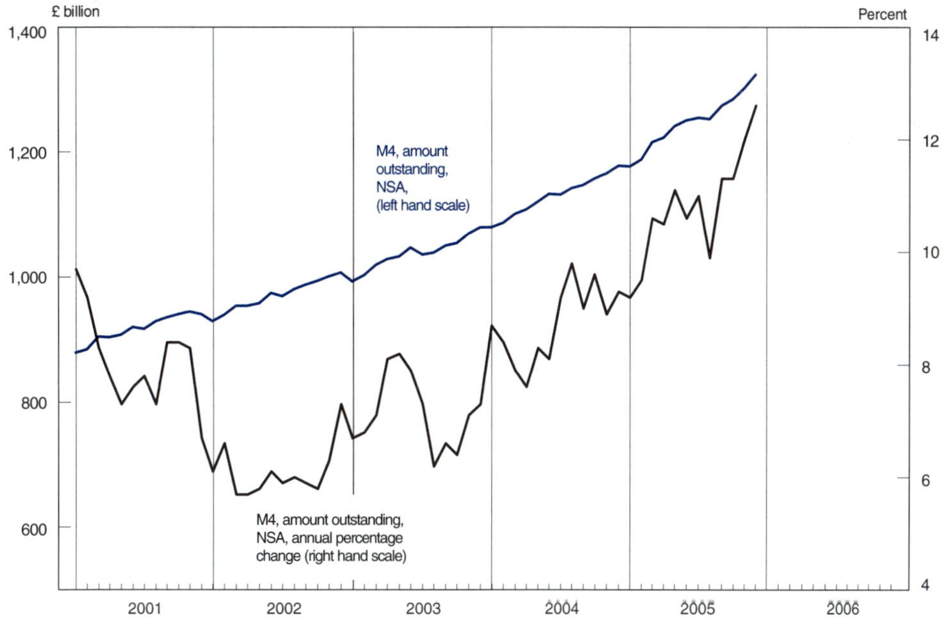

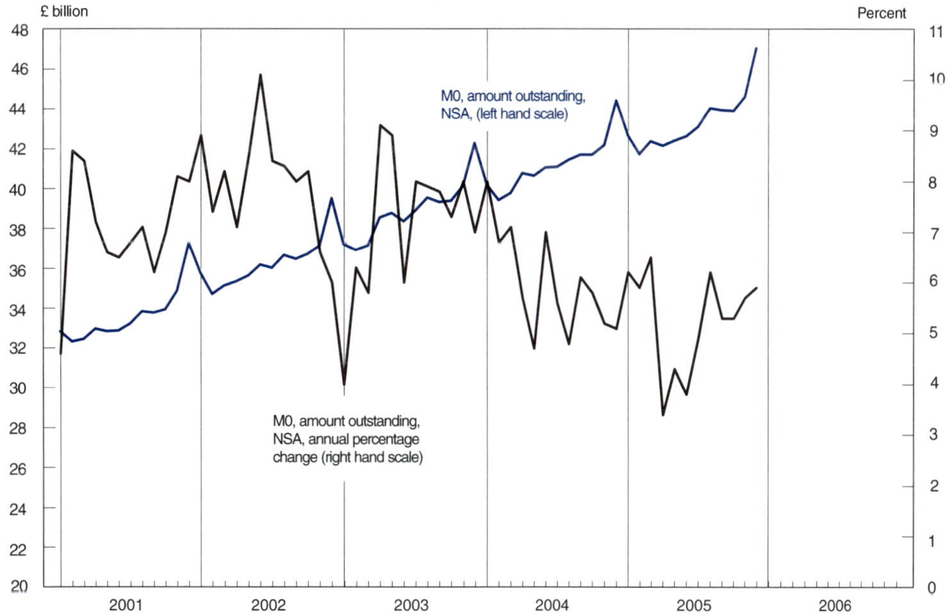

6.3 Counterparts to changes in money stock M4[1,2]

£ million, not seasonally adjusted

	Public sector net cash requirement+[3]	Purchases by the M4[4] private sector of: Central government debt	Purchases by the M4[4] private sector of: Other public sector debt	External and foreign currency financing of public sector: Purchase of British government stocks by overseas sector	External and foreign currency financing of public sector: Other	Public sector contribution M4	Banks' and building societies' sterling lending to the M4 private sector	External and foreign currency transactions of UK banks and building societies	Net non-deposit sterling liabilities of UK banks and building societies	External and foreign currency counterparts	M4
	1	2	3	4	5	6	7	8	9	10	11
	ABEN	RCMD	AVBV	AVBZ	AQGA	AVBF	AVBS	AVBW	AVBX	VQLP	AUZI
2001	–2 750	7 526	191	318	4 194	8 842	82 446	–21 607	–10 815	–17 732	58 868
2002	18 316	–9 148	–110	–897	1 588	11 543	107 655	–25 113	–25 149	–22 627	68 936
2003	38 829	–31 962	–473	10 378	–3 067	–7 048	127 712	–27 161	–20 341	–40 602	73 163
2004	41 389	–30 771	–1 182	2 235	–158	7 042	156 087	4 463	–67 477	2 070	100 115
2005	41 557	–2 836	–644	38 970	84	–810	155 934	27 388	–34 362	–11 500	148 151
2001 Q1	–12 408	3 243	–268	–2 356	3 734	–3 343	31 075	–7 719	1 254	–1 629	21 267
Q2	6 421	2 972	233	4 549	1 000	6 078	21 194	–7 262	–4 325	–10 811	15 685
Q3	–6 103	4 439	95	–2 931	1 287	2 648	15 710	7 221	–8 836	11 438	16 744
Q4	9 340	–3 128	131	1 056	–1 827	3 459	14 467	–13 847	1 092	–16 730	5 172
2002 Q1	–6 179	2 873	–260	–1 045	2 398	–124	24 732	–7 089	–3 172	–3 646	14 347
Q2	7 087	–4 266	101	–266	–1 001	2 188	24 507	1 613	–8 069	879	20 239
Q3	399	–2 120	93	–1 960	208	540	34 214	–8 547	–11 077	–6 379	15 131
Q4	17 009	–5 635	–44	2 374	–17	8 939	24 202	–11 090	–2 831	–13 481	19 219
2003 Q1	–318	–4 248	31	1 934	430	–6 038	21 783	2 357	–4 432	854	13 670
Q2	16 293	–8 454	–210	2 855	–2 099	2 676	34 559	–1 532	–6 969	–6 485	28 735
Q3	5 852	–10 522	–184	980	–1 222	–7 056	30 591	–2 300	–17 743	–4 501	3 492
Q4	17 002	–8 738	–110	4 609	–176	3 370	40 779	–25 686	8 803	–30 470	27 266
2004 Q1	282	–11 958	–534	978	1 670	–11 519	34 934	30 405	–33 204	31 096	20 616
Q2	11 692	–1 846	–343	2 204	–136	7 162	37 475	4 663	–16 199	2 323	33 101
Q3	7 216	–11 055	–26	125	–1 441	–5 431	51 828	–15 857	–16 348	–17 423	14 192
Q4	22 199	–5 912	–279	–1 072	–251	16 830	31 850	–14 748	–1 726	–13 926	32 206
2005 Q1	–2 504	–4 814	–394	8 258	1 411	–14 558	31 683	18 380	1 980	11 533	37 485
Q2	16 505†	–6 020	–228†	5 428	–306	4 523	35 072	17 836†	–21 131	12 102†	36 300†
Q3	8 305	1 301	105	12 752	–815	–3 856	52 687†	–11 328	–13 537	–24 896	23 966
Q4	19 251	6 697	–127	12 532	–206	13 081	36 492	2 500	–1 674	–10 239	50 400
2003 Jul	–6 066	–2 472	–235	–1 339	880	–6 555	7 726	–900	–11 352	1 319	–11 081
Aug	3 454	–5 675	53	228	–771	–3 166	5 309	–9 972	11 432	–10 971	3 603
Sep	8 464	–2 375	–3	2 091	–1 331	2 665	17 557	8 572	–17 823	5 151	10 971
Oct	–1 576	–5 271	–96	–1 161	3 016	–2 766	23 106	–21 906	5 433	–17 729	3 867
Nov	5 551	1 071	–41	7 050	–49	–518	9 928	8 850	–2 980	1 751	15 281
Dec	13 026	–4 538	28	–1 280	–3 143	6 654	7 744	–12 630	6 350	–14 492	8 118
2004 Jan	–14 375	493	–292	–786	3 019	–10 368	20 959	7 287	–18 931	11 092	–1 054
Feb	–68	–4 662	237	1 267	225	–5 536	4 713	12 060	–3 581	11 018	7 656
Mar	14 724	–7 789	–479	497	–1 574	4 386	9 263	11 057	–10 691	8 986	14 014
Apr	–2 239	–2 121	–158	–1 908	80	–2 530	10 350	6 592	–7 175	8 580	7 237
May	3 207	–1 617	–26	1 168	–68	328	8 737	3 242	325	2 006	12 631
Jun	10 724	1 892	–159	2 944	–148	9 364	18 389	–5 171	–9 349	–8 264	13 234
Jul	–6 886	–4 326	139	–947	–117	–10 243	14 260	941	–5 114	1 771	–156
Aug	3 256	2 294	–106	3 248	409	2 605	15 348	–6 241	–1 700	–9 080	10 013
Sep	10 845	–9 023	–58	–2 176	–1 733	2 208	22 219	–10 557	–9 534	–10 114	4 336
Oct	–1 486	–2 332	–118	1 345	–56	–5 337	14 820	–5 608	5 877	–7 009	9 751
Nov	9 024	190	–43	–1 944	286	11 401	2 130	–1 075	–2 775	1 155	9 681
Dec	14 661	–3 770	–118	–473	–480	10 766	14 901	–8 065	–4 828	–8 072	12 773
2005 Jan	–16 815	–4 508	–2	927	1 714	–20 539	16 670	–3 684	6 033	–2 897	–1 519
Feb	651	2 042	–161	2 650	–406	–523	4 483	14 852	–7 241	11 797	11 571
Mar	13 660	–2 348	–231	4 681	103	6 504	10 530	7 212	3 188	2 634	27 433
Apr	–963	1 289	–260	1 939	–37	–1 909	8 761	2 610†	–2 485	635†	6 978†
May	5 154	–4 115	181	–677	–129	1 768	14 415	18 935	–14 651	19 482	20 467
Jun	12 315†	–3 194	–150†	4 166	–139	4 664	11 896	–3 709	–3 995	–8 015	8 856
Jul	–8 426	1 184	57	2 820	–551	–10 556	18 281	–2 501	–542	–5 872	4 682
Aug	4 760	2 773	108	4 042	–150	3 449	5 085	–14 270	3 911	–18 462	–1 825
Sep	11 970	–2 656	–59	5 890	–114	3 250	29 321†	5 442	–16 905	–562	21 108
Oct	–4 838	889†	–253	3 444†	–187†	–7 833†	12 015	1 453	5 126†	–2 178	10 762
Nov	9 100	–174	138	3 058	–210	5 795	63	14 108	–1 904	10 839	18 062
Dec	14 989	5 982	–13	6 030	191	15 119	24 414	–13 061	–4 896	–18 900	21 576

For most periods the relationships between the columns are as follows:
6=1+2+3-4+5; 10=4+5+8; 11=1+2+3+7+9+10

1 A wider range of figures is published monthly in *Financial Statistics*.
2 These figures fall outside the scope of National Statistics.
3 Formerly the public sector borrowing requirement.
4 The M4 private sector comprises all UK residents other than the public sector, banks and building societies.

Source: Bank of England; 020 7601 5467

Counterparts to changes, in money stock M4

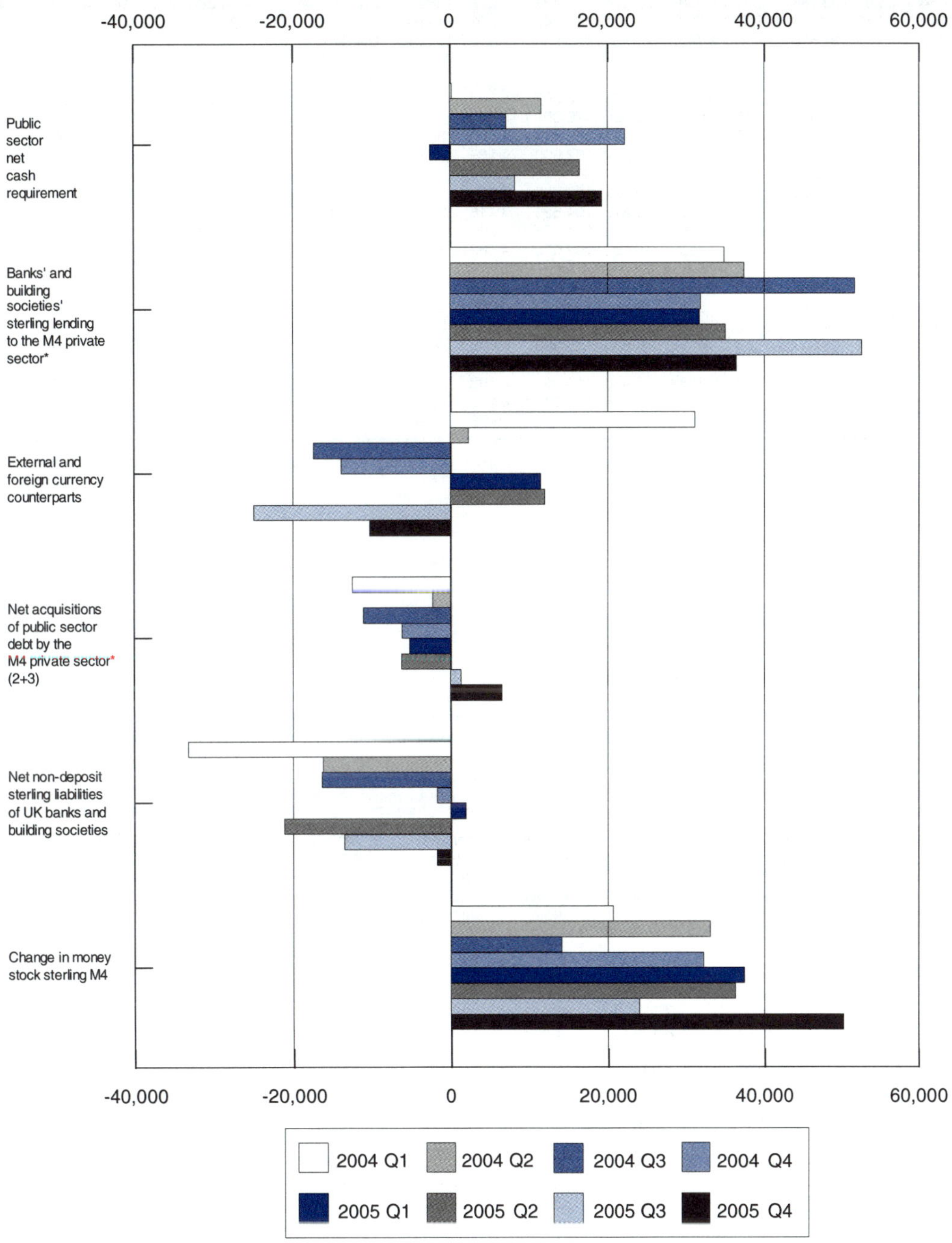

*Private sector other than banks and building societies

6.4 Public sector receipts and expenditure

£ million, not seasonally adjusted

	Public sector current expenditure							Public sector current receipts								
	Current expenditure on goods and services	Subsidies	Net Social Benefits	Net current grants abroad	Other current grants	Interest paid to private sector and RoW	Total current expenditure	Operating surplus	Taxes on production	Taxes on income and wealth	Taxes on capital	Other Current taxes	Compulsory social contributions	Interest/dividend from private/RoW	Rent and other current transfers	Total current receipts
	GZSN	NMRL	ANLY	GZSI	NNAI	ANLO	ANLT	ANBP	NMYE	ANSO	NMGI	MJBC	ANBO	ANBQ	ANBS	ANBT
2002	210 654	5 266	123 288	–539	24 218	21 534	384 421	16 278	138 450	142 716	2 381	20 360	63 410	4 852	2 426	390 873
2003	231 543	6 243	130 308	–855	28 780	22 721	418 740	17 293	145 894	144 021	2 416	22 660	71 540	4 836	2 123	410 783
2004	246 869	6 603	137 508	–428	31 745	23 557	445 854	17 172	154 525	154 968	2 881	24 171	78 069	5 475	2 033	439 294
2002 Q1	50 871	1 204	30 075	12	5 409	5 236	92 807	4 037	32 685	45 805	556	4 812	17 103	1 158	670	106 826
Q2	52 712	1 332	29 977	–126	6 067	5 437	95 399	3 933	33 940	28 544	607	5 172	15 142	1 187	512	89 037
Q3	53 264	1 360	30 500	–375	6 845	4 631	96 225	4 099	35 828	35 492	619	5 221	15 278	1 230	743	98 510
Q4	53 807	1 370	32 736	–50	5 897	6 230	99 990	4 209	35 997	32 875	599	5 155	15 887	1 277	501	96 500
2003 Q1	56 276	1 207	30 829	–75	7 227	5 321	100 785	4 217	34 077	46 210	545	5 204	17 222	1 243	661	109 379
Q2	57 925	2 044	31 540	–185	7 388	5 813	104 525	4 118	36 490	29 368	606	5 807	17 670	1 169	484	95 712
Q3	58 272	1 461	32 810	–295	6 709	5 398	104 355	4 269	36 546	36 110	631	5 829	18 245	1 173	491	103 294
Q4	59 070	1 531	35 129	–300	7 456	6 189	109 075	4 689	38 781	32 333	634	5 820	18 403	1 251	487	102 398
2004 Q1	60 284	1 489	32 922	–222	8 197	5 467	108 137	4 444	36 887	47 564	650	5 703	20 830	1 260	487	117 825
Q2	61 118	1 800	33 743	–187	7 533	5 651	109 658	4 023	38 407	31 745	731	6 135	18 454	1 347	526	101 368
Q3	61 998	1 503	34 210	–36	8 598	5 796	112 069	4 072	38 791	39 334	759	6 188	18 893	1 399	510	109 946
Q4	63 469	1 811	36 633	17	7 417	6 643	115 990	4 633	40 440	36 325	741	6 145	19 892	1 469	510	110 155
2005 Q1	64 212	1 863	33 597	–374	9 328	6 436	115 062	4 393	37 342	54 325	713	6 004	22 096	1 454	504	126 831
Q2	65 734	1 616	34 476	71	7 634	6 516	116 047	4 123	39 517	34 825	804	6 379	19 820	1 288	487	107 243
Q3	65 738	1 653	36 163	–117	8 146	6 292	117 875	4 678	40 917	43 664	844	6 678	20 503	1 375	470	119 129

Sources: Office for National Statistics;
Enquiries 020 7533 5987

6.5 Public sector key fiscal indicators[1]

£ million[2], not seasonally adjusted

	Surplus on current budget[3]		Net investment[5]		Net borrowing[6]		Net cash requirement		Public sector net debt	
	General government[4]	Public sector	General government[4]	Public sector	General government	Public sector	General government	Public sector	£ billion[7]	% of GDP[8]
	ANLW	ANMU	-ANNV	-ANNW	NNBK	ANNX	RUUS	RURQ	RUTN	RUTO
2002	–4 978	–7 331†	10 752	10 487†	–16 011†	–17 818†	16 421	19 310†	349.0†	32.5†
2003	–20 454	–22 331	15 037	15 103	–35 806	–37 434	38 214	38 521	380.2	33.5
2004	–20 254	–21 339	17 499	17 067	–37 713	–38 406	41 321	42 324	423.2	35.6
2005	..	–15 190	..	28 358	–43 500	–43 548	41 443	41 583	464.6	37.5
2002 Q1	11 284	10 701†	4 891	4 515†	6 248†	6 186†	–6 383	–6 119†	314.6†	30.4†
Q2	–9 168	–9 750	1 068	997	–10 481	–10 747	7 126	7 045	321.5	30.7
Q3	–730	–1 165	2 618	2 463	–3 448	–3 628	–145	1 329	325.5	30.6
Q4	–6 364	–7 117	2 175	2 512	–8 330	–9 629	15 823	17 055	349.0	32.5
2003 Q1	5 839	4 952	5 942	6 186	–331	–1 234	–1 305	–208	346.3	31.8
Q2	–11 834	–12 358	2 015	1 824	–14 083	–14 182	16 404	16 266	354.8	32.1
Q3	–4 247	–4 623	3 444	3 440	–7 753	–8 063	6 036	5 903	360.1	32.1
Q4	–10 212	–10 302	3 636	3 653	–13 639	–13 955	17 079	16 560	380.2	33.5
2004 Q1	6 467	5 998	5 514	5 598	727	400	486	1 003	381.5	33.2
Q2	–11 574	–11 933	3 281	3 071	–14 914	–15 004	11 577	11 690	394.4	33.9
Q3	–5 485	–5 796	3 969	3 733	–9 447	–9 529	6 968	7 370	400.7	34.0
Q4	–9 662	–9 608	4 735	4 665	–14 079	–14 273	22 290	22 261	423.2	35.6
2005 Q1	8 269	7 954	8 596	9 174	–470	–1 220	–2 098	–2 552	421.0	35.1
Q2	–12 042	–11 260	2 895	5 089	–15 905	–16 349	15 266	16 559	436.7	36.1
Q3	–2 641	–1 871	5 253	6 448	–8 405	–8 319	8 455	8 348	444.6	36.3
Q4	..	–10 013	..	7 647	–18 720	–17 660	19 820	19 228	464.6	37.5

1 National accounts entities as defined under the European System of Accounts 1995 (ESA95).
2 Unless otherwise stated.
3 Net saving, *plus* capital taxes.
4 These series are not always updated in line with aggregate general government net borrowing.
5 Gross capital formation, *plus* payments *less* receipts of investment grants, *less* depreciation.
6 Net borrowing equals surplus on current budget minus net investment.
7 Net amount outstanding at end of period.
8 Net debt at end of the month, gross domestic product at market prices for 12 months centred on the end of the month.

Sources: Office for National Statistics;
Enquiries 020 7533 5984

Public sector finances

£ billion, not seasonally adjusted

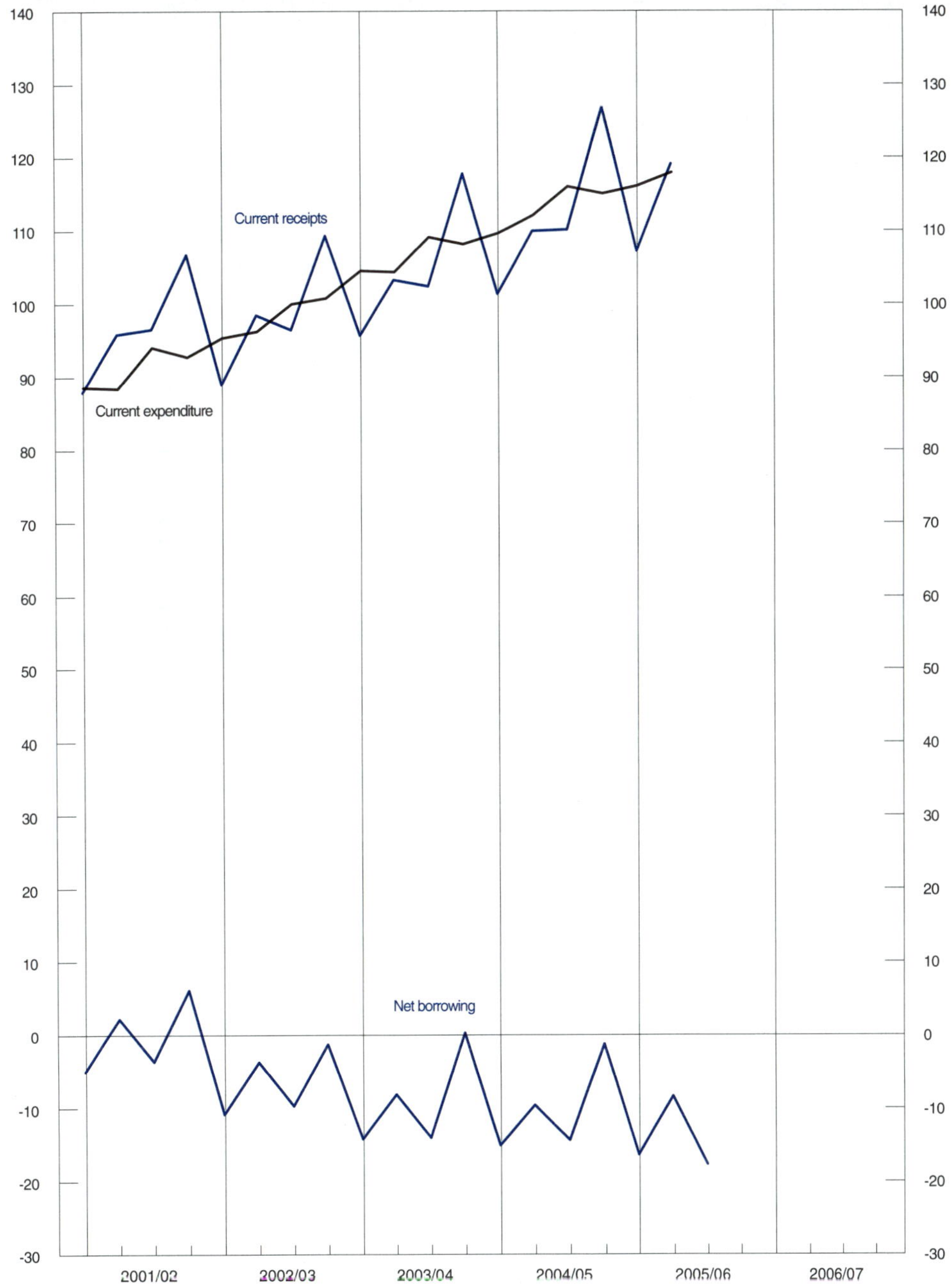

6.6 Consumer credit and other household sector borrowing

£ million

	Consumer credit								
		of which							
	Total consumer credit	Credit cards[1]	Other[1]	Banks	Building societies' class 3 loans	Other specialist lenders	Retailers	Insurance companies	Loans secured on dwellings (NSA)[2]
Amounts outstanding	VZRI	VZRJ	VZRK	VRVV	VZRG	VZRH	RLBO	VZQZ	AMWT
2000 Q1	119 191	33 454	85 773	85 942	314	28 853	2 663	1 415	503 376
Q2	121 978	34 925	87 073	88 684	314	28 938	2 613	1 310	514 638
Q3	124 249	36 286	87 998	90 989	349	29 131	2 555	1 273	525 523
Q4	127 306	37 625	89 567	94 276	391	29 005	2 502	1 197	535 391
2001 Q1	129 096	38 016	91 146	95 840	411	29 124	2 523	1 229	546 179
Q2	133 022	39 407	93 611	100 378	423	28 331	2 509	1 221	561 121
Q3	135 991	39 997	96 000	103 415	446	28 472	2 522	1 206	576 957
Q4	140 854	41 766	99 045	107 704	435	29 099	2 478	1 178	591 152
2002 Q1	144 226	43 405	100 885	110 948	462	29 194	2 504	1 183	606 222
Q2	147 159	43 418	103 727	113 118	458	29 634	2 575	1 193	625 670
Q3	152 987	45 950	106 997	118 391	520	30 409	2 562	1 196	652 553
Q4	157 115	47 255	109 874	120 975	606	31 833	2 531	1 182	675 180
2003 Q1	156 404	43 810	112 587	116 654	622	35 669	2 521	1 033	695 615
Q2	160 961	45 779	115 119	119 493	668	37 433	2 221	933	718 271
Q3	164 242	47 606	116 590	121 833	732	38 759	2 169	824	746 267
Q4	166 313	47 790	118 658	122 775	762	39 980	2 142	701	774 548
2004 Q1	170 154	48 977	121 143	127 033	750	39 692	2 071	690	798 758
Q2	174 491	50 439	123 983	130 711	777	40 082	2 040	698	826 122
Q3	178 128	51 695	126 397	133 791	836	40 872	1 991	676	853 738
Q4	182 212	53 759	128 600	137 203	904	41 588	1 934	661	876 880
2005 Q1	186 492	55 217	131 223	140 247	947	42 829	1 866	651	892 813
Q2	189 190	55 806	133 313	141 649	978	43 974	1 812	642	916 634
Q3	190 519	55 912	134 583	141 818	1 066	45 311	1 775	538	946 413
Q4	192 536	56 730	135 982	142 535	1 110	46 742	1 747	520	..
2003 Jan	157 778	47 515	110 263	121 349	598	32 033	2 542	1 143	..
Feb	154 739	43 670	111 069	119 886	613	30 348	2 539	1 089	..
Mar	156 077	43 694	112 383	116 283	630	35 462	2 511	1 033	..
Apr	157 339	44 165	113 174	116 799	654	36 549	2 492	990	..
May	159 042	45 031	114 010	117 936	654	36 706	2 472	959	..
Jun	160 541	45 633	114 907	119 162	681	37 534	2 216	933	..
Jul	162 053	46 300	115 753	120 633	694	37 697	2 199	904	..
Aug	163 201	46 867	116 335	121 592	709	37 677	2 198	868	..
Sep	163 997	47 571	116 426	121 659	721	38 821	2 160	824	..
Oct	165 219	47 980	117 239	121 889	727	39 884	2 152	776	..
Nov	166 091	47 892	118 199	122 651	725	40 128	2 151	732	..
Dec	166 079	47 569	118 510	122 618	735	39 994	2 135	701	..
2004 Jan	167 627	48 158	119 469	125 417	745	38 524	2 089	686	..
Feb	169 316	48 614	120 702	126 909	750	38 831	2 039	684	..
Mar	169 978	48 903	121 075	126 911	759	39 491	2 064	690	..
Apr	171 373	49 827	121 547	128 358	770	39 534	2 064	697	..
May	172 598	49 876	122 722	129 104	785	39 794	2 040	700	..
Jun	174 155	50 278	123 877	130 601	790	40 208	2 036	698	..
Jul	175 977	51 336	124 641	132 004	801	40 353	2 023	692	..
Aug	176 910	51 415	125 496	132 356	809	40 772	1 993	684	..
Sep	177 944	51 628	126 315	133 786	821	40 991	1 984	676	..
Oct	179 195	52 226	126 969	135 281	831	41 000	1 967	669	..
Nov	181 023	53 003	128 020	136 265	847	41 526	1 945	664	..
Dec	181 988	53 521	128 467	136 991	878	41 498	1 926	661	..
2005 Jan	183 946	54 424	129 522	138 388	895	41 755	1 906	658	..
Feb	185 223	54 962	130 262	139 264	913	42 128	1 881	655	..
Mar	186 356	55 173	131 183	140 239	959	42 668	1 859	651	..
Apr	186 858	54 990	131 868	140 583	941	42 936	1 834	648	..
May	187 926	55 513	132 413	141 067	965	43 129	1 823	645	..
Jun	188 819	55 633	133 186	141 582	993	44 099	1 808	642	..
Jul	189 367	55 785	133 582	141 802	1 029	44 152	1 790	638	..
Aug	190 160	56 062	134 099	142 035	1 048	44 437	1 790	544	..
Sep	190 357	55 800	134 557	141 657	1 051	45 477	1 768	538	..
Oct	191 112	56 187	134 925	141 443	1 071	46 646	1 760	532	..
Nov	191 739	56 293	135 446	141 821	1 081	46 805	1 745	526	..
Dec	192 404	56 502	135 902	142 501	1 081	46 590	1 739	520	..
2006 Jan	193 183	56 982	136 201	143 120	1 098	46 516	1 726	514	..

1 From January 1999 onwards, a more accurate breakdown between credit card and 'other' lending is available. Credit card lending by other specialist lenders can now be separately identified and is included within the credit card component. Data from January 1999 onwards are therefore not directly comparable with earlier periods.

2 These figures fall outside the scope of National Statistics.

Source: Office for National Statistics; Enquiries Columns 1-8 01633 812782

Consumer credit and other household sector borrowing

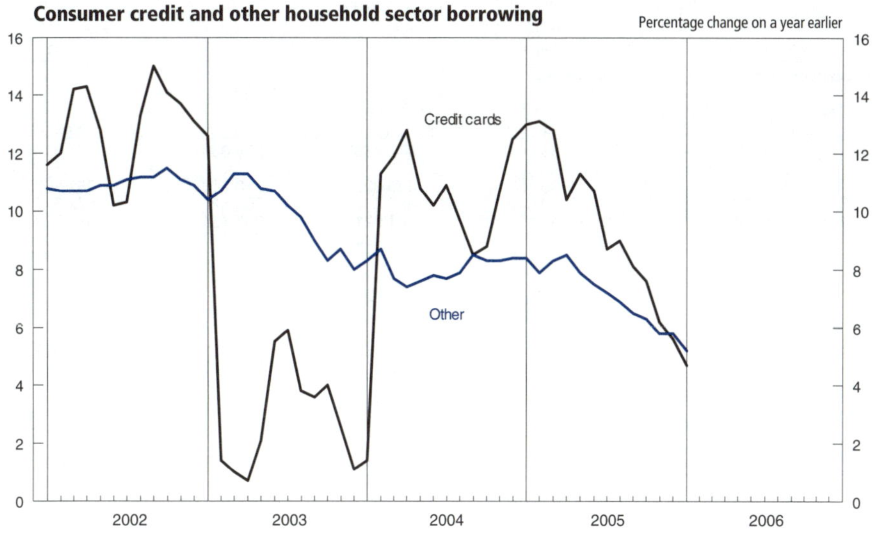

Consumer credit: amounts outstanding

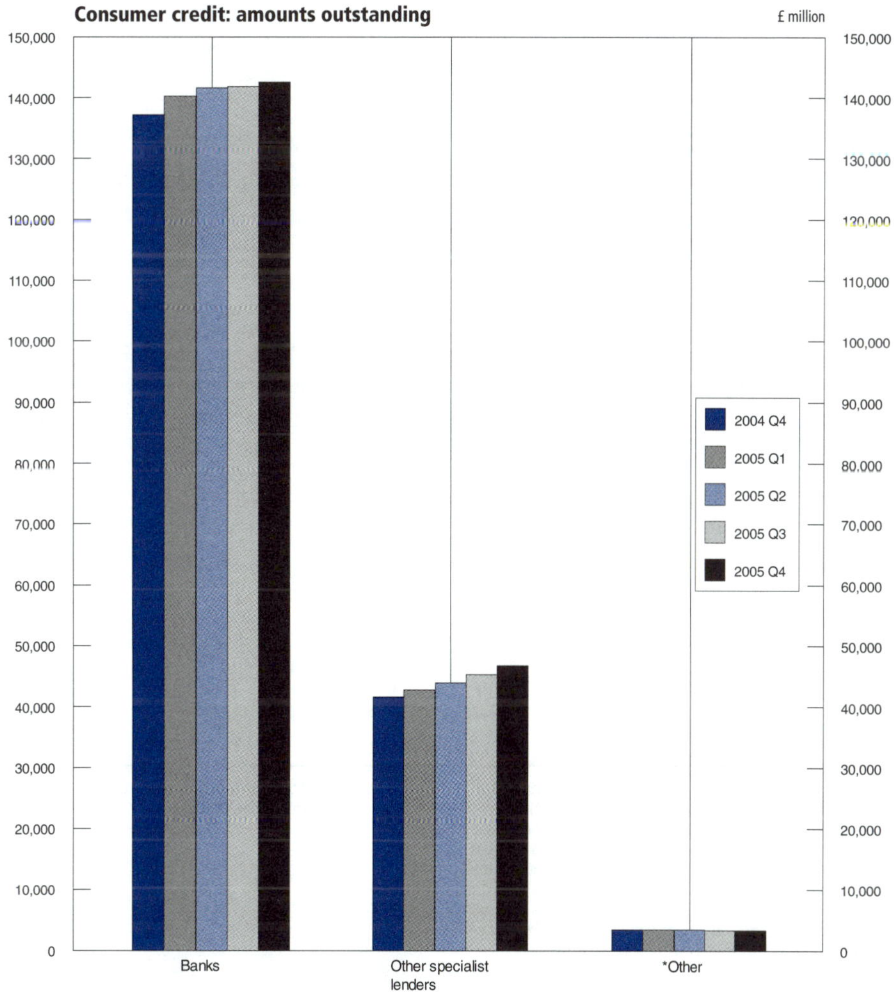

*Other is the sum of Retailers, Insurance companies and Building society class 3 loans

6.7 Analysis of bank lending to UK residents[1,2]

Amounts outstanding

£ million, not seasonally adjusted

	Manufacturing[3]	Other production	Financial	Services	Individuals	Total loans, advances and acceptances
Total loans, advances, acceptances and sterling commercial paper						
Amounts outstanding						
	TBSF	BCEX	BCFH	BCFR	TBTW	TBSA
2004 Q4	41 315	33 801	472 689†	276 838	667 615	1 492 258
2005 Q1	41 160	36 157	490 833	280 213†	667 560	1 515 924
Q2	43 892	40 642	497 342	296 820	674 527	1 553 222
Q3	44 538	41 118	501 621	307 164	689 722	1 584 162
Q4	48 569	38 312	526 272	318 447	703 205	1 634 803
Of which **in sterling**						
	TBUF	BCEY	BCFI	BCFS	TBVW	TBUA
2004 Q4	29 102	30 870	244 248	258 166	666 816	1 229 202
2005 Q1	29 449	32 943	243 282†	261 801†	666 693	1 234 167
Q2	30 466	36 853	250 928	277 027	673 685	1 268 959
Q3	31 060	37 571	260 562	284 904	688 579	1 302 676
Q4	31 510	34 754	272 454	294 997	702 249	1 335 964
Changes in sterling						
	TBWF	BCEZ	BCFJ	BCFT	TBXW	TBWA
2004 Q4	–424	–476	5 318	7 083	16 490	27 991
2005 Q1	347	2 073	–3 040†	3 635†	2 351	5 366
Q2	1 285	3 933†	11 816	15 835	8 498	41 368
Q3	594	718	9 634	7 985	16 492	35 424
Q4	450	–2 927	11 892	11 797	14 710	35 922
Changes in foreign currencies						
	TBYF	BCFA	BCFK	BCFU	TBZW	TBYA
2004 Q4	50	230	5 208	1 024	64	6 577
2005 Q1	–383	296	21 428	–109	75	21 307
Q2	1 488	517	–4 193	1 096	–42	–1 133
Q3	–116	–288	–8 164†	2 249	292	–6 028
Q4	3 269	–64	8 252	788	–270	11 975
Facilities granted						
Amounts outstanding						
	TCAF	BCFB	BCFL	BCFV	TCBW	TCAA
2004 Q4	80 540	67 658	532 527	387 539	754 796	1 823 061
2005 Q1	81 873	69 889†	548 189†	392 410†	754 583	1 846 944
Q2	85 567	73 990	556 131	413 779	762 253	1 891 719
Q3	83 697	75 025	565 990	422 977	782 659	1 930 349
Q4	87 321	75 903	592 080	439 004	794 014	1 988 320
Of which **in sterling**						
	TCCF	BCFC	BCFM	BCFW	TCDW	TCCA
2004 Q4	51 962	53 583	284 725	347 690	753 817	1 491 778
2005 Q1	53 213	54 298†	281 451†	351 019†	753 551	1 493 532
Q2	53 016	57 655	286 953	369 369	761 236	1 528 229
Q3	51 639	58 229	300 707	375 208	781 324	1 567 107
Q4	52 314	57 978	311 304	388 427	792 798	1 602 820
Changes in sterling						
	TCEF	BCFD	BCFN	BCFX	TCFW	TCEA
2004 Q4	741	1 556	5 837	12 516	15 823	36 473
2005 Q1	1 251	715†	–5 348†	3 329†	2 209	2 155
Q2	80	3 381	12 278	18 984	8 978	43 701
Q3	–1 377	573	13 754	5 948	21 687	40 584
Q4	675	–361	10 597	14 922	12 513	38 347
Changes in foreign currencies						
	TCGF	BCFE	BCFO	BCFY	TCHW	TCGA
2004 Q4	–69	704	4 803	983	85	6 506
2005 Q1	158	1 487	21 216	1 621	60	24 543
Q2	3 023	194	644	1 884	–35	5 710†
Q3	–898	245†	–6 965†	2 812	306	–4 501
Q4	2 219	712	10 422	1 789	–206	14 936

1 Comprises loans, advances (including under reverse repos), finance leasing, acceptances, facilities and holdings of sterling commercial paper issued by UK residents, provided by reporting banks to their UK resident non-bank and non-building society customers. This analysis is based on the 1992 Standard Industrial Classification and excludes lending to residents in the Channel Islands and the Isle of Man who are classified as non-residents for statistical purposes from end-September 1997. Holdings of investments and bills and adjustments for transit items are no longer included. For a more detailed breakdown of these data see *Financial Statistics* Table 4.5B.

2 These figures fall outside the scope of National Statistics.

3 Includes lending under the DTI special scheme for domestic shipbuilding.

Source: Bank of England; Enquiries 020 7601 5360

Analysis of bank lending to UK residents: total loans, advances, acceptances and sterling commercial paper

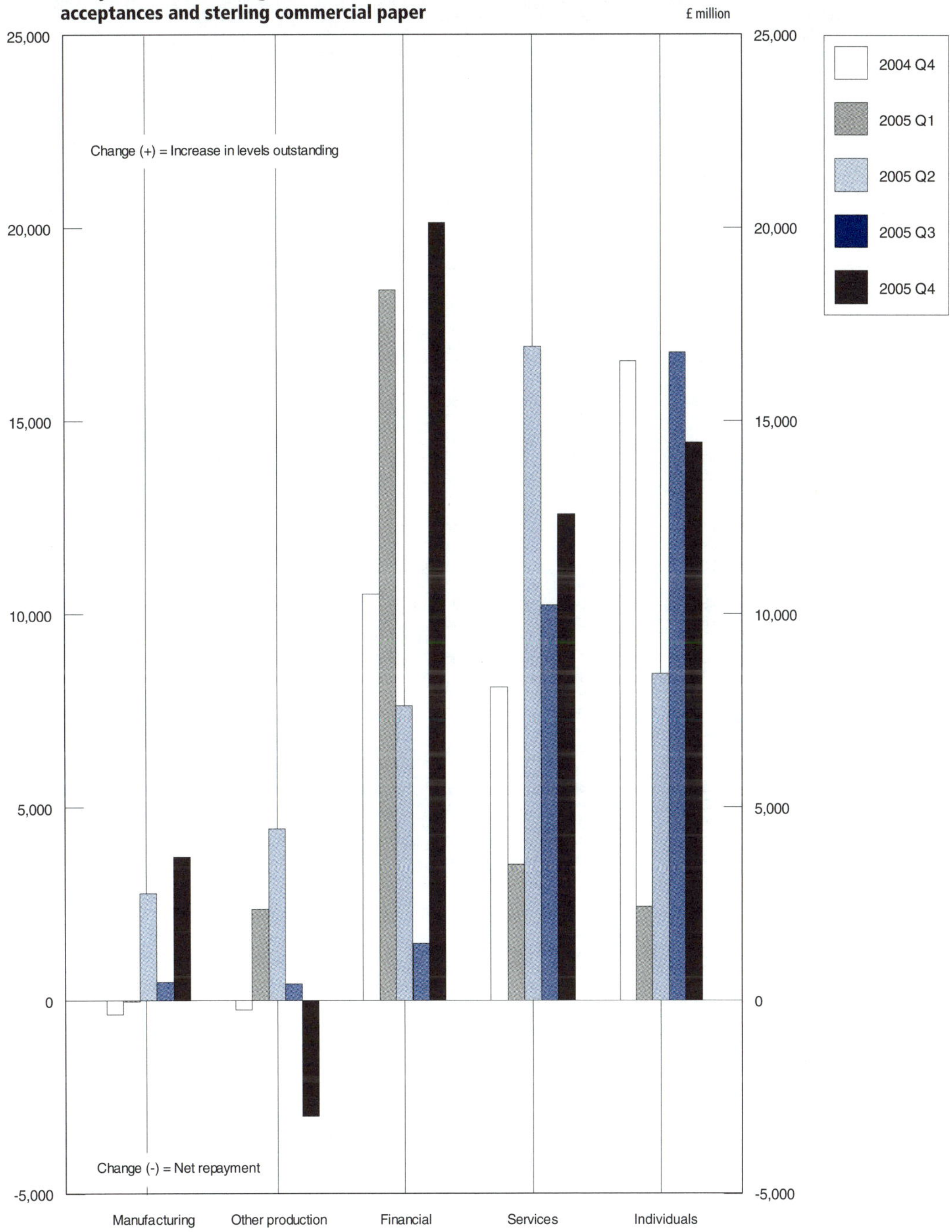

6.8 Interest rates and yields[1]

Percentage rate

	Last Friday						Last working day	Average of working days
	Treasury bill yield[2]	Inter-bank 3 months bid rate[3]	Inter-bank 3 months offer rate[3]	Sterling certificates of deposit 3 months bid rate	Sterling certificates of deposit 3 months offer rate	Selected retail banks: base rate	Euro-dollar 3 month rate	British government securities: long-dated[4] - 20 years
	AJRP	HSAJ	HSAK	HSAL	HSAM	ZCMG	AJIB	AJLX
2002	3.92	3.94	3.96	3.90	3.94	..	1.35	4.83
2003	3.90	3.95	3.98	3.95	3.98	..	1.10	4.64
2004	4.75	4.81	4.84	4.78	4.82	..	2.56	4.77
2005	4.48	4.57	4.59	4.57	4.61	..	4.51	4.39
2002 Jan	3.90	3.97	4.03	3.97	3.99	4.00	1.86	4.81
Feb	3.91	3.97	4.00	3.91	3.95	4.00	1.85	4.83
Mar	4.04	4.09	4.16	4.09	4.11	4.00	2.00	5.11
Apr	3.98	4.06	4.13	4.05	4.06	4.00	1.86	5.13
May	4.04	4.09	4.13	4.09	4.11	4.00	1.82	5.18
Jun	3.97	4.06	4.09	4.05	4.07	4.00	1.83	5.02
Jul	3.75	3.94	3.97	3.92	3.94	4.00	1.75	4.90
Aug	3.86	3.91	3.97	3.91	3.93	4.00	1.80	4.64
Sep	3.81	3.88	3.91	3.85	3.86	4.00	1.74	4.45
Oct	3.73	3.88	3.91	3.85	3.87	4.00	1.64	4.59
Nov	3.86	3.94	3.98	3.94	3.95	4.00	1.42	4.64
Dec	3.92	3.94	3.96	3.90	3.94	4.00	1.35	4.62
2003 Jan	3.79	3.88	3.91	3.88	3.89	4.00	1.29	4.44
Feb	3.49	3.59	3.64	3.60	3.62	3.75	1.30	4.39
Mar	3.51	3.57	3.61	3.57	3.59	3.75	1.25	4.54
Apr	3.47	3.55	3.58	3.54	3.56	3.75	1.28	4.67
May	3.44	3.54	3.57	3.55	3.55	3.75	1.22	4.46
Jun	3.50	3.55	3.59	3.55	3.56	3.75	1.09	4.39
Jul	3.32	3.36	3.40	3.36	3.38	3.50	1.06	4.65
Aug	3.53	3.54	3.57	3.54	3.56	3.50	1.11	4.68
Sep	3.59	3.66	3.67	3.63	3.65	3.50	1.13	4.76
Oct	3.81	3.86	3.90	3.85	3.87	3.50	1.13	4.88
Nov	3.86	3.90	3.94	3.90	3.92	3.75	1.12	4.95
Dec	3.90	3.95	3.98	3.95	3.98	3.75	1.10	4.83
2004 Jan	4.00	4.05	4.10	4.06	4.08	3.75	1.08	4.75
Feb	4.11	4.11	4.16	4.12	4.14	4.00	1.07	4.78
Mar	4.24	4.30	4.33	4.30	4.32	4.00	1.05	4.67
Apr	4.31	4.35	4.39	4.35	4.37	4.00	1.11	4.87
May	4.54	4.56	4.59	4.55	4.59	4.25	1.24	4.98
Jun	4.65	4.77	4.79	4.74	4.78	4.50	1.56	5.00
Jul	4.80	4.86	4.89	4.87	4.88	4.50	1.64	4.92
Aug	4.77	4.88	4.90	4.88	4.90	4.75	1.78	4.81
Sep	4.73	4.82	4.86	4.83	4.85	4.75	1.98	4.76
Oct	4.73	4.81	4.84	4.82	4.84	4.75	2.14	4.68
Nov	4.69	4.77	4.80	4.76	4.80	4.75	2.38	4.58
Dec	4.75	4.81	4.84	4.78	4.82	4.75	2.56	4.44
2005 Jan	4.71	4.79	4.81	4.77	4.81	4.75	2.75	4.44
Feb	4.79	4.87	4.90	4.86	4.90	4.75	2.90	4.53
Mar	4.82	4.90	4.93	4.88	4.92	4.75	3.04	4.74
Apr	4.75	4.86	4.88	4.85	4.89	4.75	3.18	4.60
May	4.70	4.79	4.81	4.78	4.82	4.75	3.31	4.41
Jun	4.57	4.69	4.73	4.69	4.73	4.75	3.51	4.29
Jul	4.48	4.54	4.56	4.53	4.57	4.75	3.67	4.33
Aug	4.43	4.52	4.54	4.51	4.55	4.50	3.84	4.34
Sep	4.45	4.52	4.55	4.52	4.56	4.50	4.07	4.26
Oct	4.47	4.54	4.56	4.53	4.57	4.50	4.24	4.36
Nov	4.46	4.55	4.58	4.54	4.58	4.50	4.41	4.25
Dec	4.48	4.57	4.59	4.57	4.61	4.50	4.51	4.14
2006 Jan	4.45	4.52	4.54	4.51	4.55	4.50	4.69	3.81

1 These statistics fall outside the scope of National Statistics.

2 Average discount rate expressed as the rate at which interest is earned during the life of the bills.

3 Spread of rates over the day in the inter-bank sterling market; from June 1982 rates are the spread at 10.30 am.

4 Averages of Wednesdays until February 1980; from March 1980 figures are the average of all observations (3 a week); from January 1982 average of working days. Calculated gross redemption yields - see *Financial Statistics Explanatory Handbook.*

Sources: Bank of England; Enquiries 020 7601 4342.

Interest rates and yields

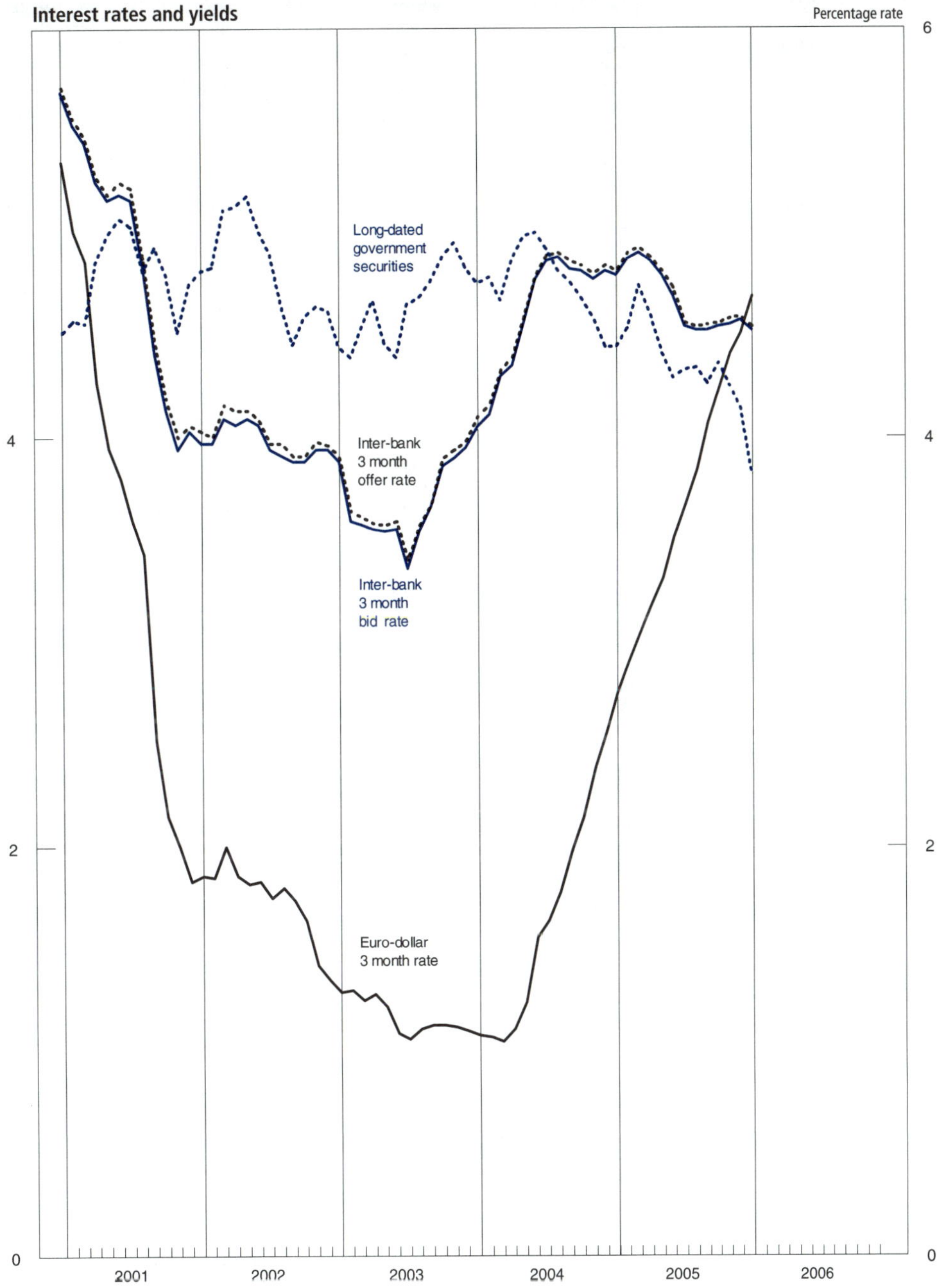

6.9 A selection of asset prices

Not seasonally adjusted

	Producer price indices (2000 = 100)		Housing: ODPM all lenders mix adjusted house price index (2002 = 100)			
	Plant and machinery bought as fixed assets by motor vehicle industry	Manufactured output: motor vehicle industry	New dwellings[1]	Second-hand dwellings[1]	All dwellings[1]	Average price of agricultural land in England (1995 = 100)[2]
	PVJL	PQIR	WMPN	WMPP	WMPQ	BAJI
2001	102.0	95.4	90.3	95.7	95.1	155
2002	100.2	95.2	108.7	111.6	111.2	144
2003	99.5	94.6	126.4	129.0	128.7	147
2004	98.9	96.1	138.6	144.6	143.9	162
2005	99.5	97.3	147.6	152.4	151.8	..
2001 Q1	102.9	95.4	90.8	92.1	92.1	156[3]
Q2	103.1	95.5	90.8	96.0	95.4	148[3]
Q3	101.2	95.4	94.1	99.4	98.8	160[3]
Q4	101.1	95.4	95.4	96.9	96.8	154[3]
2002 Q1	101.0	95.6	100.0	100.0	100.0	130[3]
Q2	100.5	95.5	106.5	108.4	108.2	139[3]
Q3	100.0	94.9	111.0	116.1	115.5	152[3]
Q4	99.2	94.9	117.1	121.8	121.3	148[3]
2003 Q1	99.1	94.6	119.3	124.0	123.4	136[3]
Q2	99.7	94.1	127.2	127.3	127.2	148[3]
Q3	99.9	94.5	127.9	131.1	130.7	179[3]†
Q4	99.5	95.1	131.8	133.7	133.4	141[3]
2004 Q1	98.8	95.5	130.8	135.2	134.6	155[3]
Q2	99.3	96.2	137.8	143.1	142.5	155[3]
Q3	98.9	96.3	143.1	149.6	148.9	175[3]
Q4	98.8	96.5	142.6	150.7	149.8	170[3]
2005 Q1	99.2	96.9	145.1	150.1	149.5	211[3]
Q2	99.0	97.0	146.5	151.6	150.9	189[3]
Q3	99.7	97.5	149.0	154.5	153.8	..
Q4	100.0p†	97.8p	149.6	153.7	153.1	..
2004 Jan	98.8	95.0	131.5	136.0	135.4	..
Feb	98.2	95.4	129.4	134.7	134.1	..
Mar	99.3	96.2	131.6	134.8	134.4	..
Apr	99.1	96.3	135.9	141.1	140.5	..
May	99.5	96.3	136.7	142.9	142.2	..
Jun	99.2	95.9	140.9	145.3	144.7	..
Jul	98.8	96.2	142.5	148.5	147.8	..
Aug	98.9	96.3	142.3	150.4	149.5	..
Sep	99.1	96.3	144.5	149.9	149.2	..
Oct	98.9	96.5	144.4	151.1	150.3	..
Nov	99.1	96.5	143.0	150.9	150.1	..
Dec	98.4	96.5	140.4	150.1	149.0	..
2005 Jan	98.9	96.6	143.9	149.6	148.9	..
Feb	99.4	96.9	144.0	148.7	148.1	..
Mar	99.2	97.1	147.4	151.9	151.3	..
Apr	98.9	96.9	144.6	150.8	150.1	..
May	99.3	97.1	146.9	151.3	150.8	..
Jun	98.9	97.1	148.0	152.6	152.0	..
Jul	99.9	97.4	149.7	154.3	153.7	..
Aug	99.5	97.4	148.8	154.4	153.7	..
Sep	99.8	97.6	148.5	154.8	154.0	..
Oct	100.4p	97.8	151.1†	153.0†	152.7†	..
Nov	99.9p	97.7	146.9	154.2	153.4	..
Dec	99.7p†	97.8p	150.9	153.8	153.3	..
2006 Jan	99.8p	97.9p	..	..	..	..

1 Series based on mortgage lending by all financial institutions rather than building societies only, as previously published. This change has been made necessary because of the mergers, takeovers and conversions to plc status affecting the building society sector. The series is based on the Office of the Deputy Prime Minister's 5% survey of mortgage lenders (at completion stage), but now includes all mortgage lenders rather than building societies only. From February 2002, monthly data has been obtained from the enlarged survey and quarterly data from 2002Q2 are based on monthly indices. From September 2005, figures are based on the new Regulated Mortgage Survey (CML/BankSearch).

2 Please note that because of some changes in coverage, the revised series from 1993Q1 is not directly comparable with the old series. From 1993Q1 prices of all sales of agricultural land exclude some transfers in order to come closer to estimates of market determined prices. However the new series does not represent exactly competitive open market values. Sales are now analysed and recorded on the basis of when the transactions actually took place. Further information is available on the DEFRA Website (www.statistics.defra.gov.uk/esg/default.htm) accessible through the Internet. Data before 1993 remain on the previous basis.

3 Provisional estimates.

Sources: Office for National Statistics, Enquiries Columns 1-2 01633 812106; Office of the Deputy Prime Minister, Enquiries Columns 3-5 020 7944 3325; Department of Environment, Food and Rural Affairs; Enquiries Column 6 01904 455326

Measures of variability of selected economic time series[1]

	Table	Period covered	Average percentage changes $\overline{CI}$	$\overline{I}$	$\overline{C}$	$\overline{I}/\overline{C}$	MCD or QCD	$\overline{I}/\overline{C}$ for MCD (or QCD) span
Quarterly series								
National income and components: chained volume measures, reference year 2002								
Gross value added (GVA) at basic prices	2.1	Q1 1990 to Q3 2005	*0.6*	*0.1*	*0.6*	0.2	1	0.2
Households' final consumption expenditure	2.5	Q1 1990 to Q3 2005	*0.8*	*0.3*	*0.7*	0.4	1	0.4
Gross fixed capital formation	2.2, 2.7	Q1 1990 to Q3 2005	*1.6*	*0.8*	*1.3*	0.6	1	0.6
Exports: goods and services	2.2	Q1 1990 to Q3 2005	*2.0*	*1.1*	*1.4*	0.7	1	0.7
Imports: goods and services	2.2	Q1 1990 to Q3 2005	*1.9*	*0.9*	*1.6*	0.6	1	0.6
Real households' disposable income	2.5	Q1 1990 to Q3 2005	*1.0*	*0.8*	*0.7*	1.1	2	0.3
Current prices								
Gross operating surplus of private non-financial corporations	2.11	Q1 1990 to Q3 2005	*2.6*	*1.9*	*1.6*	1.1	2	0.4
Other quarterly series								
Construction output[2]	5.2	Q1 1990 to Q3 2005	*1.2*	*0.7*	*0.9*	0.9	1	0.9
Households' saving ratio[3]	2.5	Q1 1990 to Q3 2005	*0.9*	*0.7*	*0.5*	1.5	2	0.4
Monthly series								
Retail sales (volume per week)[2]								
Predominantly food stores	5.8	Jan 1990 to Sep 2005	*0.6*	*0.6*	*0.2*	2.4	3	0.8
Predominantly non-food stores	5.8	Jan 1990 to Sep 2005	*1.0*	*0.9*	*0.4*	2.4	3	0.7
Non-store and repair	5.8	Jan 1990 to Sep 2005	*2.1*	*2.0*	*0.5*	3.7	4	0.9
Index of industrial production								
Production industries	5.1	Jan 1990 to Sep 2005	*0.6*	*0.5*	*0.2*	2.9	4	0.8
Manufacturing industries	5.1	Jan 1990 to Sep 2005	*0.6*	*0.5*	*0.2*	2.4	3	0.8
Average earnings: whole economy[2]	4.6	Jan 1990 to Sep 2005	*0.5*	*0.3*	*0.4*	0.7	1	0.7
Exports: value, f.o.b.[4]	2.13	Jan 1990 to Sep 2005	*2.8*	*2.7*	*0.7*	3.6	4	0.9
Imports: value, f.o.b.[4]	2.13	Jan 1990 to Sep 2005	*2.2*	*2.1*	*0.7*	2.9	3	0.9
Money stock - M0[5]	6.2	Jan 1990 to Sep 2005	*0.6*	*0.3*	*0.5*	0.6	1	0.6
Money stock - M4[5]	6.2	Jan 1990 to Sep 2005	*0.7*	*0.3*	*0.6*	0.5	1	0.5

1 For a fuller description of these measures see article 'Measuring variability in economic time series' in *Economic Trends*, No 226, August 1972.
The following are brief definitions of the measures.
$\overline{CI}$ is the average month to month (quarter to quarter for quarterly series) percentage change without regard to sign in the seasonally adjusted series.
$\overline{C}$ is the same for the trend component.
$\overline{I}$ is the same for the irregular component, obtained by dividing the trend component into the seasonally adjusted series, except for those series which are seasonally adjusted using an additive model, see footnotes 3 and 5.
$\overline{I}/\overline{C}$ is therefore a measure of the size of the relative irregularity of the seasonally adjusted series.
The average changes $\overline{I}$ and $\overline{C}$ can also be computed successively over spans of increasing numbers of months (quarters). MCD (QCD), months (quarters) for cyclical dominance, is the shortest span of months (quarters) for which $\overline{I}/\overline{C}$ is less than 1 and therefore represents the minimum period over which changes in the trend, on average, exceed the irregular movement.
MCD cannot exceed 6 even if $\overline{I}/\overline{C}$ exceeds 1 for 6-month periods.

2 Series relate to Great Britain.

3 The figures in the tables were obtained from an additive analysis of the households' saving ratio so CI, $\overline{I}$ and $\overline{C}$ are differences in percentage points.

4 The figures have been updated as described in an article in *Economic Trends*, No 320, June 1980.

5 As the irregular component for M0 and M4 is obtained by subtraction of the trend rather than by division, the figures for CI, $\overline{I}$ and $\overline{C}$ are expressed as percentages of the trend level in the preceding month.

Source: Office for National Statistics: Enquiries 020 7533 6294

Index of sources

Abbreviations

DEFRA – Department for Environment, Food and Rural Affairs.

ODPM – Office of the Deputy Prime Minister.

Gross domestic product	2.1	Office for National Statistics	First Release
			Monthly Digest of Statistics
			UK Economic Accounts
At basic prices	1.1, 2.1, 2.3, 2.4		
At market prices	2.1, 2.2		
By category of expenditure	2.2		
In relation to output	2.8		
In relation to stocks	5.7		
Per head	2.4		UK Economic Accounts
Gross fixed capital formation (see also Fixed investment)	2.2	Office for National Statistics	First Release
			Monthly Digest of Statistics
			UK Economic Accounts
By sector and type of asset	2.7		
Dwellings	2.7		
Gross household disposable income	2.4, 2.5	Office for National Statistics	First Release
			Monthly Digest of Statistics
			UK Economic Accounts
Gross national income (per head)	2.4	Office for National Statistics	
Gross operating surplus of non-financial corpoirations	2.11	Office for National Statistics	First Release
			Financial Statistics
			UK Economic Accounts
Gross saving (corporations)	2.10	Office for National Statistics	First Release
			Financial Statistics
			UK Economic Accounts
Household final consumption expenditure		Office for National Statistics	First Release
			Consumer Trends
			Monthly Digest of Statistics
Component categories	2.6		
In relation to personal income	2.5		
In relation to total final expenditure	2.3		
Per head	2.4		
Households' income before tax	2.4, 2.5	Office for National Statistics	Monthly Digest of Statistics
Housing			
Average price of new dwellings at mortgage completion stage	5.4	ODPM	Housing Statistics
Fixed investment in dwellings	2.7, 5.4	Office for National Statistics	
Orders received by contractors for new houses	5.4	Department of Trade and Industry	Monthly Digest of Statistics
			Press Notice
Starts and completions	1.1, 5.4	ODPM	Housing Statistics
		The Scottish Executive	
		National Assembly for Wales	
Imports			
Of goods	1.1, 2.13	Office for National Statistics	First Release
Price index	1.1, 2.14		Monthly Digest of Statistics
Volume indices	2.14		
Of goods and services	2.2		First Release
			Monthly Digest of Statistics
			UK Economic Accounts
Price competitiveness (manufactures)	2.15	Office for National Statistics	
Incomes		Office for National Statistics	
Households' gross disposable income	2.5		First Release
			Monthly Digest of Statistics
			UK Economic Accounts
Households' income before tax	2.5		First Release
			Monthly Digest of Statistics
			UK Economic Accounts
Income from employment as a percentage of gross domestic product (see also Wages: Earnings)	2.3		Monthly Digest of Statistics
Inventory holding gains (non-financial corporations)	2.11	Office for National Statistics	First Release
			Financial Statistics
			UK Economic Accounts

Industrial production: index of output	5.1	Office for National Statistics	First Release Monthly Digest of Statistics
By main industrial groupings	5.1		
By selected industries	5.1		
In relation to output (gross domestic product)	2.8		
In relation to stocks (manufacturing industries)	5.7		
Inter-bank 3-month rate (see also Interest rates)	6.8	Bank of England	Monetary and Financial Statistics
Interest rates	6.8	Bank of England	Financial Statistics
Eurodollar 3-month rate			
Inter-bank 3-month bid and offer rates			Bank of England
Selected retail banks base rate			
Sterling certificates of deposit 3-month bid and offer rates			
Treasury bill yield			
International Reserves	6.1	Bank of England	Financial Statistics
Key fiscal indicators	6.5	Office for National Statistics	
Labour Force Survey	4.1, 4.2, 4.3, 4.5a	Office for National Statistics	First Release Labour Market Trends
Manufacturing industries		Office for National Statistics	Monthly Digest of Statistics
Change in inventories	1.1, 5.6		First Release
Inventory ratios	5.7		
Output (constant prices)	5.1		
in constant prices	1.1		
per filled job, per hour worked	4.7		
Money stock	1.1, 6.2	Bank of England	Financial Statistics Press Notice
Motor vehicles			
New car registrations	1.1, 5.8	Department of Transport	
Production of passenger cars and commercial vehicles: total and for export	1.1, 5.3	Office for National Statistics	News Release Monthly Digest of Statistics
National accounts	2.1 - 2.15	Office for National Statistics	First Release Financial Statistics UK Economic Accounts
National disposable income at market prices	2.1	Office for National Statistics	
Non-financial corporations (see also Corporations)	2.10, 2.11, 2.12	Office for National Statistics	First Release Financial Statistics UK Economic Accounts
Operating surplus (see also Corporations)	2.3, 2.11	Office for National Statistics	First Release Financial Statistics UK Economic Accounts
Orders received			
By construction industry (see also Construction)	5.2	Department of Trade and Industry	Construction Statistics
By engineering industries (see also Engineering)	5.2	Office for National Statistics	News Release Monthly Digest of Statistics
Output			
By construction industry (see also Construction)	1.1, 2.8, 5.2	Office for National Statistics Department of Trade and Industry	Construction Statistics
By engineering industries (see also Engineering)	5.2	Office for National Statistics	News Release Monthly Digest of Statistics
Gross value added by category of	2.8		First Release Monthly Digest of Statistics
Gross value added at basic prices service inds.	2.9		
Per filled job (see also Productivity)	4.7		
Overseas trade (see Exports; Imports; Trade in goods)			
Petroleum (see also Energy)	5.9	Department of Trade and Industry	Energy Trends
Population			
Estimates per capita, income, product and spending	2.4	Office for National Statistics	

United Kingdom macro-economic statistics

Published by ONS

Annual publications

Economic Trends Annual Supplement

Input-Output Analyses

Overseas Direct Investment

Financial Statistics Explanatory Handbook

Share Ownership

UK Balance of Payments (Pink Book)

UK National Accounts (Blue Book)

First releases

- Share Ownership
- Foreign direct investment
- UK trade in services

Recent editions

Quarterly publications

UK Economic Accounts

Consumer Trends

Overseas Trade analysed in terms of industry

First releases

- UK Balance of Payments
- UK National Accounts
- UK Output, Income & Expenditure
- GDP Preliminary estimate
- Business investment
- Investment by insurance companies, pension funds and trusts
- Govt Deficit & Debt under the Treaty (bi-annual)
- Profitability of UK companies
- Productivity

Consumer Trends 2005 quarter 3
www.statistics.gov.uk/products/p242.asp

United Kingdom Economic Accounts: 2005 quarter 3. Palgrave Macmillan, ISBN 0 230 00322 2. Price £32.
www.statistics.gov.uk/products/p1904.asp

UK Trade in Goods analysed in terms of industry (MQ10): 2005 quarter 3
www.statistics.gov.uk/products/p731.asp

Monthly publications

Consumer Price Indices

Economic Trends

Producer Price Indices

Financial Statistics

Monthly Review of External Trade Statistics

First releases

- UK Trade
- Public Sector Finances
- Consumer Price indices
- Producer Prices
- Retail Sales Index
- Index of Production
- Index of distribution

Financial Statistics: February 2006. Palgrave Macmillan, ISBN 0 230 00279 X. Price £42.50

Focus on Consumer Price Indices: January 2006
www.statistics.gov.uk/products/p867.asp

Monthly review of External Trade Statistics (MM24): December 2005
www.statistics.gov.uk/products/p613.asp

Other publications

- Retail Prices 1914–1990
- Labour Market Trends
- National Accounts Concepts Sources and Methods -
- Sector Classification Guide for the National Statistics